The per̶ ̶ ̶ ̶'is material is re-
s'

Jews of the Latin American Republics

Jews
of the Latin American
Republics

JUDITH LAIKIN ELKIN

The University of North Carolina Press

Chapel Hill

The author acknowledges with gratitude the courtesy of the
American Jewish Historical Society to reprint the following
article which is published in somewhat different form in this
book: "Goodnight, Sweet Gaucho: A Revisionist View of the
Jewish Agricultural Experiment in Argentina," *American Jewish Historical Quarterly* 67 (March 1978): 208–23.

Library of Congress Cataloging in Publication Data

Elkin, Judith Laikin
  Jews of the Latin American republics.

  Bibliography: p.
  Includes index.
    1. Jews in Latin America—History. 2. Latin America
  —History. I. Title.
F1419.J4E43   980'.004'924   79-17394
ISBN 0-8078-1408-3

SOL

Contents

Illustrations

Tables

Map

Preface

Jews do not figure in the postindependence history of Latin America as presently written. Overlooked by Latin Americanists as too few and too marginal to affect the area's development, they have likewise been regarded by Jewish scholars as outside the course of Jewish history. So we find that Latin American historians omit mention of a Jewish presence within the independent republics once the fires of the Inquisition have been banked. Historians and sociologists of the Jewish people, for their part, tend to overlook Latin America, grouping its Jewish communities under "Others" after more salient groups have been investigated. The Jews of Perpignan in the thirteenth century have been the subject of a monograph, as have also the Jews of Washington, D.C., in the twentieth; but there is no history of the Jews of Latin America.

Is there in fact any such entity as Latin American Jewry? The life of Jews moves within the lives of nations among whom they live, is shaped and altered by them. In the case of Latin America, without underestimating the differences that characterize the various republics, we may agree that there are also broad similarities. Cultural congruence, rooted in the phylogeny of their peoples, is the base upon which studies of such continentwide phenomena as race, the military, the church, and the system of latifundia have all been founded. Immigration, too, is subject to continental analysis. Generally speaking, immigrants have had to integrate into societal molds that were Iberian and Catholic, that demanded of them not only conformity but complicity in a hierarchical social order that consigned them to a specialized and subordinate category. In accommodating to such social orders, Jews all over Latin America faced similar constraints and opportunities. Molded by their own cultural heritage, they made similar adaptations. The result was the emergence of an identifiable Latin American Jewry, sharing certain economic, cultural, and social characteristics that distinguish them both from their matrix populations and from the Jewries of other continents. These shared characteristics include their origin as immigrants, a distinctive demographic profile, characteristic life style, and mode of acculturation. Despite differences of nuance, Latin American Jews constitute an identifiable group, the study of which enlarges our understanding of Latin America and expands the universe of Jewish diaspora.

The reasons for Jewish invisibility have partly to do with the small number of people involved. There are probably just half a million Jews scattered through the Latin American continent and adjacent islands. In all countries save Argentina, Jews comprise fewer than 1 percent of the population, so that recognition of their presence may strike some as an academic nicety.

But Jews have been numerically insignificant in all countries where they have dwelt. The vital Jewish community of seventeenth-century Amsterdam numbered no more than two thousand. Jews comprise rather less than 3 percent of the population of the United States, yet they have profoundly influenced arts and letters, science, the economy, the administration of justice, the posture of foreign policy, to name only major areas. Have Jews wielded a like influence within Latin America? If they have not, how may this be explained? If they have, why is this not perceived?

Emergence of a Jewish entity to take its place beside the Indian, black, and Iberian populations that have already marked out the major areas of Latin American ethnic studies is hampered by the lack of a proper name for the group. Most Spanish and Portuguese terms for "Jew" are in varying degrees impolite, pejorative, or defamatory. Usage varies in different sectors of the continent and among different population strata: *judío, israelita,* and *hebreo* may all be used benignly. Ambiguous usage reflects the ambiguous status of the Jews themselves and provides a clue to the reasons for their invisibility: one does not discuss what one cannot name.

As a concept of Latin American Jewry emerges, it becomes apparent that invisibility is a function of ambivalence in these societies that have not yet reexamined the medieval stereotype of the Jews and consequently cannot decide how to regard contemporary Jews. Traditional social structures rebuff and marginalize Jewish elements that are viewed as inconsistent with the national norm, and the evidence is that accommodation of the immigrants proceeded at a slower pace than the immigrants' own acculturation. Yet, absorption of immigrants into national life must be a reciprocal process: immigrants must be willing to acculturate, society must be willing to accommodate.

How do Jews acculturate to Catholic societies that reject cultural pluralism as a valid ideal? Subjected to the cultural imperatives of Hispanic Catholicism, can Jews survive as Jews, or are they destined to assimilate or emigrate? The effort to arrange a modus vivendi between Hispanic and Judaic cultures, each containing elements historically antagonistic to the other, lends to the subject its peculiar interest.

Numerous historians, sociologists, and enthusiasts have attempted to describe particular Latin American Jewish communities, using voluminous published and unpublished materials produced, largely in Yiddish and Hebrew, by these communities themselves. For the most part, these studies present portraits of Jewish communities set uneasily upon landscapes that bear little or no resemblance to reality and that emphasize Jewish detachment from national life. No scholarly attention has been focused on that large proportion of Jews who merge into the matrix populations each year, nor has any attempt been made to reconcile these apparently contradictory phenomena.

Till now, information derived from community and private surveys has not flowed into the field of Latin American studies because of the language barrier. The absence of communication between Jewish historians (for whom Latin America is peripheral) and Latin Americanists (for whom Jews are beneath the perceptual threshold) has prevented incorporation into the body of universal scholarship of that small amount of work that has been done. Here lies another reason for the invisibility of Latin American Jews. Synthesis of Jewish and Latin American data was required in order to establish the dimensions of Jewish life and to relate it to that of the national societies within which it moves.

This task is here undertaken for the first time. The present study offers data relating to Jewish life in all the Latin American republics over a span of more than two hundred years. Some of the data were generated by scholarly studies. Where these are lacking, personal reminiscences, newspaper accounts, and other subjective materials were utilized in order to present as comprehensive a picture as possible. Data were supplemented by extensive interviewing in the United States and Latin America, which served to bridge gaps and test interpretations. Needless to say, the interpretations are my own. Some, I believe, will withstand challenge; others are offered as provocations to other scholars to investigate the disjuncture between two cultures that are in ambiguous contact with one another.

Preface

My purpose in writing this book was to stake out the relatively new field of Latin American Jewish studies and thus to encourage the entry of new scholars into it. The desired result of this effort is twofold: to establish the Latin American diaspora as a distinct branch of world Jewry; and to render visible the Jewish component of Latin America's complex racial and ethnic scheme.

Because of the scope of this work, sources were more than usually scattered. Without the cooperation of staff at many institutions, it would not have been possible to assemble so many disparate fragments. My appreciation goes to the entire staff of the Albion College Library, who bore with patient good humor my numerous requests for their assistance; to the staff of the Hatcher Library of the University of Michigan, and particularly to Frank J. Shulman, formerly archivist for the Center for Japanese Studies of the University of Michigan; to Hannah Desser of the American Jewish Committee; Rose Klepfisch of the archives of the American Joint Distribution Committee; Dina Abramowicz and Marek Web of the YIVO Institute for Jewish Research; Myrtle Prescott, formerly librarian of Congregation Adat Shalom in Farmington, Michigan; Sarah Bell, librarian of the Midrasha College of Jewish Studies in Southfield, Michigan; and Walter Rehfeld, librarian of Congregação Israelita Paulista.

The experience of others who had trod this path before was generously made available by Jacob R. Marcus, director of the American Jewish Archives; and Lawrence Marwick, now retired, who was the head of the Hebraic Section of the Library of Congress. A special debt is owed Charles Gibson, Zvi Gitelman, Robert Mattoon, and Bradford Perkins for their critique of the manuscript; Martin A. Cohen and Seymour B. Liebman for their suggestions on the colonial period; and G. Robina Quale for her critical reading of the whole. The extensive interviewing carried out in the course of this research was facilitated by the cooperation and courtesy of Jacobo Kovadloff, Dr. D. Eduardo Schteingart, Henrique Rattner, Rabbi Mauricio Pitchon, and Max Weiser. To them, as to all those who agreed to be interviewed, I am heavily indebted. Cora Burcham typed the manuscript and was of constant aid in matters of form. The writer is responsible for all translations, with the assistance of Rabbi Steven Chester and Shari and Yael Buxbaum for some of the Hebrew sources.

Research within the United States was partially funded by a Rackham dissertation grant. Travel in Latin America was made possible by award of the Minnie Cumnock Blodgett fellowship of the American Association of University Women. For the confidence and support extended to me by AAUW throughout the period of my fellowship, I am most deeply grateful.

Finally, I wish to thank Sol, Alissa, and Susannah, who endured with love and understanding the many inconveniences this project caused them.

Ann Arbor   Judith Laikin Elkin
1979

Jews of the Latin American Republics

1

Jews in the Spanish and Portuguese Dependencies

Despite the elusive nature of the history of Jews and Jewish converts in the Spanish and Portuguese New World, it is appropriate to open a narrative of modern times with a glimpse into the earlier period. Only in this way can we understand the mentality of the Jews who settled in Latin America following the attainment of independence and discover the preconceptions that greeted them on their arrival.

It is a truism of Latin American history that events and ideologies of the colonial period imposed lasting patterns on the independent republics. In the case of Jews, the pattern is ill-defined. Both the Spanish and Portuguese crowns pursued policies that were intended to exclude Jews and the descendants of Jews from society, their purpose being to create a populace united in both political and religious allegiance. Jews and converted Jews were prohibited by law from entering the colonial dependencies of Spain. In reality, many of them did. *Conversos* were tolerated in Brazil, but eventually they found themselves fearful for their physical survival. Because society dealt with Jews by proscribing them, Jews and their descendants figure in the history of the colonial period only as objects of legal or ecclesiastical procedures designed to reduce them to conformity, as penitents and impenitents exhibited to the people as examples of the horrors of deviance. This encounter between Jews and conversos, on the one hand, and a church-state system bent on their physical and spiritual eradication, on the other, provides the psychological backdrop to the presence of Jews in the Latin American republics in modern times.

Iberia

Jews lived in the Iberian peninsula when Spain was a remote province of the Roman Empire. Before 1492, they functioned as a separate caste under Visigoths, Christians, and Moors, alternately integrated into general society and marginalized from it, subjected to periodic pogroms, but also appointed to high public office. Characteristically, special legislation ordained and circumscribed the Jews' participation in public life, protected them from excessive religious violence, and kept intact their communities that were important sources of revenue for contending princes and princelings.

In 1391, popular zeal for the total Christianization of the peninsula erupted in pogroms and the forced conversion of many thousands of Jews. In 1412–15, a wave of voluntary conversions overtook another considerable number,[1] probably because conversos were able to integrate themselves into Spanish life, whereas Jews suffered heavy legal disabilities. For the rich and well educated, conversion was an open sesame into lives of influence and public service. At a time when rationalism was challenging the religious beliefs of intellectuals, it may have seemed less important to retain one's allegiance to "the dead law of Moses," as the church called Judaism, than to collaborate with the dominant society in the creation of tolerable living conditions. Intermarriage with the best families of the land was common, and by the sixteenth century there was scarcely a noble family in Spain without its converso or Jewish connection.

Thousands of Spanish Jews, however, continued to adhere to their ancestral faith, and so the original body of Jewry divided into two groups living side by side: conversos and Jews. Related to one another by blood and marriage ties, the two groups found themselves cast into very different roles by society; yet their fates remained intertwined, for the church saw the Jews as a threat to the adoptive faith of the conversos.

As the eight-hundred-year civil war of the Reconquest drew to its close, a thirst for religious as well as national unification gripped the victorious Catholics. Within weeks of the fall of Granada, last Moorish bastion on the peninsula, the process of sieving Jews out of Spanish life culminated in the Edict of Expulsion. The Edict, issued in 1492,

4

forced Spain's remaining Jews to choose between conversion to Catholicism and exile from Spain. Thousands of professing Jews now fled Spain for North Africa, Portugal, Italy, and the Ottoman Empire.

Converts were allowed to stay on in Spain, and these now swelled the existing converso population.[2] But the quality of the conversos' faith had by now become a matter for official inquiry. The Holy Office of the Inquisition, the institution charged with defending the Catholic religion and Spanish culture against heresy, operated on the assumption that many conversos were not true Catholics, but Judaizers, practitioners of Jewish rites in secret: in short, heretics. Motivated by religious zeal and by greed—for the property of those arrested fell forfeit to the Holy Office—the Inquisition moved against the conversos with all the combined power of church and state. Arrest without a right of habeus corpus; the application of judicial torture; bounty payments to informers; interminable periods of imprisonment without opportunity to learn what charge had been brought, and by whom; all were standard operating procedure, and all were duly recorded in the *procesos* (court records) of trials. Every conceivable method for extracting confessions from prisoners was brought into play, and yet the procesos fail to answer the fundamental question of the true nature of converso belief. In fact, if it had been impossible to determine how many Jews became Christians, the number of New Christians who remained secret Jews can only be a subject for speculation.

Jewish historians who have memorialized the Jews and conversos imprisoned and tormented by the Inquisition have tended to operate on the same assumption as the Catholic establishment: these were secret Jews who had converted to save their lives and property, but they continued to practice their old religion in secret. Just who first called the conversos swine (Marranos) is not known, but the name stuck as a badge of honor. The Marranos are heroes in Jewish history.

Conversos, however, were not at any time a cohesive group. There were surely genuine converts to Catholicism among them. Indeed, as early as 1499, the rabbis to whom such questions were addressed ruled that the Spanish conversos were voluntary converts and renegades and wrote them off as lost to Judaism.[3] The closing of Jewish religious academies, the flight of Jewish scholars abroad, the destruction of Hebrew books, all prevented conversos, whatever their inclination, from experiencing a genuine Jewish religious life. Their chief source of information about the Jewish religion came from the Bible in its Catholic version and the Edict of Grace which the Inquisition issued periodically in order to exhort the Catholic faithful to detect and denounce Judaizers in their midst. Some stigmata noted in the Edict were bathing on Fridays and stripping the vein from the leg of an animal before cooking it. Consideration of such habits as heresy gives point to Benzion Netanyahu's remark that "the aim of the Inquisition . . . was not to eradicate a Jewish heresy from the midst of the Marrano group, but to eradicate the Marrano group from the midst of the Spanish people."[4]

Following this line of thought can lead one to the conclusion that Marranism in its origin was a myth that satisfied the very different longings of the Jews and of their tormentors: the Jews for heroes they could idealize, the Inquisition for grounds to arrest conversos and enjoy their property. Netanyahu's work on the subject opens with the question: who were the Marranos? and quickly confronts the reader with the challenging response: they were Christians.[5]

What, then, is one to make of the unrefuted record of murderous activity directed against the Marranos by the Inquisition? Why was the Catholic church engaged in the business of killing Catholics? It has been suggested[6] that this came about as a result of class warfare against the rising middle class, many of whose members were conversos. It is probably just as incorrect to assume that all New Christians were crypto-Jews as it is to affirm that there were no Judaizers at all among them and that the entire case against them was conceived in paranoia and dedicated to greed.[7] The Judaism of persons who had been baptized into the Catholic faith had to differ profoundly from the Judaism practiced openly by Jews in other countries. Whatever may have been the belief system of individuals who experienced conversion in their own flesh, Judaism must have been very attenuated among their descendants of the third, fourth, fifth, sixth generation. Indeed, we know that the beliefs of individuals who admitted to Judaizing under torture were far different from the beliefs of normative Jews.

Yet, the definition of Jewishness has never been wholly confined within the limits of rabbinic law. Persons who consider themselves Jews, who act upon this conviction, and who suffer punishment for it, cannot be defined out of the Jewish people by legal rulings. The texture of converso religious life, like the song the sirens sang, may be beyond conjecture. The operative fact for our present history is that the ambiguity of Marrano mentality obscures the history of "Jews" in Spain and her possessions because we do not really know who they were.

The case was somewhat different in Portugal. Here there was no

6

long, drawn-out period of forced conversion alternating with voluntary conversion. In Portugal, Jews had lived in relative peace, and consequently many of the Spanish refugees of 1492 crossed over into that country. Pressures soon began to be exercised against them. When the Jews resisted conversion, hundreds of their children were kidnapped, forcibly baptized, and sent to the island of São Thome in the Gulf of Guinea to be raised as Christians.[8] With the accession to the throne of Emanuel III (1495–1521) and his engagement to a daughter of Ferdinand and Isabella, Portugal was pressured by the Catholic monarchs to rid itself of Jews as Spain had done. But Emanuel viewed his Jews as an economic asset and did not wish to lose them. Instead, he had them all forcibly baptized in 1497. Thus, overnight, one-fifth of the Portuguese population became New Christians, *cristãos novos*. By the end of the sixteenth century, the line between Old Christian and New was so unclear that in both Europe and Latin America the names "Portuguese" and "Jew" had become synonymous.

It is a peculiar paradox of history that in the century leading up to these events, the Spanish prepared for themselves a set of rules to live by that ensured the survival of the old distinction between Jew and Christian long after there were no Jews left in the kingdom. This they did by developing and elaborating the concept of *limpieza de sangre*, cleanliness of blood, according to which any Jew or descendant of a Jew, or any person penanced by the Inquisition, and all his descendants, carried a taint of impurity in his blood and was to be excluded from public life.[9] Thus a caste of persons came into existence—the conversos—who were no longer Jews, but who were not accepted as Catholics either.

The preoccupation with limpieza de sangre emerged among different population sectors in the Iberian peninsula in the fifteenth century. It became official policy during the reign of Philip II (1556–98)[10] by which time the standard of "clean blood" was being applied by the crown, the church, the military orders, the universities, and all social strata according to their circumstances to the end of excluding the descendants of Jews and Moors from public life. New Christians were barred from holding office in any corporation, public or private. They were prohibited from entering an ecclesiastical career or joining a military order; they were barred from the university and from careers in medicine or pharmacy. They could not negotiate on the stock exchange, and measures were under consideration to prevent their marrying Old Christians.[11]

When Philip II brought Portugal under his rule, the policy of limpieza was extended to that kingdom as well as to all its dependencies overseas. By the end of the sixteenth century, it was popularly believed that neither the sacrament of baptism nor the practice of Christian virtue could change the fact of a person's Jewish origin. The ineradicable stain was in the blood, and there it stayed.[12]

Considering the pressures exerted on New Christians continually to prove and reprove their religious orthodoxy and the increasing barriers placed in the way of their integration into national life, it would not be surprising had some of them looked abroad for new homes. As the age of exploration dawned, the newly unified Spain was ready to play a role in competition with Portugal. A vision of redemption in far-off lands, of "lost tribes settling in New Canaans," can be drawn from certain apocryphal writings, particularly the Book of Esdras. Authentic Jews viewed messianism with suspicion, but it would not be surprising if New Christians, who had opted out of Jewish life but who were denied access to the messianic promise of Christ, picked up on quite a different vision of messianic deliverance. The age of exploration now dawning offered a surrogate religious experience by presenting the possibility of the founding of new societies that would prefigure the nobility and innocence of paradise. In such a vision, Catholic, Protestant, and Jew could share and share alike.[13]

The money that financed Columbus's first voyage of discovery was lent to Queen Isabella by conversos who were closely associated with the court of Aragon, after the Catholic monarchs had turned down the would-be explorer "for the last time." Columbus's first letter home was written, not to the king and queen, but to two of these patrons, Luis de Santangel, secretary of the exchequer to Ferdinand of Aragon, and Gabriel Sanchez, Ferdinand's treasurer general. Both were New Christians; de Santangel's cousin had been burned at the stake, and he himself was saved from the Inquisition only by the intervention of Ferdinand.[14]

Several historians have tried to draw from these and other circumstances the inference that Spanish conversos were actively looking for a new land where they could live in peace.[15] Conversos had chosen Spain and exile from Judaism in preference to Judaism in exile from Spain. Now that Spain was rejecting them, some may have looked outward for a resolution to the intolerable contradictions of their lives. The theory that the discovery of the New World had a converso (even a crypto-Jewish) hidden agenda is enticing. But the proof of it has been concealed with all the cunning the conversos mustered in order to protect their identity and their lives.

8

The Indies

If conversos hoped that the age of discovery would open up new lands for settlement, the crown was equally intent that the new lands should remain free of any Jewish or converso taint. From the start, the monarchs attempted to apply the policy of limpieza to the Indies. As early as 1501, Queen Isabella instructed Nicolás de Ovando, governor of Hispaniola, to bar Jews, Moors, heretics, New Christians, and persons penanced by the Inquisition, their children or grandchildren from settling in the Indies.[16] Charles V repeated the order in 1522, singling out "recent Jewish converts." The instructions were included in the comprehensive Laws of the Indies and were repeated frequently over the next three centuries, illustrating both the continued hostility of the crown to settlers of Jewish descent and the persistence of New Christians in their efforts to share in the destiny of their homeland. Those who arrived in the New World were technically illegal immigrants who were committing a crime merely by virtue of being there, and they were subject to action by the state and by the Inquisition if they were caught. Nevertheless, the intense pressures exerted in Spain and Portugal against persons of Jewish descent resulted in the flight of numerous conversos and crypto-Jews to the New World, where the opportunity for anonymity was considerably greater than at home. Those who managed to elude the authorities in their quest for survival sought only to disappear, and consequently left no written trace. What is known of them comes from the dossiers of the Inquisition.

Seven years after Cortés landed in Mexico, the first two persons fell victim to the policy of limpieza in the New World. One of these was Hernando Alonso, a blacksmith and ship's carpenter who helped build the brigantines on which Cortés's army embarked for the siege of Tenochtitlan (Mexico City). In the ensuing years, Alonso became a rancher and purveyor of meat to the Spanish army. Denounced for having rebaptized a child in wine and for having told his wife to stay away from church while menstruating, Alonso was convicted of Judaizing and burned at the stake in 1528.[17] The actions Alonso was accused of are not Jewish customs; there is no evidence that he followed any Jewish beliefs; on balance, his prosecution may have been more a political than a religious event, an attempt by the Dominican Order to tame the power of the conquistadors. Characteristically, of the first "Judaizer" executed in the New World, we do not even know that he considered himself a Jew. The ambiguity of the Jewish presence within Iberian history was tranferred to the New World intact.

9

The crown was committed to restricting immigration to the pure of blood, but like everything else that lay within the royal power to grant or withhold, permits of exemption could be bought. Exclusion was difficult enough to enforce, and exemption from the law provided a ready source of cash to the perennially empty royal treasury.[18] In 1509, the exclusion was partially lifted in consideration of a tax of 20,000 ducats. This benefit, extended for reasons of avarice, was periodically suspended for reasons of bigotry. Sometimes, the effect of tightening the regulations was simply to drive up the price of the necessary certificate of limpieza. Also, because soldiers, sailors, and servants were not required to obtain a certificate, some conversos entered New Spain in these roles. Thus, despite the hazards, numerous persons of Jewish descent did in fact settle in Mexico by the mid-sixteenth century, but they lacked assurance that they could live out their lives there. What proportion of these were faithful Catholics, and what proportion were Judaizers, remains a subject of scholarly dispute.

The occupations of conversos who came to the attention of the Inquisition in New Spain (a skewed sample, because not all conversos were denounced) indicate that they had come to the New World for the same reasons as everyone else: to earn a living and perhaps to strike it rich. Suspected judaizantes included merchants, buyer and seller of Negro slaves, mine owner, ship's carpenter, purveyor of meat, monk, mortician, fencing master, clogmaker, peddler, carpenter, miner, tailor, seamstress, innkeeper, breeder of pigs, pharmacist, clergyman, public scribe, confectioner, merchant to China, Dominican priest, mayor of Tecali, secretary, owner of a sugar mill, doctor, army captain, vicar general of Michoacan, dealer in cattle, farmer, silversmith, handyman, shopkeeper, juggler, chief constable of Cuazualco, weaver, jeweler, and the owner of a hacienda.[19] Conversos, in other words, ran the gamut of occupations, reflecting their former integration into the economy of their homeland. They had skills needed in the new colony, but it was considered less important to nourish these skills than to confine or expel the persons who practiced them. Women prisoners were listed by family relationship rather than by occupation. There is record of one who was the sister of a Jesuit priest and mother of a Dominican monk. Having been raised in a Catholic household and having raised her own children as Catholics was not a sufficient warranty that a converso would be allowed to take her place in society.

The chief prize of the Holy Office of the Inquisition in New Spain was Luis de Carvajal y de la Cueva, conquistador, pacifier of the northern frontier, first governor of the province of Nuevo Leon, and faithful

Catholic. He had been awarded a contract for the conquest and pacification of a vast territory stretching northwest of Mexico City; this contract, unlike most, did not specify that settlers going out with him had to produce certificates of limpieza. The governor recruited over a hundred of his relatives and their friends to settle in Nuevo Leon, evidently ignorant of the fact that some of them were Judaizing, or perhaps calculating that, if they were, he was well advised to have them near, where he could keep an eye on them. These accompanied him, whether in the hope of improving their fortunes or in the hope that in that distant waste they could revert to their ancestral religion. Eventually, the Inquisition arrested, tortured, penanced, and executed most of the Carvajal family, including the governor's nephew and namesake, Luis de Carvajal the younger, who became a martyr to the Jewish faith. His brother Gaspar, a Dominican monk and authentic Catholic, was convicted of abetting and protecting Judaizers but was allowed to repent in the privacy of his monastery. The governor, stripped of office, honor, and property, died in jail.[20]

Better known to Mexican history are conversos who succeeded in making their contributions in a Catholic mode. These probably include Sor Juana Inés de la Cruz (1651–95), writer of lyric and mystical verse, who was known in Mexico as the "Tenth Muse"; and the Franciscan friar Bernardino de Sahagún, who began an encyclopedic work on Aztec culture that is today our primary source of information on that civilization.

The Inquisition was introduced into Peru in 1570, but found few Judaizers in its early years. During the period 1580–1640 (the so-called Babylonian Captivity, when Portugal came under the rule of Spain), numerous Portuguese entered the viceroyalty, among them, conversos. Again, we find them deployed widely through the economy. According to Inquisition records, persons with the following occupations were tried for Judaizing (keeping in mind that not everyone charged with that crime was a converso): merchants, peddlers, storeowners, vendors, monks, doctors, writers, scribes, lawyers, candymakers, shoemakers, silversmiths, a swordsmith, brokers of Negroes, carters, sailors, soldiers, grocers, a bailiff, a judge, a mayor, and two professional card sharks.[21]

The largest group (twenty-two) identified in Inquisition records were merchants, the next largest (thirteen) commercial travelers. In the course of time, converso merchants came to control much of the trade of South America, buying and selling in international trade and in trade among the colonies—much of which was prohibited by the mercantilist policies of the mother country. Their wealth and conspicuous life style proved their undoing, for eventually their Old Christian competitors moved against them by impugning their faith. In August 1635, eighty-one persons were arrested by the Inquisition, sixty-four of these for Judaizing. The uncovering of this "grand conspiracy," as it was called, caused a financial panic as creditors rushed to recover their debts before the Inquisition could sequester the property of those arrested. The flight of much of the rest of the converso population threw the viceroyalty into economic chaos.

All those arrested as Judaizers, and who survived torture, appeared at the great auto-da-fé four years later, when eleven of the prisoners were burned at the stake as impenitent heretics and the rest sentenced to varying terms of imprisonment, forms of penance, or service in the galleys.[22] This was the climax of Inquisitorial activity against conversos in Peru, for New Christians were terrorized into either flight or conformity. The institution still had its uses, however. In 1736 it was employed to get rid of the adventuress Doña Ana de Castro, lover of the viceroy.

An office of the Inquisition was also opened in Cartagena in 1610, but it did a brisker business in witches than in Judaizers.

The La Plata region did not escape notice. Its economy may have been neglected by the Spanish crown, but the faith of its inhabitants nonetheless came under the scrutiny of the Inquisition, operating through its agents in Buenos Aires and elsewhere.[23] The most famous of its Argentine prisoners was the surgeon Francisco Maldonado de Silva of Tucumán, who was a crypto-Jew. Denounced by his pious sister, de Silva became the most stiff-necked Jew in the dungeon of the Inquisition, writing religious tracts on scraps of paper and passing these along to other prisoners to encourage them in their resistance. Maldonado de Silva left no doubt as to his religious loyalties, for he circumcised himself, renamed himself Eli Nazareno, and fasted and prayed continually in his cell. Imprisoned for twelve years while the Inquisitors alternately inquired into the tenets of his faith and forgot about him for long periods of time, he was taken out and incinerated along with participants in the so-called grand conspiracy of Lima.[24]

Most New Christians who came to the New World were Portuguese rather than Spanish. In Spain, conversions forced and voluntary had been going on for a century prior to the discovery of America and the descendants of Jews had largely assimilated by 1580. Jews who wanted above all to retain their religious faith had already left Spain when America appeared miraculously from out of the ocean. The Jews of Portugal (who included the Jewish faithful exiled from Spain) were forcibly converted in one blow in 1497; they were assisted in this by the fact that their children were converted first and they did not want to be separated from them. Under the circumstances, the proportion who continued to practice Judaism secretly may have been large.

Confusion over identity occurred during the Babylonian Captivity, when Portuguese could freely enter Spain and the Spanish possessions. During this period, large numbers of Portuguese conversos crossed over the La Plata into present-day Argentina. From there, many worked their way northward up the smugglers' trail to Potosí (in present-day Bolivia), where rose the silver mountain that was the treasure house of Spain and the tomb of countless Indians. Portuguese Jews who fled Brazil in the wake of Inquisitorial visitations built up the illegal commerce of Buenos Aires, importing West African slaves and exporting the silver of Potosí.[25] Everywhere, the unwelcome commercial competition of the Portuguese won for them the contemptuous appellation *judío*, or Jew; consequently, it is unclear just how many of these immigrants were in fact of Jewish or converso origin.

Considering Portugal's small population (perhaps one million at the time of the discovery of Brazil), it was sometimes deemed more expedient to banish heretics to Brazil than to forbid their going there. At various times, New Christians were prohibited or encouraged to emigrate from Portugal, each change in law being accompanied by a demand for a heavy fine on "the descendants of the New Christians of the Hebrew Nation of Portugal." The Portuguese were, after all, simultaneously trying to hold down Goa, Macao, Ceylon, and Angola. The result of this colonial policy, compounded of equal parts venality, valor, and vacillation, was that quite a few cristãos novos were enlisted in the cause of empire. These included Fernão de Noronha, who was a knight of the royal household and probably a voluntary convert and who brought an entire company of conversos to settle the land granted him by the crown; João Ramalhô, notorious fifteenth-century castaway who, together with his multitudinous halfbreed offspring eased Portuguese penetration of the continent; Gaspar de Gama, seaman and captive counselor to the Arab ruler of Goa, who was kidnapped and baptized by Vasco de Gama, and later served with Pedro Cabral on the expedition that discovered Brazil; and Tiradentes, the Toothpuller, who was a precursor of Brazilian independence and who was hanged for treason in 1789.

A large proportion of the white population of Pernambuco in the sixteenth century were probably Judaizers. They practiced a wide range of occupations: owners and managers of sugar plantations and sugar mills, teachers, farmers, owners of boarding houses. They had a synagogue (but probably no scrolls of the law) at Camaragibe. There were several authors among them, including Ambrosio Fernandes Brandao, who wrote the *Dialogos das Grandezas do Brazil* in 1618, and the first Brazilian poet, Bento Teixeira, author of the *Prosopopea*. Apparently, many officials of the Catholic church were conversos, as we know from the royal order prohibiting their assignment to Brazil.[26]

Cristãos novos were not barred from Brazil, but they remained subject to the Inquisition if they reverted to Judaism. Perhaps as a result of mixed motives, however, Brazil never had an autonomous office of the Inquisition; instead, inspectors were sent out to Brazil periodically, and suspects were remanded to Lisbon for trial.

Records of the Inquisition's visitation to Brazil in 1618–19 show that many Brazilian conversos were Judaizing and were in touch with the openly professing Jews of Amsterdam. That city was then a world trade center, and the relative tolerance of Calvinism had attracted Spanish and Portuguese exiles to Holland. Many families had branches in both Holland and Brazil, a factor that fostered trade between the two countries and kept the crypto-Jews of Brazil in touch with the living body of Judaism.[27] Nevertheless, it must be said that Brazilian conversos made the voluntary decision to stay where they were.

A variety of adjustments were made by cristãos novos in Brazil. Perhaps none fitted into society as smoothly as those who lived in Bahía in the mid-seventeenth century. They comprised 20 percent of the white population of eight to ten thousand and attained positions of wealth and prestige at the core of society.[28] Twenty percent of conversos who were brought before the Inquisition were owners of sugar mills (*senhores de engenhos*) or merchants in the lucrative international sugar trade. Although the same laws of purity of blood that excluded conversos from public life in Portugal were supposed to prevail in Brazil as well, in fact cristãos novos served on the governing Câmara and held posts in government and administration.[29] A full 32 percent of cristãos novos who were haled before the Inquisition were practicing a profession—lawyer, solicitor, scribe, judge, treasurer, or tax collector—all occupations forbidden to conversos. Ownership of land and slaves conferred status, and apparently anyone who could acquire the means to live like a lord (or a *fidalgo*) was allowed to become one—though again, conversos were not legally allowed to become fidalgos. Intermarriage with Old Christians followed as a matter of course.

The cristãos novos were aided in their effort to assimilate by the desperate need for European manpower in the face of Indians who died rather than submit to regimented labor and blacks who died of too much regimented labor. The distance from the homeland and the size of the continent to be subdued placed a premium on European skills, which the Portuguese were loath to see go to waste. The converso, who was despised at home, automatically qualified on arrival in Brazil for a higher social status owing to his white skin and European upbringing. Why be a heretic, if one could be a lord?

Nor were these persons either Jews or foreigners, but baptized Portuguese. Having been brought up in the Catholic faith, neither they nor their parents had had contact with the living Jewish tradition. After the lapse of one hundred and fifty years, they differed decisively from the Jewish people from whom they originated, even though some vestiges of "Jewish" behavior may have been retained.[30] Such a vestige might amount to no more than a futile gesture of protest, such as that of the senhor de engenho who caused to be placed in a shrine a statue of St. Teresa bearing the features of his own daughter who had been burned at the stake.

About 12 percent of cristãos novos in seventeenth-century Bahía were proletarian, including shoemakers, barbers, musicians, bakers, and sailors.[31] These tended to marry into the mixed castes and disappear from the record. The people most likely to run afoul of the Inquisition were the merchants and commercial travelers, who together made up 36 percent of the converso working population. Traveling between Brazil, Portugal, Holland, and the city of Hamburg (at that time a center for the international sugar trade), they might well have chosen to remain abroad beyond the clutches of the Inquisition. But even some of those who had been penanced preferred to return to their homes in Brazil rather than exile themselves in order to live as Jews.

In the second and third decades of the seventeenth century, the Dutch West India Company conquered the rich northeast coast of Brazil. They held onto Bahía for one year only, but retained Pernambuco, Recife, and Olinda for a quarter of a century. It might seem that the Dutch invasion, bringing with it the promise of religious toleration, would appear a godsend to cristãos novos of the country. Indeed, at the time of the capture of Bahía, the story was put about that its loss was caused by their treachery. This canard has been demolished by the Brazilian historian Anita Novinsky. Cristãos novos living in Bahía participated in the defense of their own city and of Pernambuco against the marauding heretics. Their contributions in money, manpower, and leadership were in rough proportion to their weight in the population and the economy.[32] Furthermore, of twenty-two persons denounced by contemporaries as Dutch collaborators, just six were cristãos novos. A decade later, an inquest aimed at identifying clergy who had crossed lines during the war turned up eight Catholic priests, forty-eight Old Christians, and twenty-four New Christians.[33] Evidently, people were acting according to what they conceived to be their own best interests, not some preconceived notion of what was required of them as a Catholic, a Jew, or a converso.

Inquisitorial activity was renewed with a vengeance when the Portuguese reoccupied their coastal cities. Brazilian "heretics" (Jews who had been baptized but subsequently reverted to Judaism) were the staple participants in Portuguese autos-da-fé until 1769. During this period, probably four hundred conversos were tried and penanced; of these, eighteen were executed but only one, Isaac de Castro, was burned alive. (Those who recanted and kissed the cross were garrotted before being burned.)

A great loss to Portuguese literature was sustained through the execution of Antonio José da Silva, a young law student who was on his way to becoming a major playwright. Author of fables, humorous poetry, and raunchy comedies, da Silva was burned at the stake on 19 October 1739 while one of his plays was being performed at a local theater.[34]

It was left to the clever Marquis de Pombal to suggest to King José I that the distinction between Old Christian and New be officially wiped out. The destruction of records in 1773 ended the ability of government or church to discriminate; made it impossible for historians to trace the descendants of conversos; and achieved what the Inquisition had claimed it wanted to achieve all along: the disappearance of the Jews and their descendants from Portugal and from Brazil.

Overt Jewish Communities

Identifiable Jewish life appeared during the mid-seventeenth century in regions that were captured from the Spanish or Portuguese by non-Iberian powers. Thus, when the Dutch West India Company set its sights on the northeast coast of Brazil, Jews of Holland (some of them Portuguese by birth) participated as stockholders in planning the raids, went out with the expeditions as soldiers, and settled in the conquered areas.[35] In each locale, the Dutch Reform church was established, with a grant of toleration to other religions. Thus it became possible for Brazilian crypto-Jews to move to Pernambuco or Recife and openly revert to Judaism. An unknown number of Brazilian Jews did exactly this (the Dutch destroyed their records before leaving Brazil). Some who were subsequently captured by the Portuguese were either hanged as traitors or sent to Lisbon for trial as heretics.[36]

Those who succeeded in establishing themselves under Dutch jurisdiction prospered as traders, middlemen, interpreters, and brokers of slaves. The Dutch West India Company monopolized the import of slaves, but private entrepreneurs ran the slave auctions. Among these were numerous conversos, who also provided the credit that senhores de engenho needed until the sugar crop was brought in.[37] Considering that the mill owners found it cheaper to replace a slave every seven years than to feed him adequately, business was brisk.

The Brazilian New Holland attracted settlers from the homeland, including Jews. One group of two hundred Jewish settlers came out from Amsterdam in 1642 under the leadership of Rabbi Isaac Aboab. Shortly thereafter, they were able to gain official permission to establish a synagogue in Recife. There was a synagogue in Mauricia and probably one in Paraíba, as well as services conducted in private homes.[38]

One who came to Dutch Brazil from Amsterdam and then moved on to Portuguese Bahía was Isaac de Castro Tartas. An enigmatic character, de Castro had the reputation of being a brilliant scholar. A secret Jew, he adopted a Catholic life style in Bahía but was arrested as a heretic and sent to Lisbon for trial. His defense was that he had never been baptized. (An unbaptized Jew was not a heretic, but a Jew.) His inquisitors determined to their own satisfaction that he had been baptized, and he went to the stake for it on 14 December 1647.[39] The question of why a believing Jew would move from Dutch to Portuguese jurisdiction cannot be answered satisfactorily. Perhaps, as claimed by witnesses at his trial, he wished to spread Judaism among the cristãos novos of Bahía. If so, there is no record that he made any converts.

A census of Dutch Brazil taken in 1645 showed a total population of 12,703, of whom 2,899 were free white civilians. Perhaps half of these were Jews.[40] Hostility toward them began to develop as commercial competition in the little outposts became keener. Also, as Portuguese and Dutch learned one another's languages, middlemen were no longer so important. Calvinist preachers who had opposed toleration from the start repeatedly urged the governor to close the synagogues.

In general, the Dutch safeguarded the religious rights of their Jewish subjects; however, these rights were at all times subject to the fortunes of war and diplomacy. When the Dutch were driven from the Brazilian coast by the Portuguese Brazilians in 1654, the Jews had to evacuate with them. One hundred and fifty Jewish families now returned to Amsterdam; others went elsewhere in the Caribbean; twenty-three stragglers wound up in the port of New Amsterdam, where Governor Peter Stuyvesant reluctantly admitted them on orders from his stockholders. This group formed the first Jewish congregation on Manhattan Island. They named it, appropriately, Shearith Israel, the Remnant of Israel.[41]

The Dutch also captured Curaçao in 1634, and some Jewish refugees from Brazil headed for that island when the Brazilians retook Recife. Another contingent of twelve families arrived directly from Holland, intending to establish a Jewish farming colony on Curaçao.[42] This venture failed, and they turned to commerce. Jews from Italy, Guadeloupe, Surinam, and Portugal also settled on Curaçao in the seventeenth century.[43] Thus, the first Jews to settle openly in the Western Hemisphere were Portuguese and Spanish-speaking Sephardim.[44]

By actions of 17 July 1657 and 24 September 1658, the States General of Holland recognized the Jews as Dutch citizens and defended them as such when any were captured at sea by Spaniards.[45] This was to become an important factor in the ability of Jews to engage freely in trade and shipping in the Caribbean area. Sephardim based on Curaçao worked as sailors, navigators, merchants, slavers, and pirates. In 1715 they probably accounted for 36 percent of the white population of Curaçao, and they dominated the island's shipping.[46]

This was a highly organized community, determined to retain its religious heritage and cultural identity intact. Endogamous marriage was strongly encouraged; aloofness between different segments of society guaranteed that Jewish weddings would take place in a synagogue and that the children would be raised as Jews.[47] Cousin marriage was a continuous feature of these matches, as was true for Portuguese in Brazil and for Sephardim in New York.[48]

Despite economic integration, Jews were still being referred to as "the Portuguese nation" by the Dutch government one hundred and fifty years after their settlement on Curaçao. It was only after the post-Napoleonic emancipation that the Jews, newly eligible for appointment to government positions, switched from the Portuguese language to Dutch in their synagogue.[49]

From Curaçao and other Dutch-protected areas, Sephardic merchants fanned out to other Caribbean islands and contiguous areas of the mainland. Some settled in the British Antilles, notably Jamaica, which came under British rule in Oliver Cromwell's time and thus is not usually included in the polymorphous term "Latin America." Other groups established themselves, at least for brief periods, on Barbados, St. Croix, St. Thomas, and St. Kitts; in Panama and Costa Rica; in New York City and in Charleston, South Carolina. The French monarchy granted Jews the privilege of settling in lands under French dominion in a series of *lettres patentes* issued from the sixteenth through the eighteenth centuries. Consequently, there were Curaçaoan Jews to be found in Guadeloupe and Martinique (where Brazilian exiles gave a stimulus to sugar manufacture), the Mississippi territory, French Santo Domingo or Haiti, and the Dominican Republic, which latter territory Spain ceded to France in 1795.[50]

Limiting ourselves to an area that ultimately remained within the Spanish ambiente, it appears that Sephardic immigrants to Santo Domingo were well received and that they acculturated quickly. Arriving mostly as commercial travelers for Curaçaoan firms, they became involved in the financing of Dominican political and military ventures, particularly in the war of independence from Haiti (1844).

In a letter written in 1846, the president of the republic noted that the Jews attended church and made charitable contributions through ecclesiastical authorities while at the very same time the church was praying for their conversion. That, concluded the president, would be achieved not by persecution but by sweet persuasion.[51] In the atmosphere of the republic, which had undergone a period of French occupation, Masonic lodges provided a neutral meeting ground for Christians and Jews. The president and the Jewish merchant in whose defense he wrote his letter of toleration were lodge brothers. Accepted by society and prospering in trade, Jews married local women and raised their children as Catholics. As the president predicted, the conversion of the Jews took place through sweet persuasion, and their descendants are traceable among upper-class Dominican families today.[52]

Jews were far more hesitant to enter Spanish America proper, even after attainment of independence. Though governments officially abolished the Holy Office, the aura of the Inquisition continued to shade the mentality of the population. Furthermore, there existed for some years the real possibility of a Spanish intervention to regain control of the chaotic republics, in which case the Inquisition might have been reinstituted.

Surprisingly, a few individual traders and even some families of Curaçaoan Jews took up residence in two dozen Venezuelan towns in the mid-nineteenth century. Five Colombian locations can also be documented.[53] Many of these Sephardim intermarried, passing along their characteristic names to their Catholic descendants.

As the nineteenth century progressed, Sephardic merchants moved outward from their homes in Curaçao, Jamaica, Barbados, and other portions of the Antilles into other Caribbean islands and the countries of the Spanish Main. Their peregrinations were premodern in the sense that they constituted a mobile merchant class at home anywhere in the Caribbean; they retained their ties to Curaçao, returning there to marry or to die. Because of the number of males who married while abroad, a surplus of unmarried Sephardic women remained on the island. This was one factor that kept the size of the mother community small; it numbered no more than a thousand at its height.[54]

Folklore identifies Sephardim as the founding fathers of most contemporary Latin American Jewish communities. This is probably true for the circum-Caribbean. The numbers of Sephardim, however, were not sufficient to sustain the omnipresence attributed to them.

It has also become a tradition in many parts of Latin America that some Marranos survived the colonial period and that they rejoined the body of world Jewry upon arrival of the first Jewish immigrants of modern times. This tradition, where properly investigated, has proved to be without substance. Though some descendants of Marranos may have survived the colonial period in Argentina, they did not survive as practicing Jews.[55] The conversos of New Spain were not ancestors of the contemporary Jews of Mexico. In Peru, all trace of the large and prosperous converso community had disappeared by the time the first European Jewish immigrants arrived in the 1840s. Despite certain curious relics that are regularly produced to substantiate the myth, it is likely that, consequent on the activities of the Inquisition and relentless pursuit of the chimera of clean blood, all overt manifestations of a colonial Jewish presence were legally extinguished and genetically submerged.[56]

The mythology lingers on, however, among Mexican farmers of Vienta Prieta who can read and write Hebrew; among sophisticated Chilean politicians who seek to blacken their opponents' reputations by references to their "tainted" ancestry; among prominent Catholic families who refer proudly to known Sephardic forebears. The myth of the Jew who is not a Jew, the Catholic who is not that either, overhangs the Latin American mentality. The fact is that by the end of the seventeenth century, one would have been hard put to distinguish New Christian from Old.

Yet as long as the Inquisition functioned, all suffered from a continuing insecurity. No one could be certain what a thorough investigation of his lineage might turn up. Attainment of high public office was certain to trigger an investigation of one's limpieza, and the charge of racial impurity was to retain its sting into the twentieth century.

The independent governments moved quickly to abolish the office of the Inquisition within their own boundaries, for the institution had attracted the hatred of more than Jews and conversos. But it was more difficult to abolish the Inquisition mentality, which had had free rein in the dependencies for four centuries. What was abolished was the institutionalization of limpieza, the legal qualifications for officeholding and for permanent residence. Also abolished was the incitement to denunciation which the Inquisition had provided by rewarding informers with a percentage of the property taken from those denounced. What remained, needless to say, was a certain stigma.

The Christian legend on which Iberian society had based its drive for purification was that there existed two inexorable enemies of Christ: the devil and the Jews.[57] Inevitably, it was assumed there was an alliance between the two. This medieval legend, transmitted to Latin America and imposed upon pagans who had never seen a Jew, produced a situation where the concepts "judío" and "diablo" came to be synonymous. European-derived peoples may have outgrown this legend, but in Mexican villages today, Easter continues to feature ritualized warfare between the forces of light and the forces of darkness, the latter personified by nude men painted as devils, who are called, plainly enough, "judíos."

Diabolization of Jews proceeded from medieval Europe, entered the Portuguese as well as the Spanish possessions, and persists in these societies as evidenced by both languages. Spanish dictionaries, whether published in Spain or in the Spanish American republics, retain the association between "judío" and deviltry, including actions that are illegal, immoral, or associated with witchcraft. The *Diccionario de la Academia Española*, for example, includes the following:

Judío (fig.). Ávaro, usurero [miser, usurer].
Judiada (fig. y fam.). Acción inhumana. Lucro excesivo y escandaloso. [Inhuman action. Excessive and scandalous profit].
Hebreo (fig. y fam.). Mercador [merchant]. Usurero [usurer].
Sinagoga (fig.). Conciliabulo, en su 2ª acepción, vale decir, una

junta para tratar de cosa que es o se presume ilícita. [Conspiracy. In its 2nd meaning, a meeting called to deal with something that is, or is presumed to be, illicit].

Cohen. [Name borne by priests of Israel.] Adivino, hechicero, alcahuete. [Soothsayer, sorcerer, bawd].[58]

The centuries-old linkage of Jew = usury = immorality remains embedded in Spanish dictionaries despite attempts by Jewish organizations to have definitions changed through the Real Academia Española. Often enough, witchcraft is thrown in for good measure.

Likewise, in Portuguese, the *Pequeno Dicionário Brasileiro da Lingua Portuguêsa* defines "Judeu" thus: "homem mau, individuo avarento ou negocista" [an evil man, avaricious person, one given to sharp practices]. The *Portuguese-English Dictionary* compiled by James L. Taylor and published by Stanford University Press defines "Judeu" simply as "Jew."

The standard term for Jew in government documents in modern times is *israelita*, a term that is regarded by some as a circumlocution comparable to the old-fashioned use of "Hebrews" in the United States; this term, too, is pejorative in Central America. But in Peru, "the word Jew has been considered an insult," said the president of the Zionist Federation in 1974. "We therefore avoid the word Jew in public and use instead the term Israelite." Shortly thereafter, the Jewish community of Peru let it be known that they preferred judío after all to avoid unfortunate confusion between Peruvian israelitas and Israelis. The confusion is complete and bespeaks an identity crisis of continental proportions.

Jews have been the beneficiaries of a favorable mythology as well. As victims of Spanish bigotry, they have attracted the sympathy of anti-Spanish and anticlerical factions in all epochs. Individuals in revolt against their peninsular heritage seem to find emotional support in identifying with those earlier Spaniards who suffered at the hands of their fatherland.[59] The young José Martí, later to become the liberator of Cuba, wrung from the University of Saragossa the right to offer Hebrew as his foreign language. There is a persistent legend that descendants of conversos still living in Spain in the nineteenth century lent their talents and their fortunes to the achievement of Cuban independence.

By the time independence had been achieved all across the continent, Marranos, conversos, cristãos novos, and "Portuguese" all were passing into the realm of mythology from which historians are only now rescuing them. But the era left a distinctive heritage. No Jew would henceforth enter the Spanish- and Portuguese-speaking republics without being aware of what had happened here in the past. The new republics would have to achieve independence, not just from Spain and Portugal, but from the Catholic church, before Jewish immigrants would be attracted to their shores. And when the match had been made once more between the Jewish and Iberian cultures, the nature of the relationship would be colored ineluctably by what had gone before.

Jews declared Spain anathema after the Expulsion, vowing never to return to the land that had treated them so hardly. Yet, exiled Sephardim retained Ladino and Portuguese as their home languages and continue to speak them today. The nationalist poetry of Judah Halevi remained popular among Sephardim and Ashkenazim alike. Conversos, for their part, made so profound an identification with the majority culture that they disappeared as a separate entity. As if to counterbalance this fact, the name "Marrano" took on overtones of undying loyalty to the Jewish people.

How much of this ambiguity would be transferred to American lands of Iberian culture? How closely would prospective immigrants identify contemporary Argentina or Mexico or Peru with the actions and attitudes of the Spanish Inquisition? Did fear of a recurrence of religious fanaticism deter potential Jewish immigrants?

We cannot state with certainty the motivations of all immigrants to the New World. We know that many were seeking religious freedom. What can be said with certainty is that very few Jews settled in Latin America during the first century of that continent's independence.

2

The First Jewish Immigrants
to the Independent Republics:
1830 to 1889

Jews could not have settled in the Latin American republics had not radical changes overtaken the colonies on their road from dependence to autonomy. These changes legitimated the presence of Jews, yet never led to rejection of the belief system that had previously mandated their exclusion. Consequently, the life of Jews of the Latin American republics moves in a different context from the life of Jews in the Spanish and Portuguese dependencies; but it is a context shaped by ideas rooted in the earlier era.

The Immigration Debates

The exclusivism of Spanish and Portuguese rule and the desire either to sustain or to reject it was the starting point for both proponents and opponents of immigration. The merits and drawbacks of recruiting European immigrants were debated all over the continent in the middle decades of the nineteenth century, and always the touchstone was the preexisting value system and whether to retain or to modify it. Certain central issues, overlapping but with differences of nuance, surfaced at slightly different times and in somewhat different terms in each of the republics. But wherever they were debated, the attitudes expressed by legislators, journalists, and molders of public opinion helped determine the type of legislation that would be passed and therefore determined also the type of immigrant the country would eventually receive. Viewed with hindsight, it is clear that the attitudes expressed during the debates over immigration spelled out the limits of accommodation the republics would be willing to offer their immigrants.

These attitudes can be grouped into certain universal themes that appeared in precincts of the continent that were quite unlike one another in other respects: (a) The need to break the Catholic monopoly of faith in order to attract new immigrants (preferably from northern Europe) versus the desire to retain a Catholic standard that was intrinsic to the way of life of the elite and that many did not desire to see changed; (b) The desire for large-scale immigration of farm and factory hands for the purpose of supplying a reservoir of labor, its wages continually depressed by the arrival of new boatloads of the unemployed, versus the fear that large cohorts of immigrants would make economic and social demands that would destabilize society; (c) The hope that European immigration would provide the impetus for modernization of the economies versus the fear that introduction of modernizing elements would upset existing social arrangements; (d) The desire to remake the nation biologically, to "regenerate the race" by large-scale interbreeding with Europeans, versus the fear that large, unassimilated groups of aliens would impede formation of a firm national identity in the infant republics. In sum, what was wanted was economic growth without social change.

The dialectic of the immigration debate was drawn from the social philosophy of positivism, which came increasingly into vogue in Latin America of the nineteenth century. An outgrowth of the rationalist philosophy of Auguste Comte, positivism in its Latin American manifestation held that scientific observation of society could yield knowledge of the laws that governed it. These laws, which were objectively verifiable, could be manipulated for the betterment of mankind, leading to material and moral progress somewhat along utilitarian lines of "the greatest good for the greatest number." Good government consisted of developing economic and social policies in conformity with proven principles.[1] In combination with economic liberalism, positivism came to imply support for policies calculated to increase the international mobility of labor, investment capital, and entrepreneurial skills. It was increasingly urged that these commodities be imported from Europe in order to initiate economic development in the young Latin American republics.

All of these trends did not appear full-blown or simultaneously in all precincts of the continent, but many educated Latin Americans saw in positivism a means of attaining their intellectual emancipation, of imposing a new intellectual order to replace the one that had been destroyed. As national polities and problems varied, so versions of positivism varied as between Argentina and Mexico, Brazil and Cuba. Nevertheless, varieties of positivism became the dominant philosophy of governing elites in the latter half of the nineteenth century.

What type of immigrant should Latin America recruit? In contemporary terms, all races were not created equal. The white lineage of the upper classes was more highly prized than the Indian, African, and mixed blood of the lower classes. In fact, the kindest thing one could do for the dark-skinned poor was to whiten them.[2] Mestizos were commonly regarded as inferior to their *criollo* fathers; nevertheless, over the course of time it should be possible to create a new and superior race if only enough immigrants could be persuaded to lend themselves to the operation. A subtheme in the immigration literature was the comparative virtue of different nationalities (often referred to as "races") as whitening agents. Some preferred Anglo-Saxons and Germans, believing them to have a superior work ethic; others opted for Spaniards and Italians, who as Catholics and Latins were less likely to disrupt existing institutions.

During the last quarter of the nineteenth century, race came increasingly to be discussed in Social Darwinist terms, following the teachings of such "scientific" racists as Joseph Arthur de Gobineau, Houston Chamberlain, and Gustave Le Bon. As might be expected, the propagation of racist ideas had a deleterious effect upon the image of the Jew, not only in Europe but in Latin America as well. That these ideas were not indigenous but imported is suggested by their prevalence in the most Europeanized of the republics, Argentina and Chile. The same intellectuals who idealized the English, the German, the Italian, or the Spaniard, tended to regard the Syrian, Jewish, or Oriental immigrant with disgust. The latter were frequently characterized by the press as immoral, slothful, and diseased. Biologically degenerate, they could contribute little to the task of upgrading the mestizo "race."[3]

The topic of Hispanic and Lusitanian attitudes toward Jews in modern times needs more research; there is nothing comparable to the voluminous literature available for Inquisition times. These attitudes are complex and ambiguous, becoming more so when brought into contact with the varied ethnic makeup of the republics. It would not be far-fetched, however, to suppose that the ancient doctrine of limpieza de sangre resonated in modern racist theories.

Sources of Jewish Immigration

Jewish migration to the Western Hemisphere in modern times originated in nineteenth-century Europe. It was a part of that great river of humanity that flowed from east to west impelled by the three titanic forces let loose by the Napoleonic wars: nationalism, industrialism, and democracy. This migratory movement was by far the most encompassing mankind had experienced to that date. It was motivated by an unparalleled increase in population, the advance of industrial capitalism, and ethnic rivalries intensified by economic competition. These forces caused millions of persons to abandon irrevocably their homes in Europe or the Near East, bringing their families and their possessions with them as they left the Old World in search of a new.

Among these immigrants, the Jews—advance scouts of urbanization and industrialization and among the first casualties of the new social arrangements these forces engendered—figured in numbers far greater than their proportion to the general population. Jacob Lestchinsky has documented the intensity of Jewish migration:

Of sixty-five million people who emigrated from Europe in a century and a half, about four million were Jews. This represents about 6 percent of the entire emigration from Europe. The percentage of Jews in Europe at the beginning of the nineteenth century was not more than 1½, never more than 2. The intensity of Jewish emigration was, therefore, three to four times as great as that of the general emigration from Europe. If we consider only those sections of Europe from which Jews emigrated, i.e., middle eastern and southern Europe, the intensity of Jewish emigration is not three to four times, but six to seven times as great as that of the general emigration.[4]

High birth rates and declining death rates meant that Jewish populations of eastern Europe continued to grow despite the export of large numbers to the New World. Within the time span 1881 to 1939, five million Jews are believed to have taken part in international migrations, compared with the estimated world Jewish population of 7,650,000 at the beginning of this period. This migration converted Jews from a European to an American people. Whereas 72 percent of world Jewry had lived in East Europe in 1850, the ratio of Jews in East Europe to world Jewry was diminished by 1939 to 44.9 percent. Transit

27

in and out of western and central Europe left those areas possessed of a constant 14 percent of world Jewry. But the 1.5 percent who lived in the Americas in 1850 had increased to 33.4 percent of the total by 1939.[5]

The impetus for large-scale migration was the lag between industrialization and the increase in population: people were increasing faster than the capacity of industry to absorb them. This process, which impelled Jews and non-Jews out of Europe in unprecedented numbers, worked itself out differently for the two groups. Among Gentiles, agricultural laborers and unskilled workers who could not be absorbed into the cities predominated. Among Jews, those who emigrated were mostly urbanized and engaged in urban or semiurban occupations as a consequence of having been forbidden to own land. With the rise of new semiurban elements, efforts were made to expel Jews from their urban occupations as well, through the use of terror, much of it government-sponsored. Jewish migration had a dual motivation: economic necessity and the need to find new homes where their fundamental human rights would be secure.

Jewish intercontinental migration exhibited extremely complex patterns. The annual migratory flow waxed with the pressures placed upon Jews in their homelands and waned with the barriers placed in the way of their admittance to other countries. But Jewish migration may be divided, in rough and ready terms, into three periods.[6] These refer not only to dates but to the countries of origin of the immigrants. There is overlap, as well as gaps, between categories. Any periodization tailored to the larger Ashkenazic immigration will not totally suit the Sephardic. Nevertheless, the periods reflect not only changes in the origins of the immigrants, but meaningful periods in the history of the Latin American republics. Some notice of these periods will enable the reader to relate Jewish migration to Latin America with events taking place on that continent and worldwide.

The first European migratory wave (1830s–1880s) consisted of German and French Jews. The ending of the Napoleonic wars had engendered a reactionary political current in Europe, reversing the trend toward greater civil rights for Jews that had been a product of the French Revolution. Hundreds of Jews took flight to ports in Holland, from where they embarked for the New World. Most headed for the United States, but some went to England and France. Still others took ship for ports in Brazil, Argentina, Colombia, Mexico, and Santo Domingo.[7] The pace of this emigration quickened after 1830, when industrial revolution and agrarian crisis brought starvation and dislocation to peasants and artisans, stimulating mass general emigration from Germany. Among the rest, some fifty thousand Jews (chiefly from the regions of Bavaria, Bohemia, and Posen) left Germany between the years 1830 and 1870. Only a small fraction of these headed for Latin America. An even smaller number of Sephardim, chiefly from Morocco, migrated to Latin America during these years.

The period of French and German Jewish migration coincided with the early decades of Latin American independence (nominally won between 1810 and 1824). Throughout the middle decades of the century, the new republics struggled to define their boundaries and their identities. To a certain extent, the debate over immigration policy catalyzed attitudes toward the condition of being Latin American. Acceptance or rejection of European immigrants, or of certain categories of them, would become indicators of society's capacity to absorb them. Policies developed during the debates would set the stage for the reception of immigrants up until World War I.

Numerically, Jewish immigration during this period was scant; but its importance was not negligible. These were the immigrants who tested the conditions for Jewish life on the continent and who ascertained that there was a possibility—at times precarious—for the settlement of Jews in larger numbers. Furthermore, individual Jews played a role in the early economic development of Argentina, Chile, Mexico, Brazil, Peru, and Guatemala.

Argentina

During the first decades of Argentine independence, immigration was a point of contention between men of the Enlightenment and others who continued to function within a Spanish Catholic culture that did not agree to the proposition that other religions had a right to exist. The forces for modernization, which favored lifting religious restrictions so as to facilitate immigration, won legal decisions that were not always put into practice because of the resistance offered by classes within Argentine society that were still tied morally and mentally to the old regime.

As an example of this discrepancy between word and deed, brought about by a real incapacity of these divergent forces to agree, a decree of the revolutionary government of 1810 may be cited: "English, Portuguese, and other foreigners who are not at war with us, can move to this country and will enjoy all rights of citizenship; and those who dedicate themselves to crafts and the cultivation of the countryside will be protected by the government."[8] At the time of this proclamation, the Inquisition still sat in Buenos Aires. Even after it was dissolved, in March of 1813, its orders continued to be published from Madrid or Lima.

It is likely that the majority of Argentines opposed the extension of civil liberties to foreigners. In 1825, a treaty between the federal government of Argentina and the British government provided for, inter alia, freedom of religion for British subjects. The treaty failed of ratification in all the Argentine provinces, which at that date exercised considerable autonomy. Only in the province of Buenos Aires, where most British residents were concentrated, was enabling legislation passed. The right of religious dissidents to marry was won only after a long struggle. A law of 1814 had stated that "authorities would give special consideration in marriage to increase the population," but it remained virtually impossible for a non-Catholic to marry save in a Catholic ceremony. After 1825, the right of dissidents to marry could be pressed under provisions of the treaty with Great Britain, but only in the province of Buenos Aires.[9] In short, few fundamental changes in the closed Spanish system were introduced during the first decades of independence. Cultural exclusivism and xenophobia characterized the country through the Rosas period (1835–52).

Following the battle of Monte Caseros, which brought down the dictatorship of Juan Manuel de Rosas, the policy of religious and national exclusivism that had tied the country to Spanish colonialism was discontinued. Immigration became a function of the Argentine state as the result of a conscious effort on the part of some sectors of the elite to replace the old inherited social structure with a model inspired by more advanced societies. Many of their ideas derived from the writings of Juan Batista Alberdi (1810–84), who believed that Argentina would make no progress in the modern world as long as her interior provinces remained unpeopled.

Popularized by the slogan "gobernar es poblar" (to govern is to populate), Alberdi's policy stressed the need "to make inviolable the mixed marriages which are the means for natural formation of the family in our America, called to populate itself with foreigners."[10]

Although Alberdi no doubt had Protestant immigration in mind, certain constitutional clauses that resulted laid the legal basis for the immigration of Jews. The constitution gave support to Roman Catholicism, but did not establish it, Article 19 stating that "private actions of men which do not offend order and public morality nor prejudice a third party, are reserved to God and are beyond authority of magis-

30

trates." There was not, however, a complete separation of church and state: Article 76 provided that the president and vice-president had to be of the Roman Catholic faith.

These constitutional provisions, which represent a compromise between traditional and enlightened views, did not completely resolve the issue of religious liberty. Approval of a system of state education in 1884 and of a civil register for marriage in 1888 led to a break with the Vatican. Meanwhile, until the coming into force of the latter legislation, the basic civil liberties of non-Catholics relating to birth, marriage, and death continued to be governed by laws formulated during the reactionary era of Rosas.[11]

Liberal economics provided the substructure for proimmigration views. Many members of the ruling elite believed that prosperity depended on the free movement worldwide of manpower, goods, and capital. It was particularly important that large numbers of foreign workers be brought in. "Increased population, economists . . . repeated, would stimulate expansion of the export industries, whose growth was often made synonymous with economic development."[12]

The specific economic interests that supported liberal immigration policies included most prominently the landed elite, who, according to Solberg, "were convinced that prosperity and growth required a steady flow of cheap labor. They expected, moreover, the European laborers to form a large, servile working class that would augment upper-class wealth but would not challenge the prevailing social hierarchy or distribution of economic power."[13]

Argentine expectations concerning immigrants focused upon the need for *brazos*—"arms," or farm and ranch hands. An instrumental view of the immigrants' utility to the Argentine economy pervades debates and polemics throughout the nineteenth century. Writing as late as 1909, the Argentine director of immigration recommends excluding would-be immigrants who are missing their right arm.[14] In context, this injunction clarifies the relationship between "immigrant" and "brazo."

Although the Argentine government paternalistically provided temporary housing and free transport to work areas for all "honest immigrants," they made no move to accommodate the whole man. Specifically, no legislation was passed to alter patterns of land tenure so as to satisfy the immigrants' inevitable demand for land of their own. In fact, in the very same year the basic immigration legislation was passed, 1876, there was also passed the first law of lands and colonies, which permitted land to be sold in lots of eighty thousand hectares. The result was to increase the concentration of land ownership and make it more difficult than before for a small farmer to buy a parcel of land.

In addition to the liberal economic views that prompted many Argentines to support free immigration, was the motive of "regenerating the race." In this phrase, Argentine *pensador*, educator, and statesman D. F. Sarmiento (1811–84) summed up his opinion of Argentina's gaucho population and his expectations of the immigrants. Sarmiento hoped to eradicate the violent and nonproductive life style of the gaucho by inundating the pampas with European immigrants. The latter, with their settled habits of work and modern technology, would soon turn the "desert" into productive fields. Not only would the immigrant foment economic development, but he would also spread modern European civilization throughout Argentina. Many intellectuals prior to 1905 were reacting against what they regarded as the superstition and fanaticism of the Spanish church and state, which had held sway in Argentina for three centuries. The only way to extirpate these traits from the national character was to introduce masses of Europeans who would bring with them the sweet reason of contemporary civilization.[15]

Despite the cosmopolitan appearance of such a policy, it was in essence racist, premised as it was upon the inferiority of people of mixed blood. Pseudoscientific racial theories that classified nonwhites as biologically inferior met a sympathetic response from the criollo upper classes who had come into their privileged position by defeating the Indian on the battlefield and in the church. Such hopeless human material could, however, be improved through mass interbreeding with European immigrants, preferably those drawn from northern Europe, Spain, or Italy, homes of virile "races."

It would be interesting to speculate on the origins of this race hatred. Did it represent a displacement of the contempt peninsular Spaniards had long directed toward criollos? Were criollos objectifying in the gaucho the mestizo element in their own heredity that had caused them to be so depreciated by the Spanish? Or did concepts of limpieza de sangre, elaborated upon at such length with respect to Jews and Moors, provide a model for the treatment of other "races" whose ancestors had not been Christians? Whatever the psychological mechanism, the fact is that racial and economic rationales became intertwined.

Argentina in fact attracted enormous numbers of immigrants. The total has been calculated at 6,500,000 for the years 1857–1965, counting returnees; or 4,379,000 if only those are counted who remained.[16] These were poured over an estimated base population of 1,200,000. For decades, foreigners made up almost 70 percent of the population of Buenos Aires (where up to a third of the entire population was concentrated). At the same time, almost half of the population of the provinces of greatest economic and demographic weight was also composed of the foreign-born.

These foreigners came not from northern Europe, as the enlightened faction had hoped they would, but from southern and eastern Europe where the impact of the industrial revolution was just beginning to be felt. Northerners, already conditioned to industry, tended to choose the United States, both because of its higher level of industrialization and because there were elements of cultural affiliation dating back to the colonial period. During the mass exodus of northern Europeans, Argentina had been closed to immigration. Now the southern Europeans were being displaced by the industrialization process and accompanying population growth. Their linguistic and cultural affinity, as well as the long colonial relationship encouraged them to choose Argentina.[17] In the century following the fall of Rosas, almost half the immigrants to Argentina were Italian; exactly a third were Spanish; about one-fifth consisted of Poles, Russians, French, and Germans, with Jews among the latter grouping.[18]

It is apparent that the first half-century of independence did not produce a climate favorable to Jewish immigration. In the absence of legal provisions for marriage or burial within their faith, few Jewish families were susceptible to the lure of Argentina. Various single men are known to have migrated, and these exercised the options of bachelorhood, remigration to Europe, or marriage to local women in Catholic ceremonies, followed by the raising of their children as Catholics. Interesting case histories of all these patterns have been documented.[19]

The record of the birth of a child in Buenos Aires in the year 1835, to a Jewish father whose family stemmed from the province of Lorraine, provides the first—and characteristically ambiguous—trace of Argentine Jewry. Because it is not known whether the child's mother was a Jew, the child's own Jewish status is in doubt. Sometime before 1844, one Henry Hart, an English Jew, migrated to Buenos Aires, where he entered trade and joined the organization that later came to be the Club de Residentes Extranjeros, a group whose membership included foreign merchants, stockbrokers, and persons involved in the development of Argentine railroads and the meat-packing industry. In

33

the decade of the fifties, other Jews from England, France, Germany, and Alsace arrived in Argentina, where they entered various business activities.

In 1860, the first two Jewish weddings were authorized by Argentine authorities, and this date may be set for the origins of a Jewish community. Interestingly, the lawyer who pleaded the case on behalf of the prospective brides and grooms was a conservative Catholic who opposed civil marriage and believed that extending the right of religious marriage to dissidents was necessary in order to stave off the greater evil. Records of the wedding of the two Levy sisters reveal an extended kinship grouping with links to the areas of Lyon, Alsace, and the Rhineland. These connections define the most significant body of Jewish immigrants to Argentina before 1889.[20] The origins of early Jewish immigrants are confirmed by records of the Congregación Israelita, the earliest of which date from 1873. Sixteen of the Congregación's twenty founding members have been identified. They include persons born in Germany, England, Alsace, and Romania. Only one was a Sephardi, belonging to a Portuguese family that had settled in Hamburg.[21]

By 1882, the Congregación had a membership of seventy-five, roughly one-tenth the estimated Jewish population of the city at that time. Many other Jews of the city were married to local women and were raising their children as Catholics; some of these rejoined the Congregación when the death of their wives released them from their vows. Almost all were in trade, as they had been in their native cities of Europe. In fact, 85 percent of Buenos Aires Jews in this period were engaged in retail merchandising. They owned small shops that sold European imports; or they represented European firms, sometimes owned by relatives; or they established an Argentine branch of a London or Paris shop. They concentrated in jewelry, books, clothing, and household items, particularly china and porcelain. A few were high financiers and real estate brokers, and some owned real estate in the central core of the capital or in provincial centers. Although the professions were crowded with foreigners in mid-nineteenth century, Argentina's Jews seem to have figured among them in numbers less than their proportion to the general population.

A singularly romantic figure of the 1880s was Julio Popper, Bucharest-born adventurer, explorer, and publicist, who undertook a number of explorations through Tierra del Fuego. A mining engineer by profession, Popper prospected for gold but had uneven luck with the eighty thousand hectares of land and eighteen mines he owned at his death. Though lionized by Buenos Aires society, his reputation outran his luck; his debts outweighed his assets when death (possibly with the assistance of some mortal hand) took him at age thirty-six.[22] Popper was born a Jew, but took no part in the affairs of the Buenos Aires Jewish community, which was being organized during his active years. His brother Max, who for a while supervised the Popper operation in Tierra del Fuego and who died there of tuberculosis at the age of twenty-six, was a member of the Congregación.

Moroccan Jews began arriving in Argentina in 1875, though they were few in number until after 1880.[23] There were also Sephardim from Gibraltar, many of them related to the Moroccans by marriage. A few arrived after spending some years in Brazil: because parts of Morocco had been under Portuguese rule, many Moroccan Jews spoke Portuguese. Many members of this community relocated between Argentina and Brazil. Unlike the West European Jews who favored Buenos Aires, Sephardim tended to settle in the interior of the country, beginning as itinerant merchants and ending as proprietors of variety stores in the market towns of Buenos Aires, Santa Fé, and Entre Ríos provinces. By 1889, they were established in such towns as Mercedes de San Luís, Bahía Blanca, and Santa Fé (the original port of entry for many) as well as in the pioneering agricultural colony of Esperanza.

In addition to these two communities, a number of East European (Russian, Polish, Romanian) Jews made their appearance in Buenos Aires in the decade of the eighties. Many of them were white slavers, pandering to the needs of the hordes of immigrants, the vast majority of whom were single men. The presence of these *t'maim* (unclean ones) was widely publicized in the Jewish world through such books as Sholom Aleichem's *A Mentsch fun Buenos Aires* and Sholom Asch's *Motke Ganiff*. The consequence was that Argentina acquired a bad name among Jews for years to come.[24] The Congregación's refusal to admit the t'maim to membership forced the white slavers to organize their own communal institutions. The relative strength of their religious ties is illustrated by the fact that while the free-thinking French, German, and English Jewish settlers made room for themselves in the British cemetery, the East European t'maim established their own.

The Argentine national census of 1895 found 3,954,911 persons in the country, of whom approximately one-quarter, 1,004,527, were foreign born; 6,085 israelitas were counted. Creoles were uncomfortable with all foreigners, and though the rhetoric of the immigration debate had emphasized the need for large numbers of immigrants, foreigners continued to be the object of nativist suspicion.[25] Ethnocentrism manifested itself in the slow pace at which the Catholic monopoly of civil matters dissipated, despite legislation intended to accord religious toleration. Even the provincial government of Buenos Aires, the most progressive of the provinces, never activated provisions of an 1833 law providing for the registration of births, deaths, and marriages in non-Catholic families. As late as 1877, a Jew brought a case before the Superior Tribunal de Justicia in an effort to force the registration of the birth of his children, without baptism. Only after the victory of secularist forces in 1888 was the way cleared for mass Jewish immigration into Argentina. Even so, the motive power of czarist oppression was required to get many Jews to settle in Argentina.

Chile

Many of the forces propelling Chile toward a proimmigration policy were similar to those at work in Argentina: the need for a larger work force; the belief that the European was genetically superior to the mestizo; and the theory that prosperity was a function of the free flow of capital and labor across international boundaries. There were two outstanding differences in the respective situations of the two countries. Chile's greater distance from world trade routes resulted in a smaller and tardier flow of immigrants. In the year 1895, Chile received just 665 immigrants to Argentina's 44,169, and in that year the proportion of foreign-born living in Chile was just 2.9 percent as compared with Argentina's 25.4 percent.[26] Furthermore, Chile industrialized at a faster pace than did Argentina. Large landowners were not as powerful a class in Chile as they were in neighboring Argentina, and the primary impetus for recruitment of immigrant labor came not from *hacendados* and *rancheros* but from industrialists and mining entrepreneurs. But Chileans looked down upon the *inquilino* (mestizo peon) with the same disdain with which Argentines viewed the gaucho. And the solution was the same as that sought by the Argentines: import a European work force that was already educated, habituated to industrial labor, and racially superior to the mestizo.

The first Jew, or descendant of Jews, who can be identified in nineteenth-century Chile is Stefan Goldsack, an engineer who was engaged in England by the diplomatic agent of Lord Cochrane, naval hero of the Chilean war of independence. Goldsack had worked in Woolwich with the inventor of a rocket that was put to use by the British navy in its wars against the French; he was charged with transferring the technique to the Chilean navy, which he did with little success, possibly owing to the Chilean government's having employed Spanish prisoners of war in their manufacture.[27]

Few Jews are known to have immigrated to Chile in the early decades of independence, but arrivals increased during the California gold rush, when traffic along the west coast of the two continents generally increased. The Jewish immigrants of the fifties and sixties came mostly from Germany and France, and they settled in a range of towns from Copiapó, capital of the northern mining district of Atacama, to Traiguen in the south. Some Jews established themselves in the German colonies that took root in the south of Chile; others were attracted to the mining industry of the north. Most, however, settled in Valparaíso, which had the largest foreign colony of any city in Chile.

The presence of Jewish immigrants can be traced through the records of the various German clubs that sprang up all over Chile, the first of which was the Club Alemán de Valparaíso, founded in 1838 by a group of German expatriates including Jews, as well as in the records of the companies of volunteer firemen, the first of which was founded in Valparaíso in 1850, after fire had destroyed a part of that city. The records of the customs house, combined with advertisements in Valparaíso newspapers, reveal the presence of increasing numbers of Jewish retail store owners, particularly in ready-to-wear clothing.

An interesting figure of this period is Manuel de Lima y Sola, born in 1818 in Curaçao. Following the Curaçaoan pattern of bachelor migration, de Lima settled first in Caracas, then in Hamburg, and ultimately in Valparaíso, where he and several partners opened an import house. In Valparaíso, de Lima joined an already existing lodge of French Masons that met under the name Etoile du Pacifique. Becoming conscious of the need for a lodge where no language barrier hindered the admittance of Chileans, he initiated efforts that resulted in the founding of the first Chilean lodge, Union Fraternal, in 1853.[28]

The large foreign community of Valparaíso provided an atmosphere of comparative religious toleration in the mid-nineteenth century. Not so Santiago. A German traveler to that city during Holy Week of the year 1860 reported seeing numerous dummies, elegantly dressed and labeled "Judas Iscariot," being garrotted in front of homes where Jews were known to be living. Nevertheless, intolerable situations in Europe impelled some Jews to settle there. Dr. Pedro Herzl, for example, stymied by the difficulties Jews had in obtaining medical diplomas from the University of Vienna prior to the revolution of 1848, settled in Santiago and became the first Austrian-trained physician to practice there.

In 1852, a confrontation between church and state occurred when the Archbishop of Santiago, Rafael Valentin Valdivieso, ordered communicants to denounce persons suspected of heresy. The impact was immediate in the city of Copiapó, where it became known that a list of names of Protestants and Jews was being prepared. With masses of miners due to arrive in town for the celebration of Christmas, it was feared that riots would follow. The temper of the times is illustrated by the fact that, following publication of the bishop's proclamation, the citizens rallied in defense of religious liberty and against a return of the Inquisition to Chile.

Church and state were not legally separated until 1925. Cultural isolation led many individual Jews to convert to Catholicism, either to conform voluntarily to prevailing social norms or more specifically to marry, a rite that was sometimes celebrated on the groom's deathbed. A civil register for marriages, births, and deaths was established in 1885, and all except two of the Jewish families known to have emigrated to Chile during this period assimilated into the general population. The two who remained Jewish sent their sons and daughters to France to marry.

Mexico

In no country of Latin America was the struggle between church and state as prolonged and as bitter as in Mexico. The war waged for over a century by these titanic forces shaped the Mexican nation from its inception to the present day. As a consequence of the entrenched position of the Catholic church, Mexican liberals acquired a different stamp than liberals in other countries. They became identified, not with the cause of religious liberty, but with the extirpation of church power, even though that be at the expense of religious liberty.

The first federal constitution of 1824, following overthrow of the upstart Emperor Agustín de Iturbide, declared that "the religion of the Mexican nation is and shall perpetually be the Roman Catholic Apostolic." No provision was made for the observance of other religions, and the ancient ecclesiastical privileges were guaranteed.[29]

Despite the unpromising legal setting and the extremely unsettled conditions in the countryside, a few Jewish adventurers and itinerant peddlers made their way to Mexico in the early years of independence. They were able to become citizens only after 1843, when President Antonio López de Santa Anna repealed the law that limited citizenship to Roman Catholics and prohibited Mexican women from marrying outside the church. In the following decade, the names of ten persons who may have been Jewish can be discerned in Mexican naturalization records. Of these individuals, five came from Germany, three from France, one from Poland, and one from Turkey. Three settled in Zacatecas, two in Vera Cruz, one each in San Luis Potosí, Tamaulipas, Santiago, and Mexico City. They gave their occupation as *comerciantes* and were probably itinerant peddlers.[30] What religious life they led had to be clandestine because the holding of non-Catholic religious services was unconstitutional. American soldiers serving in the Mexican-American War came upon isolated Jewish families, including one that was observing Yom Kippur. Among their company was one man who had come from a distant town disguised as a friar.

The fall of Santa Anna paved the way for the Reforma and the opening of immigration to non-Catholics. The Ley Juárez (1855) that attacked ecclesiastical and military privileges and the Ley Lerdo (1856) that attempted to destroy the church's political power by divesting it of its property in land came to be embodied in the liberal constitution of 1857. In its final form, the constitution omitted mention both of the Roman Catholic religion and of religious liberty.

Although individual Jews settled in such towns as Aguas Calientes, Jalapa, Jalisco, Durango, Vera Cruz, Oaxaca, and Mexico City, and in Baja California, this liberal period brought neither stability to the Mexican government nor relaxation to Jewish apprehensions, which were shaped more by popular attitudes than by the legal context. The church generally, the Inquisition specifically, were more determinative of Jewish behavior than any relaxation of the law.[31] Consequently, when German Jews entered Mexico as a result of the European upheavals of 1848, either they followed no Jewish forms or they did so clandestinely. And the religiously neutral constitution did not make all that much difference: letters written in 1862 show that Jewish immigrants still found it necessary to appear to be Catholic.

During these years, the capital city exhibited relatively greater tolerance than the countryside. In 1861, a group of over one hundred Jewish men organized in Mexico City and were holding regular meetings to collect funds for charitable and religious purposes. Under the guise of holding an annual meeting of a Masonic Grand Council, they met in a Masonic lodge to celebrate the High Holy Days. The development of this community was cut short by the turmoil of the French intervention.

Although the Liberals, who under Juárez restored the republic, favored immigration, only a handful of Jews are found in naturalization files for the decade 1867–77. Fear rather than law continued to govern Jewish behavior, and evidence of Jewish communal activity disappears from the record. For example, although the Jews living in the federal capital had planned to build a synagogue, this project was quietly dropped, and no organized community came into existence at this time.

The reason for such pronounced self-effacement was the change that had occurred in the Mexican political climate. The liberalism of the Reforma had been tolerant of religious differences; the liberalism of the restored republic was antireligious. The years of foreign invasion, civil war, and chaos had taught Juárez and those who surrounded him the dangers of excessive liberalism. They moved over intellectually to positivism, with its exaltation of material progress and its denigration of spiritual values. Empiricism having replaced mysticism, there was no room left in official ideology for individual religious belief. The evolution from official toleration of religious differences to official disapproval of all religions made overt expressions by Jews quite impossible, for they were caught between the hammer of governmental anticlericalism and the anvil of intense Catholicism among the masses.

When Porfirio Díaz rose to power in 1877, positivism proved congenial to his style. His dictatorial rule, lasting thirty-four years, imposed a regime of law and order upon Mexico in the interests of foreign investors and the small Mexican elite. "Liberty, Order, and Progress" was the watchword, with the emphasis on order to the detriment of the liberties of the great mass of the people. Because economic wisdom required opening the country to foreigners from industrialized countries who had capital and entrepreneurial skills, an atmosphere of religious toleration was made to prevail within the precincts of Mexico City. Thus, from 1879 onward, the number of Jewish individuals began to increase.

Most prominent among the Jewish immigrants were Alsatians, and almost without exception they considered themselves to be French. For them, religion was an accident of birth, a defect educated men should overcome, though a certain religious sentiment was not inappropriate for women and the lower classes. Many of these immigrants married Catholic wives, fathered Catholic children, and returned to France in their old age. These Alsatian Jews had no interest in organizing a community life, which might have attracted the disdain of elite circles and the hostility of the masses, still capable of being aroused to frenzy by the church. They adopted a collective "low profile" that has remained the dominant characteristic of the Mexican Jewish community to the present day.

But being Jewish did not prevent individuals from making their way successfully in Mexican society; some of them gained positions of power unmatched by Jews in any other Latin American republic to the present day. Most notable among this group was José Yves Limantour, the financial genius of the Díaz regime. Limantour achieved power second only to Díaz himself and might have been named successor to the dictator, had he not been disqualified by his parents' foreign birth. He was largely responsible for the fiscal soundness of the Mexican government in the period prior to World War I, a condition that contrasted brilliantly with the financial chaos that preceded it. Limantour put Mexico on the gold standard; abolished the sales tax (*alcabala*) that had trammeled domestic commerce since colonial days; and consolidated the Mexican railroads into one national system. His identification with Díaz brought about his own resignation along with that of the dictator when the Revolution broke out in 1910.

Eduardo Noetzlin and his associates, contemporaries of Limantour's, were members of a French banking firm with assets in Holland and Switzerland. Noetzlin founded the Banco Nacional de Mexico, which served as an arm of the Treasury Department. Jean Baptiste Jecker, a Swiss adventurer and entrepreneur, entered Mexican history in a less favorable light as negotiator of the loan to the government of General Miguel Miramon that, repudiated by Juárez, became a cause of the French intervention. The Englishman Ernst Cassel became involved in Mexican industrialization as financier of the railroads. He was a friend of Baron Maurice de Hirsch and of Jacob Schiff, president of Kuhn, Loeb and Co., which participated, along with Speyer Brothers—another Jewish firm—in the reorganization of the Mexican railroads in the 1890s.[32]

By that time, Jews were involved in Mexican mining and railroads, the Banco Occidental of Mazatlan, and numerous family businesses. Jewish immigrants were owners of jewelry stores and department stores, purveyors of crystal and glassware, and owners and managers of hotels and restaurants. A number of patents issued to Jews in 1895—for the production of photographic paper, a trouser belt, a printing press, and an apparatus to dry cement—show that Jewish immigrants had entered manufacturing. There were also intellectuals in this immigrant group, including the editor of *El Financiero Mexicano*, the publisher of *L'Écho Français,* the director of the Lycée Française, the director of the Normal School at Jalapa, and the statistician, cartographer, and social reformer Isidoro Epstein.

Sephardic and Arabic Jews had been entering Mexico in small numbers since the earliest years of independence. Some had fled Syria following the Damascus Affair of 1840, in which Jews were accused of murdering a priest to use his blood for sacramental purposes. In 1900 they were organized into four congregations in Mexico City, without their ever having come to the attention of the fashionable French and Alsatian Jews of the capital.[33] These "Turcos" lived as virtual pariahs, plying their trade as peddlers in isolated areas where popular conceptions of the Jew had not progressed much beyond medieval diabolization. They had compacted the Jewish historical experience into a highly ritualized attachment to religious form; the establishment of their synagogues did not require the hiring of a rabbi; there were enough men among them capable of conducting the services. Between this low-status community with its attachment to religious norms and the high-status French and Alsatian community of the capital, characterized by alienation from Jewish life, there was no contact at all.

Interestingly, at a time when European Jews declined to identify with their religious community for fear of calling down calumny, there was an indigenous movement to restore to public life the descendants of crypto-Jews. Francisco Rivas Puigcerver, born in Campeche, Yucatan, in 1850, was a baptized Roman Catholic who claimed to be heir to the Marrano tradition. In a magazine that he began publishing in 1889 called *El Sábado Secreto,* Rivas argued against this integrationist position and in favor of recognition of the diverse ethnic and religious elements that went into the making of Mexico. He urged the Jews of Mexico to declare themselves and to live openly as Jews; at a later date, he corresponded with publicists in Turkey in an effort to stimulate Jewish immigration from that empire to Mexico.[34] His efforts met no resonance among the Mexican people.

Most educated immigrants to Mexico did not become citizens, and among those who did, it is not always possible to distinguish Jews. Possibly one hundred Jews became naturalized Mexicans over the course of the generation 1862–99. Of these individuals, forty-five came from Germany, ten from the United States, nine from France, and six from Austria. To these must be added the French Jews, who, as stated above, tended not to take out citizenship. The Mexican census of 1895 found just .1 percent of the population to be non-Catholic, of whom .13 percent were israelitas.[35]

Brazil

European immigration to Brazil began with the flight of the House
of Bragança from Lisbon to Rio de Janeiro during the Napoleonic wars.
In 1808, the prince regent opened the ports of Brazil to direct trade
with foreign countries, and the country remained open to European
immigrants through the reign of his son, Pedro I. Brazil began her national existence as a monarchy, and church and state remained united
under royal patronage following independence. But in this country of
Catholicism "with the bones removed," in Gilberto Freyre's felicitous
phrase, there was greater freedom of religion than in the Spanish republics of the early independence period. The Imperial Constitution
of 1824 (under which Brazil was governed until 1889) recognized Roman Catholicism as the official religion, but guaranteed the right to
exercise other religions in private. In Brazil, the church gave its consent to mixed marriages, in order that Protestant immigration could
be encouraged. This was a concession not granted to any of the Spanish American republics.

Brazilian interest in immigration sprang from two motives: the
desire to create a class of small farmers who would engage in diversified agriculture and thus supply the consumer demand which large-
scale monoculture overlooked; and the provision of a pool of cheap
manpower to perform the manual labor of the coffee, cotton, and
sugar plantations as the end of the system of slavery drew near. But
despite systematic recruiting of agricultural workers and subsidies for
their travel, immigration to Brazil lagged behind that of other countries of the Western Hemisphere, no doubt because of the perceived
difficulties for immigrants in competing with the system of large estates
and the heritage of black slavery. In consequence, immigration to Brazil remained a mere trickle until 1888, the year of abolition, when the
number of immigrants jumped abruptly to 133,000.

Jews began to emigrate from Morocco to Amazonia shortly after
independence was declared. These were probably Spanish-speaking
Sephardim whose ancestors had settled in North Africa following the
Expulsion from Spain. It is curious that they should have settled in
Portuguese-speaking Brazil just when the Portuguese Jews of Curaçao
were moving over to Spanish-speaking Venezuela and Colombia. The
Moroccans seem to have adapted easily to their new circumstances,
founding a synagogue, Porta do Céu, in Belém do Pará in 1828.[36]
Staking out likely sites along the river, Moroccan traders played a role
in the development of the commerce of the region. Living at ease

among their Christian neighbors, they flourished economically, broadening their activities into export and import (particularly of textiles) and also into navigation of the Amazon and exploration of riparian lands. They entered local politics and held municipal office. With the arrival of additional Sephardim from Africa, Syria, and Arabia, other congregations were formed in Bahia, Manaus, Ceará, and Rio de Janeiro, yielding a contemporary fourth generation of Brazilian Jews.

Dom Pedro II, second emperor of Brazil (1841–89), was an ardent supporter of immigration as a means of populating the country with modernizing elements and was particularly interested in attracting Germans to Brazil. He was also a philo-Semite. No doubt interesting conversations passed between the emperor and the French envoy, Count Joseph Arthur de Gobineau. The latter regarded the Brazilian population as "corrupted in body and soul, ugly to a terrifying degree," as a result of miscegenation.[37] The emperor, who was a statuesque blond, is alleged to have told the count that the latter's racial theories, according to which all achievements of civilization could be ascribed to the Aryan race, were "not suited to our climate." With respect to Jews, Dom Pedro declared (somewhat tongue-in-cheek, perhaps), "I will not combat the Jews, for from their race the God of my religion was born."[38] The emperor studied the Hebrew language with a Swedish professor of Oriental languages named Akerblom and continued his studies under the guidance of the grand rabbi of Marseilles after going into exile in France. In the year of his death, Dom Pedro's translation into French of various Hebrew liturgical poems appeared under the title *Poesis Hebraico-Provençales du rituel Israélite contadin—traduites et transcrites par S. M. Don Pedro II d'Alcantara, empereur du Brésil.*

West European Jews began entering Brazil during the latter part of Dom Pedro's long reign. The most significant number came from Alsace and Lorraine.[39] A group of Jewish immigrants founded the town of Espírito Santo do Pinhal, in the state of São Paulo, and from the 1850s onward they are found as proprietors of coffee plantations. They took an active part in the political and administrative life of the municipalities in which they lived, and some of them joined the Brazilian army.

In the capital city of Rio de Janeiro, Alsatian Jews dominated the commerce in gems from 1856; they were also importers of pharmaceuticals, domestic articles, and luxury goods, including wines, champagne, liqueurs, and jams. By the seventies, German Jews were also engaged in sericulture, the manufacture of telephone parts, and the construction of hydraulic works. A member of this migration was Bertholdo

Goldschmidt, born in Posen in 1817, who acquired Brazilian citizenship in 1857 and assumed a post as professor of German at the Imperio Colegio Pedro II. Goldschmidt, together with a colleague, edited the first German-language journal in Brazil (*Der Deutsche Beobachter*) and translated the dramas of Schiller into Portuguese. On his death in 1893, he was buried in the cemetery of São Francisco Xavier.[40]

The defeat of France in the Franco-Prussian War and the annexation of Alsace-Lorraine by Germany propelled more French Jews to Brazil, and particularly to São Paulo, which from 1881 was taking up more than her share of immigrants. Some individuals settled in cities such as Pôrto Alegre, Passo Fundo, and Santa Maria; but the Jewish colony in São Paulo city itself, which came to number several hundred, was the largest and liveliest, with strong representation in the liberal professions. French Jews were university professors, dentists, engineers, and artists. In São Paulo in the second half of the nineteenth century were to be found the composer Alexandre Levy, the painter Berta Worms, and the biologist André Dreyfus. This French colony assimilated to Brazilian society and has now almost ceased to be Jewish.[41]

Curiously, there also arrived at this time Jews from Portugal—not conversos or cristãos novos, but persons who had survived as avowed Jews. Some came directly from Portugal, others by way of the north, where they had been trading in vanilla beans, rubber, and those exotic feathers esteemed by Parisian women of *la belle epoque*.[42] All were drawn southward by the increasing economic dynamism of São Paulo.

The assimilation of Jews into Brazilian society was facilitated by the variety of positivism that flourished in Brazil during this period. Brazilian positivists were modernizers who sought to improve educational opportunity in order to create a technocratic elite. Emphasizing material prosperity, positivists wanted to foment conditions favorable to the growth of capitalism.[43] At the same time, and for corresponding reasons, the movement was anti-Catholic in its thrust. The liberality of Dom Pedro's regime was congenial to the spread of this new "religion" that denied the existence of a personal god and took "humanity, the Great Being, as the object of its veneration."[44] The Positivist church itself attracted only a few members; but the larger number of practicing positivists had the effect of leavening the intellectual environment of the great cities of the Brazilian littoral, preparing, incidentally, a milieu that was much more receptive to Jews than was that of such tradition-bound areas as Peru.

As Dom Pedro aged, the imminent ascension to the throne of the pious Princess Isabella became a precipitant in formation of elements hostile to a continuation of the monarchy. After the emperor's abdication, positivist and other progressive influences in the drafting of the republican constitution brought about the separation of church and state and the guarantee of religious freedom.

Peru

"That the Catholic Church is the State ecclesiastical establishment of Peru admits of no question, for, indeed, the system of interdependence of State and Church is one of the most comprehensive and absolute in Latin America. Furthermore, this ecclesiastical policy has been maintained with little or no change through the years."[45] In this way, J. Lloyd Mecham describes the actual situation in Peru. The countries that formed the old viceroyalty of Peru were not active seekers of immigrants in the nineteenth century, their elite classes preferring a status quo fortified by the church to modernization and the hazards of change. Until 1915, religious toleration could not legally exist, the public exercise of any religion but the Catholic being forbidden by the constitution. A law providing for civil marriage was passed in 1897; before that date, marriage was a religious sacrament that could be performed only in a church. In the matter of cemeteries, a dent was made earlier in the Catholic monopoly over civil affairs, as a result of the need to provide a respectable burial for foreigners sojourning in the country—foreigners who were Peru's main link with international trade.[46]

The political, social, and economic upheavals in Europe in 1848, and again in 1870, propelled some immigrants to Peru even though government was not recruiting them. Among these immigrants there were some Jews, mostly from Alsace-Lorraine, but including a few from Austria, Poland, Russia, and Italy.[47] Most of the immigrants brought their families as well as employees of their firms—a sign that they intended to stay. Among the migrants were industrialists, bankers, diamond merchants, jewelers, engineers, merchants, and employees of these firms. Also included among them were representatives of European firms, such as the House of Rothschild, whose agents, the Jacoby brothers, established the first exchange bank in Lima. Other agents became involved in buying and selling Peruvian wool and cotton, as well as in mining ventures. The ties of these firms ran back to England and France.

An important figure in this nineteenth-century community was Henry Meiggs, an engineer who designed and supervised construction of the Callao, Lima, and Oroya Railroad, at that time the highest track in the world and the one that "broke the back of the Andes," in the phrase used by Oliver Wendell Holmes in his biography of Meiggs in the *Dictionary of American Biography*. Born in 1811 in Catskill, New York, Meiggs came to Peru in 1870 following a career of railroad construction and financial skulduggery in California (which he left as a fugitive from justice) and Chile (where he completed a railroad that had bankrupted other men and turned a profit too). Holmes endowed Meiggs with old New England ancestry, but that may have been the result of some Meiggsian sleight of hand: the Jewish community of Lima claims him, too.

The career of Meiggs provides some insight into the status of the Jews in Lima of the 1870s, a rather surprising one in light of the existing state-church system. The few Jews living in the city had been burying their dead in the British cemetery, but the need for a place in which to bury according to Jewish rite was becoming apparent. Meiggs, who by then was sixty-four years of age, sold a plot of land to the newly formed Sociedad de Beneficencia Israelita for one centavo a square yard for use as a cemetery. Gratitude for what amounted to his donation of land is expressed in a plaque affixed to the gate of the Cementerio de Baquijano, which is still in use. Not far distant from the cemetery is Peru's first racetrack, the land for which was also provided by Meiggs. Among those who contributed toward its construction were ten individuals and firms whose names are also to be found on the plaque at the Jewish cemetery. Many of these persons, as well as other Jews, were members of the Sociedad de Carreras, which later metamorphosed into the Jockey Club of Peru. It was apparently possible to belong both to this oligarchic redoubt and to the Sociedad de Beneficencia Israelita. Social intercourse led to intermarriage. Although members of this migration founded the burial society that would later become the cornerstone of organized Jewish life in Peru, all of its original members assimilated into the Peruvian population and disappeared from Jewish ranks within the course of three generations.

Very different from this Ashkenazic migration was that of Jewish North Africans—probably Spanish-speaking Moroccans from Tetuan and Tangier—who came to Peru in the mid-nineteenth century, attracted by the rubber boom in Amazonia.[48] The initiation of commercial steamboat service made it possible for adventurers to penetrate the interior by way of the river, and people of all nationalities trooped to the area to enrich themselves or to die unchronicled in the jungle. Jews were among their number. They lived in the region of Iquitos till about 1910, when the development of East Indian rubber plantations ended the Amazon boom. Of the 150 Jews known to have been in the province of Amazonas at that time, possibly 90 left the area. Many of those who stayed had formed unions with local women. There are therefore people living in Amazonas today with Sephardic names, such as Benzaquen, Levy, Israel, Abenzur, but with only a dim memory of their Jewish origins. This group, ignored by the organized Jewish community of Lima, was recently contacted by an outreach program conducted by the Israeli embassy of that city.

Guatemala

Despite the very different conditions of Guatemalan life, the debate over European immigration took place in terms so similar to those that engaged the Argentinians and Chileans that we are led inescapably to the conclusion that the context of immigration policy was molded by the same intellectual forces all over the continent.

Debate over the merits of immigration began while Guatemala was a member of the Federation of Central America, a union with El Salvador, Honduras, Nicaragua, and Costa Rica that coalesced after the fall of Iturbide of Mexico in 1823 and lasted only until 1838. Most articulate elements in the new republic were concerned with improving the quality of life. On the method, direction, and tempo of change, opinion diverged. Liberals generally were convinced that certain elements essential to growth were not obtainable from domestic sources, and they looked abroad for help. Consequently, they framed laws that they hoped would attract immigrants and capital to the country to aid in the development of the economy and alter existing cultural patterns. Disestablishment of the Catholic church and the proclamation of religious toleration in 1833 opened the way for admission of non-Catholics. Public lands were made available to private buyers, with one-third reserved for distribution free of charge to immigrant families or to the founders of new settlements.[49]

Legislation in support of immigration was spurred by a vision of prospective European settlers as active agents of social change, who would serve as models of entrepreneurial activity while teaching native citizens the virtues of civic responsibility. In addition to their material contributions, they were expected to alter existing culture patterns so that the modernization of Guatemala could begin. Generally, the Indian (who comprised the majority of the population) got short shrift. Although at first there was some Enlightenment sentiment that all men, even Indians, were perfectible, there was an increasing tendency during the nineteenth century to view the indigenous inhabitants as a stumbling block to economic development. The large land grants being offered to foreign developers as often as not belonged to the Indians, by usage if not by law. The cheap labor offered the colonists was that of the Indian, who had been freed from the onerous labor laws of colonial days only to be bound over under laws of vagrancy. It was considered a favor to the Indian population to Europeanize it, and this could even be done humanely: a European immigrant who married an Indian woman thereby qualified for a double portion of land.

Conservatives feared that a mass influx of foreigners might destabilize society or even lead to the alienation of national territory, as had happened in Mexico, but they did not close off immigration entirely when they came to power. Rather, they reduced the scope of institutional accommodations they were prepared to offer. Specifically, Conservatives reestablished the church and ceased support for sponsored programs of mass colonization. They retained incentives for individual settlers who conformed to existing social norms.

Both Liberals and Conservatives anticipated an immigration composed almost entirely of agricultural workers. Liberals would have recruited these en masse, whereas Conservatives considered it more prudent to attract desirable immigrants individually. But neither approach succeeded. Changes in law were ineffectual in altering the nativist attitude of Guatemaltecos, and in the absence of any strong economic attraction, the immigrants simply did not come.[50]

When the Liberal party disestablished the church and proclaimed religious toleration in 1833, the way was legally clear for Jewish as well as for non-Jewish immigrants. Of the few who came, the majority were German; among the Germans, there were Jews. The first for whom there is any record came from Posen in 1848.[51] In that city, the civil status of Jews had long been at hazard, some of them qualifying for Prussian citizenship and some not. The full emancipation glimpsed as a result of the revolution of 1848 turned out to be a chimera, and the reaction that followed compelled many Jews to emigrate.

In 1870, a congregation of German Jews was formed in Guatemala City. This was an industrial and commercial community, occupying itself in textile manufacture, the curing of hides, and export-import trade. One of its number, Luis Schlesinger (1820–1900) may be considered an industrial precursor for Guatemala as a whole. Restrictions were placed by government on the commercial activities of foreigners however, (in 1952, the Guatemalan government still withheld citizenship from German Jews), and so the country never became an attractive place of settlement for large numbers of Jews. Religious toleration was a sine qua non, but not in itself sufficient inducement.

The Jewish Population of Latin America in 1889

By 1889, only a few thousand Jews were to be found in all Latin America. Any enumeration risks the omission of individuals; however, the identifiable groups included the Portuguese Sephardim of Curaçao, who had by now dispersed to adjacent lands of the Caribbean basin; West European Ashkenazim from France, Germany, Alsace, Lorraine, Switzerland, and England, who were scattered in the metropolitan cities of Argentina, Chile, Guatemala, Mexico, Brazil, and Peru; Spanish-speaking Sephardim from North Africa adventuring in the Amazon region of Brazil and Peru; and Arabic-speaking Sephardim in provincial towns of Argentina and Mexico.

These groups differed from one another in language, social mores, and religious practices. Members of these diverse cultural groups—though they may all have been perceived as "Jews" by the majority population—in fact had nothing to do with one another. Where communal institutions formed, they coalesced on an ethnic basis; characteristically, the various synagogues and burial societies were founded by specific ethnic groups of Jews, and they formed no liaison with one another. This pattern endures to the present day.

We have seen how Portuguese Sephardim fitted into mercantile societies on the fringe of the Spanish-speaking world. Appointed to key government positions in the Dominican Republic, they utilized their oversea connections to extend the republic's slim resources, in one instance arranging for a Dutch bank to consolidate the Dominican debt. As the Sephardim of Santo Domingo assimilated to the highest social strata, they gave up their economic ethos, adopting instead the mentality of those who prefer to invest their wealth in houses and land. They chose for their sons the traditional academic preparation for physician or lawyer, in preference to business. These families did not seek to conceal their Jewish origins; on the contrary, they tended to boast of them, possibly because Jewish descent proved they were white, a matter of importance to Dominicans in the light of their long occupation by black Haitians.[52] The number of Sephardic families in the Dominican Republic had dwindled to twenty by the first quarter of the nineteenth century; the last survivor died an old man in the 1950s.

Ashkenazim were strangers to the Spanish-speaking world, but they proved almost as malleable as the Sephardim in the social setting in which they now found themselves. These western Jews came from societies that had been plowed and harrowed by the great wars of religion, of rising nationalism, and of the industrial revolution. They were imbued with the ideal of emancipation, of liberation from medieval restrictions, and of acceptance by the family of man. In accord with Enlightenment thought, they had freed themselves from the bonds of established religion in order to make themselves acceptable for citizenship on an equal footing with Christians. Indeed, a specifically Jewish Enlightenment (*haskalah*) had developed, which preached that Jews should divest themselves of attributes that made them unacceptable to Christians in order to qualify themselves for emancipation. "Be a Jew at home, a man on the street," counseled the *maskillim* (enlighteners), the implication being that the world would accept as a man the same individual it rejected as a Jew.

In the context of the European historical process, westernized Jews came to equate emancipation with acceptance by the Christian majority. If that acceptance required the rejection of Jewish tradition, so be it. Hans Kohn, the eminent historian of nationalism, describes the phenomenon: "During the first half of the nineteenth century, assimilation swept through Jewish life like a veritable hurricane; originating in Western Europe, it moved eastward, wiping out with it practically all the upper strata of Jewish society. One purpose seemed to animate Jewish life: to escape from Judaism, to become like the gentiles."[53] This dream of emancipation alternately bloomed and withered in the revolutions of 1830 and 1848. The desire to escape from Judaism may have been a factor in rendering West European Jews available for immigration to Latin America, a continent that had no history of Jewish settlement, and therefore no ready-made structures for the legal isolation of Jews.

In the major metropolitan centers of the Latin American continent to which the German, French, English, and Swiss Jews came, they found an elite class that was more attuned to the cultural emanations of Europe—particularly France—than to the rhythms of their autochthonous societies. Social circles that were receptive to Masonry and to positivism formed a milieu into which these secularized Jews could comfortably assimilate. Although the social structures of these countries were still patrimonial and clerical, those sectors of the creole elites who wished to break with the past welcomed immigrants with modernizing skills. Their nonadherence to the Catholic church made them welcome allies of the anticlerical elites. Jewish immigrants of 1830,

1848, 1870 included engineers, financiers, doctors, linguists, scientists, and entrepreneurs—all skills the continent gravely lacked. Possession of such skills facilitated the entry of the immigrants into the upper reaches of the middle class, where their mobility was enhanced by the fact that many were estranged from their religion and eager to be accepted socially. Many Jewish immigrants continued to regard themselves as Jews while paying little attention to religious ritual. Having been partially assimilated into the Gentile environment of Europe, they formed religious congregations in the New World but continued their assimilatory trend by marrying Catholic wives, sometimes in Protestant ceremonies. The opening of social circles to accommodate the newcomers was simplified by the readiness of both parties to relegate religion to a secondary status. Intermarriage, the result of social acceptance, accomplished one of the major goals the proimmigration forces had set themselves.

The expectation that immigrants would supply the Latin economies with cheap labor went unsatisfied by this migration. Few in number, Jewish immigrants were completely irrelevant to the demand for agricultural labor since they included, as far as can be determined, no farmers at all (with the exception of the landowning German coffee planters of São Paulo). On the other hand, these immigrants did provide entrepreneurial skills that many Latin Americans, particularly the positivists, wanted to recruit to give impetus to industrialization. In the process, some Jewish immigrants achieved great personal success, unhampered by their origins or religious affiliation.

Of the Oriental immigrants of this period, far less is known. They proceeded from Muslim areas that had not been reached by the intellectual currents that shaped post-Napoleonic Europe. Nationalism, secularization, emancipation were alien concepts for them. As pariahs who were alternately harassed and patronized by their Muslim overlords, the Jews had occupied extremely low status in their countries of origin.[54] They transferred their occupations, their outlook, and their status to the countries of their adoption. There is no known instance of these Oriental communities seeking to link up with the high-status Ashkenazim of the great cities. They may not even have recognized one another as Jews.

Religious toleration was not a decisive consideration for non-Jewish immigrants to Latin America. Most were from Spain or Italy, with religious beliefs so similar to those of the host countries that no alteration in ecclesiastical structures was necessary to accommodate them. The real impact of the introduction of religious toleration was to encourage a diversified flow of immigrants, including Protestants, who arrived in numbers far greater than did Jews. Once immigrants entered a country en masse, as they did Argentina, their very number and heterogeneity wrought unpredictable and irreversible changes in society, including tolerable conditions for Jewish settlement. In other words, the preconditions for Jewish settlement could in no way be created by Jews, but could arise only out of changed attitudes within the republics. These changes had to be in the direction of movement away from ancient Hispanic ideals of conformity to monolithic Catholic beliefs.

Mass immigration in fact occurred only where religious toleration combined with economic opportunity. The experience of Guatemala shows that legal toleration alone was not enough to attract immigrants, Jews or non-Jews. But if the economic possibilities seemed attractive enough, immigrants came even where there were barriers to their absorption.

For Jews, religious toleration was crucial. True, individuals found their way to the most unlikely areas when the economic stakes seemed high enough (or, in later periods, when the pressure was great enough). But for the mass of people, the absence of a legal base for their existence—for marriage, burial, registration of the birth of a child, secular education—did not create an alluring prospect. Without religious toleration, no Jewish immigration of any magnitude took place, whatever the idiosyncratic choices of individual Jews.

Thus, formation of the contemporary Jewish communities was a function of religious toleration and economic incentive, on the one hand, and of the massive immigration of heterogeneous peoples, on the other. The combined activities of the newcomers did in fact commence the industrialization of the continent so devoutly anticipated by positivists and others, while at the same time upsetting the former balance of political and social forces, as the traditionalists had feared. In this way were the expectations of liberal and conservative alike brought to reality.

3

Mass Immigration: 1889 to World War I

The contemporary Jewish communities of Latin America were formed between 1889 and World War I, largely by East European Ashkenazim. The extremely high migration figures for this period (see Table 1) reflect the intense pressures that were being exerted upon Jews within their countries of origin, at a time when international travel was relatively cheap and most countries of the Western Hemisphere followed unrestricted immigration policies.

Most migrants of this period originated in the Russian Empire, Poland, and Romania, where a dual policy toward Jews was being exercised by governments of the late nineteenth century. Toleration for the Jewish commercial and industrial bourgeoisie that was engaged in modernization of the economy was accompanied by ruthless oppression and deprivation of the majority, a policy aimed at driving impoverished Jews to emigrate. The pressure was particularly severe in Russia, where the czarist government sought to divert attention from economic upheaval and social and political struggle by encouraging a brutal wave of pogroms.

In 1881, the assassination of Czar Alexander II was made the occasion for a series of government-sponsored pogroms. The May Laws of the following year forced confinement of Russian Jews to certain towns and townships, driving them from the rural villages where many had lived. As a result of officially countenanced mass destruction, Jews by the thousand—dispossessed, bewildered, and the responsibility of no one—fled over the border into Germany. From there, many made their way, with the help of Jewish relief organizations, to the New World. These East European Ashkenazim, in their pell-mell flight westward, provided the bulk of the manpower of the Jewish communities of the United States, Canada, and Latin America, in the process shifting the balance of the world Jewish population from Europe to the Western Hemisphere. In the twenty years 1880 to 1900, half a million Jews entered the United States. But these numbers were to be eclipsed during the next fourteen years. Among the million and a half Europeans who fled their homes annually in the years 1900 to 1914, fully one-tenth were Jewish. The vast majority of these entered the United States, with its reputation for religious toleration and economic opportunity.

But the desperate need for a haven forced Jews into areas such as Latin America that had not previously been regarded as hospitable. Ashkenazim now settled in all the Western Hemisphere republics, building substantial communities in Argentina and Brazil. Accommodating themselves to the new environment, they soon outnumbered the West Europeans and Sephardim who had preceded them, stamping Latin American Jewish communities with the East European orientation they retain to this day.

Sephardic immigration also increased during this period, though at a lower level numerically than Ashkenazim because they were drawing from a smaller population reservoir. Emigration of Jews from Morocco escalated after 1880. The years 1900 to 1914 saw substantial Sephardic emigration from the Balkans, spurred by natural calamities and deteriorating economic conditions. How many Sephardim entered Latin American countries during these years is not known,[1] but Arabic- and Ladino-speaking congregations were organized in both Mexico and Cuba, countries that had not as yet attracted East European Jews.

The majority of immigrants gravitated to those countries that, out of a desire to encourage immigration, had separated church and state. Individual Jews, however, settled for idiosyncratic reasons in every one of the republics, including those with the most limited vision of religious freedom.

Argentina

More than any other country of Latin America, Argentina seemed to offer an optimal combination of religious toleration, strong government support for immigration, industrial employment, and land for farming. So great was the attraction that one-quarter of a million im-

Table 1. *Jewish Migrants from Europe according to Countries of Immigration, 1840–1942*
(Absolute Numbers)

Years	United States	Canada	Argentina	Brazil	Uruguay	Other Countries of America	South Africa	Palestine	All Other Countries	Total
1840–1880	200,000	1,600	2,000	500		1,000	4,000	10,000	2,000	221,100
1881–1900	675,000	10,500	25,000	1,000		1,000	23,000	25,000	4,000	764,500
1901–1914	1,346,400	95,300	87,614	8,750		3,000	21,377	30,000	10,000	1,602,441
1915–1920	76,450	10,450	3,503	2,000	1,000	5,000	907	−15,000	5,000	89,310
1921–1925	280,283	14,400	39,713	7,139	3,000	7,000	4,630	60,765	10,000	426,930
1926–1930	54,998	15,300	33,721	22,296	6,370	10,000	10,044	10,179	10,000	172,908
1931–1935	17,986	4,200	12,700	13,075	3,280	15,000	4,507	147,502	20,000	238,250
1936–1939	79,819	900	14,789	10,600	7,677	15,000	5,300	75,510	60,000	269,595
1940–1942	70,954	800	4,500	6,000	1,000	2,000	2,000	35,000	10,000	132,354
1840–1942	2,801,890	153,450	223,540	71,360	22,327	59,000	75,765	378,956	131,000	3,917,388

Source: Jacob Lestchinsky, "Jewish Migrations, 1840–1956," p. 1554.

migrants were admitted to the country in the five-year period 1881–85, and this number was more than doubled in the following quinquennium.[2] Yet, the number of Jews admitted to Argentina from 1881 to 1889 was probably no greater than 350.[3] At the beginning of this period, the Argentine government had authorized its agent in Milan to look into the situation of Jews in czarist Russia with a view to inducing them to migrate to Argentina. His efforts were unsuccessful, probably for two reasons: the underdevelopment of the Argentine economy, as compared with that of the United States; and fear that the religious toleration offered by the Constitution of 1853 might lack substance.

The modest effort to attract Jewish immigrants was met by opposing forces. The French language newspaper *L'Union Française* deplored the move, referring to Jews as "noxious insects and powerful parasites." *La Nación*, the prestigious paper founded by Bartolomé Mitre (president of the republic from 1862 to 1868) was more moderate. Recognizing the plight of Russian Jews, *La Nación* posed no objection to their individual, spontaneous migration to Argentina. But active recruitment was opposed: Jews were the least assimilable people in the world. In 1890, the same newspaper serialized *La Bolsa,* an anti-Semitic novel still widely circulated and read in Argentina.

The question of Jewish immigration to Argentina remained moot for the better part of a decade. The earliest mention of Argentina as a possible haven that can be found in the Jewish press of eastern Europe occurred in *Hatsefira* of Warsaw in June of 1888.[4] By that date, the first group of Jewish settlers bound for Argentina had already been organized.

In August of 1889, this group of 824 Jews sailed from Bremen on the ship *Weser* with the object of taking up farming on a plot of land they had bought from an agent of the Argentine government. They were at first denied entry at Buenos Aires as "harmful elements," having been expelled from their home country. This on-the-spot decision by the port inspector was reversed, and the immigrants were admitted. It was due to their subsequent misadventures that the intervention of Baron Maurice de Hirsch was solicited, with the resultant founding of the Jewish Colonization Association (JCA).

In Argentina's great century of immigration, we know that almost half the immigrants were Italian and another third Spanish. Jews would be counted among the remainder, but exactly how many entered the country cannot be determined. Immigrants were listed by country of birth, not by religion. The national census of 1895 asked a question concerning religion. In that year, israelitas were enumerated at 6,085, a figure considered by one qualified observer to be a "serious under-estimate."[5] The majority of these israelitas, 5,890, were foreign-born. Only 753 of them were living in Buenos Aires; the rest were in the provinces of Entre Ríos, Santa Fé, and Buenos Aires, the majority in agricultural colonies.[6]

By 1909, when JCA[7] conducted a census, 19,361 Jews were living in the agricultural colonies, 16,589 in the capital, and about 13,000 more in the cities of Rosario, Santa Fé, Carlos Casares, La Plata, Córdoba, Mendoza, and Tucumán, bringing the total of Jews in Argentina to just under 50,000.[8]

The number of israelitas in Buenos Aires and their neighborhood settlement pattern coincided closely with the number of Russian-born persons in the city. This identification was quickly made, and Jews came to be known as *rusos*.[9] Though some 85 percent of Jews did indeed come from Russia, another 15 percent were classified by JCA as Turks or Moroccans, reflecting the independent migration of peddlers into the interior. There were only a sprinkling of French, German, English, Italian, Austrian, and Romanian Jews.

These ethnic divisions became an element in occupational choice, as may be seen from observations in the JCA *Report*: "The Russians are generally engaged in the furniture trade, the Turks in haberdashery, the Moroccans in cloth and ready-made clothing, the French, Germans, Dutch, etc., in jewelry. Some of them are extremely rich but most of them are only small tradesmen."

The East Europeans felt themselves to be distinct from the Sephardim and "Orientals" (Arabic-speaking Jews), as well as from the West Europeans who had preceded them and who they sometimes took to be descendants of Marranos, so attenuated was their Jewish cultural life. A view across the gulf that separated "easterners" from "westerners" has been provided by Pinie Wald, a sheet-metal worker and socialist activist who migrated from Lodz to Buenos Aires in 1906. "Originally, these people [the west Europeans] were separated by distance from us *Jewish* Jews; from up close, nothing changed. We don't fight one another, God forbid! We live at peace with one another. But we live as separate nations."[10]

Feverish worldwide migration characterized the years 1910–14. Possibly 41,000 more Jews entered Argentina during these years, bringing the Jewish community past the 100,000 mark on the eve of World War I. About one-quarter of this population was now in the JCA farm colonies and another one-quarter in provincial towns. (Among the latter, as many as 40 percent may have been engaged at least part-time in farming.) But Argentine Jewry was becoming increasingly concentrated in the capital. The numbers of colonists continued to grow, but the urban population grew still faster, so that over half of Argentine Jews —65,000 of 110,000—were living in Buenos Aires by World War I.[11]

Among these Jews, JCA identified only one hundred who were in the liberal professions in 1909. The mass of Jewish immigrants to Argentina were skilled and unskilled workers. A description of the Jewish working class has been left by Pinie Wald: "The Jewish immigration was proletarian and arrived third class, since there was no fourth class. We were no different than the general run of people coming in, except that all the Jews came with the intention of staying. . . . The entire Jewish migration was proletarian, from the '90s of the previous century to the '50s of the present century."[12] Russian, Romanian, and (Austrian) Galician Jews had not been able to work in factories in the countries of their birth. In Argentina, according to Wald, they were hired without discrimination. Bosses treated them well, "not as Jews but as deaf and dumb and suffering immigrants."

Unlike the more numerous Italians and Spaniards, who were for the most part peasants, the Jews included a high proportion of skilled workers.[13] The fate of this Jewish proletariat would largely be a function of the capacity of the Argentine economy to absorb them into productive occupations (see Chapter 5).

By the 1890's, immigrant workers were organizing themselves into unions, a tradition already well established in Europe but still alien to Argentina. The earliest stages of labor organization in Argentina, as elsewhere in Latin America, were dominated by anarchists, making it appear to the propertied class that the organization of labor posed a direct threat to the continuance of civilized society. The salience of foreign-born labor leaders, moreover, provoked a chauvinist response, making the repression of industrial ferment appear to be both patriotic and enlightened. The unions, for their part—with no labor code to satisfy the legitimate aspirations of workers and no representation in government—oriented themselves toward forcible seizure of power and liquidation of the state as an instrument of oppression. The consequence was a series of violent strikes, violently suppressed.

The history of Jewish trade unionism in Argentina has not yet been written, though it deserves to be. A Centro Obrero Israelita (Jewish Workers' Center), founded in 1897, included both workers and bosses. By 1905, Jewish tailors, carpenters, capmakers, and bakers all had organized. The first two groups joined the Socialist-dominated Union General de Trabajo. The bakers, who from all accounts suffered the most exploitative conditions, joined the anarchist-dominated Federación Obrera Regional Argentina (FORA). By 1908, the anarchists were publishing one page of their newspaper, *La Protesta*, in Yiddish. Buenos Aires Jewish unions experienced the same heated debates as those carried on in the New York Jewish unions as to the relative merits of organizing into separate Jewish locals (with business conducted in Yiddish) or merging with the general membership in each trade union.[14] Most of the Jewish unions failed to survive wartime layoffs and the police repression of 1919.

For a while, Jewish immigrants to Argentina were active politically. Among the founders of the Argentine Socialist party in 1896 were numerous immigrants and sons of immigrants, including Dr. Enrique Dickmann, son of Russian Jews who had migrated to the agricultural colonies. Other Jews who had been affiliated with the socialist movement in Europe through its Jewish sector, the Bund, retained their ideology after arrival in Argentina. There they founded Avanguard in 1907, with the purpose of promoting socialism among the Jewish working class through the medium of Yiddish. Like other socialists, the Bund opposed resort to revolutionary solutions.

Jews were represented in all branches of the workers' movement, but most heavily in the Socialist party. The Argentine anarcho-communist movement (FORA del V Congreso) had a Jewish component known as Arbeter Freynt; so did its syndicalist spin-off, FORA del IX Congreso.[15] Together these "progressives" founded the Algemeiner Yiddisher Arbeter Farband in 1909 in Buenos Aires that took part in the May Day parade that year during which several demonstrators were killed by the police. A short while later, a Jewish anarchist named Simon Radowitski assassinated the Buenos Aires chief of police in revenge for the slayings. Antianarchist feeling erupted in the sacking of the offices of *La Vangardia* and *La Protesta*, the Bundist and anarchist newspapers, as well as the Biblioteca Rusa, the Jewish workers' library. In the police crackdown and state of siege that followed, many revolutionaries fled the country or were deported. The socialist wing of the Zionist party (Poalei Zion), founded in Buenos Aires four years earlier, virtually collapsed at this time following deportation of its leaders.

Although the mass of working-class immigrants probably had little time for ideology or politics, a general reaction against them now set in. As in the United States, labor unrest, urban crime, and declining morality all were blamed on the immigrant. Demands that immigration be curbed began to come from previously proimmigration forces.

In 1909, Ricardo Rojas began the remythologizing of the gaucho that heralded the birth of cultural nationalism. Argentina, he wrote, threatened by invasion of foreign influence and ideas, must develop a collective consciousness based on native traditions. Immigrants are tolerable as long as they can be assimilated, and Argentina is generous. But resistance to assimilation is serious. The feeling of racial superiority, originally enlisted in the war against gauchismo, was now brought into play in a struggle against the admission of more immigrants.

For that purpose, Rojas undertook to reinterpret Sarmiento, the apostle of population growth. Sarmiento, Rojas wrote, was "a partisan of immigration conceived as a procedure for creating a fatherland in consortium with humanity, and not as a factory without historical destiny, formed by individuals without flag, or collectivities without ideals. . . . Sarmiento wanted immigration in order to populate the desert, refine the race, stimulate wealth, elevate culture, correct political customs; but all this under the aegis of a nationalist ideal, without which Argentina would run the risk of moral dissolution."[16] The way was being paved for the closing off of immigration.

In light of the onslaught of criticism of the immigrant as un-Argentine, publication of *Los gauchos judíos* in 1910, Argentina's centennial year, takes on importance. Its author, Alberto Gerchunoff, was born in Poland in 1884 and brought to Argentina, where he grew up in the Jewish agricultural colony of Moisesville. Migrating to Buenos Aires at age seventeen, he became a reporter for *La Nación* and eventually its editor in chief. His best-known work, translated as *Jewish Gauchos of the Pampas*, achieved considerable success in Argentina among both Jews and non-Jews. In fact, he was not so much a Jewish writer as a writer who interpreted Jewish life to the Gentiles. In this role, he played a considerable part in the rooting of the Jewish community in Argentina. His novel represents the Jewish claim on Argentine history, a claim backed up by the expenditure of blood, sweat, and love in the agricultural colonies.[17]

Gerchunoff proposed that Jewish life in Argentina represented a continuation of the Jews' Spanish tradition, interrupted but not ended in 1492. By settling in Argentina, Jews were simply recovering what was already theirs; they even learn Spanish easily, he avers, because they already possess a Spanish spirit. To develop this line of thought, Gerchunoff had to ignore the disparate historical experience of Sephardim and Ashkenazim: the latter were never in Spain and were never expelled from there. But his effort to anchor the Jews within Argentine tradition was rewarded by the admiration of numerous critics, one of whom wrote concerning him, "que por ser judío, tenía mucho de española." (Being Jewish, he had much of the Spaniard in him.)[18] He was also rewarded by the veneration of thousands of Argentine Jews, for whom he spoke at a level of psychological, if not factual, truth.

Gerchunoff was not the only contribution of the East Europeans to Argentine culture. Samuel Eichelbaum, born to Russian Jewish parents in the town of Dominguez, was described in 1956 as "the preeminent Spanish-speaking playwright."[19] Joseph Kessel, born in Villa Clara to a physician who was among the first Jewish settlers in Entre Ríos, was received into the French Academy of History for his literary and historical works.[20] Cesar Tiempo (born Israel Zeitlin in 1906 in the Ukraine) lived a lively literary life in Buenos Aires as journalist, playwright, poet, and editor of the literary review *Columna*.[21] Other Argentine literary figures stemming from this migration include Enrique Espinoza, editor of *Babel*; Carlos Grünberg, novelist and poet; and Max Dickman, influential Buenos Aires writer. Enrique Dickmann, who was elected to Congress on the Socialist ticket, likewise stemmed from this migration. Dickmann grew up in the Jewish agricultural colonies but became a physician, one of those many of whom it was said, "We planted wheat, and grew doctors."

Chile

Despite early liberal immigration policy, Chile actually received very few immigrants in the nineteenth century. The country remained difficult of access. Prior to the opening of the Panama Canal, the options were a hazardous voyage through the Straits of Magellan or an arduous crossing of the Andes by foot or muleback (the trans-Andean railroad was not opened until 1910). There was no attempt to organize mass Jewish immigration, such as occurred in Argentina. The result was that there were scarcely enough Jews for a *minyan* (prayer unit of ten men) in Santiago in 1906, when an earthquake impressed upon the residents there the need for supernatural support.

Most of the East European Jews who came to Chile in the years just prior to World War I were moving on from Argentina, where they had not been able to sink roots. They arrived partially acculturated, with some knowledge of Spanish, and, says one author, a fear of appearing to be Jewish which they had learned in Buenos Aires. These early settlers seem to have lived in fear of the surrounding population, whom they saw as "consumed by drunkenness and dominated by religious fanaticism" (a statement contained in the Yiddish text, but not in the Spanish translation).[22] An effigy of Judas, looking suspiciously like the medieval caricature of a Jew, was still being taken out and garrotted each Holy Week. Consequently, many Jews feared to identify themselves publicly as Jews, and a social club organized in 1911 opened under the unlikely name Filarmónica Rusa.

The Chilean Jewish community gained recruits with the flight of political activists from Argentina following the police repression of 1909. Some Jewish businessmen also left Argentina during World War I for Chile, where the economy was more buoyant because of the worldwide demand for copper and nitrates. But central European Jews continued to predominate, and these were still scattered in foreign colonies for the most part. A small number of German-speaking Jews had become highly successful in banking and export-import houses in the major cities.[23]

To the south, various Sephardic families settled in Temuco, capital of Araucania, in 1914. They came from Monastir, in Yugoslavia, and they called their first club Centro Macedonia; only later was the word israelita added. From Temuco, some of these Sephardim moved to Santiago and founded a community there.

Chilean intellectual support for immigration reversed field around 1905, when the accumulation of economic power by foreigners and their consequent rise to middle-class status presented an unexpected challenge to existing interests. This reaction must have set in without much stimulus from Jews. The newly arrived East Europeans were mostly peddlers who had not yet had time to establish themselves or to draw substantial quantities of business away from established merchants. And, although under the circumstances precise numbers cannot be known, there were only from two hundred to five hundred Jews in all of Chile in 1914.[24]

Mexico

Two waves of Jewish migrants reached Mexico in the first two decades of the twentieth century. Increasing numbers of Syrian, Turkish, and Lebanese Jews were matched by increments from the Balkans, expelled by the wars of that period. In 1917, an unknown number of

Russian Jewish men who had migrated to the United States crossed into Mexico to avoid being drafted to fight a war they feared would include an invasion of Russia.[25]

Mexico was not attractive to immigrants generally, and very few Jews found their way there. Many who did attempted to obscure their identity, either out of a sense of alienation from the Jewish people or from fear that the Inquisition mentality had taken permanent root in the deeply religious countryside. In the absence of community organization, mythology takes over, and estimates of the Jewish population of Mexico in 1905–10 vary from seventy-five to fifteen thousand [sic].[26] The *American Jewish Year Book* figure of 8,972 is plausible, but the number could not have been known with certainty either then or now.

Brazil

In the last decade of the nineteenth century, Jewish immigration to Brazil increased in numbers while becoming more disparate in origin. Immigrants continued to come from North Africa and western Europe, but to these were added Jews from countries of the eastern Mediterranean (Greece, Turkey, Syria, Lebanon, Palestine) as well as from Russia and adjacent countries of eastern Europe. These immigrants organized themselves into *landsmanschaften* on the basis of country of origin; the synagogues and mutual aid societies grew up without reference to one another. Nevertheless, they established a skeletal infrastructure for Jewish life that would ease the entry into Brazil of future waves of immigrants.[27] In this respect, Mexico and Brazil stand in contrast to one another, highlighting the far more relaxed religious atmosphere of Brazil.

Most of these immigrants settled in Rio de Janeiro, São Paulo, or the state of Minas Gerais; but smaller numbers dispersed to other provinces. The Brazilian national census of 1900 located 1,021 Jews in the country. During the years 1900–1910, East European Jewish immigration increased. Many arrived in Brazil under shepherding of immigration agents, who had acquired the ships' tickets gratis from the Brazilian government upon representing that they were recruiting labor for the coffee, tobacco, and sugar plantations. The immigrants quickly sought escape from the debt slavery of the plantations, and most metamorphosed into peddlers.

Some Ashkenazim came to Brazil under the auspices of the JCA, which founded Colonia Filipson in the state of Rio Grande do Sul in

1903, beginning with forty-eight families totaling two hundred persons, most of them children. Unaccustomed to the soil and climate, the immigrants abandoned this colony within a single generation, turning to peddling and petty commerce in Pôrto Alegre, capital of the state.[28] The colony Quatro Irmãos, founded in 1910, likewise failed within a few years. Rio also served as a staging area for the introduction of Jewish girls into the white slave trade during periods when the Argentine police cracked down on prostitution in that country.[29]

On the eve of World War I, the most important Jewish communities in Brazil were still the Sephardim of the north. There were small communities in Itacoatiara and Parintins and a large one in Manaus that was not organized. The largest community was that of Belém do Pará, which possibly numbered eight hundred. Its local influence was reflected in the establishment of a chair in the Hebrew language at the Colegio Pará e Amazonas. Rio likewise had an organized Sephardic community at that date.[30]

In all, there may have been five thousand Jews in Brazil in 1917, compared with Argentina's 112,000, according to an investigation commissioned by the American Jewish Committee.[31] The scant number of Jewish immigrants into the country in this period, when pressures for exodus from eastern Europe were great, corresponds to what is known about the relative unattractiveness of the country to immigrants at the turn of the century. Immigrants arriving without capital or professional skills (and this included most of the East Europeans) had to compete on the labor market with recently freed slaves. The predominantly rural and regimented nature of plantation labor was no attraction for immigrants who hoped that, by coming to the New World, they could improve the quality of their lives.

Peru

The first East Europeans entered Peru from Poland, Russia, and the Balkans in the closing years of the nineteenth century.[32] In the first decade of the twentieth century, the pace of immigration quickened, and in 1917 Harry O. Sandberg estimated that there were three hundred Ashkenazim in the country. Most were Besserabians, coming from such towns as Novi-Selitz, Sikureni, and Yedinitsi, and in fact Besserabian Jews claim all the territory from Peru northward to Nicaragua.[33] Originally, they came as peddlers, returning home to the *shtetl* (provincial Jewish towns of eastern Europe) when they had put aside some money. But the rise of anti-Semitism in Europe after World War I put an end to their peregrinations, and those who had been able to establish an economic base in Peru settled there on a permanent basis. Most of these stayed in Lima, but some opened stores and cafes in provincial towns, where an occasional advertisement for "Casa Bessarabia" can still be seen.

All countries of Latin America received Jewish immigrants during the period 1880–1914. The repression being experienced by Jews of eastern Europe was matched by the pressures exerted against Jews in the Balkans. Ashkenazi and Sephardi alike were forced to find new homes in areas that had never before appeared attractive. Just which Latin American republic an immigrant might choose appears to have been determined partly by historical circumstance and partly by the idiosyncracies of shipping agents. Many random choices of destination were made by the immigrants, whose knowledge of the continent was slight. The result was the appearance of ephemeral Jewish communities in every corner of the continent. Only in Panama and Uruguay did communities implant themselves vigorously.

Panama

Sephardic immigrants had settled in Panama while the area was still a province of Gran Colombia. These were descendants of Portuguese New Christians, who had moved to British territory such as Jamaica and St. Thomas and there reverted to Judaism. The destruction of St. Thomas by hurricane in 1867 drove numbers of these Sephardim to relocate in Panama.[34]

More Sephardim of the Antilles entered Panama when the French began construction of the canal. The assumption of the canal project by the United States initiated a commercial boom that attracted, among others, Jews from every part of the world. Partly because of the presence of the United States in the Canal Zone, and partly as a result of the mixture of nations in the infant republic, Panama developed a relatively liberal religious policy. Catholicism was recognized as the predominant religion of the republic, but freedom of conscience was also guaranteed, and the government was forbidden to interfere in religious practices. As a result, there was no practical or legal bar to the immigration of non-Catholics.[35]

In 1917, a well-defined occupational hierarchy was observed among Panamanian Jews. The "native" Jews (descendants of émigrés from Curaçao) comprised a quarter of the Jewish population of five hundred. Owners of commission houses and of large holdings in the public utilities, these Portuguese Sephardim mingled with the highest strata of society rather more than with their coreligionists. About 15 percent of Jews were Syrians, a class of middle-sized merchants in dry goods, notions, and the like. Turkish and Egyptian Jews were peddlers and small shopkeepers, occupying a considerably lower social level than previously named groups. American and central European Jews had invested heavily in hotels, movie theaters, and furniture and clothing stores and had done particularly well since the arrival of the American canal builders. A few Jewish ranchers, farmers, dentists, lawyers, and opticians rounded out the occupational picture.

Uruguay

Although church and state were not legally separated until 1919, all Jewish observers attest to the religious toleration that prevailed in the republic in the twentieth century. Uruguay appeared to be the only Latin American republic eager to acknowledge the cultural role of the immigrant, and even to build a monument to him in a public park. Or, as one immigrant phrased it, "that faceless seeker after happiness whom fate cast upon the Uruguayan shore, . . . turned out to be a pioneer and founder of the modern national economy."[36]

Sephardim found their way to Uruguay in the early 1900s. They came, declassed and impoverished, from Lebanon, Syria, and Turkey. Although they arrived without resources, their knowledge of Ladino eased their entry into the Uruguayan economy. Most became peddlers, and their integration was facilitated by the absence of xenophobia. There was greater willingness on the left bank of the Plata than on the right to accept the immigrant innovator without concern for his religion. Immigrants received equal rights on arrival; all they had to do was obey the law.[37] In this atmosphere, the Sephardim metamorphosed within a decade into merchants, handcraftsmen, and even small industrialists. Additional Sephardim arrived after the First Balkan War (1912–13). These were economically better off and culturally on a higher plane than their predecessors, and they laid the foundations of the present Montevideo Jewish community. By 1917, there were seventeen hundred Jews in Uruguay, three-fourths of them Sephardim. About fifteen hundred of the total lived in Montevideo, and almost all were middle or working class. A few extremely wealthy merchants had left their Jewish origins behind. About 10 percent of this population was in agricultural colonies, either established by JCA or initiated independently. Numbers of second-generation youth were attending the university, and about ten Jews held low-ranking positions in government.[38]

Paraguay

Paraguay and Bolivia may be taken as paradigms of societies so intensely Catholic and so polarized between a Spanish creole elite and a subjugated Indian mass that there was no room for a non-Catholic middle class. Jews came to these countries only as isolated individuals and for the purpose of economic betterment, until the period of the Nazi holocaust exerted far more severe pressures upon them.

Paraguay has never presented itself favorably as a place of settlement for large numbers of immigrants. Most of those who came were either Italian or Argentine—both Latin and Catholic. Roman Catholicism remains the established religion of the state; civil marriage and burial are relatively recent acquisitions. Exceptionally, a colony of five thousand Mennonites did establish itself on three million acres of land along the Paraguay River, receiving special dispensation from the government to retain their self-imposed religious norms in isolation.

The second half of the nineteenth century saw the arrival in Paraguay of a small number of Sephardim, including the anthropologist Moisés Santiago Bertoni and his son Guillermo Tell Bertoni, the latter a botanist and lawyer, who became active in Paraguayan politics.[39] Small groups of Ashkenazim from Poland and Russia settled in Paraguay in the first decade of the twentieth century. In 1917, the director-general of statistics was a Jew. Additional arrivals from central Europe and the Balkans brought the community to six hundred by World War I.[40]

Bolivia

Bolivia, old Upper Peru, was one of the last bastions of the loyalist Spanish church during the wars for independence, and her first constitution amply reflected that fact: "The Roman Catholic Apostolic religion is the religion of the Republic to the exclusion of all other public cults." Half a century later, in 1871, this article was slightly revised in an effort to accommodate foreign immigration: the practice of non-Catholic cults was to be permitted "in colonies where it is tolerated." By 1905, this right had been extended throughout the republic, and over the next five years, the rights of civil marriage and of civil burial were instituted. Nevertheless, economic and social conditions were not deemed inviting by any large number of immigrants. The grant of religious toleration served to facilitate the entrance of Protestant missionaries to the country, but not of many non-Christians.

In 1904, several Russian Jewish families found their way to Bolivia. (The expression used by the Yiddish-language historian is *farblondzhet*, which carries the implication that these people had gotten lost and wandered into Bolivia by mistake.)[41] Twenty-five families were counted in that country by the representative of the American Jewish Committee in 1917. All were either owners of businesses or employees of these same firms.

Cuba

Cuba, which remained under Spanish control far longer than the other republics, is the single one in which Jews participated in the wars of independence. Filibustering raids against this last of the Spanish colonies in the New World were mounted—prematurely, as it turned out—from Gran Colombia in 1832 and from New Orleans in 1852. These included a number of Jews, who earned themselves a place in Cuban history. Of particular interest is the career of Luis Schlesinger, a Hungarian Jew who had fought in the revolution of 1848 and who subsequently fled to the United States. There he was recruited by Cuban General Narciso López, who persuaded him to lead a raid upon the island. The expedition took off from New Orleans and reached El Morrillo, Pinar del Río, on 12 August 1851. Captured by the Spanish and imprisoned in Ceuta, Schlesinger escaped and lived to write his memoirs.[42] Akiva Rolland, a Ukrainian Jewish adventurer, entered Cuban history as General Carlos Roloff and became the first finance minister of the independent republic. Substantial numbers of Jews, chiefly of Spanish origin, fought in the final war of independence in 1898. The American expeditionary force that served in that war included a number of Jewish soldiers who decided to remain on the island when the war was over. At the conclusion of the war, some Romanian Jewish immigrants (referred to as "Americans" in Cuban Jewish literature because they had been naturalized on the mainland) took up residence in Cuba and opened businesses there. By 1900, there were about three hundred Jewish families in Cuba.[43]

The years 1902–14 witnessed intensive immigration to Cuba from Turkey and Syria (fifty-seven hundred persons, according to Cuban government figures), an undetermined proportion of whom were Sephardic Jews. This group was swollen by the arrival of refugees from the Mexican Revolution of 1910 and the counterrevolution of 1913 (following the murder of Francisco Madero). By 1916, there were four thousand Sephardim in Havana, but their numbers dwindled as the world war ended, some returning to Mexico and others proceeding to the United States.

East European Jews were slow to discover Cuba as a country of settlement. Close to four thousand East European Jews passed through the Cuban offices of various Jewish immigrant aid societies between 1910 and 1917, but the best estimate of the total Jewish population of Cuba in 1919 is just two thousand. As long as the United States, and even Europe, were viable options, Cuba was no more than a transit stop for world Jewish migrations.

Venezuela

As we have seen, Jewish life in Venezuela commenced with the migration of Sephardim from Curaçao in the early nineteenth century. Some of the immigrants continued to intermarry over a period of generations with their relatives on Curaçao and Saint Thomas. A descendant of this group, David Lobo Senior, born in 1861 at Puerto Cabello, became rector of the Universidad Central of Venezuela and later chargé d'affaires of the Venezuelan embassy in Washington, D.C. Dr. Mario Capriles, born in 1872, served as president of the legislature of the state of Carabobo, then as deputy, senator, secretary, and finally president of the National Congress. Capriles was decorated with the order of Caballero of the Royal Order of Isabella the Catholic, a suitable honor in light of the fact that his mother was a descendant of Abraham Senior, last Jewish minister of the queen.[44] Other noteworthy Venezuelan Sephardim included a president of the Supreme Court, an official of the Bank of Venezuela, the man who introduced the telegraph into the country, and the founder of the Venezuelan Red Cross.

Over the course of time, increasing numbers of Sephardim contracted marriages among the surrounding population. Jewish communities at Tucacas (state of Falcón) and Barcelona (state of Anzoátegui) disappeared within the last century through assimilation. The longest-lived of the communities, and probably the oldest on the continent, was situated at Coro, whose port is opposite the island of Curaçao. The cemetery there tells the story. In contrast to the cemetery of the mother community of Curaçao, whose tombstones are engraved in Hebrew, those at Coro are in Spanish and sculpted with undeniably

Catholic cherubs. Apparently, the Coro community originally lived as Jews but lacked the ability to pass along their traditions. Gradually the community dissolved, bequeathing its descendants to the nation at large.

The cemetery at Coro was founded in 1832 by Josef Curiel for the burial of his infant daughter Iojevet. Long neglected, the site was restored in 1970 under the direction of the Venezuelan minister of public works, José Curiel, a descendant of the family.[45]

The contemporary Jewish community of Venezuela originated with the migration of Jews from Morocco, Palestine, Syria, Lebanon, and Iran, beginning in 1900. Most started their new lives as itinerant peddlers, moving up within a generation or two into the ranks of merchants and bankers.[46] Most of the Moroccans were Spanish-speakers from Tetuan. The frequency of movement between Morocco and Venezuela is shown by the fact that the principal shop in Tetuan in the 1920s was called La Caraqueña; the doctor of the Spanish legation in Caracas was a Moroccan Jew.

As far as can be ascertained, Russian Jews did not find their way to Venezuela during the period of czarist repression. The continual civil unrest to which Venezuela was subject in the nineteenth century was not conducive to immigration of any type. The intimate ties between church and state presented an additional problem. The temporal power of the church was contained in 1873, when the dictator Guzman Blanco succeeded in breaking the ecclesiastical monopoly over civil matters, including registration of births, marriages, and deaths and the administration of cemeteries. But the relationship between church and state remained symbiotic: religious liberty was guaranteed, but only under supervision of the state. The Venezuelan government continued to exercise the *patronato* (the right to appoint the church hierarchy) until 1964. In effect, the Catholic church became and remained a state church.

Portuguese Sephardim had had long historic experience with this type of situation; the Spanish Sephardim who lived as *dhimmis* in Moslem lands, alternately protected and harassed by their overlords, may have found the atmosphere of Venezuela a relief. But Ashkenazim were well aware of the possibilities for full emancipation and equal citizenship held out by the development of democracy in the United States. Fleeing from czarist oppression and Catholic reaction in eastern Europe, they would have been most reluctant to step backward in time to a country where they would have had to subordinate themselves once more to a monolithic Catholic regime.

71

The Jewish Population of Latin America in 1917

The survey commissioned by the American Jewish Committee in 1917 estimated at 150,000 the number of Jews then living in South and Central America and the Caribbean.[47] Of this number, from 110,000 to 113,000 were in the Argentine. The influx of Russian and other East European Jews had by now reversed the balance between Sephardi and Ashkenaz, so that the latter now constituted about 80 percent of Latin American Jewry. The easterners were as unlike the central Europeans who had preceded them as both were unlike the Sephardim.

The easterners arrived penniless and had perforce to fit themselves into the interstices of the host economies. There were no bankers or high financiers in this migration, no agents of the House of Rothschild. To the contrary, many were clients of Jewish philanthropies. Once arrived, they were under great pressure to make good. In addition, the easterners were more provincial than the German, French, and English Jews. Locked into the Pale of Settlement, without access to national schools or the national economies, Jews were not participants in the national life of Russia, Poland, or Romania in the sense in which Jews had participated in the national life of France, Germany, or England since emancipation. Despite the influence of the haskalah, which encouraged secularization of Jewish life in preparation for emancipation, emancipation had never come. The Jews' capacity to come out into national society depended upon the willingness of society to permit them to do so; this had not come about in eastern Europe. Consequently, eastern Jews identified as Jews, rather than as citizens of the national societies within which they existed. They were still citizens of the shtetl, that small Jewish world, traditional, introverted, closed, that balanced uneasily upon the threshold of a hostile large world they could not enter.[48] Although religion per se may have been on the defense in shtetl life as everywhere else in Europe, the grip of *Yiddishkeit* (Jewishness) was undiminished. Shtetl Jews arrived in Latin America with Yiddishkeit their chief cultural possession and no tradition whatever of free mingling with a Gentile population. The easterners' attachment to the Yiddish language had no counterpart among the German, French, and Alsatian Jews, who had already translated their private lives into a non-Jewish language. East European Jews exhibited far greater need to continue their communal life together. They struggled to preserve their way of life through myriad communal organizations patterned after those that had served their needs in the old country and appeared to be equally necessary in the new. Schools, cultural centers, libraries, burial societies, mutual aid societies—all these organizational forms came to be synonymous in the minds of the East Europeans with the concept of a Jewish community. In turn, the existence of these communal organizations demarcated the Jewish populations more clearly than had been the case before the arrival of the East Europeans.

Among this group particularly one senses a terror of Spanish-speaking lands, a rearousal of ancestral fears going back to 1391 and the terrible pogroms in Castile, not unlike those of 1881 in Russia. These immigrants needed an act of will to entrust their lives again to those whom they saw as the descendants of their old tormentors. Ashkenazim had never been in Spain, of course, and neither had most Argentinians or most Mexicans. But who knew better than Jews how strong the grip of tradition could be?

We have earlier reviewed what the Latin American expectations of immigrants were. Some of these were being fulfilled. There were thirty-five thousand Jewish farmers on the land in Argentina in 1917 and several thousand more in Uruguay and Brazil. But despite the tug of agrarian life in the "New Zion," the overwhelming majority of Jews, including three-quarters of the now substantial Jewish population of Argentina, lived in the cities.

Prior to World War I, Latin America's lack of industrialization and continued use of cities as religious and administrative centers rather than as centers for the production of goods meant that middle population sectors were small and elitist. Most Latin American cities remained limited in their functions and unintegrated by rail, canal, or road with their rural hinterlands; they exhibited little specialization of labor until the spurt of economic growth occasioned by the disruption of international trade during World War I. Buenos Aires and Montevideo were exceptions to this pattern, and these cities did become early recipients of large numbers of Jewish immigrants.

What area the Jewish immigrant chose to settle in seems to have been controlled in part by the class structure of the host society. For a Jew, the absence of a modernized middle class presented a serious obstacle. In a country of landed aristocrats and landless peasants, he could be neither. There was no social background into which he could fit. Many Italian immigrants to Argentina resolved the problem of social incongruence by migrating annually to harvest the wheat crop, returning home for the winter: the famous *golondrinas* (swallows). For the Jews, there was no returning home. They needed places of permanent settlement. Thus, although there is no country of Latin America

73

in which East European Jews did not settle, the largest cohorts headed for the southernmost republics, with their predominantly European populations, their nascent middle classes, and their social milieus that were favorable to industrialization. Modernizing economies meant employment, skilled and unskilled, for the laboring and middle classes. Secularizing values in Argentina, Uruguay, Panama, and the southern states of Brazil led to disestablishment of the Catholic church and its relegation to secondary status. Such developments made it possible for Jews either to live as Jews or to intermarry comfortably.

Peasant societies, on the other hand, characterized by an Indian or mestizo mass and a Hispanic criollo elite, presented the immigrant— Jew and non-Jew alike—with the prospect of a mass society whose way of life he could only reject and an elite that rejected him. Such countries as Guatemala, Paraguay, and Peru were unable to attract much immigration no matter what legal frame they devised because there was no social setting into which an immigrant could fit. For Jews, the matter was complicated by the prevailing religiosity of these societies, which made it difficult either to live as a Jew or to assimilate. Countries in this category did receive some Jewish immigrants in the period 1889–1917. But these individuals lived isolated as a merchant caste in a manner not dissimilar to the status of Jews in Europe of the Middle Ages. Sephardim and Arabic-speaking Jews (of whom the least is known) also migrated to the modernizing republics of the southern cone. A larger proportion of them settled in countries such as Mexico, Cuba, and the Central American republics, which Ashkenazim regarded with dread.

By the end of this period, there were few who could trace their origins to the Portuguese Jews of Curaçao. These Sephardim—Jews, Catholics, Masons—had become well integrated into the upper classes of their respective national societies. They made meaningful careers for themselves in the national economy and government of Venezuela, Colombia, and the smaller Caribbean republics, enjoying a high degree of social integration in countries that retained an intense attachment to Hispanic Catholicism, countries that never seemed to be viable options to East European immigrants.

In addition to these groups there were estimated to be another fifty to sixty thousand persons in Latin America in 1917 who had been born Jews but who had severed themselves from Jewish life.[49] Their number is obscure, though not beyond conjecture. If the estimate of ethnic Jews not identifying with their religious community is anywhere near the mark, it indicates an assimilation rate of 25 percent within two generations of arrival on the continent. The mingled hope and fear of proimmigration forces that Jews would add to the biological mixture of "races" seems to have been justified.

4

Completion of the Contemporary
Jewish Communities

Global Jewish migration was part of the great immigrant stream that coursed from east to west throughout the nineteenth century. Dammed by World War I, the migrants resumed their westward flow once the guns were silent—but in diminished numbers because barriers were now placed in their way.

The Migrants

The Jewish immigrants of postwar days were no longer "rusos." Revolution in Russia held out the promise of equal rights to all sectors of the population and forbade emigration equally to all. But to the west of Soviet borders, old attitudes of anti-Semitism were reinforced by the new ideology of fascism. As a result, increasing pressure was exerted on Jewish populations. With the number of people increasing faster than the capacity of industry to absorb them, the crisis of lack of land and lack of employment grew increasingly desperate in the interwar years. The surplus sons of peasants poured into the cities as unskilled labor. Their children, anxious to rise in the world, found that many of the leadership positions in trade, industry, and the liberal professions were in the hands of Jews, who had begun their modernizing role earlier. The very success of Jews in urbanizing themselves led to a nationalistic reaction against them.

Following the breakup of the Austrian and Ottoman empires and the fulfillment of the pledge of self-determination for small nations, national majorities gained access to the levers of power for the first time and were in a position to shape economic and political policies calculated to expel Jews from economic positions they wished to possess. From 1925 to 1939, official anti-Semitism and pogroms were calculated to make life so miserable for Jews that they would emigrate. Conditions did in fact become intolerable in central Europe long before the rise of Hitler. Discriminatory taxes, boycotts, destruction of Jewish-owned property, and officially sponsored pogroms began the destruction of the Jewish communities that the Nazis were to finish. To many Jews in Poland, Romania, Hungary, Latvia, and Lithuania, emigration seemed the only way to survive.

Sephardim had been abandoning their homes in Turkey and the Balkans ever since the Young Turk rebellion of 1908 and the Balkan War of 1912–13. That conflict left the Jewish communities ravaged and thousands of impoverished refugees piled up in Salonica and Constantinople. Major Jewish communities in Monastir, Janina, Castoria, Kavala, and Adrianople were badly damaged, and their situation was worsened by World War I. The exchange of populations between Greece and Turkey (1923–28) destroyed the economic foundations of the Jewish community of Smyrna, sundered the ancient Sephardic community of Salonica, and propelled another wave of Ladino-speaking Jews toward the New World. Of the four million Jewish migrants in the period 1840–1956, two to three hundred thousand were Sephardic and Arabic Jews. If this migration were documented, the number of Jewish migrants to Latin America would be seen to be somewhat larger than Tables 1 and 2 indicate.

German-speaking Jews began appearing in Latin America in the year of Hitler's accession to power, as the possibility dawned that the Nazi plan for a "final solution" to the "Jewish problem" might be put into practice. But the rise of fascism in Europe coincided with the adoption of exclusionist immigration policies elsewhere. Widespread visa restrictions went into effect throughout the Western Hemisphere, narrowing considerably the options of the refugees. Those Jews who sought to migrate during this period found it increasingly difficult to enter their preferred lands of destination and had to go wherever governments would grant entry. The result was to increase the celebrated dispersion of the Jews to a greater degree than ever before in their history.

Migration Patterns

If Jewish migration was a function of political events in Europe, the pattern this migration assumed was a function of United States immigration law.

The United States had been the destination of choice of the vast majority of Jewish migrants, and under free market conditions this country absorbed 90 percent of them. By 1921, however, the United States had altered its perception of itself as haven of the world's "huddled masses, yearning to breathe free." In that year, the Immigration Quota Act established an annual quota of 3 percent of the total of foreign-born of each nationality resident in the United States, based on the census of 1910. Three years later, the Immigration Act of 1924 reduced these quotas further, to 2 percent of the foreign-born resident in the United States in 1890. As there were few eastern or southern Europeans in the United States in that year, the areas from which Jews now needed to emigrate were allocated extremely small quotas.

Passage of such legislation caused the Jewish immigrant stream to be diverted elsewhere. Other countries—chiefly Palestine, Argentina, Canada, and South Africa—now experienced a rise, which although substantial in terms of impact on the receiving societies, nevertheless made only a small dent in the number of Jews who needed to leave Europe and who were cut off from escape.

Latin America, as we have seen, had never absorbed more than a tiny fraction of Jewish emigrants. In the period 1926-30, the continent received 42 percent of them—but the flow was running at a greatly diminished level (see Table 1). Beginning in 1931, Palestine emerged as the most important destination of Jewish immigrants, and from that date until the outbreak of World War II, just 18 percent of Jewish migrants settled in Latin America.

On the southern continent, Argentina had always been the recipient of the largest number of Jewish immigrants. Over the course of a century, she absorbed 5 percent of the total European Jewish migration, ranking third after the United States (71.5 percent) and Palestine/Israel (9.7 percent).

As the stream of Jewish migration was deflected from the United States, Argentina continued to absorb the lion's share within Latin America, admitting nearly 40,000 Jews in the period 1921–25 (twice as many as were admitted to all other Latin American countries combined) and nearly 34,000 in the following five years (about half as many as were admitted to all other Latin American countries). Rising xenophobia and the compelling example of the United States, however, caused Argentina also to curtail immigration, and 1923 was the last year in which a sizable number of Jews were legally admitted. The 14,000 Jews who entered officially that year dwindled to an average of 2,500 per year in the barbarous years 1939–42.[1] Larger numbers must have entered the country unofficially because subsequently, between 1948 and 1950, the Argentine government allowed nearly 10,000 illegal Jewish immigrants to regularize their status in the country.[2]

Argentina, Uruguay, and Chile received at least 150,000 Jews in the interwar period (see Table 2). These immigrants contributed numerically to the existing Jewish communities, but did not significantly alter their nature or trajectory. The closing of Argentina to legal immigration, on the other hand, altered drastically the character of the Jewish community of Brazil. That country's intake of Jewish immigrants was just 2,025 in 1924. Thenceforward, the number rose irregularly until the outbreak of World War II, the largest recorded numbers entering in 1929 (5,610) and 1939 (4,601).[3] As we shall see, larger numbers of Jews arrived during this period without the formality of stating their religion.

Fragmentary communities came into existence in Paraguay, Bolivia, Venezuela, Colombia, the Dominican Republic, and Ecuador. Most proved transient. More substantial Jewish communities formed in Cuba

Table 2. *Jewish Immigration to Latin America between World Wars*

Dates	Country	Number of Jewish Immigrants	Comment
1920-47	Argentina	109,449	plus some 10,000 illegals
1936-47	Bolivia	8,000	of whom 5,000 left in same period
1924-47	Brazil	56,204	
1934-47	Chile	15,000	
1937-47	Colombia	5,000	
1918-47	Cuba	25,000	of whom half left in same period
1924-47	Ecuador	3,500	
1918-47	Mexico	15,000	
1933-47	Paraguay	10,000	almost all of whom went on to Argentina
1927-47	Uruguay	21,500	
1933-47	Venezuela	7,500	plus an undetermined number of "Marranos"
1937-47	Others	2,000	

Source: Mark Wischnitzer, *To Dwell in Safety,* p. 288.

and Mexico. Only when the United States, followed by Argentina, excluded mass immigration did new communities form in these previously disfavored republics.

In the aftermath of World War II, about a million and a half more Jews migrated worldwide; 77.9 percent of these went to Palestine/Israel.[4] Latin America received about 37,000 persons from this migration. Some two-thirds of these were displaced persons who were admitted to various republics between 1945 and 1956. Largely kin of persons already admitted for permanent residence, their continentwide distribution meant that they made little demographic impact.

Following the Suez crisis and the Hungarian uprising of 1956, some 8,300 Jews were resettled in Latin America, 70 percent of them in Brazil. Concentrated in the cities of São Paulo and Rio de Janeiro, the immigrants had a definite impact on their communities.

All Latin American republics now have restrictive immigration laws, and the growth of contemporary Latin American Jewish communities has halted. Over the course of the century 1840-1942, some 376,-227 European Jews—fewer than 10 percent of the four million who migrated—entered Latin America. It is conceivable that larger proportions of non-European Jews, for whom data are lacking, settled on the continent during this period; but their absolute numbers would be considerably lower because of the smaller population base. In any event, it is plain that, for Ashkenazim, the largest sector of world Jewry, Latin America was not the first choice for settlement.

Changed Attitudes toward Immigrants

Latin America of the post–World War I years presented immigrants with a different prospect than had earlier prevailed. In some countries, industrialization was creating new opportunities within the expanding industrial plant, as well as broader scope for the deployment of entrepreneurial skills and capital. But the emergence of new social forces attendant on industrialization, such as organized labor, was viewed as socially disruptive and caused an elitist reaction. The rapid growth of cities and the development of an "alienated, restless, and increasingly militant proletariat" dismayed the creole elites, whose traditional notions concerning the natural servility of the laboring classes were being upset.[5] If they did not close off immigration immediately, it was because the elites still believed that immigration was essential for economic development.

By World War I, the naive faith in European immigrants as whiteners and enlighteners of inferior mestizo races had dissipated. Instead, a celebration of the native races had begun, intensified by rivalry with the immigrants, who in almost all countries achieved far greater economic success and swifter social ascent than seemed possible for any honest man. Carl Solberg interprets this change:

> The gleaming image that European immigration had once enjoyed among Argentines and Chileans was tarnished by 1914. Only a quarter century earlier the elites of both republics had welcomed the foreign influx with enthusiasm, but many of the changes wrought by immigration dismayed powerful segments of the population. Foreign-born businessmen and professionals controlled ever greater shares of both nations' economies. Immigrant urban laborers organized, struck, and became continually more militant. The spectre of anarchism, and, some thought, of bloody social revolution, loomed. . . . After 1905 influential writers in both republics were rejecting the positivist and cosmopolitan-oriented ideologies invoked by the elites since the 1850s to justify liberal immigration policies. In place of cosmopolitanism, these intellectuals began to formulate nationalistic ideologies that lauded traditional creole social and cultural values and stressed the belief that immigrants must adopt these values. Such a vindication of creole culture contrasted sharply with nineteenth-century Argentine and Chilean social thought, which had disdained the Spanish and indigenous heritages as barbaric while regarding the immigrant as the very symbol of civilization.[6]

By the end of World War I, both the Argentine and Chilean governments had officially reversed old traditions, passing laws that regulated the admission of labor "agitators." But channels for legitimate political participation did not always appear. Even so perceptive an observer as José Luis de Imaz comments that Argentine "labor leaders would naturally be left outside the prevailing system, since their coming to power through anarchist activities obviously implied the exclusion of all other sectors."[7] Despite the rhetoric of the Argentine Socialist party, labor was not to be brought into the political process until the regime of Juan Perón.

As serious as a nativist reaction was for immigrants generally, the hazard was doubled for Jews, because they were all immigrants and because feeling against them could be cynically conjoined with ancient religious antagonisms. An instance of the blending of nativist reaction with classical anti-Semitism took place in Argentina in 1919 during the so-called Semana Trágica (Tragic Week). At that time, the apprehensions of conservatives concerning the effect of immigration on the status quo were ignited by rumors of a plot by rusos to overturn the governments of Argentina and Uruguay and institute rule by workers' soviets.

The week's events began with a strike against an iron works. Violence broke out, some workers were killed, and observers were quick to allege outside agitation by Bolsheviks, immigrants, and Jews. From the perspective of the oligarchy, immigration appeared to be changing Argentine society, and changing it for the worse. Admittedly, economic progress was taking place, but many felt the price was too high.

At the very time that the strike itself was being settled, the Jewish neighborhood of Buenos Aires came under murderous attack. "Now, reactionary mobs rather than angry workers roamed the streets shouting death to *rusos*—Russian Jews—who were somehow identified in the popular mind with anarchists and Bolsheviks."[8] The assault on Jews and Catalans was led by Rear Admiral Domecq Garcia, who gave military instruction to the *guardia blanca*—volunteer squads of patriotic youth. Buenos Aires was compared with Petrograd two years earlier and "patriots" urged the volunteers to assault Russians and Catalans in their homes and neighborhoods.[9] This they did, destroying libraries, clubs, presses, and shops, while the police looked on. Pinie Wald was arrested as would-be dictator of a republic that was to be established, encompassing all of South America.

A Jewish deputation called on President Hipólito Irigoyen at this time, to disassociate the mainstream community from the actions of hotheads and to request police protection for law-abiding citizens. The deputation was chided for having made its appeal in the name of the Jewish community rather than as individual Argentines, despite the fact that it was the community that was under attack.[10] Nevertheless, the police were ordered to offer equal protection of the law to all and to put an end to attacks on Jews. In enforcing this order over the weekend following, 800 persons were arrested, 80 percent of them Russian. At the same time, 72 people were killed and 80 gravely wounded, and another 800 received minor injuries, all in the Jewish quarter of the city. No exact accounting of the human toll was ever made, but estimates ranged between 850 to 1,000 dead, with 3,500 to 5,000 wounded.[11] There is no doubt that the Jews suffered most heavily: at one point, United States Ambassador Frederic J. Stimson reported that of 182 bodies collected, 150 were of Russian Jews.

No evidence of a plot, Bolshevik or other, was ever uncovered. None of those arrested was ever brought to trial, for want of evidence. Wald himself was charged only with possession of a firearm, a charge that could have been brought against most porteños that week. Evidently, the "plot" was no more than a hoax cooked up by police and press to justify the attacks that had been made on Jews.

Montevideo police were also alerted to the existence of a "plot" by rusos to overthrow the government on the eastern bank. News of arrests in Montevideo encouraged Buenos Aires police to make more raids. Nothing, not even Bolshevism, is as contagious as panic.

Although Argentine Jews customarily downplay the events of Semana Trágica, it seems likely that a historic process was set in train as Jews proceeded to internalize the lesson of "tragic week." Evidence, though fragmentary, is suggestive. Jews learned that political activity was far more dangerous for them than it was for others and that the entire Jewish community could be attacked for the actions of anyone who had been born Jewish. This sense of collective destiny—that the entire community is hostage for the acts of individual Jews—remains strong among Argentine Jews—and among Argentines—today. It both explains and aggravates the tendency of mainstream community members to reject radical political activity by Jews and thus to split Jews along ideological and generational lines (since it is almost always the young who are attracted to radical politics).

Anti-Semitism had always been endemic among the Argentine upper class. Now elite fear of communism, Freemasonry, and liberalism began to receive external support from fascist ideology. The allure of European fascism, with its concommitant anti-Semitism, struck a responsive note among many Argentines, who were particularly attracted to the ultramontanism of Charles Maurras (1868–1952), soon to become chief ideologist of the Vichy regime. Maurras turned the word "Jew" into an ideogram that stood for modernizing attitudes that immigrants were introducing into Argentina and that threatened the continuity of creole values.[12] The ultimate libel was that the Jew was, and always would remain, an alien who did not belong to the Argentine nation. Even the agricultural colonies did not establish Jews as Argentines, for these, it was alleged, were no more than a plot to create Palestine in Argentina.

As the Argentine upper class responded to labor unrest, the great depression, and the stimulus of fascism, anti-Semitism was turned to the service of nationalist reaction, to which Jews were especially vulnerable because they were nearly all foreign-born. These attitudes were by no means confined to one class: latent feelings of anti-Semitism, derived ultimately from medieval Catholic teachings, are widely disseminated through the Argentine middle and lower classes, continually available for political activation.[13]

A decade after Semana Trágica, worldwide depression brought waves of anti-Jewish feeling to other sectors of the continent. Commercial competition in a dwindling market was partially responsible, as was the possibility of fascist victory in Europe. The anti-Semitism of professional Nazi propagandists found resonance in many sectors of South America. The threat seemed particularly ominous in countries such as Bolivia, where there was no educated middle class with which Jews could ally. The anti-Semitism implicit in the teachings of the medieval church and transmitted from generation to generation among illiterate and superstitious folk who had never seen a Jew was a daily fact of life to which Jewish immigrants had to adjust. In this case, the gap between immigrant and native-born appeared impossible to span.

While World War II was in progress, and in the context of a possible German victory, the Bolivian Movimiento Nacional Revolucionario (MNR) adopted an anti-Semitic stance.[14] A plausible explanation could be the search by the petite bourgeoisie for scapegoats who could be held responsible for the inflation that was pressing them. These could be found among big capitalists and Jewish "internationalists." Always latently anti-Semitic, Bolivian city dwellers became actively so, and the MNR pandered to their hatred to gain their support. Though anti-Semitism may have been viewed by the MNR as no more than a tactical weapon, it appeared as a distinct threat to the Jews who had sought refuge in the country and also no doubt contributed to MNR's image abroad as a fascist-inspired party.

Anti-Semitic attitudes were in no instance as strong or as violent as those that swept Europe in the same period, but Jews experienced a general feeling of threat from the right: from nationalists, from fascists, from sectors of the unreconstructed church hierarchy. Gradually an ambience was being created that was less favorable to immigrants generally, and to Jews specifically, except insofar as Jews could conform entirely to Latin American norms by ceasing to be Jewish. It was in this ambience that the present-day Jewish communities evolved.

Doors Close

Exclusionist immigration policies were adopted almost universally in the years prior to the outbreak of World War II. Pressure was so intense, however, that a number of "errant vessels" headed for Latin American ports in the hope of landing Jewish passengers whose acceptability was not established. The case of the *St. Louis* is best known. This vessel was turned away by Cuban authorities in June 1939 even though all 930 Jewish passengers aboard held landing certificates issued by the Cuban director-general of immigration; 734 of them also held visas for entry into the United States, with effective dates of from three months to three years of their arrival in Cuba. Efforts by American citizens failed to persuade the government of either the United States or of Cuba to admit the immigrants, and the vessel returned the refugees to meet their fate in Europe. The desperate drama in Havana harbor was played out to the accompaniment of violent anti-Semitic utterances in the press, radio, and in Congress, as rival political factions struggled to control the millions of dollars in ransom they assumed could be extorted from the refugees.[15]

The cases of such errant vessels are too numerous to list here, but in his history of the period, Mark Wischnitzer has recorded the dimensions of the problem and the chaotic pattern of refugee distribution that resulted.

[In March of 1939] three boats: the Italian Conte Grande and the Hamburg-American Cap Norte and the General Artigas, carried ninety-five refugees to Uruguay. Since their tourist visas were illegal, they were not allowed to land in Montevideo. But thanks to the efforts of Hicem [a Jewish immigrant aid society], the Uruguayan authorities permitted them to disembark on condition that they proceed to Chile. In May, three boats with a hundred and fifty Jews on board embarked for Paraguay, via Uruguay. The Hicem committees in Buenos Aires, Montevideo and Asuncion then exerted their efforts to assure the arrival of the refugees in Paraguay.[16]

Bribes, swindles, and clandestine landings all played a role in the drama. In May 1939, three thousand Jewish refugees entered Bolivia with documents counterfeited in Europe and sold to them for $1,500 apiece. Two Bolivian consuls were dismissed as a result, and the outstanding visas were invalidated. Those refugees who were still in transit were stranded with worthless documents. Following intervention by HICEM, an agreement was worked out whereby HICEM revalidated the visas (which implied a guarantee of support) and agreed to limit the number of such visas to four hundred per month.[17]

Chile ceased admitting refugees from Nazi-dominated territories in December 1939. In April of 1942, Mexico decreed that thenceforth only natives of the Western Hemisphere would be admitted as immigrants. Argentina, Bolivia, Chile, and Paraguay in effect barred entry to refugees from Germany and Axis-dominated countries by denying admittance to persons without passports signed or certified by the authorities of their countries of origin. Panama instituted similar restrictions. Only Ecuador and the Dominican Republic welcomed Jewish refugees throughout this period.[18] In both these countries, however, the absorptive capacity of the economy was severely limited.

Under these pressures, a new class of conversos came into existence:

Jews who submitted to baptism in order to gain entry into Colombia, Venezuela, and Brazil. In other instances, baptismal certificates were made available without religious formality. Some of these were authorized by Archbishop Angelo Roncalli, apostolic delegate to Turkey and Greece, later Pope John XXIII.

An unknown number of Sephardim entered Latin America on Spanish passports. In decrees of 1924 and 1932, the Spanish government authorized the naturalization of descendants of Spanish Jews exiled in 1492, regardless of their current place of residence.[19] In 1940, General Francisco Franco publicized the offer in Vichy France, Romania, Greece, and French Morocco, urging Sephardim to accept the protection of Spain. Many of those who did proceeded to haven in the Spanish-speaking American republics, protected by their Spanish (and neutral) nationality. Thus the Spanish dictator began the rehabilitation of Spain in Jewish history precisely at the hour when the Jews were threatened with their greatest disaster since 1492.

In such ways, thousands of Jews found themselves in countries where they had never considered settling and where very few European immigrants had ever settled. Under the circumstances, many refugees regarded their havens as temporary refuges until they could move on to places of known Jewish settlement in Argentina, Uruguay, Canada, Israel, or the United States. Many of those who moved on did so illegally: Jewish "expediters" who specialized in smuggling Jews from one country to another appeared in lightly populated areas. Nevertheless, there remain in all the Latin American republics today Jews who arrived in the stressful thirties and forties and who either chose to remain or were unable to leave.

The fastest-growing Jewish communities of the interwar period were in Cuba, Mexico, and Brazil. They developed in an atmosphere far different from that of the mid-nineteenth century. From the 1930s on, rising nationalism and accelerating rates of industrialization altered the expectations host societies placed upon their immigrants, offering enhanced opportunity for economic and social advancement but increasing the pressures for homogenization. The controlling importance of conditions within the host societies is clearly illustrated by the contrasting destinies of the Jewish communities of Cuba and Brazil. Both originated in poverty and the struggle to survive; both began to appear viable in the forties and fifties. But one came to an abrupt end in 1959, whereas the other is currently the most buoyant on the continent.

Cuba

Mass arrival of Jews in Cuba began in March 1921, when a change in American regulations enabled would-be immigrants to expedite their admission through a stopover in adjacent territory. Almost all Jewish immigrants who passed through "Akhsanie Kuba" (Hotel Cuba) during the next two years proceeded on to the United States.[20] A 1925 survey found that only one-fifth of the Jews then in Cuba had been on the island more than a year. This situation changed abruptly when admission to the United States was barred. From then on, immigrants had to adjust to Cuban society.

Adjustment proved to be difficult. The Jewish immigrants were for the most part poor and unskilled. They were thrown on an economy that was based on the large-scale cultivation of sugarcane; wage scales for field hands were far below the minimum requirement for a European life style. Consequently, immigrants settled exclusively in the towns. There they found few of the factory jobs that would have enabled them to support themselves. A survey by the (United States) National Council of Jewish Women found that 90 percent of Jewish immigrants to Cuba were unemployed in 1924. Most of those regarded as employed were engaged in peddling, which is really a disguised form of unemployment.

The condition of these immigrants worsened when in 1933 the revolutionary government of Ramón Grau San Martín enacted the Law of 50 Percent, which stipulated that half of employees in any manufacturing plant must be Cuban citizens. Jews had not been able to become citizens during the previous decade, under the regime of the dictator General Gerardo Machado. When citizenship became available, the high fees and technical barriers prevented many from attaining it. Consequently, most Jews were barred from gainful employment. Those who had found jobs were mostly employed by other Jews. These now had to let go half of their work force. It is not to be wondered that, of the twenty-five thousand Jews who entered Cuba between 1918 and 1947, fully half departed during the same period.

So large a number of migrants and transmigrants, most of them penniless, created a financial burden greater than the few established Cuban Jews could handle, and they were outside the concern of the Cuban government. In the years before the outbreak of war, anti-Semitic propaganda emanating from Nazi sources was leveled at the refugees, threatening the position of all Cuban Jews.

The Hebrew Immigrant Aid Society (HIAS) and the Joint Distribution Committee (commonly called "Joint" or JDC) stepped into the breach, providing interim aid in the form of loans, schooling, travel documents, and sponsors, all services the Cuban government did not offer and the immigrants could not provide for themselves. This "American intervention," reminiscent of United States government intervention in the larger polity, extended itself by the usual means to include interference in Cuban Jewish community affairs, which the local Jews were scarcely in a position to reject even when, as in the case of the *St. Louis,* such intervention had disastrous consequences.

Jews who had been cast away on Cuba as a result of their efforts to reach the United States identified spontaneously with Robinson Crusoe. They were overwhelmed by fear and anxiety when they found themselves stranded on an island where they had no desire to be, inhabited by people whom they regarded as their cultural inferiors. The stories of Abraham Dubelman convey this culture shock as the immigrants struggled to Cubanize themselves. "The Balance Sheet" explores the dilemma of a Jewish peddler who has passed himself off as German and married a Cuban girl. He urges her to throw away her crucifix: "We must free ourselves from these useless things." His own unconcern for religion is a legacy of the haskalah, but he finds secularism insufficient as his children grow up in a Catholic world. Though he is successful in business—as signified by his end-of-the-year balance sheet—when it comes to a final balance, all he wants is to be buried among Jews.

"But some, like Robinson Crusoe, felt Cuba had possibilities, though it was very primitive as compared to any European land that we had known,"[21] wrote Sander M. Kaplan, editor of the lively biweekly, *Havaner Lebn.* In the thirties, Jews came to realize they would have to "make their America in Cuba." With little commerce and less industry, Cuba obviously stood in need of an entrepreneurial class. Those immigrants who accepted their fate and put their hands to the task prospered. As they improved their situation, they began to see Cuba not as a desert island but as a beautiful country worthy in itself. Cuba could be a desirable home, not just a way station on the route to America. In 1934, the author of "Jewish Robinson Crusoes" exuded confidence.

The thirties witnessed the emergence of Cuban Jewish patriotism, expressed in a copious Yiddish literature of short stories, poetry, and novels, written by immigrants who had surprised themselves by falling in love with their new home. Dipping into the history of the Spanish conquest, Y. O. Pinis published an epic poem based on the resistance of an Indian chief against the invaders. Chief Hatuey is presented as a freedom fighter, spurning the hypocritical love offered by the Spanish priests as they advance with torches to perform their "act of faith."[22] *Clara*, a historical romance, commemorates the participation of descendants of conversos in the Cuban war of independence and their association with the Cuban hero Antonio Maceo.[23] Maceo himself was the subject of an epic poem by Eliezer Aronowsky, who won praise for his work from Don Federico Henriquez Carvajal, a companion of José Martí. "*Maceo*," wrote Carvajal, "projects a red symbol on the horizon of Cuba."[24]

Several books about the Liberator, José Martí, and his relations with Jews and Judaism, were also published. Among them were Abraham Matterin's essays "Martí y las discriminaciones raciales," "Martí y los hebreos," and "Temas hebreos en la obra de Martí."[25] Marco Pitchon's *José Martí y la comprensión humana* contains an essay on "Lo hebreo en el pensamiento de José Martí" that illustrates the fusion between Christian and Judaic thought in the mind of the Liberator.[26] The most arresting example is to be found in his statement that "Moisés no ha muerto, porque Moisés es el amor" (Moses has not died, for Moses is love). The fact that the founder of the Cuban nation identified with the Jews' earlier struggle against Spain eased the acculturation of the Jewish immigrants.

The economic advancement of those Jewish immigrants who remained in Cuba was spectacular. Moving perforce out of proletarian jobs into peddling or cottage industry, they became particularly important in the manufacture of furniture and shoes and in diamond cutting. (For a more detailed description of the work odyssey of Cuban Jews, see Chapter 5.) By 1948, the majority of Cuba's twelve thousand Jews were reckoned as middle class, and there were scarcely three hundred wage earners left on the island. Jews were no longer represented in the labor unions, where they had been most active on first arrival.[27] Some of the German-speaking Jews had entered Cuban national life, including several university professors: Boris Goldenberg (sociology); Heinrich Friedlander (economics); and Desiderio Weiss (languages). Jewish lawyers, artists, and writers were all functioning in the forties.[28] Oscar Ganz, prime minister under Carlos Prío Socarrás, was the son of Jewish parents, and so was the Havana representative of the Comintern.

By this date, Cuban Jews were concentrated in the capital, where a luxurious community center, the Patronato de la Casa de la Comunidad Hebrea de Cuba, was built at the then extremely high cost of three-quarters of a million dollars. The souvenir booklet published on the occasion of the dedication of the Patronato featured photographs and messages of congratulation to numerous young men and women who were completing the *bachilerato* or even graduate courses in medicine, engineering, architecture, and other professional fields.

This ebullience was to last less than a decade. The Cuban Jewish community, which in 1948 seemed well on its way to naturalization, has now almost totally disappeared. Its destruction was not the result of anti-Semitic action, but a function of the Cuban revolution of 1959. At first, Fidel Castro was warmly received by many Jews who had suffered along with everybody else from the caprices and injustices of earlier regimes. Fidel made special efforts to befriend Cuban Jews, for example, by making kosher meat available and arranging for matzo to be delivered at Passover. A Jew, Enrique Oltuski Osachki, served in the first revolutionary cabinet.

Nevertheless, the decision of the revolutionary government to re-structure Cuba's economy resulted in destruction of the Jewish community. Nationalization of commerce and industry deprived Jews of their businesses as the Law of 50 Percent had deprived them of their jobs. Former owners were left to live on compensation payments that could not equal the incomes they would have earned had they been able to continue in free enterprise. Nationalization of the economy presented East European Jews with the same dilemma they or their parents had faced in Europe of the twenties and from which they had earlier fled.

Impoverishment was not the only problem: the close relationship that had existed between Cuban Jews and the United States now seemed a source of danger in the context of strained relations between Cuba and the mainland.[29] As a result, the great majority of Jews, along with the majority of the Cuban middle class generally, abandoned the island. By 1965, there were only twenty-four hundred Jews left in Cuba. They continued to gather at the Patronato, now a splendid embodiment of the maxim, *sic transit gloria mundi.*

Brazil

There were between five and seven thousand Jews in Brazil in 1917, with the Sephardim of the Amazon region still the most important community.[30] During the decade of the twenties, some thirty thousand East European Jews entered the country, principally from Poland, the

Ukraine, Bessarabia, and Lithuania. Most headed for the southern states, where industrialization was under way, seeded by the wealth generated by coffee exports. Between the years 1900 and 1939, the state of São Paulo alone absorbed 2,215,000 immigrants, and East European Jews comprised a part of this stream.[31] Today, the pivot of Brazilian Jewish life, as of Brazilian life generally, is in the great cities of the south.

Until 1922, Jewish immigration to Brazil was individual and sporadic. In that year, because of the increasing swell of immigrants in need of aid, JDC, HIAS, and HICEM all began operations in the country, providing temporary lodging and loans for the establishment of business and professional offices and settling a few families in the agricultural colonies that had been founded at the turn of the century. One-sixth of the present Jewish population of São Paulo stems from this migration.

Most of the new arrivals settled in the district of Bom Retiro, and a description of their living arrangements was sent home by an American social worker, who had been commissioned to survey Jewish communities of Brazil and Argentina with a view to ascertaining welfare needs.

Sao Paulo is divided into districts, and Bom Retiro is the district where the majority of the residents are Jews. Here they have reproduced the typical slum district, with overcrowding, poor housing, poverty, and so forth. It is the "east side" of Sao Paulo. A visit to some of the families under the care of the Dama Israelitas (Council of Jewish Women) disclosed that they live in subbasements made up of concrete floors and walls, without windows and with poor sanitation–conditions which, in our larger cities, are looked after by well organized community agencies with trained social workers, who are totally absent in this Bom Retiro district. The minimal cost of living for a family in this district is $20.00 a month for a family of four. About 8000 Jews live in this district, and 90 percent of them are very poor.[32]

Most of the men were earning their living as peddlers: there were three thousand licensed and an estimated fifteen hundred unlicensed peddlers in the district at the time the memo was written.

The Jewish community of Rio de Janeiro developed along similar lines. Immigration of East European Jews to that city began in 1903, with the arrival at the police hostel of "e mais quatro judeos da Bessarabia," as the police blotter has it. By 1914, there were probably two thousand Jews in Rio. After the war, Polish Jews began to arrive.

By 1933, the year Hitler came to power, there were forty thousand Jews in Brazil. In that year, German Jews began arriving, and from one to four thousand entered Brazil officially each year until World War II, despite increasing restrictions.[33] The exact number who entered can never be verified, despite precise records kept by the Jewish immigrant aid societies, because numerous refugees entered with baptismal certificates. In addition, throughout most of the thirties, persons arriving in Brazil as first-class passengers and able to show the sum of $20,000 for each family member could be admitted without regard to quota restrictions. An unknown number of Jews were admitted to Brazil on these terms. Government drastically curtailed immigration in 1937, and from then on it became increasingly difficult for Jews to obtain visas for Brazil, as Claude Lévi-Strauss found, when, after the capitulation of France, he sought shelter in the country where he had performed his distinguished ethnographic research.[34] The frustrations of dealing with discriminatory visa regulations were now compounded, now eased, by the venality of consular officials, and a tragic sense of exasperation laces the reports of American Jewish relief workers assigned to Brazil during this period.

One-quarter of the Jewish population of São Paulo stems from immigration in the thirties. Many of these refugees from Nazism had been employed in industry, commerce, and the free professions. They brought with them their technical education and their work experience. Involved since birth in an industrialized society, they possessed skills that were at a premium in Brazil, then in the early stages of industrialization. Immigrants of all origins—German, Japanese, Polish —were already playing a substantial role in the country's industrialization process, and the German Jews were qualified to participate as well.

Meanwhile, the East Europeans who had preceded the German Jews by a good many years were still struggling to gain an economic toehold. The German immigrants, rich or poor, sought above all to dissociate themselves from the impoverished Poles, Lithuanians, and Bessarabians who were still immobilized in Bom Retiro. Even those without means settled far from the old Jewish ghetto, refused to avail themselves of existing social welfare agencies that had been set up for the Östjude (a term the German Jews used with contempt), and no matter how hard pressed, refused to take up the *schwarze arbeit* (black labor) that the Poles resorted to in order to feed their families.

The early years of the Vargas era (1930–45) witnessed the outbreak of anti-Semitic manifestations by Ação Integralista Brasileira, a party modeled on Italian fascism. Government policy was not specifically anti-Semitic, but Integralista attacks were tolerated as a way to appease right-wing supporters.[35] Although the Integralistas were suppressed in

1938, the Vargas regime progressively narrowed the area of civil liberties, and Jews were now confronted with a new threat.

The Third Reich was making an aggressive attempt to turn Brazil's substantial German community into a fifth column. In the course of this struggle, the Brazilian government promulgated a series of laws aimed at dissolving German, Italian, and Japanese cultural nuclei. Starting in 1938, all political activity by foreigners was interdicted. Elementary teachers had to be native Brazilians; curriculum had to focus on Brazilian history and geography. The following year, the military was called upon to enforce denationalization of ethnic groups, and the foreign-language press was given a two-year ultimatum to convert to the Portuguese language.[36]

These Brazilianization measures, aimed at aborting the Nazi initiative, struck with special force at Jewish cultural life. The East Europeans were still functioning in Yiddish. As it became dangerous to speak any language but Portuguese in public, the Yiddish theater, newspapers, libraries, and schools closed, and the rich communal life of Bom Retiro dried up.

German Jews were less drastically affected. In conformity with the haskalah tradition, they had established their religious congregation, Congregação Israelita Paulista, as a Portuguese-speaking body. Their communal life was organized for religious purposes only, and this was never interfered with by the Brazilian government.

The official census of 1940 enumerated 55,666 israelitas in Brazil, of whom 20,379 were in the city of São Paulo and 19,743 in the Federal District of Rio de Janeiro.[37] The outbreak of World War II put a stop to immigration almost entirely, but after 1946 and the fall of Vargas, a more liberal political atmosphere prevailing, it became possible once more for Jews to secure visas. During the next few years, numerous Jewish displaced persons arrived from European concentration camps. Most postwar immigrants to Brazil were self-sufficient within three to six months of arrival.[38] Rapid integration into the economy was a function of the great economic expansion taking place in Brazil at this time.

By 1950, there were some seventy thousand Jews in Brazil, one-third of whom were in Rio de Janeiro and another third in São Paulo. The five thousand Jews who migrated to the latter city during the fifties constituted the largest accretion to the community there. These were mostly Hungarians and Egyptians displaced by the international crises of 1956.[39]

The French-speaking Egyptian community seemed singularly well equipped to integrate into Brazilian life. Linguistic affinity to Portuguese enabled them to learn the language more rapidly than could speakers of Yiddish, Hungarian, or German. Cultural affinity with the large Brazilian Arab community facilitated their penetration into channels of trade and even into politics of the small towns, many of which had Arab mayors. However, Arab-Israeli hostility in the Middle East closed off many of these channels. A gulf also continues to separate the Egyptian Sephardim from the dominant Ashkenazim, who seem unable to utilize the talents of the Sephardim to accelerate integration of Jews into Brazilian life. On the contrary, Sephardim still fault the Ashkenazim for discriminating against them in Jewish communal life. In general, the Brazilian Jewish community remains profoundly divided along ethnic lines, the major divisions being the East European, German, Arabic (or French) Sephardim, Ladino-speaking Sephardim, and North Africans.

The Brazilian census of 1970 located 120,000 israelitas in the country, an increase of 50,000 over the census of twenty years earlier. Community leaders offer an estimate of 150,000 to 155,000. At the lower extreme, two professional demographers estimate the Brazilian Jewish population at just 100,000.[40] São Paulo, the continent's fastest-growing city, is today the home of the most ebullient Jewish community on the continent.

The Completed Communities

These, then, are the major tides that deposited Jewish elements on the shores of Latin America. Barring another shift of opinion in favor of immigration (which appears unlikely in view of the continent's high rate of natural increase and continued emphasis upon indigenous values), there will be no accretions to these communities from outside in the foreseeable future. They may therefore be viewed as completed products of the age of immigration.

That age being not far past, the Jewish communities are young. There are few "old families" among them, and these tend to be Portuguese Jews from Curaçao, who are not integrated into the predominantly Ashkenazic communities. There are also descendants of those Sephardim who settled in the Amazon basin a hundred years ago, as well as descendants of Argentine farmers who are now going into their fourth generation.

But the majority of Jews arrived in Latin America in the years that bracket World War I. In Argentina, the country of densest Jewish settlement, the 1960 census showed that fewer than 3 percent of Jews aged sixty-five and over had been born in the country. The younger the age cohort, the larger percentage that is native-born, with 98 percent of children aged fourteen and under having been born in Argentina.[41] Half the Jews of São Paulo were born in Brazil. Of this number, 21 percent had two Brazilian-born parents; only 3.9 percent had all four grandparents born in Brazil.[42] Thus, most Latin American Jews are not far from their immigrant origins.

From the Ashkenazi heartland in eastern Europe came the Jewish immigrants to settle the United States, Canada, and the republics of Latin America. The overwhelming majority of Latin American, as of United States and Canadian Jewry, are Ashkenazim. A survey of origins of foreign-born Jews living in Argentina and in Canada in the 1930s showed that 80.9 percent of the former and 83.4 percent of the latter originated in areas defined by the researcher as Poland, Russia, and Romania.[43] During the period of mass migration, the major initiatives in Jewish life sprang from Ashkenazim, not Sephardim, and the former were being subjected to far more intense pressures than the latter. Consequently, Ashkenazim were far more likely than Sephardim to risk all on the frightening gamble of migration to the Western hemisphere.[44]

It is interesting to speculate on the impact of the ethnic origin of these Jews. Suppose the majority of Jewish immigrants had been Sephardim? In receiving Sephardim, Latin Americans had to accommodate Spanish-speakers who had participated in a common core of Spanish history and to whom the church had long ago assigned a certain role in the scheme of things. Habituated to the life of a subordinated minority in Spanish and Arab lands, Sephardim had on the whole internalized their role as a separate, tolerated caste.

In receiving Ashkenazi immigrants, Latin Americans found themselves confronted by bearers of a culture that had never felt the impress of Spain, but had been shaped instead by forces such as industrial capitalism and the egalitarian ideal, which had never taken root in Hispanic soil and which many Latin Americans found repugnant. By the nineteenth century, Ashkenazim were participating in the modernization of Europe; they came to Latin American societies that were still in large measure traditional.

The Southern Hemisphere had not yet industrialized when the great migration landed. In fact, as we remember, the skills needed for take-off were one of the boons sought of European immigrants. Nor had Latin America undergone the "great transformation" that has been identified as the distinguishing mark between traditional and modern societies. For the most part, a traditional Hispanic value system lingered on, characterized by a hierarchical view of society and adherence to a standard of Catholicism that had reacted to Reformation with Inquisition.

European Jews, on the other hand, had reaped, as all Europe had reaped, the harvest of Reformation and Enlightenment, and they were moved by the ideal of a free and open society in which they could take their place as equals. There can be little doubt that this difference in outlook limited both the numbers of Jews who desired to settle in Hispanic and Portuguese America and the capacity of host societies to accommodate them. From the point of view of other Latin Americans, Ashkenazim differ from other European elements in the population far more than do the Spanish-speaking Sephardim. Eighty percent of all immigrants to Argentina were Spanish or Italian; but 80 percent of Jewish immigrants were rusos.

Jewish immigrants exercised their options in ways not too different from non-Jewish immigrants. The United States was far and away the major recipient of all overseas immigrants, and probably three-quarters of all Jewish immigrants came here as well. The next largest recipient was Argentina, which accepted 11 percent of the sixty million Europeans who emigrated overseas between the years 1857 and 1965.[45] Among Jewish immigrants from Europe in the century that ended in 1942, 9.6 percent opted for some country of Latin America, and more than half of these chose Argentina. The largest number of Jewish migrants settled in countries that were receiving the largest contingents of European immigrants of all nationalities and religions. The smallest Jewish communities grew in countries that did not attract many Europeans. The evidence that roughly similar proportions among Jewish and non-Jewish immigrants chose Latin American destinations suggests that Jewish migration responded to the same elements of encouragement and discouragement as did non-Jewish immigration.

The national origins of Latin American Jews are remarkably varied. Most Latin American Jewish communities count individuals from a dozen or more different countries among their members. In fact, identifying the national origins of Latin American Jews is a popular pastime. A journalist reports that the Jews of Guatemala and of El Salvador are from Posen. Nicaragua is populated by Bessarabians and Hungarians. Costa Rica is Polish, and so on and so forth.[46] In all communities, Ashkenazim are organized separately from Sephardim, and they do not worship together. The enumeration of Mexico's Jewish community in *Encyclopedia Judaica* includes Ashkenazim, Sephardim, Damascenes, persons from Aleppo, Germans, and one category of "Hungarians and Americans." Strong antipathies persist among these groups.

The cultural differences Jews brought with them to Latin America were meaningful to the individuals involved, and they quickly became institutionalized in Jewish life. One of the constants of Latin American Jewish life from its origin until the present day is its institutionalized fragmentation. The phenomenon, well known throughout Jewish history, has been explained by Rafael Patai:

A certain degree of acculturation to the non-Jewish environment has taken place in every Jewish Diaspora. In view of these acculturative processes which have been very considerable, especially since the Jewish Enlightenment and emancipation, it is quite clear that the Jewish people as a whole cannot be termed an ethnic group. There are marked cultural differences among the Diasporas, and everywhere the traits in which one Diaspora differs from the others are the traits in respect of which it is similar to its non-Jewish environment. On the other hand, no Jewish Diaspora is culturally identical with its non-Jewish host people; or, to put it positively, every Diaspora differs from its gentile environment in several respects, of which Jewish religion and tradition and Jewish group identification are the most important. In relation to the gentile majority, the Jewish Diaspora of every country thus constitutes a different ethnic group, but the Jews as a whole constitute not one but several ethnic groups.[47]

Ethnic loyalty is a more divisive factor among Latin American Jews than is citizenship. A German Jew of Buenos Aires has more cultural baggage in common with a German Jew of Lima than either has with a Syrian Jew of his own city. A major anomaly of the position of Jews in Latin America is this contrast between the Jewish self-perception of a congeries of ethnic groups whose fate is linked because of a nominal religious identification and the general Latin-American perception of Jews as a unified, cohesive group responsive to identical impulses. This fragmentation also makes mock of population figures, since there is little point in grouping together individuals who do not perceive themselves as belonging to the same group. Furthermore, these ethnic divisions minimize any influence these tiny communities might have had upon the political and social development of their adopted homelands.

The late arrival of Jews to the continent takes on added importance in light of the fact that in the period between the wars, public feeling was turning against immigrants. As we have seen, the immigrant was a convenient scapegoat for the political and social turmoil that accompanied industrialization and urbanization. In the Latin American context, anti-Semitism tends to emerge when anticipated social change fails to occur and the hopes of the poor are dashed.[48] At such times, the exclusive ideologies of the elite and the latent Jew-hatred of the mass reach a cathexis. Jews were seldom physically abused after the traumatic events of 1919, but continuous attention is paid to their foreign origins.

In societies to which entry was circumscribed by the ambit of Catholicism, landownership, and *abolengo* (good birth), only industry and commerce offered entrée to the immigrant, whether as worker, entrepreneur, or lowly vendor of manufactured goods. Arriving as they did from modernized countries, the Ashkenazim in particular found tremendous opportunity for those with skills, education, capital, luck, or a combination of all these. Arriving at a time when industry was in its infancy, many Jewish immigrants were strategically placed to integrate themselves into their new homes by way of the industrialization process. Economic expansion became the context for the burgeoning of new Jewish communities, and over the course of a generation or two, some individuals and some communities flourished economically to a degree that no one could have predicted.

During the nineteenth century, the tug of war between the Catholic tradition and the anticlericalism of some sectors of the middle class created a small middle ground where Jews could live comfortably as a secular minority. Many Jews who were in flight from the religiosity of the shtetl were prepared to move over to a secularized version of Judaism, provided they were not required to merge with another religion that had been historically hostile to them. In Latin America's metropolitan centers they found a comfortably secular milieu.

Since World War I, however, Latin America generally has experienced a growth in nationalism that is characteristic of all developing areas. Though secular in nature, it is inevitably tinged by the Catholic heritage. Nationalism on the ascendant exerts pressure on all within its orbit to become part of a new, all-embracing nationality, be it Argentine, Brazilian, or any other. This pressure leaves little room for a minority group that conceives itself as related to a different tradition than the majority population. The result has been to increase the pressure on Jews, particularly Jewish youth, to assimilate entirely to the general population. We shall look more closely at this question of Jewish identity in Chapter 8.

The majority of Jews arrived in Latin America as triple strangers: by religion, by ethnic origin, and by historical experience. Their arrival on the continent was almost in its entirety a product of modern forces: the advance of industrial capitalism from western, to central, to eastern Europe, and its impact upon populations living there. Jewish communities of Latin America are anchored, not in the colonial past of their respective countries, but in the more recent past of their own countries of origin. This incongruence between time frames of the Jewish immigrant and the Latin American society into which he attempted to fit cannot be overstressed if we are to come to an understanding of the Jewish dimension of Latin American history.

5

Making America:
Jews in Commerce and Industry

From the 1890s on, Jews entered the Latin American economies as farmers, peddlers, artisans, and workers in cottage industry. The agricultural movement deserves a chapter of its own, but the other three occupations are linked to one another. The peddler (often perceived by local residents, along with his Syrian and Lebanese counterparts, as a *turco*) was the typical figure at the turn of the century. But he was increasingly supplemented by the artisan and, particularly after the arrival of German immigrants, by the owner-worker in cottage industry. The marginality of these occupations meant that breadwinners were frequently forced to shift from one to another, with displaced artisans becoming peddlers, peddlers saving up their money to buy machines to produce the goods they sold, and cottage workers peddling their products door-to-door. The combination of means employed by the immigrants in their struggle to "make America"[1] varied from one country to the next and from one time period to another; but the reciprocal nature of their adaptation must be kept in mind. What were the immigrants equipped to do? What gaps in the local economies permitted them to find a place?

Peddling

Packs on their backs and account books in their pockets, Jewish peddlers trudged the streets of major cities and provincial towns, selling small portable items of mass consumption such as matches, scissors, sandals, knives, razor blades, religious articles, tableware, jewelry, and cloth. They sold their wares for a small down payment and an agreement that the customer pay weekly installments. Thereafter the peddler returned weekly to collect on his debts and to sell more goods. Because of the risk involved in extending credit without collateral, the peddlers took a high profit margin—probably 100 percent of the value of the goods. If they were lucky and the number of bad debts was small, they could save up enough money to establish themselves in a fixed place of business and perhaps hire newer immigrants to go out and peddle for them. If they were unlucky, they lost their investment. Initial parcels of goods for peddling were usually acquired on loan from some peddler who was already well enough established to be able to spare some. In addition, small loans were customarily made available without interest by the mutual aid societies that were among the first organizations to be established by the immigrants.

From their weekly visits to collect accounts, the peddlers acquired their folk name of *cuentanik* (Spanish *cuenta*, account, with a Russian suffix). In some countries, they were *semanalchiks* (from Spanish *semana*, meaning week). Successful cuentaniks graduated to the status of *clientelchiks*, spending their time on accounts collection and hiring more recent immigrants to serve as their *klappers*, or (door-) knockers. Klappers who worked their way up to become full-fledged cuentaniks often used this vantage point to buy a stall in the marketplace; from that point, the aspiration was to buy a respectable store.

Peddling is by its nature a solitary occupation. There was no central administration to keep records of what was going on, but contemporary writers observe that "90 percent of the Jews here are peddlers," or "most of the Jewish immigrants started as peddlers." An abundance of autobiographies, newspaper accounts, and fictionalized histories persuade us that peddling was the accommodation Jewish immigrants typically made to the Latin American scene, at least between the years 1880 and 1939. Their choice of occupation was dictated by two sets of factors: one internal—the heritage of skills and attitudes the immigrants had brought with them; the other external—the economic and social structures they found in their new homelands. As one former peddler wrote:

Perhaps a Colombian would want to ask how and why we entered national life the way we did. The truth is that we have arrived at being a very old people, enduring and experienced, because of our ability to orient ourselves in life; and that we have been forced by very difficult circumstances to invent ingeniously or else perish. . . . Our old activities, our property, our customs, had been left behind . . . [and so] we had to learn a new modus vivendi. We went out on God's streets, loaded down with merchandise, in an epoch when Columbia produced very little of her own; and we offered it on the install-ment plan, house by house, receiving in exchange, and by virtue of private contract, our daily bread.[2]

The internal factors that enabled Jews to enter peddling were their familiarity with commerce, their literacy (which made it possible to keep accounts), and their extreme poverty (which prepared them psy-chologically to undertake the most arduous work). The external fac-tors were to be found in the gap between production and distribution of consumer goods that characterized the entire continent during the years of heaviest migration, the absence of credit for the small man, and the consequent exclusion of masses of people from the market for consumer goods.

The interaction of these factors can be observed in every country of Latin America. In Argentina, for example, the formation of eco-nomic policy was dominated by the interests of wheat and beef pro-ducers throughout the nineteenth century. In conjunction with the import-export houses and representatives of foreign firms, these inter-ests favored low tariffs and a free field for the importation of foreign goods. These goods, because of their foreign origin and the lack of domestic competition, were priced at luxury levels, which, in combi-nation with the practice of Argentine merchants of dealing in small volume at high profit margins, resulted in extremely high prices, which the poor were unable to afford. Because all sales were made in cash, many people simply could not buy ordinary consumer goods.

Jewish immigrants to Argentina, fresh from the cities and towns of Europe and already experienced in petty trade, were quick to per-ceive the opportunity that this uneven system of distribution left open for them. The introduction of credit was risky, as the poor had no collateral; but the immigrants were literate and market wise and able to contain the risk. In the absence of other employment opportunities, large numbers of Jews entered peddling and petty trade.[3]

The goal of every peddler was to accumulate enough savings to buy a fixed place of business and get off the road. Some, with stamina, per-spicacity, and luck, managed to do so. Their life stories generated a rags-to-riches mystique about the itinerant figure of the peddler. But success was by no means universal, and the peddlers were subjected to constant personal harassment. Conditions in the 1920s were described in *Havaner Lebn*:

> When the situation in Poland forced Jews out into the world, Central America got her portion too. The Jews found there a great field for work and also the sympathy of the inhabitants. The latter spent their days in the bar and their nights with their mistresses, and they were astonished at these Jewish immigrants who were willing to undertake all kinds of work. Benefiting from their new social freedom, the Jews established nice communities in all five countries of Central America.
>
> But suddenly three years ago, things changed. The established merchant saw danger in the Jewish peddler who drew clients away from him. Patriots couldn't stand seeing Jews who had come here naked and barefoot and who were in a short time able to save money. The Jews of Guatemala got the first blow, when that country forbade peddling. Many Jews lost their money and had to leave the country, at a time when there was nowhere else to go.
>
> Even worse happened in El Salvador, where the mob was roused by charges that the Jews were Bolsheviks and had come to root out Christianity. Some Jews were killed, and the community went through tragic days.[4]

Sephardim and Ashkenazim alike began their new lives as peddlers, Ladino-speakers being aided in their penetration of the market by their knowledge of the language. Turkish, Syrian, and Lebanese Jews entering Uruguay at the start of the century followed this trade, and so did the East Europeans who followed in the 1920s. They moved up through three levels: klapper, cuentanik, clientelchik. Far from being destructive elements, they were a welcome social factor, for they disseminated not only articles that fulfilled a tangible need but also books, pictures, and other cultural artifacts.[5]

Jewish commerce imparted a foreign look to parts of cities. "Rua de Alfândega, the street of Jewish merchants in Rio de Janeiro, is full of narrow, crowded shops standing cheek by jowl, just as in Warsaw," writes a correspondent of *Havaner Lebn* in 1935.

> Most of these merchants came as shoemakers, tailors, or teachers; but arriving without means, they could not set themselves up in their trade. But one could begin as a klapper, with merchandise taken on credit.
>
> You knock on a door, open your pack, recite the few words you have memorized, ask the housewife to buy. Prices are 100 percent over cost, to cover losses. When you find a customer, you set up a timetable for collecting the installment payments. Then you set out with your pack both to sell and to collect. You struggle to set up a territory with regular customers . . . the sun

is fierce and sweat eats up your clothes . . . but the climate holds up the market for cloth.

When the klapper has put together a few hundred customers, he becomes preoccupied with collecting installments on his capital, which is entirely tied up in the customers. He seldom goes out with his pack any more; now he is a clientelchik. Ninety percent of the Jewish population of Brazil, and more than half of Jews in other South American countries, are occupied in this trade.[6]

Peddlers were often accused by shopowners of robbing the poor. The peddlers' reply was "A lefl is tyer tsum essen"—

> *Doblemente cara*
> *al almuerzo*
> *la cuchara*

"a spoon is dear at suppertime." No existing sector of the business community had previously provided items of common household use to the large mass of the population that had not enough cash to enter a real store. The peddler appeared at the housewife's door with the items she needed, when she needed them. The provision of credit meant that, for a few cents down, many a family could eat with table utensils for the first time in their lives.

Competitors for the workers' paycheck naturally complained. In Chile, as in many other areas, a high rate of alcoholism prevailed among the working class. The factory worker customarily stopped in at the tavern on his way home, often leaving a good part of his paycheck there. When the peddler caught the worker at the factory gate and wrested his money from him, he antagonized the tavern owners, who were quick to spread stories about Jewish usury. But the peddlers gave goods in return for the workers' money, commodities that enhanced the quality of life for the workers' families. By bringing merchandise into the home and initiating housewives into installment buying, the semanalchik helped raise the standard of living of the poorest class, who had until then not been able to buy for cash the clothing and furniture they could now obtain on terms.[7]

Two-thirds of the Jewish immigrants who entered Mexico during the peak immigration years 1924–29 and who had been gainfully employed in their countries of origin had been merchants and traders. These were Polish Jews, who were being systematically extruded from their economic positions by the ethnic Poles, as well as declassed members of the Jewish petite bourgeoisie who took advantage of a temporary relaxation in the law to leave the Soviet Union.[8] These merchants, small manufacturers, and independent artisans brought along their skills and experience, but no financial means. Having been expropriated in their home countries, they arrived paupers. The B'nai Brith Organization of the United States opened offices in Mexico City and Vera Cruz to supply such social services to the immigrants as finding jobs, housing, schooling, providing legal aid, teaching Spanish, and granting loans—all services the Mexican government itself took no interest in providing.[9]

In almost any terms in which the immigrants could be described— socially, psychologically, financially—they were not prepared to join the Mexican industrial scene as it then existed. Mexico's industry in the twenties and thirties was concentrated in oil wells and metal mining. To join the owning class required vast amounts of capital which the immigrants did not have. They could not join the industrial proletariat because as foreigners they were excluded from the labor unions, which were as much *cofradias* as unions; and most companies ran a closed shop. In existing small and medium-sized industries of an urban type, such as textiles and clothing, workers were extremely ill-paid and kept in a dependent relationship to both boss and labor leaders, which went down ill with these once-independent storekeepers and tradesmen. In such a social constellation, there was no room for foreign workers.

To fit into his new homeland, the Jewish immigrant had to continue along the lines of his previous career as an independent businessman. For this, conditions in Mexico were propitious because the economy contained gaps the newcomers were qualified to fill. The same conditions that prevented formation of a Jewish proletariat encouraged formation of a Jewish merchant class.[10] But lacking capital to become a merchant, the Jew had first to become a peddler.

Most male immigrants to Peru were peddlers until government prohibited that activity in 1939, and so were the early immigrants to Colombia. Even mountainous Bolivia was tackled by the intrepid peddler. In 1940, a Joint representative to Bolivia wrote: "In Bolivia you see the Eastern Jew who does not attend courses to learn Spanish, but who speaks the dialect of the Indios. They appear in the most outlying villages, where hardly any Europeans have ever been, and manage to eke out an existence, sleeping in their wagons under the stars. Hardly a German immigrant has dared or would dare to do this. . . . Without wishing to be critical, but to complete the picture, I must say that the first care of each German is to get an apartment. As far as the German is concerned, an apartment must have a bath."[11]

Peddling was the chief means of support for newly arrived Jews in

Havana until the police began arresting them for blocking traffic in 1928. The hostility of established shopkeepers, who continued to be comfortable with the privileges the crown had endowed them with four centuries earlier, resulted in the raising of the fee for a peddler's license from the equivalent of $6.25 to $125 per year. These peddlers seem to have been somewhat more militant than their coreligionists elsewhere, for they formed a Shutzfarain far Peddler (Peddlers' Protective League) and succeeded in having the sum reduced. But despite its success, the Farain soon dissolved because its members either bought fixed places of business or went into cottage industry.[12]

A correspondent of *Havaner Lebn* recalls those days:

When we first came to Cuba, we were mistaken for Germans, and since we didn't know the language well enough to explain, we kept that name. Besides it might be better not to say we were Jews, or the grandchildren of the Grand Inquisitor would have our bones. Those were happy days, for we were on our way to America. Our career: writer (for relief). Those who had no one to write to for assistance became peddlers. . . . Every ship brought 600–800 Jews, and they all became peddlers. We lived twenty or thirty families to a house, and candle-lighting on the Sabbath gave out that we were Jews. But where were our horns? Incredible! Then Eskimo Pie hit Cuba, and we all carried ice boxes around Havana resting on our stomachs, bound with a cord to our shoulders. Since the name "German" had by now worn out, the Cubans began calling us "Eskimo Pie."[13]

The change in status was jolting to many. Among the peddlers were men who had been skilled craftsmen but who, for lack of capital, were forced out onto the street. There were numbers of learned men from Polish religious academies, accustomed to a life in which the respect accorded them by the community compensated for their poverty. There was no demand whatever for their knowledge now, and they were particularly demoralized by the indignity of their new way of life.

Severe personal disorientation was a common problem. The Cuban Yiddish press abounded in stories of Jewish peddlers enticed by fishermen and "taken for a ride" in the shark-infested waters surrounding the island. A story poignantly titled "Oif Nort" (In the North) portrays a young man arriving in Chile with a bundle of borrowed neckties to begin his career as a klapper. Freezing to death on that "northern" coast, he is terror-stricken by a display of aurora borealis.[14] Disjoined from the ecology, ignorant of language and customs, isolated from all that was formerly familiar, the immigrant while still in a high state of confusion had to set about earning his living. That was the meaning of "making America."

Making America

The figure of the peddler, who in his time attracted such mixed feelings, has almost disappeared from the Latin American scene. His obituary was written recently by Alberto Lleras Camargo, former president of Colombia and former secretary general of the Organization of American States. The occasion was a review of the memoirs of a Jewish peddler in Colombia:

Colombia is a craggy, mountainous land, like the lands of the Himalayas. The Andes Cordillera, on entering our territory from the south, fans out, from a tangle of volcanoes, into three cordilleras. These fragment the land into something like islands, a condition that endured for about four centuries after the Spanish invasion. Bogotá, the capital, is on a high plateau at 2600 meters of altitude. In the '20s Bogotá was still village-like; its inhabitants villagers. Hardly anyone but the oligarchy with intellectual airs, had any acquaintance—direct or through reports—with the delights of civilization like shoes, laces, or fine textiles and the many other products which were already in common use in the Europe of the 16th and 17th centuries. The immense difficulties in the way of import and export made of this trade a heroic adventure, crowned by glory when not frustrated by bankruptcy and other disasters beyond count. To bring a piano up to Bogotá was a task for the likes of the ancient Romans or the Carthaginians, perhaps, similar to the crossing of the Alps by Hannibal's elephants. The merchant had to be wealthy, daring, adventurous and illustrious in order to rate credit and persuade European manufacturers to take the risk. The clientele of the retail stores of Bogotá were the families of presidents, ministers or candidates for such high posts. Their prices covered the cost of sending sons to Oxford and Cambridge, or Harvard and Yale, or financing the European travels of daughters who had studied French or English. This trade, therefore, couldn't provide the needs of the people at large. They just about managed to ruin the native artisanry, producing crude products for the use of Colombians. Else, one had to walk about nude. Until the Jews came.

Those Jews like Guberek invented credit for people who always thought of themselves as insolvent. Probably because they were so. On selling to anyone, they would set a scale of very minimal weekly payments: fifty centavos or one peso. Each Sunday they would return to collect the payment (never on Saturday, their sacred Sabbath, though Saturday was payday for their clients). They sold to humble persons, artisans, unskilled laborers, and the poorest of the lower middle class. These people the Jewish traders put into new shoes, clad in new clothes, changing the appearance of a nation of peasants into something better, less picturesque, more uniform, but also more equalitarian.

Merchandise not only came down in price; it came within everybody's reach. Their successors or the survivors of that pioneer generation may well say that they shod a whole country, that they dressed a whole people, that they taught this people how to save in order to be able to meet payments due

on the credits they had never previously known since the arrival of the Spaniards in the Americas.[15]

Prostitution was the feminine counterpart of peddling, in that
women with no tangible resources supported themselves selling a product the public desired. The 1895 Argentine census turned up 61 Jewish
prostitutes. In the following two decades, 3,243 Russian women registered with the authorities as prostitutes. In a survey conducted by the
Argentine Department of Labor in 1917, 94 percent of the total group
of prostitutes gave an economic motive for their actions.[16] In fact, 44
percent had no previous work experience.

Among Jewish prostitutes with previous work experience, most had
followed the needle trades: 14.6 percent had been seamstresses, and
from 6 to 7 percent had followed each of the trades of milliner, presser,
and tailor. An additional 6 percent had been servants, a role traditionally subject to sexual exploitation in Latin America. These
working-class women suffered the same downward pressures as men
and ended up prostitutes.

Some of these women and girls were recruited in Europe by pimps
masquerading as bona fide grooms in search of brides; the marriage
consummated, the groom departed for the New World and shortly
after dispatched a ticket enabling the bride to follow. On her arrival,
she was met not by a husband but by a representative of the organization, who forced her into "the life."

There was no doubt a certain attraction after the first shock. Pimps
were the mainstay of Yiddish theater and night clubs in Buenos Aires
and were able to promise their recruits a more swinging existence than
could be had in sweatshops or in the struggling agricultural colonies.
Furthermore, white slavery had the protection of the Buenos Aires
police, which brought with it certain perquisites. During the periodic
crackdowns staged as much for show as for controlling the racketeers,
prostitutes were spirited off to Rio de Janeiro for a vacation.

Starting in 1908, Jewish organizations began to campaign against
the t'maim (the term included both the women and the men, the victims and the victimizers). The Khevrah Kadisha barred them from
membership (which meant they could not get a Jewish burial), and
finally—the last straw—the theaters denied them admission. The trade
was brought to an end in the 1930s, probably as much because of improved economic conditions as for any other reason. Women could by
that date find employment elsewhere. No identifiable Jewish women
prostitutes turned up in the 1960 census.

Artisans

In Argentina, whose Italian and Spanish immigrants came for the most part from agricultural backgrounds, proportionately more Jews than non-Jews arrived as skilled craftsmen. Jewish immigrants were qualified garment workers, carpenters, and furniture makers.[17] They were also tin and sheet metal workers, jewelers, watchmakers, masons, coopers, shoemakers, capmakers, and bakers—all skills that could be utilized by an industrializing economy.

In addition to those who arrived with marketable skills, there were others whose skills were not so transferable. Clerks were hampered by their lack of knowledge of Spanish. Students excluded from Russian universities when quotas were imposed were not qualified for any kind of work. Underground conspirators against the czar, exiled in the bloody reaction that followed failure of the revolution of 1905, had no peacetime trade, but they had to learn one in short order. As Wald

1. The first shoemakers' shop in Moisesville, Santa Fé province, Argentina, at the turn of the century. A large proportion of Jewish workers who emigrated to Latin America were cobblers. (Courtesy of the American Jewish Committee)

writes, "They had escaped from prison, from Siberia, or from the gallows. If they weren't proletarian before, they were now, either from need or from ideology. Their proletarianization took place in Argentina."[18] Buenos Aires of the period offered hundreds of jobs that were peripheral to the industrial process, such as tram conductor, hygiene inspector, and layer of electrical cable. Jewish immigrants found work with relative ease in the larger cities. Some went out as hired hands to the JCA colonies at harvest time or worked for Jewish furniture manufacturers in Córdoba, where their desire to work in a Jewish environment laid them open to grosser exploitation than in factories run by non-Jews.

Workers who were able to accumulate capital set up workshops for the manufacture of consumer goods, working alongside their employees and often indistinguishable from them. Unable to compete with imported luxury goods, they produced items of cheap apparel and furniture for the mass market. These beginnings of Jewish industry in Argentina are usually viewed as the start of occupational and social mobility for the immigrants, corresponding to the mobility experienced by immigrants to the United States during the same period. And indeed there were success stories. By 1940, thirty spinning and weaving mills were owned by Jews, employing some four thousand Argentine workers. The pioneering role of Jewish immigrants in the knitwear industry is attested to by the existence, at the same date, of one hundred workshops, sixty medium-sized factories, and three large factories for the production of underwear and sweaters.[19]

As Sofer has shown, the picture of Argentina as a land of unlimited opportunity was as much a product of optimism as it was of reality. The Argentine economy was not sufficiently industrialized to generate opportunities for great upward mobility. As the period of immigration progressed, opportunities for advancement narrowed rather than broadening. Economic and political factors constrained those with ambition, elaborating structural difficulties they could not overcome. "Inflation, the high cost of living, the lack of sufficiently protective tariffs, the reliance of domestic industry on foreign products, the high cost and frequent unavailability of raw materials, and the ever-present spectre of foreign competition, made the position of workers and petty proprietors precarious."[20] The onset of industrialization led to displacement of skilled artisans, yet locally owned industry did not expand sufficiently to absorb all those who were displaced. Driven out by the operations of the machine, skilled craftsmen had two choices:

to enter a factory or sweatshop, accepting the loss of status that entailed, or to go into business for themselves. The latter route resulted in rather less success than might be anticipated by those familiar with parallel developments in the United States. More Argentine Jewish entrepreneurs advanced and then slid back into the working class than advanced and stayed there. In spite of individual success stories, the bulk of those who began their lives in Argentina as workers and who had ended their careers by 1945 ended as workers.[21]

Cabinetry was the skill that predominated among Bessarabian Jews in Rio de Janeiro in 1910. The manufacture and sale of furniture became their principal means of support. Those who could not carpenter could vend, and craftsmen or their relatives got their goods to market without submitting to the tyranny of wholesale houses. Also among

2. *World* ORT *(Organization for Rehabilitation and Training) supports vocational training for Jewish youth in dozens of locations around the world. This workshop was functioning in Buenos Aires in 1946. According to the 1960 national census, there were 25,000 Jewish factory workers in Argentina that year. (Courtesy of YIVO Archives)*

the artisan-peddlers were dressmakers and shoemakers, as well as turners, who produced common household utensils. When they took these products door-to-door for sale to their neighbors, they were breaking the time-honored taboo against manual labor that still held back the upper classes from full immersion in the industrial century, and they stamped themselves as irretrievably lower class. But they survived. One means of survival in the days of no bank accounts and credit ratings was to drive a nail into the eaves of the home of a defaulter, as a warning to any klapper who might come after.[22]

The Polish Jews who began arriving in Rio after World War I included watchmakers, dressmakers, and compounders of cosmetics. Their wares, too, went to market in the peddlers' packs, increasing the amount of inexpensive consumer goods available to the Rio populace. The work habits the immigrants had developed in Europe, where labor from sun to sun was a necessity in order to stay alive, sufficed in Brazil to generate comfortable incomes for the immigrants within a relatively short time.

The German immigrants who reached Brazil in the years leading up to World War II included quite a few with transferable skills. Among these were tailors, shirtmakers, and hairdressers. Women often proved more employable than men, for with their language skills they found jobs as tutors, governesses, and salesclerks. Seamstresses able to interpret European styles for Brazilian taste found themselves in demand. The "craft" that suffered most from exclusionist legislation was medicine: doctors found obstacles placed in the way of their practicing in Brazil.[23]

Jewish immigrants to Cuba included locksmiths, watchmakers, mechanics, bakers, tailors, carpenters, painters, garment workers, and —most numerous—shoemakers.[24] Gaining employment in factories when they could, they sought admission to Cuban labor unions where these existed, or formed new ones in industries where there were none. Between 1929 and 1943, Cuban Jewish workers founded at least eight trade unions: shoemakers, peddlers, barbers, street photographers, tailors, seltzer-water vendors, merchants, and diamond workers.[25]

But union activity exacted a price: many immigrant labor leaders, including Jews, were arrested and deported by the Machado regime (1925-33). Under the revolutionary regime of Ramón Grau San Martín that followed, matters grew worse: new labor laws created a near-monopoly of jobs for the native-born, forcing Jewish workers either to reemigrate (if they could) or to become piece workers at home, outside the protection of the labor laws. In many cases, they moved from the domination of the foreman to the tyranny of the supplier of their raw materials. Specifically, the Law of 50 Percent, requiring that half of every employer's work force must be native-born, hit Jews the hardest because they were almost all foreign-born and the employers who hired them tended also to hire other Jews. The result of the law was to deprive hundreds of immigrants of their jobs.

Many Jewish immigrants had belonged to unions in Poland and Russia, often affiliated with the Bund, the Jewish sector of the socialist movement. The exploitation to which they, along with all Cuban workers, were subjected, radicalized many, causing them to abandon the mild social democracy with which they had arrived and move closer to the communist position. The situation was described by the sociologist Boris Sapir, who spent the war years on the island:

> The Jewish workers in Cuba provided a ready ground for Socialist and Communist propaganda. They resented the exploitation to which they were exposed, and this feeling evoked in them a trend toward social rebellion and a longing for a better world. The colonial milieu with a gulf dividing the rich from the poor, and the absence of skilled industrial workers, were not conducive to the emergence of a social-democratic movement. Social Democrats in Cuba have always been a small and uninfluential group. But the seeds of Communist propaganda have freely germinated among Cuban workers.
>
> These circumstances favored the expansion of radical tendencies among the Jewish workers, too. The Bundists (members of the Jewish Social Democratic Party "Bund") played a negligible part. But the Jewish Communists succeeded in capturing the imagination of large Jewish strata. Their own organization was small. They gained influence, however, by availing themselves of neutral organizations.[26]

Other Jewish workers, with more luck and less ideology, became manufacturers of the goods they had formerly produced in other people's factories. Prior to 1933, the Cuban market for shoes had been supplied by American producers. Only a small quantity were produced on the island, largely by hand labor, and these were in the nature of luxury goods. Jewish shoemakers who were forced out of factories set up their own shops. Soon they were mass producing a shoe that was both cheap and serviceable, bringing down the price of footgear and at the same time creating jobs for other Cubans. Within a few years of passage of the Law of 50 Percent, 150 shoe factories owned by Jews were employing six to eight thousand workers and producing two million pairs of shoes annually. Eventually, Jewish firms accounted for 50 percent of all shoe manufacturing in Cuba, ending Cuban dependence on foreign suppliers.[27] During the thirties, Cuban Jews laid the basis for several other industries as well, including clothing manufacture, tricotage, and diamond cutting. This most recent industry, established in 1943 with the arrival of Polish diamond workers from Antwerp, resulted in the founding of twenty-four workshops employing twelve hundred persons.[28] The Jewish proletariat, unable to survive in the social and legislative climate of Cuba, turned instead to cottage industry and became an important factor in industrialization of the island.

The Move to Industry

Jewish immigrants moved into industry by way of two paths: that of the peddler (often a displaced artisan to begin with), who began to produce the items he took for sale; and that of the practicing craftsman, who (by choice or force of circumstance) began to manufacture goods in his own home or workshop, using the sweated labor of his own family.

Peddlers were under considerable pressure to change their occupation because of the difficult life it entailed, the marginality of the income it produced, and the vulnerability to police and popular harassment. Only in Chile did peddling die what might be termed a natural death. There, the itinerant peddler was a casualty of the great depression. Chile was more advanced industrially than other Latin American countries, and more of its employment depended upon industry; so did weekly payments to the semanalchik. Most peddlers went bankrupt rather quickly. "A blessing in disguise" was the verdict of the *Chilener Yiddisher Wochenblatt*. In its issue of 12 January 1933, the editor wrote: "This is the time for Jews to go into industry. There are resources here, labor is cheap, and the industrial giants are only beginning to develop: so we can compete."

As of that date, there had long been Jews in Chilean industry. As early as 1884, a skilled Jewish metallurgist who had migrated from Lithuania was asked by the government to open a metal foundry in the Santiago prison. Here he taught his skills to a succession of young men, one of whom became his son-in-law and head of a large steelworks. In 1901, the immigrant opened his own foundry, where he produced the first agricultural implements to be manufactured in Chile, using a technique he had invented himself.

Other firsts of Jewish immigrants in Chilean industry include factories for the manufacture of wagons (1906), mirrors (1908), leather clothing (1910), and gramophone records (1910). Jewish immigrants opened ready-to-wear clothing factories, plants for making furniture, hats, raincoats, and fur coats, and printshops. Chile's first plastics factory was opened in 1924 by Jewish immigrants. Ultimately, this plant manufactured over 1,500 parts, employed 350 workers, and had 30 salaried employees. In 1925, a mill for making thread was opened by Jewish immigrants.[29]

When the depression finished off the semanalchiks, many more Jewish immigrants went into manufacturing, for which a good climate already existed. Lacking large amounts of capital, they began with cottage industry. Working as families in their own homes, they produced such common items of apparel as shirts, underwear, ties, socks, and suspenders, which at that time were not available on the mass market. The arrival of German-speaking Jews in the thirties added more entrepreneurs to the clothing industry. Ready-to-wear, thread, patterns, elastic, and silk were some of the items produced. European Jews clothed the Chilean poor, and the *roto* (the "broken" man) disappeared from Chilean streets. In 1956 it was estimated that Jewish-owned plants in the clothing industry alone employed between seventeen and eighteen thousand people.[30]

By the fifties, there were Jewish entrepreneurs in sugar refining, tobacco plantations, lumber, chemicals, patent medicines, olive oil, perfume, steel, thermoelectric plants, packing plants, eyeglasses, zippers, air conditioning and heating, Bakelite, and glass utensils for laboratories. Jewish managers were employed in foundries and construction firms, carrying on a long tradition of Jewish technicians involved with Chile's development. A Jewish engineer, Adolfo Weiner, built Chile's national library, as well as various streets in the capital. N. Rachitoff, a Jewish engineer, directed the construction of the main railroad station in Santiago, Mapocho, and collaborated on the electrified line to Valparaíso. Engineer Akiva Pommerante built the railroad line to Curicó and later worked at Los Condes copper mine. Engineer León Levi worked on the naval base at Talcahuano.[31] This group of Jewish industrialists and technicians figured in the growth of native Chilean industry. By producing domestically goods that previously were imported at high prices, they helped make inexpensive goods available to a mass market, while providing employment to Chilean workers. As Chilean citizens themselves, they had no need to repatriate profits to other countries in the style of foreign-owned firms. Participating as they did in the modernization of the country, Jewish immigrants integrated quickly into national life, with a facility they attributed to the tolerance of the Chilean people.

The phasing out of peddling among Jewish immigrants to Mexico came as a response to antiforeign agitation that made these isolated merchants feel too vulnerable to continue in their occupation. Xenophobia became apparent in Mexico in 1930 as the depression took hold. The price of silver dropped, thousands of Mexican workers were expelled from the United States, and economic pressures built up within Mexico that found an outlet in hatred of Chinese and Jews. Many newspapers, including the *Nacional Revolucionario* of the country's ruling Partido Nacional Revolucionario, published anti-Jewish articles. Merchants publicized such slogans as "Buy from Mexicans—boycott Jews."[32]

On 27 March 1931, the Mexican government published regulations that limited the location of market booths to certain areas and imposed onerous licensing requirements. Although the new requirements were met by the Jewish merchants, they were nevertheless forcibly evicted from Lagunilla market the following month, and all the peddlers' licenses were revoked. Panic suffused the Mexican Jewish community, intensified by a "Day of Commerce" parade that featured anti-Jewish slogans. Tensions abated when the president of Mexico declared that Jews were in Mexico legally and were free to pursue any occupation they chose.

The American Jewish Committee, a New York–based organization, sent an observer to Mexico in May of 1931 to investigate the situation. His confidential report names as the principal irritant in Mexican-Jewish relations the "desire of the poor immigrant to become independent and rich," an ambition he declares is incomprehensible to the average Mexican. The antagonism does not extend beyond the limits of the small peddler and market merchant. Only these are being called "judío," a standard Mexican term of opprobrium. Jewish professional men and representatives of foreign firms are not thought of as "judíos." Economic conflict àmong merchants is being taken advantage of by various government officials, the report continues, who exploit the opportunity to force people to buy more licenses. In the end, they evicted 220 Jewish merchants to make room for their competitors. But "let it be said again that [the officials'] purpose was not so much discrimination against the Jews as the desire to mulct them, legally or illegally, and at the same time give greater opportunities and ample market space to native Mexicans."[33]

The ousting of Jews from the occupation of peddling or selling in the marketplace appears to have benefited Jewish merchants in the long run, for it gave them a needed push to enter occupations in which they could succeed far better economically and, just as important, remove themselves from direct contact with religious fanaticism. When their market stalls were destroyed, Jewish merchants used capital they had accumulated to invest in fixed places of business or in small manufacturing plants, where they began producing a variety of consumer goods that had previously been imported, such as paint, furniture, leather goods, plastics, pharmaceuticals, sweaters, stockings, underwear, film, and fishing gear. Jacob Levitz assesses their economic role in this way: "The Jews have since their settlement in Mexico a quarter of a century ago, brought into the uneven, unbalanced social structure of class-ridden, semi-feudal, industrially retarded Mexico, a pioneering spirit. With social, economic and political conditions entirely favorable toward industrial and commercial expansion, the relatively small Jewish community, with its accumulated experiences, skills and enterprises, can be said to have served as a catalytic agent in the economic life of Mexico."[34]

The number of Jewish ventures in import substitution increased at an accelerated pace during World War II, when normal sources of supply were cut off. Backed by a communal bank (Banco Mercantil de Méjico), a credit union, and two small savings and loan associations, the Jewish immigrants continued their strong movement out of commerce and into industry and the free professions. By 1950, 12.6 percent of Mexican Jews who were gainfully employed were industrialists. Some were pioneering in industries, such as tricotage, that formerly had not existed at all in Mexico.[35]

Even when they succeeded in removing themselves from direct contact with masses of people in the marketplace, Jews still did not escape anti-Semitic manifestations. The classic entanglement between commercial rivalry and religious hatred surfaced in Ecuador in 1948 in the form of the medieval blood libel. A Jewish immigrant, owner of a sausage factory, was accused of intending to kidnap a Christian boy in order to use his flesh in making sausage. (The charge was subsequently altered to an intent to kidnap the boy for homosexual purposes.) The case was publicized in a sensational manner by the local newspapers. A letter from the Joint representative in Quito reports the incident while the accused was still being held without bail and continues without transition:

Applying for an import licence Jewish importers are required to produce preliminary invoices, samples, and sworn statements, provisions which are not mentioned in any decree and which are taken arbitrarily. The clearance of goods of Jewish importers is attended by special officials and special inspectors are appointed for the examination of the merchandise. . . .

The Minister of Interior is an open anti-Semite, although the motives for his attitude are unknown. From a political point of view he is striving for success in the direction of the least resistance. Being influenced by the national merchants he makes himself the mouthpiece of national trade interest. Mr. Lima, President of the Quito Chamber of Commerce, personally suffered considerable economic losses on account of the Jewish competition. . . .

Mr. Apunte, sub-chief of the Commercial Department of the Foreign Ministry stated that the *Jewish immigration had forced the country without transition from patriarchal forms of life into the modern era,* and that the country should be cleaned as fast as possible of Jewish immigrants. (Emphasis supplied.)[36]

We have seen that the ability of Jewish immigrants to apply skills they had acquired in Europe to the production and sale of consumer goods was the key to their integration into local economies. For this to occur, the economic and social climate of the matrix society had to be receptive to immigrant entrepreneurial initiative.

The German immigrants to Brazil in the days just preceding the outbreak of World War II made a particularly good adjustment. Their careers illustrate most clearly the reciprocal nature of immigrant integration. Many German Jews arrived in Brazil with a lifetime of experience in the business and industrial world of the Continent. They came at a time when circumstances in Brazil were propitious for industrial take-off and starting up a new plant required less capital than would have been needed in a fully developed economy. Habitual Brazilian tolerance made the Germans sought-after partners by the rising Brazilian middle class. Consequently, we find German Jews and their Brazilian partners investing in the fashion and textile industries, producing cotton, silk and linen cloth, and ladies' ready-to-wear. Certain construction materials, electrical hardware, and locks were now manufactured in Brazil for the first time. The immigrants undertook for the first time the construction of houses of more than three stories in height, utilizing local materials. Elevators, porcelain plumbing fixtures, paper, and newsprint were first manufactured in Rio by Jewish immigrants. It was as though the industrial revolution had finally opened its cornucopia to Brazilians, who formerly either paid high prices for imported goods or went without.

During World War II, Jewish immigrants started up a refrigeration industry that began the preservation of foodstuffs in this country that had hitherto been a net importer of food. Aluminum factories provided important stores of this metal for the allied forces.[37] The firm of Klabin e Lafer built a diversified industrial empire on the base of their paper manufacturing plants, including the largest newsprint producer in Latin America. The two families, now joined by marriage ties, are among the wealthiest in Brazil. Horacio Lafer, born in São Paulo, served thirty years in the federal Chamber of Deputies, was majority leader under President Eurico Dutra, finance minister under Getulio Vargas, and foreign minister under Juscelino Kubitschek. He and his associate, Mauricio Klabin, who came to São Paulo in 1887, remained integrated in Jewish life while participating in Brazilian politics and industry.

An Analysis of Jewish Economic Integration

The economic decisions made by private individuals participating in a spontaneous migration are not wholly open to investigation. Individuals participate in the economy as producers and consumers, not as Jews. But there does exist a theoretical framework for analysis of the economic structure and life of the Jews that may be used to organize and render coherent the vast amount of humanistic literature available on this subject for Latin America.

The perception of Jews as a minority in an economic, as well as in the usual religious sense, is a fruitful node with which to begin. The salient economic characteristic of Jewish communities is their minority status. These are permanent minorities: neither immigration nor the natural rate of increase will ever significantly raise the proportion of Jews to total population, given their initial tiny numbers. Certain economic consequences flow from permanent minority status. Such a minority cannot reproduce the full range of occupations. Their recency of arrival means that most sectors of the economy are already fully manned; immigrants therefore concentrate in remaining sectors, where old residents will resent them less and where the selection of occupation is further limited by their own historical heritage. They arrive poor (having been pushed out elsewhere) and therefore start at a low level. Beginning at this lower level, immigrants have more room to rise: since they entered new areas with greater growth potential than the old, their economic rise may be of greater magnitude than that of the general population. As newcomers, they are more free of tradition and have more room for maneuver. But the immigrants' concentration on a narrow occupational range, plus the absolute increase in their numbers, lead to numerical domination and apparent capture of some sectors of the economy.[38]

As applied to the Latin American scene, we may certainly agree that Jews represent a minority of such numerical insignificance that it would not be possible for them to man all sectors of an economy if that option were open to them. In point of fact, their late arrival in most cases excluded them from traditional sources of wealth—particularly ownership of land—and confronted them with basically urban options. Within urban parameters, immigrant Jews, like immigrants of other nations, tended to move into sectors that were less developed, for here they met less resistance from established folk. The Jewish migration, as we have seen, was propelled out of Europe by a series of convulsions whose source lay in the industrializing process. Jews, who had been factors in European industrialization and urbanization, were technically equipped and strategically placed to take part in the industrialization of Latin America.

These immigrants arrived in Latin America within a modernized mind frame, bringing with them skills and habits of thought shaped by the economic history they had lived through. They were confronted by societies that had not as yet begun to industrialize on a grand scale. What industry there was tended to be the product either of foreign investment or of immigrant endeavor. Their fortunes would depend on the extent that society had moved far enough away from traditional behavioral norms to tolerate entrepreneurial activity.

Lacking capital, Jewish immigrants had to begin operating at very low economic levels. This meant taking jobs as workers in industry, where such existed. But the industrial base was small, industrial wages far below those of Europe, and the worker lacked the protection trade unionism had won for him on the older Continent; therefore this option was not exercised by many immigrants or tolerated by many governments.

Commerce, too, was underdeveloped, and the opportunities for advancement correspondingly great. But here, the immigrant starting out without capital could be his own boss. So he became a peddler. Jewish peddlers flowed into the interstices of commerce, extending credit to consumers and purveying cheap manufactured goods to a mass market. For many *campesinos* and marginal families of the big cities, the peddler brought the largesse of the industrial revolution to the door—and at a price the poor could afford. Modernization of dress began to blur class lines, and differences between countryside and city, between poor and rich, became less pronounced.

Competition from peddlers who were products of a capitalist, risk-bearing economy aroused shopkeepers, who continued to operate in the Hispanic colonial mode, selling few goods at high prices. Commercial rivalry has been identified as a chief cause of the revulsion against foreign immigration that took place after the turn of the century. Its impact was most sharply felt by Jewish immigrants, who had entered the economies at such low levels that they were extremely vulnerable to boycott or police actions. As a result, Jews abandoned peddling within two or three decades of arrival in Latin America.

Typically, former peddlers chose one of two paths in order to establish themselves on firmer economic foundations. One was to buy a fixed place of business and expand sales to a wider market. The other was to go into manufacturing, utilizing skills brought from Europe to process local raw materials. In every country of the continent, Jewish entrepreneurs were among the first to see the potential for turning local commodities into salable merchandise, thus reversing the historic trend, which had been to export raw materials for manufacture abroad and subsequent resale at high prices on the Latin American market. This process of import substitution is generally regarded as having been the first step toward loosening the dependence of Latin America upon foreign markets. Having cut their ties to their countries of origin, Jewish immigrants had no need to export capital to pay off foreign investors, but were free to reinvest their earnings in the expansion of industrial plants. The result for many Jews personally was a meteoric rise to affluence.

Many immigrants achieved spectacular success by filling the commercial and industrial vacuum into which they came. The neglect of commerce and industry has been so persistent throughout Latin American history that it has attracted the attention of sociologists seeking to link this economic aberration to cultural characteristics of the people.

Weak achievement orientation and a view of work as a necessary evil are two characteristics continually singled out by scholars as hallmarks of Latin American society. The peninsular Spaniards who came out to rule the Indies had to dissociate themselves from any type of manual or productive labor. Even applicants for admission to the university in colonial days had to prove the purity of their blood and provide legal proofs that none of their ancestors had ever engaged in trade.[39] The requirement of limpieza de sangre, as we have seen, referred in part to the question of Jewish ancestry while trade in the Iberian peninsula had been associated with Moors and Jews. The defamatory definitions of "Jew" in Spanish and Portuguese dictionaries revolve around alleged business practices, and, as we have just seen,

Jewish peddlers on Mexico City streets were called "judío" while wealthier merchants were not. In republics that inherited Iberian culture, prestige is traditionally tied to land ownership, sufficient wealth to generate conspicuous consumption, and a life of contemplation. Technical and scientific careers have been until recently the object of condescension. Innovations that might upset traditional social and economic arrangements have been suspect as subversive.[40] Even the growth of corporate industry and the visible accretion of wealth derived from it need not change the picture materially, as has been shown most effectively for Argentina.[41] Acceptance of technological advancement is diluted by the fear that it threatens traditional values.

Yet economic development undeniably has occurred in Latin America. Whence did it come? The evidence is that much of it stems from the activities of immigrants. Not, of course, Jewish immigrants only; but immigrants generally, who in their overwhelming majority were not Jewish. According to Gino Germani, "It was the immigrant population which provided most of the labor and entrepreneurship in the beginnings of industrial development."[42] The situation does not vary greatly from country to country: immigrants took the lead in initiating the industrialization process in all sectors of the continent prior to World War I. The process began early and has continued to the present time. In 1895, 80 percent of Argentine commerce and industry was already in the hands of the foreign-born. At that date, there were barely seven thousand Jews in the country, and two-thirds of them were in the agricultural colonies of Entre Ríos. The predominance of immigrants and sons of immigrants in Argentine industry is documented through 1959, when 45.5 percent of prestigious Argentine entrepreneurs were foreign-born, while a goodly percentage of the rest were first-generation born in the country.[43] A similar situation prevailed in Chile, where by 1914 immigrants comprised a majority of owners of industry. Although they had been able to buy little rural property, they had acquired large amounts of urban real estate.[44] Many thousands of immigrants had already entered the Chilean middle class by that date, when there appear to have been no more than five hundred Jews in the country. Whatever commercial or industrial success Jews achieved in Chile may well have been a function of their status as immigrants rather than as Jews.

In countries that were slower to industrialize, the picture is not greatly different. A survey of sixty-one Bogotá executives of medium-to-large firms turned up the interesting fact that although Colombia has had very little immigration, 41 percent of her entrepreneurs are foreign-born. By way of comparison, the United States, with 10 percent foreign-born in the population at large, exhibits a mere 5 percent of foreign-born in executive positions in medium-to-large firms.[45]

Colombia provides an exceptionally interesting limiting case, in that there exists within this country of generally Hispanic value orientation a pocket of entrepreneurial activity centered in the region of Antioquia with its capital city at Medellín. Attracted by the salience of this community, E. E. Hagen studied 148 Colombian businesses, seeking the roots of achievement orientation. He found that three times as many *antioqueños* as other old Colombians became entrepreneurs. Why should this be?

Colombians have a ready answer: antioqueños are descended from Jews. The belief is widespread, and I was so told by every person interviewed in Colombia, including some who themselves came from Medellín. ("Of course, I'm not, personally, but . . .")

The myth of Marrano descent has no basis in fact.[46] Other causes led to the emergence of entrepreneurial talent among antioqueños. The interesting thing for our purposes is the persistence of the myth. As Hagen remarks, it is convenient to be able to look down on the antioqueños for their business acumen by explaining that they are New Christians.

It was by no means preordained that Latin America should recruit its entrepreneurs so heavily from among immigrants. What seems to have mattered was the contrast in value systems of the immigrants and their host societies.

Latin American value systems left commercial and industrial sectors unmanned, and immigrants in their effort to "make America" proceeded to man them. Latin America proved vulnerable to immigrant economic innovators because the host culture was hostile to rational entrepreneurial orientations. The immigrants, untrammeled by local tradition and desperate to find means of subsistence, made substantial gains. They rose economically with startling rapidity, a mobility that was shared by Jews. The latter's late arrival, small numbers, and concentration in a narrow occupational range led to the apparent capture of some sectors of the economy at certain times and certain places, calling down upon their heads ancestral antipathies that had remained embedded in Hispanic Catholicism. What in fact had happened was that Jewish immigrants supplied needs that had not previously been recognized and for which they were suited by ex-

perience. Adjusting themselves to local conditions, they entered economies as peddlers or artisans, then, adjusting again, moved into fixed
commerce and manufacturing. They thus became a part of that much
larger immigrant force that was beginning the modernization of Latin
America.

6

Agricultural Colonies:
The Burden of the Dream

Many thousands of Jewish immigrants established themselves as farmers in Argentina, Brazil, Uruguay, the Dominican Republic, and Bolivia. For the most part, they settled in groups, often under sponsorship of the Jewish Colonization Association (JCA). Only the colonies in Argentina and Brazil lasted long enough to mold the character of Jewish immigration to these countries and, in the case of Argentina, to leave an impress on the nation's history. Other colonies that were projected for areas as distinct as Baja California and Surinam never came into existence.

Despite their evanescence, the Jewish colonies are worth examining as a means of furthering our understanding of the ways Jewish immigrants could and could not adapt to Latin American society. The successes and the failures alike provide insight into the capacity of these societies to absorb European immigrants.

Argentina

We have seen that Argentine expectations concerning immigrants focused persistently on their value as farmers. Despite high expectations, the social and legislative climate was never adapted to meet their needs. The aggregation of enormous tracts of land in the hands of a few families was already a permanent feature of the landscape by the time immigrants began to arrive. The large leased tracts characteristic

of the early independence period were converted to permanent ownership under Rosas, and in 1876 the first law of lands and colonies permitted the sale of land in lots of eighty thousand hectares. This was
the same year basic immigration legislation was passed, and successive
governments never provided for the need of immigrant farmers to buy
homesteads. Between 1882 and 1912, land values increased one hun-
dredfold because of the subjugation of the Indian and the consequent
expansion of the agricultural frontier. Newly opened land was sold at
public auction, in tracts so large that the price was beyond the reach
of ordinary farmers or immigrants, who lost out to speculators and investors.[1] As a result, the process by which *latifundista* families extended their domains actually intensified during the years when proimmigration forces were calling most vocally for recruitment of farmers.

Since land was not to be made available to individual immigrants,
colonization became a corporate concern. Government allotted large
tracts to foreign entrepreneurs, who in turn contracted with European
firms to supply specified numbers of settlers. These were then allocated
plots of land within the colony, together with the right to claim ownership after a given number of years. The entrepreneurs made their
profit from shares in the harvest and by keeping a part of the land
grant for themselves.

We may now ask why Jews should have decided to cast themselves
in the role of agricultural pioneers in Argentina, a country that had not
previously attracted their attention. The motivation was partly survival and partly ideology. The former is sufficient to account for Jews'
emigrating to Argentina, but the latter is vital to an understanding of
why they came as farmers.

The renewed outbreak of pogroms in Russia in 1881 forced Jewish
intellectuals into a redefinition of their Jewishness that depended less
upon amelioration of the Gentile world's hatred of the Jew than upon
alteration of the Jews' own state of consciousness, shaped ineluctably
by objective reality. Several elements figured in what came to be called
auto-emancipation, after the title of a tract published in 1882 by Leon
Pinsker. One was Zionism, which offered a political solution. Another
was cultural nationalism, stressing the spiritual unity of scattered Jewish communities. The third was a return to nature and to productive
labor on the land. These themes were to dominate Jewish life for the
next ninety years and to result, inter alia, in creation of the state of
Israel.

Apart from the nationalist mystique of Zion, there was nothing
intrinsically attractive about Palestine, at that time a forsaken corner

of the Ottoman Empire. The appearance on the scene of Argentina, with its offer of religious toleration and land for the farmer, presented the émigrés who were interested in normalizing the situation of the Jewish people with an alternative destination. Thus Argentina, because of its policy of recruiting European farm immigrants, became a link in the chain of migrations that was converting the Jews from a European to an American people.

In 1889, one group of Russian Jews arranged their own emigration, negotiating a contract with the Argentine government that provided for their settlement on land suitable for farming. Sailing from Bremen on the ship *Weser*, they found on arrival in Buenos Aires that their land had been assigned to others. With the money that was returned to them, they made a new contract with a latifundista of Santa Fé Province, an area that was at that date attracting a larger proportion of immigrants than any other in Argentina. But this landowner proved either unwilling or unable to carry out his part of the contract, which included supporting the immigrants through the crucial first year. Reduced to poverty, without food or housing, the immigrants hovered near the railway station, sustaining themselves with handouts from passengers. Many children died the first winter, and numbers of girls went off with the white slavers. The entire enterprise would have died aborning had it not been for the passage of Dr. Wilhelm Loewenthal, a Jewish sanitary engineer, through Santa Fé on the newly opened railway. Investigating on behalf of the Alliance Israelite Universelle, he brought the plight of the settlers to the attention of Baron Maurice de Hirsch, one of the great philanthropists of the day.[2] Thus began one of the most remarkable adventures in immigration the world had seen to that date.

Hirsch's intervention was prompted by a philanthropic urge whose manifestation in practical deeds earned him considerable status among Jews worldwide, for whom the giving of *tzdakah* (charity) is a meritorious act. But his philanthropy had a practical bent. Although Hirsch sent money for the temporary relief of the impoverished Jews of Santa Fé, he went considerably farther and established the Jewish Colonization Association, an organization he envisaged as a way of restructuring the lives of diaspora Jewry. The guiding idea behind JCA was to accomplish the moral and physical regeneration of the Jews through agricultural labor. "What I desire to accomplish," wrote Hirsch, "what, after many failures has come to be the object of my life, and that for which I am ready to stake my wealth and my intellectual powers, is to give to a portion of my companions in faith the possibility of finding a new existence, primarily as farmers and also as handicraftsmen, in those lands where the laws and religious tolerance permit them to carry on the struggle for existence as noble and responsible subjects of a human government."[3]

The question is sometimes raised as to why Baron Hirsch fixed on Argentina rather than on Palestine. But the dream of a renaissance of the Jewish people in the land of its birth had not yet been formulated. The man who was to do that, Theodor Herzl, was still fumbling to give shape to his inchoate ideas when he met with Baron de Hirsch at the latter's Paris home in June of 1895. A week later, Herzl noted in his diary some arguments against Jewish settlement in Palestine: the proximity of Russia; the lack of opportunity for expansion; the climate.[4] The baron no doubt would have added the necessity of dealing with the Turks, with whom he had had scarifying experiences in the course of building the oriental railways that were the foundation of his fortune.

Hirsch, though no visionary like Herzl, had his own ideas about a Jewish renaissance. What was needed was to wean Jews away from urban occupations and intellectual preoccupations and get them back on the land. Herzl indeed faulted him for deprecating the finer qualities in Jewish life. But Hirsch was more than an imperious philanthropist. His style was to intervene in specific situations where he felt that money and organization could make the difference between success and failure of Jews to root themselves locally. Hirsch was to initiate similar ventures in Canada, the United States, and Brazil, but he favored Argentina and determined to give the project every possibility of success. The presence of stranded Jews in Santa Fé Province, on the edge of Argentina's wheat belt, provided the sort of opportunity he relished. There the lure of virgin land, which was attracting settlers in large numbers, meshed with the worldwide rise in the price of wheat to present prospects of a profit to be made through large-scale cultivation of grain. How better to combine philanthropy with good business practice than by transferring displaced Jews from Russia and settling them as farmers on land suitable for growing wheat? Thus Jews would become self-sufficient in the one occupation that, according to the baron's philosophy, could accomplish their "moral and physical regeneration." The refugees were about to acquire a good manager.

JCA was founded 10 September 1891 as a British joint stock company, with an initial capital of $10 million (furnished by Hirsch, who later added another $30 million). On his death, Hirsch's shares were divided among the Jewish communities of Frankfort-on-the-Main,

Berlin, and Brussels, the Alliance Israelite Universelle (founded in 1860 at Paris as an educational and rehabilitation agency), and the Anglo-Jewish Association of London, which became the administrator. Article 6 of its charter prohibits the taking of any profit from the company; any surplus is to be dedicated to "facilitating the emigration of Jews from the countries . . . where they are persecuted . . . , to other regions of the world where they may enjoy the rights inherent in mankind."

In negotiations with the Russian government, Hirsch assumed responsibility for the transport of colonists from various European and Turkish ports. The Russians, for their part, agreed to issue passports to the refugees, which they had hitherto refused to do. These were one-way documents, invalid for return to Russia, but they facilitated the immigrants' entry into Argentina.

Previous colonizers had received their land free from the Argentine government; in many cases, they had also received funds for their maintenance during the first year of settlement, as well as seed and tools. On 21 May 1891, however, the alienation of public lands ceased. All the land that JCA came to control had to be purchased either from the government or from private owners.

JCA organized and paid for the immigrants' transportation to Argentina, allocated land, tools, and farm animals, and provided shelter for the colonists during the transition years. It hired administrators to run the colonies and represented the colonists in their dealings with the Argentine government. JCA conformed both to Argentine law and to Jewish necessity by serving as colonizing agent for agrarian immigrants. Moreover, as Scobie notes, "the [Jewish Colonization] association introduced paternal protection and guidance totally lacking in private, company, or official immigration schemes."[5]

To start the project off, agents of Baron de Hirsch fanned out through the ports of Germany and Turkey, spreading word about the new land of promise, interviewing and selecting immigrants whom they considered fit for agricultural labor. One Constantinople contingent of two hundred families was organized into seventeen brigades, under captains who were responsible for the comportment of their charges. The JCA role in mediating between East European Jewish and Argentine cultures was immediately apparent in the edict that no one was to be permitted to embark who would not shave his beard and earlocks. On the other hand, a *shokhet* or ritual slaughterer was shipped with the immigrants. The enlightened administrators would permit their colonists to be Jews at home, if only they would behave as men on the boat. The migrants were exhorted to regard themselves as a self-conscious vanguard: "You are going in order to open a path for your brothers in captivity, accused of depreciating honest agricultural labor. Baron de Hirsch wishes to demonstrate to the world through your mediation that the accusation is false, and that Hebrews also can be good workers when they have the means to be so."[6] Thus, at the very start of the migration, the future relationship between administration and colonists was prefigured: the role of the administrators as big brother; the desire to transform the colonists' image; and the expectation that these migrants would prove a point that was very important in the ideology of the day: that Jews were capable of productive labor on the land.

Because restrictions on Jews had prevented them from owning land in most countries of Europe, few practicing farmers could be found. But stevedores, blacksmiths, ironworkers, tailors, and shoemakers were enlisted, if they were in good physical condition and had sons who might be expected to work alongside them. Although most of the recruits were not farmers, they were not city dwellers either. Most Russian Jews at that date lived in farming villages or rural towns (the shtetl), where they were intimately linked with the agricultural cycle.

The original plan was to resettle 25,000 Jews in Argentina during 1892, the first year of JCA's existence. In the course of twenty-five years, it was hoped that 3,250,000 Jews would escape from the Pale of Settlement to the Argentine pampas. In point of fact, just 2,500 Jews, one-tenth the projected number, were resettled the first year. In no year did total Jewish immigration into Argentina exceed 15,000, including those who went to the city as well as those who went to the farm. Although Argentina was the major destination for Jewish farmers under the JCA program, the colonies at their peak had only 33,000 Jewish farmers.[7]

The original scope of the settlement scheme had to be scaled down as a result of the failure of the Argentine government to approve the sale of additional adjacent tracts of land and a dawning realization on Hirsch's part that the climate and soil in the areas where he was able to buy land were not totally suited to agriculture. Hirsch therefore shifted from his original project of one vast territory to one of scattered colonies that would not raise the apprehension of Argentines that a portion of their national territory might be alienated. This move also enabled JCA to try out agricultural conditions in other parts of the country. The accompanying map indicates the location, ultimate extent of land purchased, and date of installation of the first

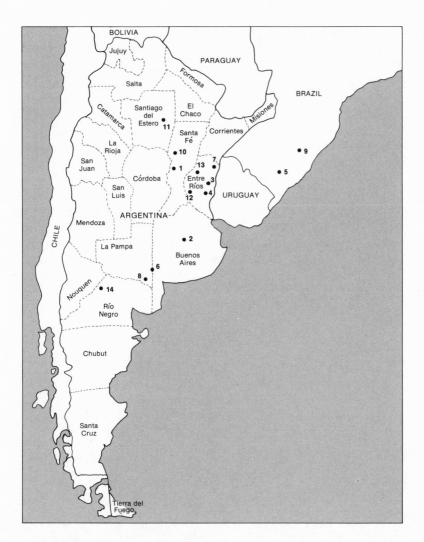

Jewish Colonization Association
Colonies in Argentina and Brazil

	Name	Settled	Hectares				
1.	Moisesville	1891	118,262	8.	Narcisse Leven	1909	46,466
2.	Mauricio	1892	43,485	9.	Quatro Hermãos	1910	93,885
3.	Clara	1892	102,671	10.	Montefiore	1912	29,075
4.	Lucienville	1894	40,630	11.	Dora	1912	2,980
5.	Philippson	1903	5,764	12.	Cohen-Oungre	1925	23,074
6.	Baron Hirsch	1905	110,866	13.	Avigdor	1936	17,175
7.	Santa Isabel	1908	47,804	14.	San José (not colonized)		156

SOURCE: Adapted from Morton D. Winsberg, *Colonia Baron Hirsch*, p. 6.

Jewish farmers in the Argentine JCA colonies. First to be settled were
the remainder of the *Weser* group who still wished to go into farming
after their rude initiation. Hirsch purchased a part of the tract on
which they had settled under contract, and it was there that the first
colony of Moisesville was established in 1891. In succeeding years, five
colonies were established in the province of Entre Ríos, another in
Santa Fé, two in the province of Buenos Aires, and one each in the
Chaco, La Pampa, and Río Negro. The early pace of settlement was
rapid; four colonies were established in the 1890s and seven more before the outbreak of World War I.

Five years into its lifetime, in 1896 (the year of Baron Hirsch's
death), the JCA project consisted of 302,736 hectares of land, settled by
a Jewish population of 6,757. The years up to World War I witnessed
JCA's greatest expansion; its area almost doubled while its population
practically tripled. The largest population—20,382 Jewish farmers
and their families, 13,000 Jewish artisans, businessmen, professionals,

*3. A group of Jewish colonists near Buenos Aires Province, about 1905. Most
still wear beards, but their uncovered heads signify that they are moving away
from Jewish tradition. (Courtesy of YIVO Archives)*

and their families, plus a non-Jewish population of about 5,000—was reached in 1925, following which the Jewish population began to diminish while the non-Jewish population continued to increase.[8] Although the population of the colonies appeared to be growing throughout the twenties, the statistics obscure the turnover in personnel as disappointed settlers departed for the city and were replaced by new immigrants, not a few of whom settled on the farm because they were admitted to the country on agricultural visas. From 1936 to 1940, the colonies underwent a revival as JCA recruited German and Austrian Jewish refugees. Most of these persons, however, were middle-class professionals with no background of manual labor, and they tended to leave as soon as economic conditions permitted.

The total land area eventually acquired by JCA in Argentina came to 617,000 hectares or a million and a half acres. This was transferred in settlement only in part; one-fourth was held in reserve for future immigrants or was not suitable for agriculture. The colonists were settled as family units. Although conditions varied somewhat from time to time and from place to place, the terms imposed upon settlers in Colonía Baron Hirsch were typical. Each colonist was awarded a lot varying in size from 75 to 150 hectares (185 to 370 acres), together with a house (two rooms and a kitchen), fencing, a well, poultry run, ten to twenty cows, eight to ten horses, twenty-five to fifty fowl, a wagon, plow, harrow, harness, and miscellaneous farm implements, seeds, and maintenance for the first few months. In return, the colonist signed a contract that obligated him to pay all land taxes and rent at the rate of 4 percent of the value of the land, 5 percent of the value of the buildings. The contract was to be reviewed after five years, and after eight the colonist would be given a definite title deed with a mortgage at 4 percent interest—if he had meanwhile succeeded in paying off 50 percent of the value of the land.

For a few years, the JCA colonies captured the imagination of the Jewish world, for they seemed to hold the promise that, here in the New World, the Jewish condition of rootlessness could be remedied. In fact, during the decade of the thirties, a larger proportion of the Jewish working class was engaged in agriculture than was the case either in their countries of origin or in other major countries of destination. In the decade preceding World War II, the percentage of Jews gainfully employed who worked in agriculture was 4.3 percent for Poland and 4.2 percent for the USSR. The corresponding percentage for Jews of the United States was 2.2 percent. But 5.8 percent of Argentine Jews gainfully employed were in agriculture in 1935.[9] This certainly justi-

fied the baron's belief that Jewish settlement on the land might succeed in Argentina.

Jewish agricultural colonies, however, were not to become a permanent feature of Argentine life. Today the colonies are in a state of decay. Just 2,373 Jewish farmers (including independents) were counted
in the 1960 Argentine census. To understand why the colonies failed,
it is necessary to examine both their internal life and the Argentine
social structures into which they had to fit.

The dominant theme of most memoirs of life in the JCA colonies
is the struggle between settlers and administrators. The administrative
apparatus of the colonies was established quickly, and it operated in
near-autonomous fashion, despite (or because of) the imposing pan-
theon of its board of directors. Staffed largely by French Jews, products
of the haskalah, the administration saw itself as "always . . . preoccupied with facilitating the assimilation of the people settled in their
colonies with the object of their becoming good agriculturists and patriotic Argentinians, though conserving their religious faith."[10] Most
diarists and historians among the East European colonists depict the
administrators as anti-Semites. Officials, believing themselves to be culturally superior to the settlers whose affairs they had been hired to
administer, displayed a contempt for the mores of the shtetl that was
at all times galling and occasionally brutal. According to one historian
of the colonies, Hirsch's fundamental principle—that the project must
not be handled as charity but must be utilized to reconstruct Jewish
life—was perverted by the JCA administrators into a conviction that
they must protect the project against the settlers, who, as East Europeans, were lacking in culture and not worthy of trust.[11] So, for example, Hirsch's stricture that JCA help only those who helped themselves
emerged from the administrators' hands in the form of a contract that
many settlers had to sign by which JCA remained sole owner of the
land up to the very last payment.[12] JCA retained the right to expel any
farmer who was tardy in his current payment, without consideration
for sums paid up to that date. The right was often exercised. This
philanthropic feudalism turned the colonists into tenants rather than
independent farmers.

The rigid bureaucratic mold, a product of the transfer of European
attitudes to Argentina, left no room for participation by the settlers in
the determination of their own affairs. With JCA legal owner of the
land, farmers found they could not get credit at the bank but were
forced to borrow from JCA, a situation that intensified their depen-

dence. Gradually, Jewish tenants found themselves being pushed into the same dependent relationship to their *patron* as *minifundistas* all over Latin America. Jews, however, had arrived on the land with financial and organizing skills; to evade this dependence, they founded cooperative credit associations. Originally organized with JCA support for the purpose of buying seeds and supplies, the cooperatives turned into a weapon of struggle against the JCA as the settlers endeavored to gain representation in the decision-making process.[13]

JCA had reason to impede colonist participation in decision making. As a charitable organization, it was selling land at prices far below those charged by commercial companies. As the price of land rose steadily, colonists watched the value of their assigned property rise several-fold over the price at which they had agreed to buy it. Colonists who received title to their land before they had adjusted to rural life were tempted by the increased value of the land to sell it, invest the money in other occupations, and establish themselves in the city. In fact, just such a fate overtook the colony of Mauricio, where victory of the colonists in a lawsuit claiming title to their land resulted in the exodus of nine-tenths of them between the years 1919 and 1930.[14] Such a development obviously ran counter to the philosophy of Baron de Hirsch and of the organization he founded.

With hindsight, it is possible to relieve the JCA administrators of the charge of anti-Semitism without thereby declaring them to have been sensitive to the settlers' problems. Two of these were the source of continuous friction: the pattern of settlement and the allocation of land to the second generation.

The pattern of settlement was crucial because Jewish life is communal in nature. The scattering of farmers on their land, combined with poor means of transport, would make it impossible to create the Jewish social institutions—synagogues, religious schools, libraries, facilities for slaughtering kosher meat, cemeteries—on which Jewish life depends. Opinion differs as to how well JCA handled this matter. Morton D. Winsberg writes that "from the beginning, the JCA and the inhabitants of the colonies in Entre Ríos . . . worked together to establish a Jewish cultural environment similar to that left behind in the ghettos of East Europe. Despite the vast difference between the two areas, they were surprisingly successful, at least in the early years of colonization."[15] This success was achieved by settling the immigrants in agricultural villages, a pattern typical of eastern Europe but not then in use in Argentina. Here the familiar old institutions were recreated—

but at the price of agricultural efficiency because farmers spent a good deal of time getting to and from their land. Subsequently, JCA gave up the village pattern of settlement in favor of locating each family upon its own land. The increase in efficiency was then accompanied by atrophying of Jewish institutions as the isolation of the Argentine countryside closed down around Jewish, as around non-Jewish, farmers.

The hostile eye of Ariah Tartakower emphasizes the latter development. In his view, JCA administrators, by scattering colonies over the Argentine map "as though for fear of the evil eye," deliberately inhibited the growth of Jewish cultural life, which they despised as inferior to their own and as an embarrassment before the gentiles.[16]

Perhaps the most short-sighted aspect of JCA policy was the refusal to grant land from its reserves to the grown sons of established colonists. The policy was adhered to over a period of many years, despite considerable agitation on the part of those colonists who foresaw that stable settlement depended on making provision for the next generation. The JCA contended that it was concerned with settling new Jewish immigrants from abroad and that Argentine-born sons ought to strike out on their own. The difficulty was that, as we have seen, it was virtually impossible for an individual to buy farm land in small plots. This was true throughout the nation and for all immigrants. So little success did colonists enjoy in establishing themselves on the land that the very word *colono* came to be generally used as a synonym for peon, a term that has more the connotation of debt-serf than of freeholder. As a result of JCA policy, grown sons of colonists who wished to remain farmers had to become tenants of other latifundistas, accepting the same short-term leases then being offered other rural proletarians. Analysts of the Argentine economy generally point to these leases, which bore no assurance of renewal, as a major cause of rural poverty. With insecure tenure, the colonists had no incentive to make improvements to the land, but tended to drift off toward the city.

Among external factors affecting the viability of the Jewish colonies, the system of latifundia was primary, in that it provided the context within which the colonies had to function. Of equal importance was the marginal utility of the land JCA was able to buy, as described by Winsberg:

The JCA colonies were generally established in the less attractive agricultural regions of the country, because most of the best land in Argentina had entered the private domain years before, and either was not for sale or was too expensive. Taking advantage of a brief economic depression in 1890, the JCA began purchasing large tracts of land, in some cases entire ranches, on the outer margin of the fertile humid Pampa. Among the largest purchases were those made in the province of Entre Ríos. . . . The land purchased by the association has at best only marginal value for agriculture.[17]

Winsberg found the region of the Entre Ríos colonies to be better suited to cattle raising than to crop production. But the small size of the farms allotted to individual families precluded their use for ranches and forced the colonists to concentrate on agriculture even though they could not do so profitably. Similarly with Colonía Baron Hirsch, which is on the border between Buenos Aires and La Pampa provinces. The 150-hectare farms issued to the colonists were inadequate to sustain wheat production in this area's dry climate. Yet the colonists were constrained to grow just that crop because it was the only product that, if the harvest was satisfactory, would bring them a profit large enough to meet the payments on their farms, as well as provide for other expenses. Paradoxically, the problem in this wheat-growing colony arose from the contemporary boom in the international market for wheat. By 1905, when Jews settled Colonía Baron Hirsch, Argentina was in the midst of an agricultural boom that saw her total crop acreage expand from sixteen million to fifty million acres between 1899 and 1911. The high price of wheat on the international market had driven up the price of land, particularly any on which the valued commodity could be grown. Consequently, Colonía Baron Hirsch is situated beyond the climatic frontier of stable wheat production.

Increasingly, the JCA colonies became part of Argentina's persistent latifundia-minifundia complex of problems. An Argentine government agronomist had held that 500 hectares were the minimum necessary for economic self-sufficiency in agriculture, 5,000 hectares the minimum for efficient cattle production. The 75- to 150-hectare farms allotted to the colonists represented no more than one-fifth of the recommended minimum, "too little to live on, too much to die from" [Tzum lebn tzu veinik, tzum shtarbn tzu fil]. To complicate matters, the settlers were totally lacking in ecological orientation. Even those who had been farmers in their old homes were unfamiliar with the soil and climate of Argentina. The lands were virgin and difficult to cultivate by hand or with the old-fashioned machinery that some immigrants brought with them from Russia. In fact, this was precisely why the cattle barons left these lands to farmers—so they would break up the tough pampa grass and eventually plant the area to alfalfa for the cattle.

Under other conditions, the settlers might have benefited from the example of neighboring farmers. Agriculture in Argentina, however, was in a primitive state owing to the system of latifundia that did not require owners to cultivate efficiently in order to reap substantial returns. The absence of a class of family farmers left a social gap between the immigrants and the large landowners that could not be bridged from the immigrants' side. Consequently, the colonists' most intimate contact with native Argentines was with that "peon on horseback," the gaucho. It was the gaucho who taught Jewish immigrants how to ride, how to herd cattle, how to shelter against the elements, how to shoot. In the end, the gaucho taught the colonist his own primitive methods of agriculture—a rude twist to Argentine hopes that European immigrants would educate the gaucho to more advanced techniques. The legend of the Jewish gaucho emerged at the turn of the century: a person midway between the cultures of the ghetto and of the pampa. The number of such Jews who existed is less important than the grip the image exerted upon people's minds: the Jewish gaucho symbolizes the settlers' physical and psychic investment in the upbuilding of the Argentine interior. As for the impact Jews made on gauchos, some of them apparently learned Yiddish in order to communicate with their exotic neighbors.

The fact that the settlers' contact with the native Argentine population was restricted to the gaucho, who was still in that condition of barbarism in which Sarmiento found and so well described him, undoubtedly contributed to the colonists' conviction that they themselves stood at a far higher cultural level than the surrounding population and that their sons and daughters must be educated, even if this meant abandoning the farm that had represented in the first place the expectation of a new and better way of life. The problem of education generally, and Jewish education specifically, emerges as crucial to the Jewish agricultural experience.

Despite the avowed commitment of the Argentine government to a system of free and universal public education, there were no schools in the areas settled by JCA. The Jewish settlers, still involved in an inherited tradition of learning, demanded that JCA establish schools for their children, and these in fact were set up at an early date. (Chapter 7 describes these schools.) Under the circumstances, however, neither the settlers nor JCA were able to provide for quality higher education, and this limitation is cited by all informants as the prime reason for moving to the city.

Scobie identifies isolation as a factor in driving all immigrants out of the countryside:

In the countryside the immigrant could not form a cultural or social group with his countrymen as he had in the city. Most of the colonies were economic ventures and only occasionally, as with the early Santa Fe colonies or the Jewish Colonization Association, did they provide religious and cultural unity. Extensive tenant farming did not permit even accidental unity or contact. The very isolation and transiency of the agricultural immigrant's life retarded his assimilation into the national culture, not because he formed groups outside that culture but because he himself was so remote.[18]

Isolation was probably felt more acutely by Jews than by non-Jews because of their centuries-old attachment to education as a way of life. "There wasn't a book to read or a light to read it by," was the answer of one old colonist when asked why he had moved to the city. For Jews, education was a cultural imperative, overriding the territorial imperative of hanging onto the land that was so marked a feature of peasant life. The departure of young people was accelerated by the decision of JCA not to make land available to the second generation. But if the decision had been made to make such land available, one suspects that in the continuing absence of a national system of schools, departure from the countryside would only have been delayed a generation.

Many forces antagonistic to all the agricultural colonies operated during the period under review, affecting Jewish settlement only because it was a part of the whole. 1895–97 were exceedingly poor crop years: these were the years when the first four Jewish colonies were started. After that, it became increasingly difficult for small farmers to get out of debt. One informant told me that his father, an original settler of Lucienville, died after forty-three years' labor on the land, still not the legal owner of it. By the turn of the century, the period when small owner-operated farms could produce wheat profitably was drawing to a close everywhere. As the world price of wheat dropped in relation to the cost of labor in Argentina, only large-scale, mechanized producers could stay in business profitably. In drought years, marginal farmers were wiped out, and a succession of droughts in the 1930s forced many farmers off the land in a pattern made familiar to us by the plight of the Okies. The worldwide depression of 1929–33 had its effect on all commodity producers. As the price of wheat on world markets dropped, colonists could no longer clear enough to make their farms pay. Often the sale or rental of their property provided a stake that enabled them to start a new life in the city, while the more successful farmers strengthened their position by adding to their own holdings. Following World War II, peronista economic planning, aimed at increasing industrial production, resulted in low farm prices and high tenant wages that again squeezed out small owners, leaving behind the familiar pattern of large-scale ownership of land by people who rarely farmed it and a class of tenant farmers lacking the political or economic means to acquire land.

The result of Argentine agrarian policy, despite the stated desire to conquer the interior, was to furnish hands to the city. Up to 1890, 70 percent of immigrants to the Argentine were peasants. Presumably, at least some of these retained an affinity for rural life despite their transatlantic transplantation. Over the years, however, decreasing proportions of immigrants actually engaged in agriculture. Maldistribution of land foreclosed on the possibility of populating the countryside with immigrants, and sent those immigrants, willy-nilly, to the cities.[19] The migration of Jewish farmers to the city must be seen in the context of the urbanization of both native and immigrant that is a prominent feature of Argentine history. In 1914, native-born Argentines were distributed almost evenly between rural and urban areas, but 70 percent of the country's foreigners were living in cities,[20] despite the asserted government policy of "internalizing" immigrants on the land and despite the fact that most immigrants were rural in origin.

Urbanization on such a scale indicates the presence of compelling economic and social forces that could not be resisted by that small segment of the migration that consisted of Jews. If they had succeeded in staying on the land, that would indeed have called for explanation. As it is, the partial and short-lived success of the JCA colonies reflects the ephemeral success of Argentine immigration policy, which was aimed at peopling the countryside with European farmers but was fatally limited by traditional social structures: the system of latifundia and the exclusion of the rural populace from national life through the failure to provide an infrastructure of schools, hospitals, and highways.

A 1958 census of the 332 colonists who still owned farms in Colonía Baron Hirsch revealed the profile of the urbanizing movement among Jews. Of a total of 857 children, 571 were twenty years of age and over. Of these adult children, 55 percent were living outside the colony. Among the 316 adult children who had left their families, 207 or 66 percent were living in Buenos Aires. The largest group of "expatriates" were housewives, showing a high tendency among daughters to abandon farm life. Among sons gainfully employed, only 9 percent, having obtained land outside the colony, were engaged in agriculture.

Departure from the colony came most frequently between ages twenty and twenty-nine, with a resulting drop in the number of children under age ten in the colony. The diminishing Jewish population is being replaced by Gentiles, who in 1960 comprised 67 percent of the colony's population.[21] From the point of view of the national economy, of course, it makes no difference whether the colonists are Jewish or non-Jewish. From the point of view of Jewish settlement, the urbanizing movement has converted Argentine Jewry into an almost entirely urban element.

In 1920, 22 percent of Argentine Jews were on the farm. During the next fifteen years, while the Jewish population of Argentina rose from 120,000 to 225,000–230,000, the proportion in the agricultural sector slipped to 11 percent. In 1960, only 2 percent of Argentine Jews declared themselves to be farmers.[22]

The departing settlers moved not only to such major metropolitan areas as Buenos Aires, Córdoba, and Tucumán, but also to the small towns located within the borders of their colonies. In 1934, there were 2,850 Jews in the town of Moisesville and 2,800 in Basavilbaso, Entre Ríos—fondly known as Varsovia Pequeña (Little Warsaw).[23]

Although the JCA colonies did not produce a large and stable middle class of Jewish farmers, they did result in the rooting of Jewish Argentines in cities of the interior. Argentina is the only country in Latin America where considerable numbers of Jews reside elsewhere than in the national capital. The Argentine national census of 1960 found nearly fifteen thousand Jews living in Santa Fé and nearly nine thousand in Entre Ríos, provinces that were the site of seven of the colonies. Sixteen districts outside of Greater Buenos Aires have populations of one thousand Jews or more, and there is no district in the republic without its Jewish citizens.[24]

The decay of the colonies, usually attributed to a stereotypical inability of Jews to relate to agricultural labor, can now be seen to have taken place within the context of a massive urbanizing movement that caught up the majority of immigrants and transformed Argentina from a rural to an urban nation. The primary factors in this movement were nationwide in scope and had nothing to do with Jews: the system of latifundia that squeezed small buyers out of the market; the steadily increasing efficiency of latifundia as machinery made possible economies of scale; the war between agriculturist and cattle baron, in which the latter used the former to open up new grazing lands for him.

Associated with the latifundia complex was the vital mediatory figure of the patron. His presence humanized the system but also furnished a convenient target for the farmers' wrath, personifying as he did the whole system in which the small man did not stand a chance. The JCA administration was, of course, the patron. Without JCA there would have been no group Jewish settlement. But its wealth and the control over the lives of the settlers this wealth conferred made life intolerable for the colonists. They left with an attitude of resentment against JCA that persists to this day. It should be recognized, however, that at a time when, nationwide, farmers were being pushed into marginal areas by the aggressively expanding cattle industry, JCA could not successfully withstand pressures exerted from within and from without. In order to develop agricultural efficiency, the association scattered the colonists' homesteads, thus inducing in the colonists a sense of isolation that most of them could not endure. For those second-generation families prepared to endure the isolation, JCA failed to provide land, conserving it instead for the expected onrush of new immigrants that never materialized. Thus, even those who would have preferred to stay on the land were driven to the city. The net result of JCA policy, as of government policy, was to stimulate the flow of immigrants from farm to city.

There can be no doubt that there was a massive failure in human relations and that this was important in the general failure to realize large-scale, permanent Jewish colonization. JCA had taken on the task of Argentinizing the settlers, a function they felt had to be performed if Jews were to find a permanent home in that country. The settlers resisted the effort as an attempt to deprive them of their culture, which was all that remained to them of their former lives. The balance that was to be struck between assimilation to an Argentine standard and conservation of the Jewish heritage at once became a matter of bitter contention between colonists and administrators, who were at opposite ends of the haskalah experience. The emancipated Jews who set the standards imposed changes on the colonists in order to speed their acculturation. Had acculturation not taken place, collision with the larger society would have been inevitable.[25] But the colonists found the process exquisitely painful in the vacuum of the pampas, where there seemed nothing of value to acculturate to. Gauchismo had little to offer. Argentina lacked the great nationalizing institutions—schools, adult education, especially, and a homogenizing industrial plant—that might have served to integrate the immigrants into national life. The absorption of immigrants was retarded by the absence of social structures with the capacity to integrate them into the intellectual, economic, or patriotic life of the republic.

In retrospect, it can be seen that the Jewish agricultural colonies acted as cultural decompression chambers, where European Jews underwent transmogrification from European shtetl to Argentine city. In this sense, the JCA performed a function more properly exercised by government, but which the Argentine government had neglected to undertake. By the time the sons and daughters of the colonists emerged into city life, they were no longer frightened, insecure Jewish refugees who felt themselves to be at the mercy of assimilated administrators, wandering gauchos, and descendants of the Grand Inquisitor, but secure, acculturated Argentines of the Jewish persuasion. The generations of youngsters whom the colonists sent to the city appeared, not as exotic strangers, but as Spanish-speaking Argentines capable of participating in the national secular culture. The lodestone that brought the colonists—or, more pointedly, their children—to the city was the prospect of an education.

Today, colonists and their descendants constitute a sort of aristocracy among Argentine Jews and are a visible reminder that Jews participated in the building of the nation. The relatively high degree of integration of Jews into Argentine life is in my view due to the fact that the colonies satisfied both the Jewish and the Argentine belief that forging a nation is a job that must begin on the land. The colonies' major contribution to the Argentine nation was the colonists themselves.

Dominican Republic

Mass settlement of Jews in agriculture is an idea that has manifested itself twice in Dominican history: in 1881 and again in 1939. The earlier plan came to naught, but it probably prepared the way for the later project, which did meet with some success. The closing decades of the nineteenth century witnessed a debate in the Dominican Republic on the value of European immigration that took place in terms that are by now familiar to us. Proimmigration forces controlled the government when the exodus of Russian Jews began in 1881. The former president, General Gregorio Luperón, approached the Alliance Israelite Universelle and the Barons Gustave and Edmond de Rothschild with the proposition that some of them be resettled in the Dominican Republic. They would be received "with open arms. They will obtain land for farming purposes and secure citizenship."[26] While the Alliance delegated an agent to investigate the offer, the Dominican government prepared a list of Dominican personalities of Jewish descent who could inform the Alliance about conditions in that Republic. The list is impressive, attesting to the acculturation of Sephardic settlers since the eighteenth century. It included the Dominican ambassadors in Paris and in the Low Countries; the consul general in Paris and in Saint Thomas; the consul in Haiti; wealthy merchants in Paris and other European capitals.[27] Evidently, the death of the agent of the Alliance caused a break in negotiations, and the matter was dropped despite continued interest on the part of successive presidents of the Dominican Republic.

The second project for mass resettlement of Jews was broached at the Evian Conference on Refugees, which assembled during the week of 6–15 July 1938, at the initiative of Franklin D. Roosevelt. Only one government represented at the conference committed itself to admit Jewish refugees from Nazism. On behalf of General Rafael Trujillo, the representative of the Dominican Republic offered to admit one hundred thousand Jews to his country.[28]

In January of 1940, an agreement was drawn up between the government of the Dominican Republic and the Dominican Republic Settlement Association of New York (DORSA). On land donated by El Benefactor himself, DORSA was to settle Jewish farmers whom it had selected as suitable candidates. The expenses incurred were to be underwritten by voluntary (in practice, Jewish) agencies and to be repaid by the settlers. A bill of rights guaranteeing freedom of religion was included in the contract.[29]

The active partner in DORSA was Agro-Joint, a subsidiary of the Joint Distribution Committee. Founded in 1914, Joint was a relief and rehabilitation agency. It had no colonizing ideology (unlike JCA or the Zionist movement), but tried to help its clients overcome handicaps imposed by the objective conditions in which they found themselves. Where an agricultural solution was needed, Agro-Joint provided the social and technical framework for its realization. The organization and its administrator, Joseph E. Rosen, had cut their teeth in the Crimea, where they had offered technical assistance to Jews of the Soviet Union who were trying to establish themselves on the land.

Having been granted quasi-diplomatic privileges by the Dominican government, DORSA representatives were able to visit European refugee camps to select "suitable" persons for the project. Just how this was done is a matter of some controversy. Some maintain that any refugee was free to sign up at an office that was opened for this purpose in Switzerland. That so few chose to do so was due to their own refusal to believe in the reality of Hitler's "final solution." There was nothing particularly attractive about going to farm on some island in the tropics. Others maintain that DORSA recruiters were indulging in social experimentation and were more eager for their project to succeed than they were interested in saving human lives. Their insistence on imposing high standards of health and capacity for physical labor resulted in the rejection of candidates at a time when rejection was tantamount to a death sentence. Wherever the truth lies, it is clear that the project early acquired an aura of social experimentation.

Eventually, several hundred suitable persons were selected and Dominican visas issued to them upon the posting of a $500 bond in New York against the likelihood of their becoming public charges. The first contingent of settlers was to consist of five hundred families, but the total population of the colony never reached that number. The first settlers reached the hacienda at Sosua two years after the conclusion of the Evian Conference. They were mostly German and

4. German Jewish colonists at Sosua in the Dominican Republic. Having arrived as refugees from Nazism, most departed at war's end. Those who remained have prospered as dairy farmers. (Courtesy of YIVO Archives)

Austrian and included substantially more men than women. The majority were of urban background; their sound physiques and clear complexions had enabled them to gamble on another chance at life.

The settlers were endowed individually with two hectares of land apiece, a house, a horse or mule, two cows, furniture, tools, and $500 credit. This was all to be repaid on terms; as with JCA, the project was designed as rehabilitation, not as charity. Each settler was required to work his own farm: no Dominican labor was to be hired. As DORSA Director Rosen said: "We did not bring refugees here to add more white landowners to exploit the peons." This proletarian sentiment, imported by Rosen from his experience in the Crimea, condemned the settlers to life as minifundistas. In this status, they joined the approximately 85 percent of Dominican farmers who are also in this category.[30] The Jewish immigrants, however, unlike their Dominican neighbors, were not bound to the soil by ties of kinship, debt peonage, and all the other social arrangements that keep the peon in his place and make the latifundia-minifundia complex so difficult to break. The result was that most of the homesteaders drifted away from their farms to the cities, where they lived as clients of Joint.

Disintegration of Sosua was accelerated by the rigid ideological strictures of the administrators. Quite early in the project, Rosen had decided to limit the total number of colonists to five hundred, since his experiment could be worked out on a small, as well as on a large, scale. Thus there were few arrivals to balance departures. The problem of settlement pattern that had plagued JCA was resolved in favor of scattering the farm plots to prevent urban clustering. This exacerbated the settlers' poignant sense of abandonment. Having just undergone traumatic experiences in Europe, they were not to have the solace of one another's company. To compound the problem, there was a severe shortage of women. Bachelors preponderated among the settlers, and those who were unable to form families provided a continually destabilizing element; in 1942, Rosen evicted fifty "malcontents"— mostly young men in their productive years. The administration's mania for social experimentation extended to setting up cooperative work groups, each of which included one woman to do the laundry, but provision for marriage and the founding of families was beyond them.

Although the Yiddish press of New York was apprehensive over Sosua, dependent as it was on the beneficence of the dictator, Trujillo kept faith with the colony. To the closing years of his reign, El Benefactor continued making friendly gestures toward Jews. He donated

$60,000 toward construction of a synagogue in the capital and issued a postage stamp honoring Sosua. It bore the legend, "Sosua, R.D., Primera colonía de refugiados en América."

DORSA later claimed to have saved thousands of Jewish lives, but it is probable that no more than 800 refugees passed through the colony; perhaps another 3,000 obtained Dominican visas on the strength of the colony but never actually settled there. The largest number of settlers at any one time was to be found in 1943, when 476 Jews occupied Sosua. Most of these were German or Austrian and had regarded themselves as well assimilated in their home countries. In the Dominican countryside, however, there was no one for them to assimilate to. The landed aristocracy were beyond their reach, the campesinos all too close. Numbers of Jewish settlers married local girls, with conversions running both ways, but those who were concerned about their Jewish identity tended to leave the island when the war ended.

Life at Sosua stabilized on an agricultural base after DORSA was dissolved. With the limit on the size of landholdings removed, the remaining families went into dairy farming; the Sosua cooperative markets milk and cheese throughout the island. The Jews and their descendants who remain bid fair to contribute to the Republic's variegated ethnic constitution, along with descendants of the Sephardim of Curaçao, long since assimilated.

Bolivia

Jewish agricultural settlement in Bolivia was an accident of World War II, unpremeditated by the Bolivian government or by the immigrants. As a colonization effort, it was a total failure. It had no permanent effect on Bolivia or on Jews, except for one fact: several thousand refugees owe their lives to their willingness to pose as farmers and to the venality of Bolivian officials who issued them visas under this guise. As Sholom Aleichem observed, there is no one so hard on Jews as an official who won't take graft.

In 1937, there were some 250 Russian, Polish, and Sephardic Jews in Bolivia. About 100 of those lived in La Paz, 50 or so in Sucre, and the rest were scattered in the vicinity of the tin mines. For the most part, they were merchants and lived a life as segregated from the elite as they were from the mass of the population. In the ensuing years, possibly 5,000 German Jews entered Bolivia. Some estimates place the number of arrivals as high as 20,000, with the number of departures not far behind. In May of 1939 alone, with the lights going out all over Europe, 3,000 Jews entered Bolivia, mostly on counterfeit documents.

For most of the refugees, Bolivia was only a transit stop on the way to Argentina, the United States, or any other country that would admit them. Many of those with documents had been issued agricultural visas, which carried the obligation to settle in that occupation. But lacking the means to buy land or the know-how to place it under cultivation, they were thrown on the charity of local Jews. Accumulating in the cities, the refugees attracted the critical attention of the press. Tension was heightened by the existence of considerable pro-Nazi sentiment within the Bolivian German community, all in the context of the contemporary possibility of a German victory in the war.

On 6 May 1940, the Bolivian government forbade issuance of visas to "persons of Semitic origin," thus bringing legal Jewish immigration to an end.[31] In the same month, the Sociedad Colonizadora de Bolivia (SOCOBO) was founded for the purpose of colonizing Bolivia on a nonsectarian basis. The initiative in this venture was taken by a leading Bolivian industrialist, Mauricio Hochschild,[32] who subscribed half the capital of $200,000. The remaining two quarters were subscribed respectively by the Refugee Economic Corporation and by Agro-Joint.

The new Jewish agricultural colony was established at Buena Tierra, sixty-two miles from La Paz in the province of North Yungas.[33] The site comprised one thousand hectares, of which just four hundred could be cultivated, the remainder being used as a water reserve. Located at an altitude of four thousand feet in hilly terrain, the land could be worked only by relatively primitive methods. Isolation was reinforced by the treacherous condition of the mountain roads. The trip to La Paz took from three to nine hours, depending on the weather. Plans were made to grow cocoa, coffee, peanuts, bananas, corn, sugarcane, oranges, tangerines, lemons, limes, pineapples, and lumber. In 1940, a start was made in cutting timber and dropping it by chute down the mountainside to the river. A necessary bridge, estimated to cost $20,000, had been promised by the government. An observer, visiting the site, believed that there could be from 75 to 100 colonists on the land by the end of the year and that ultimately the colony could absorb 250 families permanently.

This evaluation proved overly enthusiastic. Three years later, the colony reached its peak with just 42 families on the land. A real problem was presented with the fact that women comprised more than half of the work force (61 out of 112 adults aged 16 to 50). Even so, the colonists had brought 243.85 hectares of land under cultivation and had another 95 hectares in reclamation projects by 1944. In addition, they had built some fifty houses and a thirteen-kilometer road connecting Buena Tierra with the town of Coroico. The same report notes that Agro-Joint had expended a total of $338,150 on this project as of June 1945. Despite the optimisitc tone of the report, as of that date there were only 50 persons remaining on the settlement. By the end of the following year, all but a few had left, helped on their way by a bonus of $175 per family paid out by Agro-Joint. The experiment lasted just six years.

The obstacles to absorption of Jewish immigrants into Bolivia were the small farms allotted them, the isolation, and a generalized feeling of insecurity. Bolivia at this date was a prime example of the latifundia-minifundia complex. In 1950, 0.2 percent of Bolivian farmland was owned by 59.3 percent of farmers, in holdings of five hectares or less; 81.8 percent of farmland was owned by 3.8 percent of the population—latifundistas—in holdings of 2,500 hectares or more.[34] Joint's estimate that 250 Jewish families could be settled on four hundred arable hectares would become reality only if the immigrants adopted the standard of living of the highland Indian, which is one of the most depressed in the world.

In general, conditions within the country as a whole failed to satisfy the needs that had driven the refugees there. The primary impulse had been flight for survival, and the immigrants had selected Bolivia in preference to the concentration camp. But the refugees found the Bolivian political atmosphere less than reassuring. In 1942, the Congress debated an immigration bill that would have excluded Jews, Negroes, and Orientals from the country. In the course of congressional debate, Deputy Siles Suazo, representing the Movimiento Nacional Revolucionario (MNR), declared that Semitic immigrants "laugh at their obligations and are convinced of the impossibility of throwing them out because there is no country which would resign itself to support them."[35] The bill was never taken up in the Senate and so failed to become law. But its debate, together with the anti-Semitic tone of accompanying newspaper reports, had an impact on the immigrants, who had actually felt safer under the reactionary regime of Gualberto Villaroel. According to a Joint representative, "The explanation of this paradox is that the government of Villaroel had to justify before the world its democratic conditions, which is no need of the Herzog government, which originates in a union of left-wing parties." The same observer ascribed the desire of Jews to reemigrate to two reasons: the difficult climate and anti-Semitism. "[Recently] there was issued a decree by the Supreme Government ordering an investigation of the books of 'semitic' merchants who had entered the country since 1938.

. . . It can also be noticed that there is an intensive anti-semitic propaganda in the press and radio, without any attempts being made to curb it."[36]

The Bolivian revolution of 1952 brought to power the MNR, a radical grouping of mixed leftist and fascist components. Whatever the meaning of the MNR for the native-born, its hegemony could only intensify feelings of insecurity among the Jews of Bolivia, who identified it as the party that had sponsored the excluding legislation a decade earlier and countenanced anti-Semitic propaganda in its party press. In conditions of such uncertainty, it is not surprising that the pioneers of Buena Tierra did not feel the strong sense of identification with the country that would have sustained the necessarily long period of self-sacrifice required to root themselves in the land. In Bolivia, which is itself isolated from the rest of the world and where Jews were therefore in a very exposed position, the rural isolation that Argentine and Dominican settlers had found insufferable was intensified beyond endurance. The difficulties of relating to Argentine gauchos and Dominican campesinos were naught before the enigma of the Aymara Indian.

In the 1950s, Bolivians were beginning to confront the issue of their own ethnic identity. The majority Indian population, hitherto passive tenants of the countryside, were emerging to make their demands upon the national polity. The miners, foundation of the country's wealth, had emerged as a political force. The social forces let loose by the revolution of 1952 completely swallowed up the minor conundrum posed by acculturation and absorption of a tiny number of displaced urban European Jewish immigrants into the Bolivian agricultural sector. Bolivia had become involved with Jewish immigration only accidentally, through the venality of its consular officials. Jews had come to Bolivia only accidentally and because they had no alternative. Neither party was prepared to cope with the problems that resulted.

The departure of colonists to the city was followed by the departure of almost all able-bodied Jews from the country as a whole. Fewer than a thousand remain today. These are almost all merchants, fulfilling a function that highly stratified, not to say feudal, societies have traditionally proffered to Jews.

An Appraisal of the Agricultural Colonies

All the Jewish colonization ventures had their origin in the calamitous uprooting of Jewish populations in Europe and North Africa, events that occurred far from Latin America and that were not the responsibility of any of the nations of that continent. Jewish refugees from these calamities were well received in countries that welcomed heterogeneous immigration, such as Argentina and the Dominican Republic, and were rebuffed by Bolivia, which did not encourage such immigration.

There was no prima facie reason for Jewish farmers to prefer Latin American countries of destination as opposed to such areas as Canada, the United States, or Palestine. Their involvement with the Latin American countryside was fortuitous in that these countries, at pivotal points in Jewish history, happened to present the prospect of available land combined with comparative religious toleration. But the advantage of the prospect was relative to other choices available and could not always be assessed accurately from the distance. The ability to acquire land turned out to be circumscribed by existing patterns of landholding; toleration in Bolivia and elsewhere was severely limited by the culture.

Those nations that became host to Jewish agriculturists did so because they had adopted as an element of national policy the recruiting of European farmers. Jewish colonists were trying to become farmers, either for reasons of idealism or to escape persecution, or both. Inevitably, the expectations of the parties failed to mesh, leaving the immigrants open to the charge that they had beguiled their hosts. Much, however, depended upon the flexibility of the host societies in accommodating immigrant farmers. We have seen how negligent policies of the Argentine government allowed destruction of the agricultural sector and led most of the immigrants to relocate in the city; it is equally important to note that Argentine social and economic structures were flexible enough to accommodate immigrants within an urban setting. This was because the country was absorbing so many immigrants of different races and nationalities that its nature inevitably had to change. In Bolivia, on the other hand, where social patterns had not changed notably since the first century of the Conquest, Jews could fit into society only as they had in the sixteenth century.

The primary motivation of the colonists was physical security, or, more precisely, a desire to be exposed only to those hazards that are the common lot of mankind. They stayed on (whether as farmers or not) in countries where their physical survival as human beings and as Jews seemed assured (Argentina), but abandoned places where they felt humanly insecure (Bolivia) or unable to continue living as Jews (the Dominican Republic).

All the agricultural experiments attempted to settle Jews on minifundia. This came about for a variety of reasons: the necessity to settle
in groups under the aegis of a patron organization; limits on the fi-
nances of these organizations; preconceptions about the size of family
farms drawn from experience in Europe; and an ideological bias
against having Jews enter the Latin American agricultural scene as
landlords. That the colonists were unable to produce efficiently as
minifundistas should have come as no surprise, given previous experience concerning the disutility of small farms in Latin America. Acceptance of the fact that the experience of Jewish farmers was no different
in kind from the experience of non-Jewish farmers would relieve historians of the Jewish community of the compulsion for breast-beating
that always arises in connection with the colonies. Today, Jewish farmers and cattle ranchers exist in both Argentina and the Dominican
Republic. Independent Jewish farmers and cattlemen in Argentina
presently own some eight hundred thousand hectares, including land
within the original colonies. This development came about through
the purchase by successful settlers of land belonging to colonists who
failed and left for the city. The process was particularly notable among
Germans, some of whom invested reparations payments from the West
German government in land and equipment. Other estates have been
bought by previously urban Jewish families for reasons of status. Jews
survive as latifundistas precisely as do non-Jewish farmers and ranchers.

The roles of JCA, DORSA, and SOCOBO are traditionally the most con-
troversial elements in accounts of Jewish agricultural settlement in
Latin America. Yet, those who are most critical of these organizations
concede that colonization could not have been attempted without
them. In the case of the Dominican Republic, it was only through
DORSA that refugees were able to get there at all. SOCOBO was a sorely
needed organizing force on the chaotic Bolivian refugee scene. Criticism of these organizations as inept, overly paternal, short-sighted, and
so on, are beside the point. They filled a function that the local economic and social scenes required. These international Jewish rescue
organizations became the patron, that venerable figure of the Latin
American countryside, and criticism of the patron might better be
directed against the system that makes him indispensable. The organizations loomed as large as they did in the lives of the Jewish immigrants
because they provided services that were essential to the immigrants
and that were not available from any other source. The accidental
meeting of Jewish need with Latin American ambience found host
governments unequipped to deal with ensuing problems in social wel-

fare. Only Jewish organizations stood ready to fill the gap. These organizations were global in scope, nongovernmental in nature, Jewish in orientation, and not indigenous to the countries in which they operated. Their lack of knowledge of the local scene caused innumerable problems. Nevertheless, their sole concern in each case was the integration of their charges into the country of their settlement. They were not responsive to foreign governments. In view of the oft-expressed fear that immigrants might import and retain their old national loyalties and mount a threat to the nationality of their host state, it may be said that Jews were the only immigrants to arrive in Latin America unburdened by ties of allegiance to a foreign government.

There were severe limitations on what the Jewish patron organizations could accomplish. In no instance did appreciable numbers of Jewish farmers remain on the land. None of the organizations succeeded in attracting large numbers of immigrants relative to the number who were seeking an immigration outlet; none succeeded in establishing permanent, viable Jewish colonies; and in the case of both DORSA and SOCOBO, the most they could do was to process immigrants in and out of the country in orderly fashion.

Ideology appears not to have been a factor in success or failure. Colonies withered whether founded by idealists of the 1890s or by refugees of the 1930s. More important was the provision, or lack of provision, of outside material and moral support. As the historian of one moribund Argentine colony wrote: "The kibbutz movement in Palestine also would have foundered without the support of the entire nation. In countries of Latin America, no such general support existed."[37] The writer of those lines had in mind the support of the Jewish community of Argentina. We may extend that observation to include the support—or lack of support—of the Argentine government and people for its agricultural sector.

There were structural barriers to integration that immigrants, Jew or non-Jew, could not overcome without the active collaboration of the entire society. This collaboration, in the form of revision of patterns of land tenure, provision of schooling, and extension of the infrastructure through the countryside, was not forthcoming. Isolation made the Latin American agricultural sector no more promising for Jewish immigrants than it was for native-born Catholics, who likewise abandoned the countryside in droves. The passion of urban European Jews to fling themselves upon the soil was misspent in resisting entanglement with preexisting conditions that antedated their arrival on the continent and over which they could exert no influence. These were, of course, the same entanglements that wasted the energies of native-born campesinos in their struggles with the landowners. To take the point a step further, they were the social arrangements that had created the campesino rather than the yeoman farmer.

The desire to normalize the Jewish condition by return to the soil can be seen in retrospect to have been romantic. The yearning for a life of rustic simplicity was a reaction against the brutalities meted out to Jews in the cities and towns of Europe. It was not a reasoned rejection of the modern world as a whole. The movement for autoemancipation through agricultural toil took hold in an age when all over the world the agricultural sector was yielding up its manpower to the demands and challenges of industrialization. We need not accept the evaluation of the philanthropic effort as "misanthropic" in order to agree with the rest of Irving L. Horowitz's statement: "The European Jewish bourgeois failed to take into account traditional Jewish social aspirations: educational achievement, economic security, occupational mobility and cosmopolitan orientation—aspirations which can far more readily be realized in an urban and suburban environment than in a rural life style."[38]

Jewish farmers, in abandoning the land, were bringing to a close the epoch of belief in the possibility of autoemancipation through self-labor, an idea rooted in the age of Maxim Gorky and of Leon Pinsker. This is why the shift of so small a number of persons out of farming and into city life—a shift that millions of people round the globe have made during the past hundred years—attracted so much attention from diagnosticians of the Jewish condition. It was the death of the dream, not the death of the colonies, that mattered. The impact of this death was felt the more directly as Jewish farmers of Latin America abandoned their farms within the context of societies whose rural and urban sectors are among the most polarized in the world. Thus, their abandonment of rural life was visible, abrupt, and irreversible.

The ending does not negate the beginning. As European Jewry entered the Holocaust Kingdom, each individual who found his way to the Dominican Republic or to Bolivia represents a triumph. Jewish farmers of Argentina (and the paradigm will serve Brazil and Uruguay as well) found not only secure homes, but also time and space in which to orient themselves to their new environment linguistically, ecologically, behaviorally. They gained a breathing space before returning to the modern world or sending their children out into it. The colonies, in their short life span, nationalized the Jewish immigrants and turned them into citizens of the country of their adoption, where existing social systems were flexible enough to receive them. In this sense, they were a success even when—perhaps especially when—their inhabitants abandoned the farm for the city.

7

Community Life on
"The Jewish Street"

Jewish immigrants to Latin America were quickly faced by a variety of needs that were fulfilled neither by government nor by that traditional agency of social welfare, the Catholic church. In order to satisfy these needs, as well as to sustain their Jewish identity in alien lands, the immigrants founded communal organizations patterned on those they had left behind in Europe and the Middle East. These organizations enabled Jews to extend mutual aid to one another and prevented the immigrants from becoming a burden on their host societies.

Burial

Commonly, the first need to impress itself upon the immigrants was for a place to bury the dead. A church monopoly of cemeteries existed in all parts of the continent when immigrants first arrived; access to them required not just death but baptism. At first, the Jewish dead were shipped to Curaçao or Jamaica for burial. Enlightened German and French Jews of the late nineteenth-century migration made local adjustments, particularly in Chile and Brazil. In the German colonies of southern Chile, for example, Jews were buried among their Christian fellows inasmuch as the religion of corpses was not regarded as an interesting matter.[1] A partial solution also was found in those areas where non-Catholic cemeteries were licensed as the result of treaty arrangements with Great Britain. None of these, however, provided specifically for burial in accord with Mosaic law.

With the arrival of the East European Ashkenazim, the problem grew more pressing. For this group, burial among their fellows was a strong compulsion. The continuity of tradition can be seen in the transfer of the rule book of the burial society of the Jewish community of Novo-Poltavka, in southern Russia, to the emigrants who were leaving for Basavilbaso (Lucienville) in Entre Ríos. There it survives to this day, long after destruction of the community that wrote it. Henry Meiggs, who was so assimilated to Gentile society that Oliver Wendell Holmes endowed him with New England ancestry, arranged for his own burial among Jews, an act that required him to establish a cemetery. In most of the republics, a bitter legal battle had to be fought to gain the right to bury the dead without the ministrations of the church. The traditional organization for provision of burial services among Jews is the Khevra Kadisha (Burial Society), and typically this was the first organization to make its appearance on "the Jewish street," that agglomeration of clubs, newspapers, shops, schools, and theaters that came to make up the Jewish life style on the continent. At the start, the sole aim of these societies was to arrange for the burial of Jews according to Mosaic law. Gradually their functions expanded into other aspects of Jewish life, and a monopoly over burial remains at the heart of organized Jewish life today. This monopoly is the counterpart of the church monopoly that exists in society at large, and it gave to the Khevra Kadisha a power over people's lives that mimicked that of the church itself.

Charity

Charity was a discrete function for which the Jewish immigrants organized very early. When the Khevra Kadisha formed in Montevideo in 1915, there was already in existence a Sociedad de Damas de Beneficiencia Ezra, which contributed to the purchase of land for the cemetery. This women's organization provided material aid to the needy, founded a night school and library, and functioned as a savings and loan association. The one area in which it offered no services was religion, for the members were antireligious in orientation.[2] The founding of Jewish cemeteries often was not a function of religious feelings so much as it was a function of exclusion from the general society.

All the Jewish communities have either a volunteer Ezra (Assistance), a Gmilus Khassodim (known in the United States as the Hebrew Free Loan Association), or a Bikur Kholim (Calling on the Sick). Many also maintain a Hakhnosset Kalah to provide dowries for indigent brides. The Buenos Aires Ezra society is now over seventy years old and maintains a major hospital in the city. Half a million dollars are spent annually by the Jewish community of Buenos Aires on social welfare, including free medical aid, clothing, hot meals, and home care for the aged; summer camps for deprived children; and a free kitchen for the Jewish indigent. In 1970 alone, 6,211 people applied for direct relief to the various Ashkenazic agencies in the city. These were persons who were kept from becoming a burden on the state.

With the passage of time, social welfare became professionalized. The Jewish community of São Paulo, for example, maintains the following services, financed from within the community: a centralized hospital service to take responsibility for persons who need to be hospitalized for prolonged periods of time; social and economic assistance to new immigrants; a loan association; summer camp; Ezra Society, originally for assistance to the tubercular poor and now directed toward psychiatric care; home for the aged; a polyclinic offering medical assistance at home, including an x-ray clinic, ambulance service, physiotherapy, dental care, and a pharmacy; a children's aid center, offering special services for abnormal children; the Brazilian branch of National Council of Jewish Women, which subsidizes and trains workers in rehabilitation through productive work; a children's home for orphans and the maladjusted; and Alberto Einstein Hospital, whose facilities are open to the public. The professionals who staff these multivariate organizations are for the most part Jewish graduates of the Escola de Serviço Social da Pontificia Universidad Católica de São Paulo.

Many charitable and social welfare efforts among Latin American Jews are subsidized by international Jewish organizations. Their interventions during the immigration period have already been mentioned. Two additional instances may be cited as representative. Many impoverished Russian Jews, adrift in Mexico after 1924, attempted to enter the United States illegally. If caught, they were subject to deportation to their port of embarkation—in most cases, Russia. To prevent such an outcome, B'nai B'rith gave assurances to the United States secretary of labor that they would care for Jewish "illegals" if the border patrol would deport them only as far as Mexico.[3] Together with the Industrial Removal Organization (a spin-off of the Baron de Hirsch Fund, created in 1904 to spread Jewish immigrants out over the United States instead of permitting them to pile up in East Coast slums) B'nai B'rith then went to work to create "contented Jews," who would not be tempted to try crossing the border again. These organizations remained at work in Mexico until 1931, when immigration into the country from non-Latin areas was phased out and there were no more new arrivals to rehabilitate.

Similar international concern has been shown for Jewish communities that dwindled in size, leaving behind a residue of persons unable to care for themselves. The end of World War II found seven hundred Jews in Cochabamba, Bolivia. Over the next twenty years, most of these left. There were two hundred Jews in the city in 1965, 10 percent of them in the Jewish home for the aged. Six other Jewish institutions also existed in the city: a temple, a cemetery, a sports center, a community hall, a kindergarten, and a public dispensary that had been opened by the community as a philanthropic measure. The number and status of the Jews remaining in Cochabamba was inadequate to sustain all these institutions. Nevertheless, such social services were necessary to make life tolerable. The obvious solution was for the Joint Distribution Committee to subsidize the community.

Such charitable interventions had a variety of outcomes. On the one hand, many individuals and families were sustained over extremely difficult periods in their lives. This was particularly important considering that there was no possibility of government aid and the immigrants did not qualify for assistance from the church. Under these circumstances, the attrition of Jewish communities was not permitted to result in the abandonment of the helpless and the nonproductive. For those capable of supporting themselves, agencies funded by United States Jews speeded their integration into their new environment and enabled them to become self-supporting (and taxpaying) citizens.

On the other hand, the cumulative impact of these "American interventions" was to identify the Jewish communities with the United States. This was a result of historical accident, in that a free Jewish population had survived intact in the United States and was financially able to help. Identification with the United States could not help but have specific consequences in Latin America, however, where intervention by the United States has often been viewed as sinister. The result of the postwar resettlement period, when United States Jewish charities were most influential, was to create a community of interest between some Jews in Latin America and official representatives of the United States government. For example, the program of nationalization and land reform initiated by the government of Bolivia toward

the end of 1952 included the expropriation of all Hochschild proper-
ties. There were some indications that the Bolivian authorities might
consider the socobo settlements as part of the Hochschild patrimony
as well, and therefore socobo administrators contacted the United
States embassy in La Paz to certify that the American Joint Distribution Committee was owner of the land. Although this did no more
than register a preexisting fact, it had the effect of placing local Jews
under United States, rather than Bolivian, protection.

Credit

Notoriously, credit in small amounts, to people of no name, is nonexistent in Latin America. Provision of credit to the impoverished
immigrants was a matter of immediate concern, and it was tackled at
a variety of levels in all the areas of settlement.

The first successful agricultural credit cooperatives in Argentina
were founded by Jewish farmers of the Baron de Hirsch colonies.[4]
Founded at Lucienville in 1900, the Ershter Yiddisher Landwirtschaft-
licher Farein started as a co-op for buying and selling produce and
later became a representative organ for presenting the colonists' grievances to the JCA administration. In the following decade, co-ops were
founded in Clara, Moisesville, and Baron de Hirsch colonies. Typically, they marketed farm produce, operated a general store, issued loans
and insurance, and disseminated agricultural information. As the
colonization process accelerated, a movement grew to unite the co-ops
in order, as it was said, to provide the colonies with an address on the
Jewish street. This was accomplished, and the movement issued its own
newspaper, *El Cólono Cooperador*, for more than fifty years (1917-70).

Leadership in the co-op movement was taken by Miguel Sakharov,
who is credited with uniting the Jewish colonists behind the idea of
agrarian cooperation. Sakharov was the individual who had led negotiations with JCA over the provision of land for colonists' sons. The
co-op leaders then tried to buy land on the open market, but were unable to do so. The co-ops spun off credit unions, hospitals, libraries,
schools, sports clubs, and sick funds. They were prepared for political
action when a strike of farm workers at Villagua gave rise to a show
of anti-Semitism in the Entre Ríos Chamber of Deputies in 1920. At
that time, co-op leaders joined officers of JCA in presenting to the Chamber a memorandum listing the contributions of Jewish farmers to the
province. In addition to providing a census of Jewish landholdings,
schools, co-ops, and communal institutions, the memo reminded legis-

lators that 220 Argentine-born Jews were serving in the armed forces or had already completed their service.[5]

The Fraternidad Agraria, as it was known in its ultimate incarnation, served its members well during the agrarian crisis of the 1930s, when proportionately fewer Jewish than non-Jewish farmers were forced into bankruptcy because of availability of credit. In his assessment of Jewish agricultural colonization in Entre Ríos, Winsberg concludes that "the Jewish colonies in Argentina have made their greatest contribution to the rural economy through their leadership in agricultural cooperatives. . . . Lucienville's cooperative became the model not only for the cooperatives which were established in all the other Jewish colonies but for the entire Argentine cooperative movement."[6]

Another operation, typical for its time, was that of the Asociación Femenina Hebrea de Cuba, which started up a Caja de Préstamos (Loan Fund) in 1937. Its twenty-three founding members bought

5. *Descendants of Jewish gauchos pose in front of their cattle cooperative. Associations such as this one blended Jewish financial experience with the needs of the pampas and sparked development of a cooperative movement nationwide. (Courtesy of the American Jewish Committee)*

shares totaling $350, then sold additional shares to members of the community for a grand total of $900. Their purpose was to aid the rehabilitation of small merchants, industrialists, widows and orphans, by providing interest-free loans. Funds were lent to individuals to enable them to buy merchandise to peddle on the street so that, in the words of one informant, "our husbands could earn our daily bread and avoid becoming a burden on the public." In the first year of its existence, the Caja made forty-six interest-free loans ranging in size from $5 to $50, repayable in weekly installments. This type of home-made banking was the characteristic mode of self-help during the peddling era.

A far more sophisticated operation was the loan fund begun in La Paz on behalf of refugees through the agency of the American Joint Distribution Committee. When Leon Aronovici, the Joint representative, arrived in La Paz in 1940, he found already functioning a Hilfsverein—a relief organization for German Jewish refugees founded, funded, and staffed by officers of the Hochschild tin mining company in association with other wealthy German Jews of the city. The Hilfsverein stood aloof from the East European Jews, some of whom could have contributed to the relief effort but whom they regarded as their social inferiors. The East Europeans, for their part, did not rush to aid the new immigrants, who were Germans, nor could they see themselves working with the Hochschild group, whom they regarded as snobs. Aronovici realized that if he was to form a loan association and help the immigrants to become self-supporting, he would first have to bring these warring groups together. This he was able to do (he regarded it as the most important outcome of his mission), and the loan fund was established, having on its board of directors both Germans and "Easterners." The fund offered loans at 12 percent annually. That rate might seem high, Aronovici conceded, but the prevailing interest rate in Bolivia for small loans was 4 percent monthly, or about 50 percent per year.

Having reported establishment of the fund, Aronovici looked into the future to assess the possibilities for permanent settlement of Jews in Bolivia and found these in the manufacture of needed goods from local raw materials: "Bolivia lives from the mines, i.e., from the export of tin. The sacks for this are imported. . . . There is no good vinegar, no decent ink, no bone buttons, no cartons, paper, etc. These articles, which would require relatively small capital, but proper expert knowledge, could provide a livelihood for many. Bolivia imports all kinds of canned vegetables and fruits from the States, whereas beautiful fruits grow in certain districts which are not made use of industrially."[7] This expression is typical of those who became involved with the founding of loan associations. Their object invariably went beyond charity or even temporary succor. They intended to enable individuals to become self-supporting and to establish themselves economically in their new homes.

Publishing

Cultural integration presented special problems for immigrants who arrived without knowledge of Spanish and who therefore could not read the national press. But Jewish immigrants had arrived in Latin America with a well-developed sense of the importance of the printed word, and their desire to stay informed and to express their own opinions led to the development of a vigorous press in the Yiddish language. Most communal institutions began publishing newsletters and magazines as soon as they opened their doors. All ideological factions—anarchist, Bundist, Zionist, syndicalist, cooperativist, assimilationist, religious, secular—established their own periodicals and newspapers. Additionally, scores of creative writers, poets, and journalists found an outlet in the party press closest to their own orientation or created literary vehicles for self-expression. In Argentina alone, thirty-seven newspapers and periodicals can be counted that were published between 1898 and 1970 and that lasted more than six months or six issues.[8] Among the longest lived were *Di Folks Shtime* (1898–1914) and *Di Yidishe Zaitung* (1914–73). Until the failure of the latter, the Jewish community of Buenos Aires boasted two Yiddish-language dailies, and at this writing, *Di Presse* (1918–) continues to appear.

The Yiddish language predominated in Latin American Jewish publishing until the 1920s, when Spanish began to emerge as a competitor. The early Spanish-language publications originated from within the Sephardic community, but the increase in their number and circulation paralleled the passing of the immigrant generation and the narrowing of the cultural gap between Ashkenazim and their matrix societies.

Unfortunately, the scope and the depth of Jewish publishing has, for a variety of reasons, become impoverished over time. As Jewish readers gained access to the national press, they needed their own communal publications less. Many creative Jewish writers and radio and television personalities have entered the national mainstream and by and large ceased to think of themselves as specifically Jewish contributors to the intellectual scene. Unlike the writers of their parents' generation, they do not have to associate themselves with the low-status Jewish media in order to gain an audience. Probably the decisive factor, however, is the self-censorship of editors, who understand that the entire Jewish community may be held responsible for the political views expressed in their papers. The result has been contraction of the political horizon and a rigidifying of views. The current Jewish press concerns itself almost exclusively with two categories of information: that relating to the situation of Jews in other countries, particularly Israel; and that relating to internal Jewish concerns, such as community elections and social news. Almost without exception, they carry no news of the republic in which they are published. The Jewish press in all the republics has atrophied. Communal newspapers, whether published in Yiddish or Spanish or both, are similar to one another in format and editorial perspective. Their orientation is overwhelmingly Zionist, with the exception of two diehard Stalinist organs in Buenos Aires and Montevideo. Journals of opinion that enjoyed many years of popularity have lost readership and either failed financially or contracted the scope of their efforts. Their disappearance represents a net loss to both Jewish and Latin American belles lettres, for while it was in its prime, the Jewish press was a vehicle for astute political observation and considerable literary creativity.

Viewed externally, the most noteworthy feature of the Jewish press in Latin America is that it has gone unnoted. No Jewish periodical, nor any that can be identified as emanating from a Jewish source, is listed in the *Indice general de publicaciones periodicas latinoamericanas* that is prepared by the Pan American Union and the New York Library and which occupies eight folio volumes. This is remarkable, considering that some Jewish periodicals were published over a period of fifty years and more. In the two-volume supplement, the judgment of the researchers who made the selections was expanded to include *Comentario* of Buenos Aires, but not the equally interesting *Comentario* of Rio de Janeiro. These two magazines were sister publications of the North American *Commentary*, generally regarded as one of the most influential journals of opinion in the United States.

Of the 250,000 entries in the *Indice*, some 50 are grouped under the subject heading "Jews of Latin America." These citations fall into two groups: articles about Jewish agricultural settlement in Argentina and Christological speculation on the Jewish religion. No references appear for any literature emanating from Jewish sources, nor are there references to Latin American political or social developments as these relate to Jews. This singular lapse (Japanese in Brazil, for example, are well reported in the *Indice*) confirms the invisibility of Jewish Latin America and the isolation—might one say, quarantine?—of Jews by the majority culture.

This isolation stands in total contrast to the experience of Jewish intellectuals in the United States, who have profoundly influenced contemporary American literature, contributing to it a distinctively Jewish component. In searching for the causative factor, one cannot attribute the apartheid of Jewish life in Latin America to any greater religiosity on the part of Latin American Jews that might have placed them voluntarily beyond the pale. To the contrary, all indications are that the majority of Jewish immigrants to Latin America were less observant than their cousins who migrated to the United States. One clear indication comes from the late formation of synagogues.

Religious Practice

The reasons religious congregations were not immediately organized by Jewish immigrants lie both in the nature of the immigrants and in the character of the societies to which they came. Many of the early immigrants to Latin America were drawn from sectors of world Jewry that were already partially assimilated to the Gentile world. Such was the case with the French, German, and Alsatian Jews of the 1870s-80s. Those who settled in profoundly Catholic environments in Mexico and Chile apparently viewed the founding of synagogues as needless provocation. Many East European Jews were more observant of religious practices, but here, too, the haskalah had made headway.

The East European migration occurred at a time when religious and antireligious factions had the shtetl in turmoil. Even those who had been traditionalists at home were likely to throw away many elements of ritual when they landed in the New World. Secularism was fortified by the intellectual atmosphere of the metropolitan centers of Argentina, Brazil, and Uruguay, where routinism had eroded the religious passions of the urban masses. As long as they were not forced into a defensive reaction by an overbearing church presence, many Jewish immigrants were content to follow a secular orientation. Perhaps relieved at finding Catholic influence so nominal, they saw no need to agitate the religious question and generally remained apathetic toward it. ·

This is not to deny the existence of a religious impulse among all Jewish immigrants to Latin America. The East Europeans who settled the Entre Ríos agricultural colonies were observant; in their isolation, religious traditions continued of their own momentum until attenuated by time and the passing of the immigrant generation that had included religious personnel. But secularism won out. By 1959, there was no rabbi, circumciser, or ritual slaughterer in the entire province of Entre Ríos.[9]

Sephardim are known among Jews for their faithful attachment to organized religion, usually associated with a traditional style of family life. Congregação Porta do Ceu (Gates of Heaven) was founded by Sephardim from Africa, Syria, and Arabia in Belém do Pará at the turn of the century. There were four congregations of Syrian Jews in Mexico City in 1905, while the Alsatians still feared to declare themselves publicly. At the other end of the time scale, German Jews entering São Paulo just prior to World War II made it their first order of business to found their own synagogue, Congregação Israelita Paulista. The instantaneous adoption of a Portuguese rather than a Hebrew name conforms to the haskalah orientation of this group, for whom Judaism had become a religion and little more.

There have been instances of an astonishing persistence of religious belief and practice. In Buenos Aires, Jewish communists formed their own synagogue. In Montevideo, communists supported their own ritual slaughterer, who provided *linke shekhitah* (leftist ritual slaughter). And in São Paulo at the date of writing, there is a religious congregation whose members are aged Jewish prostitutes, remnants of the white slave trade, and their offspring. But these groups are in the minority; the majority of Jewish immigrants were in no hurry to establish synagogues.

Another circumstance that delayed the founding of synagogues was that observance of the Jewish religion does not depend upon an institutionalized structure; the presence of ten adult men (a minyan) is a sufficient condition for holding a religious service. This prayer unit can be brought together on an ad hoc basis to celebrate weddings and circumcisions, memorialize the dead, or observe the holidays, without any special framework. Indeed, the presence of a rabbi is not required. Therefore, in the early days when immigrants were few and far between and no sense of community united them, efforts to generate community participation were made only in times of personal crisis or during the High Holy Days (Rosh Hashanah and Yom Kippur, which occur in September or October). Thus we find the first minyan in Santiago gathering in a private home in 1906 to celebrate Rosh Hashanah. The following year, it was necessary to have a Jewish policeman released from duty in order to complete a quorum. The incident confirms a generalized lack of concern for religious activities: at the founding of the Sociedad Unión Israelita de Chile the year before, eighty-seven persons were present and signed the charter; and two years later, fifty-four persons signed the charter of the Jewish social club, Filarmónica Rusa.[10]

Overt organization of Jewish religious life in Mexico had to await the revolution of 1910, and then it occurred within an anticlerical context. The Constitution of 1917 vested ownership of churches and church property in the nation (Article 27); religious institutions possess no juridical personality, and only persons born in Mexico may serve as priests or ministers of religion (Article 130). These are deprived of political rights. The strictest enforcement of these constitutional provisions occurred during the presidency of Plutarco Calles (1924–29), whose administration coincided with the greatest influx of Jewish immigrants. These, coming at Mexico with an anti-Catholic perspective, would have been attracted at first to the radical anti-Catholic policies of Calles. At the same time, the very elements of that policy which non-Catholic settlers found attractive also operated to impede the organization of Jewish community life. There was, for example, no such thing as a native-born Jew (at least, none who spoke Yiddish) and therefore no possibility of recruiting a rabbi. Measures taken by the Mexican government to decrease popular fanaticism were equally effective in blocking transmission of the Jewish heritage. In an environment that remained ineradicably Catholic, if unchurched, Jewish children would inevitably cease to be Jewish. In this situation lay the motivation for the formation of religious congregations by persons who were not religious. Secularism in Mexico did not block the establishment of synagogues as much as it permeated them, turning the synagogues into further expressions of Jewish secularism. This is demonstrated by the fact that the synagogues were established within distinct ethnic communities, without the acknowledgment of any religious linkage between them. The numerically small Mexican Jewish community divided itself into seven watertight sectors, each representing different national origins and each barricaded behind the impenetrable fortress of its ancestral language (see Table 3). For the Americans, securalism was expressed more overtly by the formation of a "community center" in place of a house of worship.

The Jewish community of Buenos Aires is similarly characterized by a multitude of religious congregations, all based on ethnic origin. In 1954, a survey of Buenos Aires synagogues located from eighty to a

Table 3. The Seven Jewish Communities of Mexico City

Date Organized	Name of Community	1970 Family Membership	Ethnic Composition
1912	Alianza Monte Sinai	700	Arabic-speaking Sephardim from Damascus
1922	Nidje Israel	2,521	Yiddish-speaking Ashkenazim from Russia, Poland, Lithuania
1923	Union Sefaradi	844	Ladino-speaking Sephardim from Turkey, Greece, the Balkans, Italy
1930	Tsedaka U'marpe	1,150	Arabic-speaking Sephardim from Aleppo
1939	Hatikva-Menora	115	German-speaking Ashkenazim from Germany, Austria, Czechoslovakia
1942	Emuna	40	Hungarians
1953	Beth Israel Community Center	130	English-speaking Jews, largely from the United States

Source: Harriet Sara Lesser, "A History of the Jewish Community of Mexico City, 1912–1970," pp. 40–55.

hundred.[11] Two years later, an observer identified twelve Russian, five Romanian, fourteen Polish, two Galician, and five German congregations. He viewed these as being "geared to preserve particularist trends in Judaism rather than preserve Jewish life as a whole."[12] Matters have not changed substantially since that time; *Comunidades Judías* for 1971-72 claims "about 50" synagogues for Buenos Aires, fewer than half of which have rabbis. A North American rabbi serving a Buenos Aires congregation has called Latin American Jewish life "the most secularized in the West."[13]

Compartmentalization by ethnic origin is the rule: La Paz, with a thousand Jews or less, has three synagogues, one East European and two predominantly German. Guatemala City, with an estimated thirteen hundred Jews or less, likewise has three synagogues, Ashkenazi, German, and Sephardi—a large number of synagogues for a population that is so secularized that it does not produce rabbinical students. Religious congregations seem to be part of a search for identity, rather than specifically religious institutions.

The existence of a synagogue does not imply the presence of worshipers. "Santiago," commented one respondent, "has five synagogues and no *minyan*." Nor does the existence of a synagogue imply the presence of a rabbi. The shortage of rabbis and other religious personnel is comparable to the shortage of priests in the same area. Recently, the Rothschild Foundation imported a rabbi to provide religious services to the Jews of Entre Ríos and Santa Fé. In 1970, only forty-five rabbis were officiating on the entire continent. Many of these are elderly persons trained in a Europe that no longer exists. Others are Ladino-speaking Sephardim from the United States and Israel. The Brazilian congregations are in a peculiarly difficult position inasmuch as there is no worldwide reservoir of Portuguese-speaking Jews from which their rabbis might be drawn. Nowhere do native sons come forward in any number to train for the rabbinate and spiritual leadership of their communities. As Rabbi Marshall Meyer (a North American) concluded in 1970, "It is evident . . . that (a) the influence of the rabbinate is practically nil; and that (b) no one has demonstrated urgency to change this situation."[14]

The rabbis who came with the nineteenth-century immigration represented the Orthodox tradition and apparently did not include persons capable of exercising religious leadership. Reform, and the Conservative movement that attempted to bridge Reform and Orthodoxy, did not arrive in Latin America until the twilight years 1938-39. By then, these movements for modernization of the Jewish religion had been well established in Europe and North America for over a hundred years. Despite some openings toward change, it would be fair to say that Jewish expectations of reform within the Catholic church in conformance with decisions of Vatican II are not matched by expectations of reform within Judaism.

A start toward *aggiornamento* was made in 1954, when the few Conservative synagogues on the southern continent affiliated with the Conservative movement in the United States. This was followed a decade later by formation of a Seminario Rabinico in Buenos Aires. Not, strictly speaking, a seminary (its students must go on to a rabbinical seminary in New York or Jerusalem to qualify for ordination), the Seminario has begun to fill the need for religious personnel having a Spanish-language competency and educated in both religious and secular modes (seminary students must study simultaneously at the University of Buenos Aires). Presently, four synagogues in Buenos Aires, with a combined membership of some twenty-eight hundred families, have adopted the Conservative custom. These include the prestigious Congregación Israelita, where haskalah influence has persisted since the early days of its founding. There are also individual Conservative congregations in Chile, Peru, Brazil, Venezuela, Colombia, and Mexico.[15] The 130 members of Congregación Kol Shearith Israel in Panama City retain a rabbi of Reform tendencies.[16]

Apart from these few, the majority of synagogues remain in the

hands of the ultra-Orthodox, who view such innovations as the introduction of Spanish or Portuguese into the service, or mixed-sex seating,
as heretical. Far more seriously, the Argentine rabbinate has taken the
position of refusing to perform conversions to Judaism. This prohibi-
tion was instituted in the 1920s by both Sephardic and Ashkenazic
rabbis. As a result, during a period of high and rising rates of intermarriage, there is no way for a couple of mixed faith to found a Jewish
family.

A 1966 survey of Jewish university youth in São Paulo revealed a
strong tendency to abandon the patterns of traditional Judaism. Only
45 percent of a sample of Jewish students declared a belief in God,
while 38 percent declared themselves to be atheists and 17 percent un-
decided. Synagogue attendance every Saturday was reported by only 4
percent of Jewish youth. Of all those who attended synagogue either
occasionally or frequently, only 31 percent stated that they actually
prayed; 66 percent declared they did not know how; and 3 percent that
they knew how but were not motivated to pray. "In face of such results,
it is inevitable to conclude that the young Jewish university student is
abandoning religion. . . . [He] is not anti-religious but simply unre-
ligious. . . . His abandoning of religion does not occur due to an ideology contrary to religion, but simply due to indifference."[17]

Education

The absorption of immigrants into Latin American societies was
retarded by the absence of that most effective of acculturating institutions, the tax-supported public school. Whatever may have been the
verbal dedication of successive governments to the cause of universal
education, many areas of the "interior"—an evocative word—remained
without schools during the nineteenth century. Pleas by educators that
governments take cognizance of the poor and train their sons for productive labor—that they "colonize the country with its own inhabitants"—went unheeded. Education in Latin America was confined to
a relative few and retained an elitist bias inherited from colonial days.

There is, by contrast, almost universal literacy among Jews. Literate Jewish immigrants for the most part entered Latin American societies at a very low socioeconomic level. Their initial contact was with
unschooled gauchos and campesinos, the "broken" men in transition
from countryside to city, illiterate denizens of *villas miserias*. Confronted by the prodigious gap between themselves and the people they
met, Jews worried lest their own children adopt a culture whose mani-

festations they regarded as inferior to their own. They had come to a new world to give their children a better chance in life than they had had, not to watch them sink to the level of marginal men. The small, educated criollo elite comprised a sophisticated haute monde with which immigrants were most unlikely to come in contact. The schools they had created for their children were deemed untenable by Jewish families for Catholic norms prevailed even where lay control had been established. Jewish parents dreaded having their children cast in the role of deicides. Even worse was the possibility that conversion would turn their children into their own worst enemies. Interviews with Jewish families living in the Cuban countryside in 1933, published in *Havaner Lebn*, the Yiddish-language Cuban newspaper, shed light on the situation of immigrants living in isolation well into the twentieth century.

This Jewish family seized upon the visitor from Havana to ask about the availability of Jewish education in the capital. They are prepared to sacrifice everything in order to move their daughter out of her present ambience. Her friends attend a convent school, but tell this child she cannot go there because her parents killed Christ. Naturally, she cannot be allowed to become Christ's bride, as they shall all be. The daughter has begun to call her parents *judío* in the common pejorative way. And these parents–who are not even religious! –find the traditional hatreds imposed upon their child, turning her into their enemy.[18]

The need to provide education for Jewish children in a mode that would not traumatize them was the principal reason for the formation of Jewish *communities*, as contrasted to the settlement of individual families. Schools were needed in areas where existing schools were private and Catholic, admitting non-Catholic children either capriciously or not at all; these often purveyed an education that was unacceptable to Jewish parents. Schools were needed to provide basic education in areas where private and public schools were simply nonexistent. Schools were also needed to transmit the Jewish heritage and enable Jewish children to form a positive self-image. The story of the creation of these schools is largely the story of creation of Jewish communities because a critical mass of parents was required to start a school, and the school once started attracted to itself children from outlying families.

Different ethnic groups among Jews responded differently to the educational challenge, and differences were enlarged by the passage of time and factors relating to locale. Ladino-speakers had already developed a symbiotic relationship to the Catholic world at the time of their arrival in Latin America. Typically, they enrolled their children in existing state or private schools and arranged minimal after-school instruction for boys in sufficient Hebrew to enable them to say their prayers. German Jews arriving in the 1930s were able to follow a similar course because by that time most nations had made considerable progress in extending their school systems, particularly in the urban areas of Brazil and Chile, locations favored by this migration.

The problem of education was most intractable for East Europeans. There were few secular school systems in the years of heaviest Ashkenazic immigration; these immigrants did not know Spanish or Portuguese; they were unfamiliar with Catholic institutions and deeply fearful of them; and many were endowed with a strong sense of Jewish peoplehood that stimulated the desire to ensure Jewish survival in this alien environment. It was almost always the East Europeans who took the initiative in founding "integral" schools—all-day schools integrating secular and religious curricula.

The need for schools became apparent immediately in the colonies of the Jewish Colonization Association. Despite the avowed desire of the Argentine government to provide free universal education, there were no government schools in the villages near which the colonies were situated. The original settlers were Yiddish-speaking Ashkenazim from eastern Europe, and, left to themselves, they would probably have reconstructed the *heder* and *talmud torah* systems with which they were familiar (a system of combined religious and secular study, carried on in the Yiddish language and with emphasis on the learning of Hebrew for the purpose of prayer). The JCA administrators, as we have seen, regarded themselves as emancipators who wanted to hasten in all possible ways the assimilation of the settlers into the Argentine countryside.

When the colonists demanded schools, JCA set them up on the model of schools then being run by the Alliance Universelle Israelite in the Middle East. These were secular in orientation and used Spanish as the language of instruction. The administration imported the only Spanish-speaking teachers they had, graduates of the Paris teachers' seminary of the Alliance. These happened to be North Africans. Relations between teachers and parents became strained, each group being firmly attached to its own version of Judaism. After considerable agitation, the colonists, who were footing an increasing percentage of the costs, acquired control over the religion classes. At that point, Hebrew and Yiddish were given a larger role in the classroom.

In 1904, the government of the province of Entre Ríos sent an inspector to visit the JCA schools. He found 850 children attending sixteen different schools,[19] which were supported with an annual budget of 33,200 pesos. The Argentine curriculum was being taught in Spanish, with courses in the "3 Rs," calligraphy, geography, history, and singing. The inspector applied to the children the Lockean stamp of approval: *mens sana en corpo sano.* "From the beginning," he added, "they learn three languages: Spanish, Hebrew, and their jargon [Yiddish]."[20]

Nevertheless, it was these schools which in 1908 attracted the hostile attention of Argentine jingos, who charged that they were un-Argentine in character and staffed by foreigners who despised Argentina.[21] Such charges continued to be launched over the years as part of the campaign to discredit immigration. But the idea that JCA schools were impeding the acculturation of Jewish children could have been disproved by a reading of the reports emanating from Jewish educators. It was clear from the start that the children would not learn Yiddish, and the atrophying of this language can now be documented thoroughly. Several surveys of language use were conducted among Jews living in cities of the Argentine interior during the 1950s. Many respondents were descendants of settlers in the JCA colonies. Their responses show that Spanish had already become the universal language of the Argentine-born. Analysis produced a pattern of rapid movement from Yiddish to Spanish, accelerated in the case of East Europeans who married Argentine-born mates. The speed of the turnover is illustrated by the finding that Yiddish-speaking parents who used both languages when talking to their grown children used only Spanish with younger ones. In almost all cases, children who reported speaking Yiddish with their parents spoke Spanish with their siblings.[22] The general attractiveness of the Argentine landscape, the comparative malleability of society in face of the massive onslaught of immigrants, and the natural desire of second-generation immigrant children to be accepted by society at large were quite enough to start Jewish children speaking Spanish, even in the absence of state-supported schools.

Similar evidence of rapid linguistic turnover comes from Mexico, where a Jewish school system was established that for a while was regarded as the finest in the diaspora. The conditions for its creation were similar to those surrounding formation of the JCA schools in that an educational void existed at the time of the immigrants' arrival. Mexico had disestablished the church and prohibited clerical personnel from taking part in the educational process. But the state did not suddenly develop the capacity to provide schooling for all children.

Therefore, the various national groups in the federal district (Spaniards, French, Germans, and others) were encouraged to start their own schools. The Yiddishe Shule, or Colegio Israelita, was founded in 1924, the first year of large-scale Ashkenazic immigration. In keeping both with official Mexican secularism and the worldly orientation of the immigrants, the Shule followed a secular curriculum. Families of the original twenty-six students "represented all ideological tendencies," a

6. Students and teachers of the Max Nordau School, colony of Narcisse Leven in Argentina in 1946. The selection of Nordau's name for the school exemplifies the secular orientation of the founders and indicates that their interests lay more along the lines of protecting their children from possible trauma in Catholic schools than in transmitting a specifically Jewish religious orientation. (Courtesy of YIVO Archives)

174

situation that, the essayist remarks, "could not last long."[23] An ideological struggle smoldered within the school for years, ending with the exodus of several dissident groups. Ultimately, ten separate schools were established. In 1955, these schools enrolled 3,200 children, and 84 percent of them were being taught in Yiddish. In 1970, Jewish schools claimed 5,475 children, a smaller percentage of the now larger Jewish population of the capital city. Only 10 percent of them were receiving instruction in Yiddish.[24]

The substitution of Spanish or Portuguese for Yiddish occurred all over Latin America. A survey of the Jews of Valparaíso, Chile, in the 1950s, showed the same trend as that revealed for Mexico and Argentina. Two-thirds of children under eighteen reported knowing no Yiddish at all, a proportion that rose to 90 percent for children both of whose parents were born in Latin America.[25] A more recent survey of language spoken in the home among Jews of São Paulo showed an even more rapid adaptation. Fifty-eight percent of respondents gave Portuguese as their main language, while 33 percent named it as their second; Yiddish placed next, with 15 percent listing it first and 27 percent second.[26] Despite the placement of Israeli teachers in many Latin American Jewish schools, Hebrew has fared no better. The languages the Ashkenazim brought with them have everywhere yielded to Spanish and Portuguese, bespeaking the voluntary acculturation of Jews to Latin American society.

As secular schools, both public and private, appeared in the various republics, the Jewish schools have atrophied. The association is not often made by Jewish educators, who tend to attribute the drop in attendance to some moral failing in their pupils. But the fact of the matter is that these schools, founded at a time when there was an educational vacuum, no longer serve a legitimate function when that vacuum is filled. The test of this hypothesis lies in a comparison of Jewish school systems in secularized societies with Jewish school systems in republics where the church retains a controlling interest.

In relatively secularized Argentina, Jewish education has been the subject of eighty years' effort and expense. Yet, fewer than 20 percent of Argentine-born Jews have had any Jewish education at all, and that mostly on a part-time basis. The most astonishing fact is that the proportion of Jewish children enrolled in Jewish schools rises from one-half of children eligible for nursery school to a majority of first-graders. Thereafter, there is a steady and unrelenting erosion of enrollment until completion of the secondary cycle; for 1,885 children entering first grade, only 126 graduate the twelfth, or 1 in 15.[27] These children are not leaving the educational process altogether, but are transferring to government or private schools.

In Chile, where overtly secular norms prevail, fewer than 25 percent of Jewish children attend Jewish schools of any kind. Chilean Jews credit this fact to the high degree of acceptance their children find in national and private schools. It is frequently pointed out to the visitor that Chile is the only country in Latin America where a Jew could legally become president. Lack of a religious bar to office is not unrelated to a secular educational system that has accommodated Jews and other immigrants and made parochial school systems irrelevant.

The story from another secular, industrializing country, Brazil, is similar. Matriculation figures for Jewish integral schools in 1969 show 50 percent of Jewish children enrolled in preprimary, kindergarten, and primary; 38.5 percent at the gymnasia level; and 9 percent at the level of the colegio.[28] Jewish schools are funneling their students into the national schools of the republic.

The situation in republics where the school system is dominated by the church is totally different. Peru's Jewish school system embraces 95 percent of Jewish school-age children in Lima. The near-total enrollment is credited locally to the school's high academic standards, the economic health of the community, and the unity of Ashkenazic, German, and Sephardic communities, which means that there is no fallout of children. The likelihood is that this high enrollment also reflects lack of acceptance of Jews by Peruvian society.

The name of the school is itself an interesting indicator. Most Jewish schools bear the names of Jewish writers (such as Y. L. Peretz) or national leaders (such as Chaim Weizmann), but the Lima school is named for a converso whose grandfather was burned at the stake.[29] The ambiguity of the identification that Jewish children of Lima are daily asked to make at Colegio León Pinelo is apparent.

In countries where the educational process is in the hands of the church, Jews must make adjustments that are not required of them in societies that have disestablished the church. The modus vivendi arrived at in Colombia is distinctive enough to warrant attention here. That republic's constitution guarantees freedom of religion as long as its practice "is not contrary to Christian morals or laws." The Concordat with the Vatican states that "education and public instruction in Colombia will be organized and directed in conformity with the dogmas and morals of the Catholic religion." Within these parameters, Jews have worked out solutions to their educational dilemmas.

A recent study shows that an overwhelming majority of Jewish children are enrolled in Jewish integral schools: 92 percent in Cali,[30] 84 percent in Medellín, 68 percent in Barranquilla (in the latter city, Sephardim did not join the day school movement).[31] All three schools offer Colombian and Jewish curricula; half of the teaching staff are Colombian Catholics, including the principals of the three schools. Social studies are taught from texts prescribed by the Ministry of Education and sanctioned by the Curia. Religious education is compulsory for the Catholic students, numbers of whom are attracted to the schools by their high academic standards. In an interesting illustration of the capacity of the church to make room for Jews in a prescribed status, Jewish students are required by law to take one hour a day of Hebrew, Jewish history, or Jewish religion. The schools fly the Jewish flag on Fridays and manage to retain within a Catholic legal framework a Jewish presence that is largely religious and symbolic.

Thus the controlling factor in the popularity of Jewish schools seems not to be the amount of effort and funds expended by parents or the moral fortitude of their children, but rather the extent to which secular educational options exist. In relatively secularized societies with large immigrant populations (Argentina, Chile, Brazil), the proportion of Jewish children enrolled in Jewish schools is low despite the expenditure of prodigious effort and substantial funds for the maintenance of communal schools. The highest enrollments in Jewish schools are to be found in small Jewish communities situated in countries where church and state are united or incompletely separated and that do not have large immigrant components in their populations (Peru, Colombia). It is no exaggeration to say that the determining factor in success or failure of Jewish schools to retain their students has been the degree to which Jewish children have been able to attend national or private schools without undergoing protracted psychological trauma.

The Catholic church thus emerges as a prime enforcer of Jewish identity. Restricted opportunity for Jews in ecclesiastically dominated societies results in the formation of a protected reserve, within which Jewish parents attempt to preserve the dignity and identity of their children. Conversely, where society is relatively open, Jewish children enter the national educational mainstream as soon as they are old enough to vote with their feet and despite great efforts by their elders to slow them down. There is no evidence whatever that Jewish schools obstruct the acculturation of immigrants, as it was feared they would. Jewish educators believe the schools have failed to forge a functional

Jewish identity among second- and third-generation Latin American Jews. From this situation arises concern for the future of Jewry on the continent.

The success of the Jewish educational system lies in its record of integrating Jewish children into the mainstream of society. Jewish schools provided basic education at times and in settings where governments failed to fulfill this function. By offering the necessary elementary and secondary education, these schools enabled Jewish youths to qualify for admittance to the national universities, nearly all of which are open to applicants on the basis of merit. Thus, by continuing the traditional emphasis on learning, the Jewish schools qualified their students to enter into their national societies at successively higher levels.

The *Kehillah*

Discussion of Latin American Jewry is usually dominated by description of the *kehillah* (plural: *kehillot*). This is another venerable institution imported from the European experience, and its distinctive organization and style merit attention in this study. It is mistaken, however, to believe that the kehillah subsumes the totality of Jewish life on the continent. Historically, it played an important role in Jewish life in Europe, but in Latin America the kehillah never acquired the autonomy and vitality that characterized its prototype. Today it is declining in absolute as well as relative importance.

The kehillah is the organized Jewish community, and it exists in one form or another in most lands of the diaspora, adapting to local political conditions and to the needs of its members. In some countries and in some periods, the organization of a kehillah was mandated by the state, which used it to tax Jews collectively, to draft a quota of men for the army, and in general to deal with Jews as an organized entity apart from the rest of society. In modern times, following the emancipation of the Jews, kehillot survive as voluntary associations.

Latin American kehillot came into existence voluntarily, in response to a felt need for coordination of social services and also as a reaction to specific occurrences. The largest of the kehillot—Asociación Mutual Israelita Argentina, or AMIA—had its origins in a complex legal struggle to obtain a permit for purchase of land to establish a cemetery in Buenos Aires, and a monopoly over burial according to Jewish rite remains at the heart of the association. AMIA activities now cover the range of services that have been mentioned in this chapter, as well as television programs, youth counseling, Jewish book month, the rabbinical seminary, an outreach program to Jews living isolated in the provinces, an arbitration panel. AMIA's constitution prohibits it from undertaking political action, and functions in that area adhere to a separate organization, the Delegación de Asociaciones Israelitas Argentinas, or DAIA.

These and other services required an AMIA budget in excess of five million dollars in 1974. Revenue comes from membership dues as well as from extremely high burial fees, exacted even from families who have paid their dues. The fee, viewed as extortionate by many, is the source of great bitterness.

"My father was a good Jew," a young man told me. "He worked on all the [fund-raising] campaigns, served as officer in a number of organizations, and always contributed generously. When he died, AMIA cleaned my mother out."

7. *Where the Jewish community is, there is the* kehilla. *AMIA occupies an imposing building in Buenos Aires. (Courtesy of the American Jewish Committee)*

"We are constantly in need of money," explained an AMIA official. "When a rich man dies, we sock it to 'im."

Monopoly over the cemetery enables AMIA not only to finance kehillah services, but also to impose its interpretation of Judaism upon the community. The kehillah continues to back the orthodox version of Judaism to which few Argentine Jews remain attached; it has retained Yiddish in the Jewish school system long after it was apparent that that language's lack of relevance to Argentina was keeping children away; and it has refused to offer acceptable terms to the Sephardim for affiliation with the kehillah.

Recently, AMIA extended its control nationwide by way of formation of a Board of Communities (Va'ad Ha-kehillot). As a result, the president and other officers of AMIA now fulfill these roles nationwide. The exclusion of Sephardim from the kehillah was also continued and extended, indicating the increasing rigidity of ethnic lines rather than their erasure.

8. *The* kehilla's *importance derives from its monopoly over the Jewish cemetery, a situation that mirrors the Catholic monopoly that existed when the immigrants arrived. (Courtesy of the American Jewish Committee)*

AMIA is characterized by a highly centralized and rigid bureaucracy.[32] Some of this rigidity stems from the fact that decision-making offices are occupied by the largest donors of funds. These tend to be businessmen who gain social status by performing community work on a volunteer basis. Although there is a cohort of professional staff, such as teachers, religious counselors, and social workers, by and large these are underpaid, lack status, and have no input into policy making. The lack of social esteem for professional workers extends to rabbis. All the chief organizations of the community are secular in character, and a rabbi's influence is probably weaker in Argentina than in the United States. This fact does not alter the kehillah's unrelievedly Orthodox posture on questions pertaining to burial, marriage, dietary laws, and so forth.

The characteristics of kehillah organization that have been ascribed to AMIA are by no means confined to Argentina. The picture may be rounded by referring to the organization of the Jews of Mexico City. In 1952, Jacob Shatzky counted sixty-three Jewish organizations in that city, all affiliated with a Comité Central. Ten of these were religious, nine communal, eight cultural, ten charitable, ten Zionist, ten juvenile, and six had various other functions. The Comité's board of directors was meticulously divided among sixteen Yiddish-speakers (providing a majority), five Ladino-speakers, three German Jews, two Hungarians, and two Sephardim from Damascus and two from Aleppo.[33] Ideologically viewed, Zionists were in the majority, with "progressives" proportionately represented.

At that date, Nidje Israel, the congregation of the Russians and Poles, was trying to convert itself into a kehillah, an effort that was being resisted by the other sectors. Already it had established a Khevra Kadisha, an old folks home, ritual baths, and an arbitration panel (Beth Din). Within the next few years, the Nidje Israel group was successful in forming a kehillah, a feat it accomplished by excluding the Sephardim. This kehillah is now "the Jewish address in Mexico," the Sephardim having been pushed to the background. Each kehillah maintains its own schools, religious congregations, cultural activities, social welfare agencies, home for the aged, and the ancillary financial and administrative services.

Ethnic diversity was a principal barrier to the formation of a unified kehillah. The difficulty was usually overcome by the formation of separate kehillot for Ashkenazim and for Sephardim. This, of course, turned this form of organization into a bulwark of disunion and gave its principal officers an investment in the maintenance of ethnic differences. Though historically the kehillah played a cohering role in Jewish life, the kehillah in Latin America has arguably operated as a divisive force.

Another obstacle to unity was the diversity of political opinion that prevailed among Jewish immigrants, particularly at the turn of the century. Although the East Europeans give the appearance of a petite bourgeoisie because so many found it necessary to enter the local economies as peddlers, many in fact felt strong links to the working class. There were numbers of socialists, Bundists, anarchists, social democrats, and social revolutionaries among this group.

In Uruguay, as many as 20 percent of Jewish immigrants were probably factory workers and artisans. They arrived with a working-class consciousness that had been formed in Europe. Once in Uruguay, they continued to identify with leftist political doctrines. At the same time, having given up their religious faith in favor of a universalist ideal, they felt that they had little in common with shopkeepers and tradesmen who made up the bulk of the Jewish migration.

Following the Bolshevik Revolution, with its promise of Jewish emancipation, the various ideological trends crystallized among the Jews of Uruguay. In 1917, the "linke" organized the Kultur Verein Morris Vintschevsky, dedicated to the spread of Yiddish culture, which it activated through the founding of Yiddish schools for children, a public library, and a dramatic troupe. (Drama, in the eyes of the Verein, was no entertainment for the idle rich, but a means of exciting the class consciousness of the workers.) In addition, the Kultur Verein operated a free soup kitchen for the unemployed and funded a free loan association. The Verein was affiliated with the Yevsektsia, the Yiddish-speaking sector of the Communist party of the Soviet Union. Also affiliated with Yevsektsia at this time was Avanguard, a Jewish workers' movement.[34]

The Jewish Left was radicalized by the events of January 1919, when Semana Trágica spilled over the La Plata into Montevideo. Headquarters of several Jewish clubs were raided, about 80 percent of the Jewish population was under arrest at one moment or another, and a considerable but unknown number of Jews were deported. From that time forward, the Yevsektsia seems to have exerted greater influence over Jewish workers' organizations in Uruguay, possibly because they felt so exposed to government repression.

Poale Zion (pz, the socialist wing of the Zionist movement) also organized in Montevideo in 1917. When this party split into right and left factions worldwide, the Uruguayan Poale Zion likewise split, each half remaining tied to its respective counterpart abroad. The Left PZ established an Imigranten Arbeiter Heim and an Arbeiter Imigranten Kuch in Montevideo during 1927–28. The Right PZ was more closely allied with the Uruguayan Socialist party, and its members were active in Uruguayan trade unions. Both factions cooperated with Histadrut (the organized labor movement in then Palestine); both factions published newspapers and opened schools.

In 1929, the Jewish Socialist party (Bund) organized in Uruguay. One of the founding elements of the Russian Social Democratic Labor party in 1898, the Bund since then had been by turn wooed and rejected by the Communist party of the Soviet Union, its leadership alternately promoted and imprisoned. In Uruguay, the Bund preoccupied itself with following from afar events within its sister organization in Poland; locally, it engaged in cultural work on the Jewish street. In addition to publishing a party newspaper, the Bund founded schools and concentrated on retention of Yiddish as the Jewish workers' language. These actions were in accord with Bund policy elsewhere, which was to create an enveloping social system within which Jewish workers could experience a full range of cultural and social events presumed to be helpful in forming their ideology. The Bund in fact provided workers with a complete life style, ineradicably Jewish, yet apart from the traditional Jewish community.[35]

The linke of Montevideo divided between communist and Zionist camps, mutually antagonistic because Marxists opposed the development of a separate Jewish national identity, whereas Zionists, Marxist and non-Marxist alike, believed that the problems of the Jewish people could be resolved only within the framework of a Jewish national homeland. Rivalry between these "progressive" and "national" Jews prevented formation of a kehillah, since each faction wanted to dominate the finished community. Communists, opposed to Jewish "chauvinism," challenged the presence of Zionists on the governing board; while moderates and conservatives feared that, if a kehillah were formed, the communists with their superior organizing skills would dominate it.[36]

In 1931, an entity called the Yiddishe Kehillah fun Montevideo was brought into existence. Based on the old Khevra Kadisha, its goals were to provide Jewish burial, represent the Jewish community of Montevideo, subsidize Jewish schools, create an orphanage and home for the aged, provide medical assistance to needy members, help the unemployed and the handicapped, and support Jewish agricultural colonization in Uruguay.[37] This kehillah incorporated East European

Jews only. Sephardim, German-speakers, and Hungarians each maintained their own kehillot during the thirties, as well as two chief rabbis (an Ashkenazi and a Sephardi) and three separate school systems
(religious, religious-Zionist, and secular-Zionist). All these organizations were sustained by a population of barely thirty thousand Jews.
During the thirties, a struggle took place for control of this Yiddishe
Kehillah. The linke had developed one of several small free loan associations into the Banco de Goias and attempted to use it as an instrument for takeover of the kehillah. The bank was far more than a financial institution. With six thousand members and a capital of several
million pesos, it was also a fundamental organ of the community. It
offered credit, ran an ambulance service and pharmacy, sold health
and life insurance, supported numerous cultural endeavors, and organized an agricultural colony.

Failing in their effort to take over the kehillah, the Moscow-
oriented leadership of the Banco set up a rival kehillah, offering membership at lower rates, another cemetery, and, as noted above, meat
slaughtered according to both religious and communist writ. Tres
Arboles, the agricultural colony, was patterned after a Soviet *kolkhoz*.
After three years of turmoil brought on by maladministration and
strained feelings between the administration and the colonists, the
colony collapsed and took the bank with it amid cries of malfeasance.
Many depositors, progressive and otherwise, were wiped out by the
bank's failure. The credit of Jewish merchants in Montevideo was
harmed. And the fact that the government had to intervene to restore
the situation was viewed as a humiliation by most members of the community.

In 1936, these warring sectors managed briefly to form a united
front, called Council against Nazism and Anti-Semitism (Vaad Neged
Hanazism Vha-antisemiut). [38] This front broke down with the withdrawal of support by the Yevsektsia, and the atmosphere of the Jewish
community of Montevideo came close to one of civil war. Any attempt
at neutrality was suspect by both sides.

The linke, having lost their representative institution and with it
the hope of dominating the kehillah, apparently were forced out of
Jewish communal affairs and assimilated to general society in Uruguay. This facilitated formation of a "roof" organization in 1940, following mediation by officers of the World Jewish Congress. This Comité Central Israelita was recognized by the Uruguayan government
as spokesman for the entire Jewish community.

Having united all ethnic sectors and expelled the linke, the kehillah now found itself controlled by centrist forces. Zionism won out over the progressive line, and the Montevideo kehillah today is invincibly Zionist, as are also the AMIA of Buenos Aires, the Nidje Israel of Mexico City, and all other kehillot on the continent that were investigated.

In the 1950s, Jews all over the world came to regard as imperative the expulsion of the linke from kehillot. The survival of Jews and the survival of the noncommunist "free world" seemed interdependent as the nature of Soviet anti-Semitism became apparent. Additionally, within Latin America, the activities of the linke had again and again endangered entire Jewish communities because radical activity by individual Jews tended to draw down the wrath of the police and the superpatriots on all Jews. The kehillot took upon themselves the task of cleaning up the Jewish street so that right-wing governments would not be tempted to do that job. In the short run, results were favorable, in that Jewish communities were able to exist under conservative regimes that did not tolerate egalitarian movements.

In the longer run, expulsion of the linke left the kehillot without ties or inclinations toward the radical and revolutionary parties that came increasingly to the fore in the sixties and seventies. Expulsion of the linke left the latter's children and spiritual heirs without ties to the Jewish community, free to assimilate and to join third-world groupings that now claim the allegiance of masses of university youth. These movements have become anti-Zionist, if not plainly anti-Semitic, and the phenomenon of cross-pressured Jewish university youth becoming anti-Semitic is a major problem in Argentina today.

The linke themselves presumably retained their ideological tendencies that had brought about their expulsion from the kehillah and from the Jewish street. But two historical forces operated to cause many of them to cease identifying as Jews. One was the increasingly rigid line that the kehillot drew around the question of who was a Jew, particularly as this related to intermarriage and the impossibility of converting the non-Jewish partner to Judaism. The other was the increasingly anti-Semitic nature of Soviet communism as revealed in such incidents as the Prague trials and the blood libel against Jewish doctors that occurred in the 1950s. To be a Jew and to be a communist were no longer perceived by many as compatible states.

Expulsion of the linke cut the ties of Latin American Jews to European ideologies. Jews, however, have not been admitted to the politics of their adoptive homelands. One observer attributes this lack of participation in national politics to self-absorption in kehillah politics.[39]

This seems most unlikely, and I suggest that the reverse is closer to truth: exclusion from national political life intensifies intramural politics. The phenomenon of exclusion will be examined in Chapter 9, but for now it may be suggested that kehillah politics represent a displacement of political energy that finds no outlet on the national scene.

Within communal institutions, politics have become increasingly mimetic of the politics of Israel. Kehillah boards of directors are elected by their constituent organizations according to a system of proportional representation that was perfected within the World Zionist Organization. The parties that put forward candidates on "lists" are replicas of Israeli political parties, and they mate, reproduce, and divorce along with their prototypes. Marxist parties compete (and do fairly well), but their ideology relates to Israel, not to the politics of Latin America. This electoral pattern gives the kehillot a foreign appearance, and indeed their internal politics would not be intelligible to a knowledgeable reporter on any of the great metropolitan newspapers.

Kehillah elections, though nominally democratic polls of the membership, obscure the reality of Jewish life on the continent. It is wholly unlikely that Latin American Jews are marshaled politically along the lines indicated by kehillah elections. In the case of Buenos Aires, not all Jews belong to AMIA; those who do are not a representative sample of Argentine Jewry. Seventy percent of AMIA members are over fifty, and 17 percent are over seventy years of age. Twenty percent of AMIA membership had no formal education or only a few grades of elementary, while another 32 percent graduated elementary but proceeded no farther with their education.[40] Forty-five percent of the membership sampled did not vote. These included a majority of those under fifty and a majority of those with a college education. In other words, AMIA represents the elderly, the foreign-born, the Yiddish-speakers. The young, the native-born, the better-educated, and the Spanish-speakers are alienated from AMIA as a moribund institution.[41]

In the light of continued bureaucratic rigidities, political irrelevancy, and ethnic feuds, the organized Jewish communities increasingly are perceived by native-born Jews as irrelevant to their lives. Young, ambitious persons are not attracted by communal obligations or the lure of status obtained through officeholding in the community. The archaic forms of Jewish religious and cultural life offered to them by the kehillah compare poorly to the attractive secular world of the university that brings Jewish as well as non-Jewish youth into confrontation with issues of concern to them as Argentines, Chileans, Brazilians.

As the rate of intermarriage rises, no avenue of compromise opens: one must be either inside the fold or outside it.[42] Increasing numbers of Argentine youth are opting out of Jewish life by entering into marriage by civil contract only. They care less where they are buried than how they are to live their lives.

Institutionalizing Ethnicity

A pattern of intra-Jewish discord emerged as soon as Jews of different provenance came in contact with one another.[43] The rivalry between Lithuanians and Galicians, which is no more than a source of humor among North American Jews, was set in concrete in the Latin American communities by the founding of separate institutions for these groups. The Russians, who claim to speak better Yiddish than either, are patronizing of them both; all share a passionate dislike of Germans, who "aren't even Jews."[44] For their part, Germans have a tendency to believe all Jews would be better off if the East Europeans were not so Jewish.

Ethnic rivalry permeates the Sephardic as well as the Ashkenazic camp. Ladino-speaking Jews regard themselves as living on a more rarefied cultural plane than Arabic-speakers and do not consent to organize jointly with them. Antagonism between Jews of Aleppo and Jews of Damascus led to the duplication of services for each of these groups.

The most obvious breach is between Ashkenazim and Sephardim. Over and over again, Ashkenazic observers consulted in my research omitted Sephardim in enumerating populations or describing communal institutions. Sephardim, for their part, have developed little taste for history, relying on their symbiotic relationship with the Catholic world for protective coloration. Members of both camps freely express their low regard for one another, and their mutual repulsion made it impossible for them to cooperate. Since each group insisted upon each jot and tittle of its religious liturgy, separate synagogues were required. The Yiddish-language schools, pride of Ashkenazim, by their nature excluded Sephardim. The very active Yiddish literary world met no more appreciation among Spanish Jews than among Spanish Catholics. Despite prolonged negotiations, Sephardim and Ashkenazim could not even agree to bury their dead in the same cemetery.

This internecine hostility sapped the vitality of Jewish communities. It diminished the number of Jews available for political and social action and rendered them even smaller minorities than they were. The total number of "Jews" was irrelevant because they could not cooperate with one another or present a united front to non-Jews. In no instance that could be discovered were the cultural affinities of Sephardim to the Latin American *ambiente* utilized to ease the entry of Ashkenazim into the matrix society.

A perceptive observer has explained these antagonisms in the following way: "The difficulties of assimilation to the customs and language of the new home were already so great that it was unnecessary to create other problems in order to live with Jews who originated from different countries. Also, the Jewish immigrant from a Mediterranean country was as little familiar to the immigrant Jew of Western Europe as to other non-Jewish citizens of Brazil. Many factors contributed to the isolation of each group, among which [was]—why not say it?—prejudice."[45]

One looks in vain in this picture for a nationalizing mystique that might have absorbed the devotional energies of Jewish immigrants, overcoming their parochial loyalties. During the period of heaviest immigration, the most all-embracing institution of the republics was the Catholic church. Immigrants who were Catholic could be received into it with relative ease, thus relieving the trauma of the migratory process. For Jews, identification with the church was impossible. Thus many immigrants emphasized their Jewish tradition in order to provide themselves with needed social and psychological support and to provide their children with an identity capable of sustaining them in a milieu that was felt to be fundamentally hostile to them. This Jewish tradition, or better, these Jewish traditions, were narrowly defined as *Russian, Syrian,* and so on, because it was the only kind of Jewishness each individual knew. In recreating their home life style, they inadvertently walled themselves off from coreligionists whose life style differed from their own. These barriers endured in the absence of national traditions with which the immigrants could identify.

In all of this, one feels that a great opporunity has somehow been missed. As the distinguished editor of *La Luz* put it in 1960: "Argentina was a new world for Sephardim: it returned us to the Spanish-speaking world, and at the same time brought us once more into contact with Ashkenazim."[46] Jewish migration to Latin America presented the possibility of a reunion between these two branches of the Jewish people who had lived apart for centuries. For some, it opened the vista of a great reunion with the Spanish world, abandoned in such sorrow 450 years earlier, and the dawn of a neo-Sephardic renaissance. This reunion did not occur, whether for lack of vision, overly rigid attachment to tradition, failure of nerve, or lack of leadership. Jewish failure to heal the breach within accounts in part for the lack of vitality in their communities.

Salvation through Sports Alone

Institutionalized defense of the Jewish past may have been an adequate response in those republics and in those periods that were dominated by a monolithic church presence. It proved less adaptive in secular societies where religion was relegated to secondary status and upward mobility lay open, or partially open, to Jews. In these secular societies, Jewish youth are abandoning the communal institutions they perceive as rigid, desiccated relics of an outworn age. As they enter the broader society, they find few ways of identifying as Jews without paying dues to the Khevra Kadisha. Many simply stop identifying as Jews. Their assimilation is eased by the fact that, unlike the situation in the days of their parents and grandparents, they are no longer coming into contact with semibarbarous gauchos, marginalized slum dwellers, and the criminal underworld, but with middle- and upper-middle class representatives of the most attractive elements in criollo culture.

There is one institution that is now beginning to supply Latin American Jews with a secular Jewish identity. This is the Jewish sports club. Variously called the Estadio, Centro Deportivo, or Hebraica, the sports club is a hybrid between Jewish and Latin American institutions. Sports clubs organized along national lines (the Italian Club, the Syrian Club, and so on) are to be found in all Latin American cities; sports are a central fact of Latin American life. Thus it is quite in order for the Jews to have their sports club, too, and every Jewish community surveyed has one. Typically these offer a library, auditorium, restaurant, nursery school, and offices of the Jewish social welfare agencies, in addition to facilities for tennis, soccer, swimming, golf, and bowling. They are likely to offer such activities as continuing education for adults, dances, art exhibits, concerts, lectures, children's day camps, and psychological counseling. Many clubs field teams for the Macabiad, the Jewish counterpart of the Olympic games. Some are located on very choice real estate: Hebraica of Buenos Aires in the downtown business district, Estadio of Santiago on the outskirts of the city with a stupendous view of the Andes. The physical plant of the clubs tends to be impressive (in Chapter 4 I have described the scope of the Patronato in Havana). Even more impressive is their record for attracting members. "There may be 7,000 people at the Club on a fair Sunday," an Argentine social worker commented to me. "That is more than you will find at the Congregación on Yom Kippur."

Not least among its distinctions is the fact that the sports club is the only Jewish institution at which Jews of different ethnic communities mingle with one another. For the native-born generation, European and Levantine quarrels are irrelevant, and so are their languages. At the clubs that are their creation, the language spoken is Spanish or Portuguese. Increasing numbers of native-born Jews are in fact unaware of the ethnic origins of their parents and do not care to know about them; in assimilating to their national societies, they are also assimilating to one another. The result is an increasing incidence of what Latin American Jews call "intermarriage"—unions between Ashkenazim and Sephardim. Fully half the marriages registered at the Sinagoga Sefardi Maguen David in Santiago are of "mixed" couples.

The sports club, curiously enough, has become Latin American Jewry's last best hope for maintaining a Jewish presence on the continent. In keeping with the secular thrust of Jewish life since the arrival of the first Jewish immigrants, Latin American Jews have placed their money on survival as a secular, rather than as a religious, entity.

8

The Demography of
Latin American Jewry

Some 550,000 persons who were identifiably Jewish were living in the
Latin American republics in 1960, 310,000 of these in Argentina. Brazil, with 120,000, was the home of the second largest contingent. Uruguay, Mexico, and Chile rank next with 48,000, 35,000, and 28,000
Jews, respectively. In each of these republics, the transformation of
economies from agrarian to industrial modes of production had begun
by the time of World War I, the period when the largest number of
immigrants were looking for new homes. Each of these republics has
accomplished the separation of church and state, and each exhibits a
nascent middle class, at least in a limited statistical sense of the term.

Venezuela (17,000) and Colombia (14,000) have moderate-sized
Jewish communities. These republics have not completely separated
church and state and did not for the most part encourage immigration.
But the process of industrialization has attracted modernizing elements
from abroad, and the size of their Jewish populations is growing.

Republics that today are the home of tiny Jewish communities are
those that either failed to encourage, or actively discouraged, heterogeneous immigration. Nor have they for the most part committed
themselves as yet to economic and social modernization. These are
countries with large indigenous or black populations, high rates of
illiteracy, and grave polarization between elite and mass (Peru, Bolivia, Ecuador, Paraguay, the Dominican Republic, Haiti, and the
Central American republics).

Table 4. Latin American Jewish Population Centers

Location	Urban Population	National Population
Argentina		310,000* (1960)
Buenos Aires	246,000*	286,000* (1970–80 projected)
Rosario	8,384	
Córdoba	7,823	
La Plata	3,534	
Santa Fé	3,208	
Tucumán	2,882	
San Cristobal	2,406	
Bahía Blanca	2,188	
Paraná	2,051	
Mendoza	2,023	
Concepción	1,798	
Concordia	1,746	
Villaguay	1,562	
Gen. Pueyrredón	1,311	
San Fernando	1,280	
Corrientes	1,130	
Adolfo Alsina	1,024	
Bolivia		1,000
La Paz	650	
Cochabamba	200	
Santa Cruz		
Tarija		
Oruru		
Sucre		
Rural areas		
Brazil		120,000
São Paulo	57,600†–70,000‡	
Río de Janeiro	35,000*–50,000‡	
Porto Alegre	5,000‡	
Belo Horizonte		
Curitiba		
Recife		
Salvador Bahia		
Belén		
Niteroi		
Manaus		
Brasilia		
Santos		
Campinas		
Santo Andre		
São Caetano		
Nilópolis		
Campos		
Petrópolis		

Table 4. continued

Location	Urban Population	National Population
Chile		28,000
Santiago	"90%"	
Valparaíso		
Concepción		
Valdivia		
La Serena		
Arica		
Colombia		14,000
Bogotá	5,000	
Cali		
Barranquilla		
Medellin		
Costa Rica		1,500
San José	"nearly all"	
Dominican Republic		200
Sto. Domingo	100	
Sosua	100	
Ecuador		1,500
Quito	"nearly all"	
Guayaquil		
Cuenca		
Ambato		
Riobamba		
El Salvador		300
Guatemala		1,500
Guatemala City	"most"	
Quetzaltenango		
San Marcos		
Honduras		150
Tegucigalpa	86	
Choluteca		
Comayaqua		
Tela		
Mexico		35,000
Mexico City	"95%"	
Guadalajara		
Monterrey		
Tijuana		
Nicaragua		0 [§]
Managua		
Panama		2,500
Panama City	2,000	
Colón	300	
David	100	

Table 4. continued

Location	Urban Population	National Population
Paraguay		1,000
Asunción	"nearly all"	
Peru		5,300
Lima	"nearly all"	
Uruguay		48,000
Montevideo	"nearly all"	
Paysandú	250	
Venezuela		15,000–17,000
Caracas	"80%"	
Maracaibo		
Valencia		
Macacay		

Sources: Comité Judío Americano, *Comunidades Judías de Latino-américa*, 1971–72, except where noted.

* U. O. Schmelz and Sergio Della Pergola, *Hademografia shel hayehudim be-argentina ube-artzot aherot shel America halatinit.*

† Henrique Rattner, *Tradiçao e Mudança*, p. 23.

‡ Marcos Marguiles, "Ayer y Mañana," p. 328.

§ As of 1979.

Table 4 shows the distribution of Latin American Jews according to the best information available at this time. The table should be used with discretion, for no official census of the Jews of Latin America has ever been conducted, nor is one likely to be. Special problems beset the field of Jewish demography.

Fundamental to any enumeration of Jews is the determination of who is a Jew. According to Jewish religious law (*halakhah*), a Jew is a person born of a Jewish mother and who has not accepted conversion to another religion, or who has been converted to Judaism according to *halakhic* procedures. In practice, some persons in marginal categories regard themselves as Jews while others do not: for example, persons born of Jewish fathers and non-Jewish mothers. Also, there is the question of persons who qualify under halakhic definition, but who choose to dissociate themselves from Jewish life. Are such individuals to be counted as Jews? Because of the existence of "marginal" Jews, the practice has arisen of adding to Jewish census data an estimate of the number of such persons, thus occasionally producing an error equal to that which would arise were no correction attempted. Reliance on estimates is, however, a necessity for all Jewish populations outside the State of Israel.

In countries that have separated church and state, the collection of information regarding religious preference is regarded as invidious.[1] The registration of individuals as Jews has on occasion been used as the basis for discrimination. This is the case in the Soviet Union today and was a factor in the holocaust, when official records were used to identify Jews for transport. Many Jews living in Latin America entered their present countries of residence on baptismal certificates and would be unwilling to compromise their position for the sake of a census. Such life experiences combine with more remote memories of the Spanish Inquisition to limit the willingness of Latin American Jews to check the category "israelita" on a census.

In recent years, five Latin American nations have included a question on religion in the national census. Most of these produced puzzling results. The Chilean census of 1960 showed 11,700 Jews in the country, or about one-third the number actually affiliated with Jewish institutions at that date.[2] Conversely, the Mexican census of the same year showed 100,750 Jews, a startling 470 percent increase over the 1950 census considering there had been no Jewish immigration in the interim.[3] Despite the theoretical possibility of deriving information on Jewish communities from national censuses, these must be handled with extreme care. Until recently, most of our knowledge has come from studies prepared by Jewish community service organizations. The American Jewish Committee and the World Jewish Congress have made periodic attempts to assess the size and viability of Latin American Jewish communities. Some of these studies were prepared by highly qualified scholars, and they are cited throughout this work, providing as they do invaluable information for the projection of demographic trends through time. From 1966 to 1975, the series *Comunidades Judías* was compiled biannually by community leaders and social welfare professionals in each republic and edited by staff of the Comite Judía Latinoamericana. This work has now come to an end, due to the harassment and flight of staff.

Community records, however, are never complete. There is no centralized record keeping for births, marriages, or deaths among Jews. Thus, Jews who are not organized do not get counted. Gaps in data are difficult to fill in because of uncertain political conditions that make field work impracticable. In practice, some efforts to fill in lacunae in Jewish census data, if not objectively verifiable, are logically persuasive. For example, Jewish births can be estimated by consulting the records of the *mohel* (ritual circumciser) and adding the number of females presumed statistically to have been born during the same time period. Circumcision, however, increasingly is performed in hospitals by surgeons, and so this method is of decreasing value.

Nevertheless, much Jewish history has been written without the assistance of official information-gathering agencies. It would be self-defeating to assert that, where there is no certainty, there can be no knowledge. Much can be learned from the sources that are available and even more from integrating information derived from them all. In undertaking this task, most weight will be given to three excellent demographic studies, for the reasons that they encompass the bulk of the Latin American Jewish populations and that they were carried out by qualified scholars. The precise demographic dimensions of the Jewish community of Argentina were defined through computer analysis of the national census of 1960.[4] São Paulo's Jewish population was surveyed in 1969 under the direction of a trained sociologist.[5] In Mexico, an astute humanistic analysis of the census of 1950 was executed by a Jewish demographer.[6] It is not necessary to impose on the data—derived from widely different sources by way of a wide variety of techniques—an artificial gleichshaltung that in the nature of things would only intensify inaccuracies. The data as found present a startlingly clear pattern. When this pattern in turn is compared with the demography of the matrix populations, the distinctive profiles of Jewish and non-Jewish populations appear in sharp relief.

The dimensions of the Latin American Jewish population appear to be less ample than previously believed by those who embrace the most generous definition of Jewish identity. In recent years, the best-received estimates were from 800,000 to 825,000 for Latin America as a whole, some 500,000 to 550,000 of these in Argentina alone. To understand why these figures must now be scaled down, it will be instructive to understand how they were arrived at in the case of Argentina, home of the largest Jewish community in Latin America.

The 1936 municipal census of Buenos Aires identified 120,195 Jews, comprising 5 percent of the population of the city. This figure was credited by Ira Rosenswaike, the researcher who analyzed the census for its Jewish component.[7] He further enlarged this figure by a factor of from 8 to 12 percent to include persons who were ethnic Jews but who had declared themselves to be without religion. The Jewish population of the country as a whole he assessed at 230,955.

In an effort to arrive at a rate of natural increase, Rosenswaike utilized data derived from national and municipal censuses, as well as the records of Jewish institutions, particularly the Jewish Colonization Association, which had conducted its own census in 1909. From these, Rosenswaike inferred three decreasing rates of natural increase during the twentieth century. The 1.5 percent rate of natural increase computed by Simon Weill, director of JCA, was accepted for the early years of the century. "However, after World War I the Jewish rate of natural growth throughout the western world suffered a sharp decline. Everywhere the birth rate reached unprecedented lows, while the mortality rate generally fell but slightly."[8] Seeking to confirm or refute the existence of this worldwide trend among Argentine Jews, the demographer returned to the Buenos Aires municipal census of 1936. In that year, native-born israelitas of less than fifteen years of age accounted for 23.5 percent of the israelita population; by comparison, 21.8 percent of the total population were under fifteen. Assuming a lower rate of infant mortality among Jews, Rosenswaike inferred that the Jewish and non-Jewish birth rates in the city were about the same. That figure stood at 19.3 per 1,000 for the general population in 1931–35, and it was accepted for the Jewish population as well. The Jewish death rate was ascertained from the number of burials in Jewish cemeteries: 9 per 1,000 population in 1934. Taken together, the figures indicated a rate of natural increase of 10 per 1,000 per year, or 1 percent for the Jewish community of Buenos Aires in the 1930s.[9]

Despite this evidence of a low birth rate, Argentine Jews as well as outside observers refrained from crediting official census returns that showed fewer israelitas in 1947 than in 1935: 249,330 compared to 253,242. Reasoning that Jewish and non-Jewish demographic trends were similar, it was assumed that the figures were in error. Estimates of the number of Jews living in Argentina continued their steady upward trend. In 1947, the *American Jewish Yearbook (AJYB)* suggested 350,000; thirteen years later, the same publication increased this to 400,000, although the preliminary census returns for 1960 recorded only 275,913 israelitas over age five. In 1962, the *AJYB* estimate jumped another 50,000, and in 1968 yet another 50,000, with *Comunidades Judías* adding still another 50,000 for good measure in 1970, for a total of 550,000 Jews in Argentina. But a 25 percent increase in population over a period of ten years implies a growth rate of 2.1 percent annually (or even greater, considering additional factors such as emigration and outmarriage). So high a rate of natural increase is not characteristic of any developed area of the world, nor does it exist in Argentina, nor is it characteristic of Jews worldwide. The rate of natural increase among Jews of Canada (a population very similar in its origins to that of Argentina) is considerably less than 1 percent.[10] Furthermore, the fragmentary evidence that could be assembled pointed to a declining birth rate.

When the Argentine census of 1960 became available in full, it recorded 291,877 Jews. This number represented about three-fourths the number believed by the Jewish establishment to be living in the country. The discrepancy was accounted for by the fact that the census was taken on the eve of Yom Kippur: after sundown, observant Jews were not at home but at the synagogue. In addition, some 5 percent of the population, almost one million people, declared themselves to be "without confession." As a result of omission of both religious and marginal Jews, it appeared that the size of the Jewish population had been seriously underestimated by the government.

This anomaly was taken up by the demographers U. O. Schmelz and Sergio Della Pergola, who analyzed the computer tape for "Jewish" and "without confession" responses. In a persuasive analysis, they determined that the published census total might be supplemented by 6 percent to take in the proportion of respondents living in Buenos Aires (the area where most Argentine Jews are concentrated) who were born Jewish and who answered "no religion" or "without confession" to the question on religion. Having considered the data on these nonrespondents, the authors adopted a corrected total of 310,000 Jews in Argentina in 1960, with distribution as set forth in Table 4. The new total may be the most significant datum to emerge since establishment of Jewish settlement in Argentina, since it means that one-quarter of the presumed 1960 population did not exist; that presumed rates of natural increase are inoperative; and that 1970 estimates of half a million are even farther from the mark. Furthermore, it calls into question accepted population figures for Jews in other parts of Latin America. These had been rising *pari passu* with population estimates for Argentina and now must be scaled down in similar fashion. For the area exclusive of Argentina, *AJYB* estimated 237,850 in 1948, 302,250 in 1960, and 324,000 in 1970. These totals included large rounded sums for cities such as Santiago, Bogotá, Mexico City, Montevideo, and Caracas, despite the fact that in a large secular metropolis it is nearly impossible to sift out Jewish individuals without an official census. Taking into account recent findings for Argentina, it is likely that assumed rates of growth for other Latin American Jewish communities are overly generous. Quite probably, no more than 240,000 Jews presently live in Latin America exclusive of Argentina.

Birth rate. Information on the demographic characteristics of Latin

American Jewry displays an internal consistency that confirms the existence of a group that is quite distinct from the majority members of
matrix populations. The gravest difference appears in contrasting
birth rates. For whatever country we examine, the Jewish birth rate is
just half that of the matrix population. In 1965, the crude birth rate
for Argentina as a whole was 22 per 1,000;[11] during the same period,
the Argentine Jewish birth rate was 10.5 per 1,000 (See Table 5). The
number of Argentine Jews in each age cohort born since 1953 shows
steady attrition. In 1960, there were 4,434 children aged eight, but only
3,662 aged four and 3,022 aged one. In the group below the age of four
there were to be found only three-quarters of the number of children
aged five to nine. The proportion of children dwindled faster than the
number of Jewish women of childbearing age, not only because of a
continuous drop in completed fertility, but also because of a continuous rise in the frequency of mixed marriages, in the majority of which
the children are not reared as Jews. The completed fertility rate of
Argentine Jewish women in 1960 yielded a ratio of 947 daughters per
1,000 mothers, more than 5 percent short of the number required for
replacement of the parent generation.

The São Paulo Jewish community was surveyed during the five-
month period January to May 1969. The precise number of births,
extrapolated over a one-year period, yielded a birth rate of 2.4 percent
per year. This rate obtained during a period when the Brazilian population as a whole was experiencing a birth rate of 4.4 percent per year.
Ninety-five percent of Jewish families have fewer members than the
average Brazilian family. Moreover, there is a secular trend toward
fewer children in Brazilian Jewish families. In an earlier study carried
out in 1965, Henrique Rattner found that Jewish university students

*Table 5. Estimates of Vital Rates among Argentine Jews
Yearly Averages per 1,000 population, 1946–1980*

Years	Birth Rate	Death Rate	Balance
1946–50	16.5	8–9	7.5–8.5
1951–55	15.5	9–10	5.5–6.5
1956–60	11.0	10	1.0
1961–65	10.5	10–11	−0.5–0.5
1966–70	10.5	11.5	−1.0
1971–75	10.5	12	−1.5
1976–80 (est.)	11.0	15	−4.0

Source: Schmelz and Della Pergola, *Hademografia*, p. 164.

in São Paulo belonged to families with an average 2.7 children, but that their parents' families had averaged 5 children per family. The Brazilian Jewish birth rate is declining during a period when the country as a whole is experiencing accelerating population growth.

Working with the Mexican national census of 1950, Tovye Meisel found that the Jewish community experienced a birth rate of 23 per 1,000, contrasted with 46 per 1,000 among the population at large. Again, though the figure is higher, the Jewish birth rate shows up as one-half the prevailing rate.

Low fertility rates characterize all Jewish populations of the diaspora except those in Asia and North Africa. Worldwide, the birth rate, and consequently the rate of natural increase, are lower among Jews than among the general population of their respective countries. Accordingly, and considering that Latin American Jewry of all the republics proceeded from the same immigrant streams, it is reasonable to infer similar low rates for Jewish populations in those parts of Latin America for which there are no data. The inference is backed up by scattered available data on Jewish age structure in Brazil, Chile, and several small Central American communities.

This phenomenon reflects modernized attitudes toward the family, the status of women, and child-rearing practices. In modern times, Jews preceded the populations among whom they lived, according to Schmelz, "firstly, in reducing mortality, and subsequently in lowering fertility."[12] Throughout the nineteenth century, in all countries of Europe, Jewish birth rates were lower than those of their matrix populations, and the rate of increase was less than that being experienced by other European peoples. When Europe generally, and western Europe in particular, experienced a slowing down of the rate of natural increase in the period 1900–1938, the trend was led by Jews, whose rate of increase shrank faster than that of the general population. For many urbanized Jewish communities prior to World War II, there no longer was any population growth at all, but a negative balance of deaths over births.

Evidently, emigration does not change patterns of Jewish fertility. The U.S. trial census of 1957 showed that, for Jewish women still of childbearing age, fertility was 20 percent below that of the rest of the urban population, 25 percent below that of the entire white population, and almost 30 percent below that of the total United States population. Evidence from community surveys taken since that date indicates that the birth rate continues to fall. Jews imported low birth rates into their present countries of residence, and the Latin American experience has not converted them to high levels of fertility.

Death rate. A complete record of deaths among Ashkenazic Jews of Buenos Aires exists for the years 1953–63. It shows continuous increase, being 40 percent greater at the end of that period than at the beginning. In 1963, there were three and a half times more burials than marriages within the Ashkenazic community of Buenos Aires. This partially reflects increasing resort to marriage by civil contract. Nevertheless, a decline in the number of persons who identify as Jewish is undeniable.

The major cause of the rising death rate is the aging of the population. In 1963, the single year for which records are available for all Jews in Buenos Aires, 2,438 Jewish deaths are recorded. Subtracting 35 stillbirths, Schmelz and Della Pergola compute a rate of 10 deaths per 1,000 Jews of Greater Buenos Aires. The death rate for the general population of the city that year was lower, standing at 8 per 1,000. The composition of the two mortality rates was different. Infant mortality (death in the first year of life) was 9.3 per 1,000 among Jews, compared with 40 per 1,000 among the general population of Greater Buenos Aires in 1961 and 57 per 1,000 among the general population of Argentina in 1967.[13] The Jewish death rate continues low until age sixty, when mortality starts running higher than among the general population. Compounding the trend, the death rate among Jews was rising at a time when the Argentine death rate was declining.

The point has already been reached where the Jewish mortality rate has surpassed that of the general population, due to aging. It has also surpassed the Jewish birth rate, and there is now a negative balance of deaths over births within the Jewish community, with 12 deaths and 10.5 births per 1,000 population per year. Along lines of present development, the period 1976-80 should present a negative balance of −4 per 1,000 in the rate of natural increase of Argentine Jews.

The mortality rate among São Paulo Jews is 1.6 percent per year; the rate among the Brazilian population as a whole is 1.1 percent per year. The national figure includes a high rate of infant mortality. In fact, the hazards of infancy in Brazil are so great that expectation of life at birth was calculated at forty-three years in 1950.[14] The rate of infant mortality among Brazilian Jews is almost nil, and the majority of deaths occur after age sixty.

Meisel found the Mexican Jewish mortality rate to be 9 per 1,000 as compared to 15.5 per 1,000 among the general population. Both groups were growing in 1950: Jews at a rate of 1.4 percent per year, the majority population at 2.9 percent per year.[15] Over the next fifteen years, Mexican mortality dropped steeply as measures of public hygiene took hold. Mortality dropped by a third while the birth rate decreased only slightly, resulting in one of the highest rates of natural increase in the world. Among infants, the most vulnerable sector of the population, mortality continued high, with 61 infant deaths per 1,000 live births. However, there was no infant death among the approximately twenty thousand Ashkenazim of Mexico City during several years of the 1960s.

Infant mortality is at a very high level throughout Latin America. Considering only Argentina, Mexico, and Brazil, the location of a majority of Latin American Jews, the rate of infant mortality for the first two countries is 60 and 61 respectively. Brazil does not supply data on infant mortality to the United Nations; for the State of Guanabara alone (site of the former capital city of Rio de Janeiro) the rate of infant mortality in 1959 was 94.4 and in 1960, 70.0 per 1,000 live births. In these countries, as we have seen, the rate of infant deaths within the Jewish communities tends toward nil.

Here again, a global demographic pattern is working itself out. Infant mortality among Jews worldwide is extremely low, and it appears that Latin American Jews follow the pattern of other Jews, rather than the national pattern characteristic of their matrix populations. The global phenomenon of low infant mortality among Jews has been accounted for by a combination of reasons that are also persuasive within the Latin American setting: more intense urbanization among Jews over the past century and a half, when cities had better preventive facilities than did the countryside; earlier adoption of birth control among Jews, with the side effect of enabling parents to bestow better care upon each child; the low rate of illegitimacy; the comparatively high number of physicians among Jews; existence of Jewish religious observances that are supportive of good health.

There have been systematic and far-reaching changes in health care universally. These are now penetrating Latin America, as declines in the death rate show. The speed of the process differs, but because Jews in Latin America are in a more advanced time frame than their matrix populations, their infant mortality rate is considerably lower.

Infant mortality rates are a commonly accepted index of modernization. The capacity to save infants from death caused by endemic disease is dependent upon relatively low levels of technology and a

Demography

modest expenditure of funds. The inability or disinterest of governments in providing hygienic services is a salient characteristic of underdeveloped countries. Contrast between high rates of infant mortality throughout Latin America and the low rate within Jewish communities throws into relief the modernized character of Jewish life as contrasted with the traditional pattern of human wastage that continues to prevail in society at large.

Longevity. The anticipated life span of Jews is almost the same as for non-Jews in the city of Buenos Aires, being 68.9 and 73.9 for Jewish males and females respectively, and 67.9 and 74.2 for non-Jewish males and females. Uruguay and Venezuela fall into the same long-lived category as Argentina. Outside the modernized sectors of the continent, life expectancy drops sharply for majority populations but remains high for Jews. For example, in 1968, 40 percent of São Paulo Jews were over age forty; 14 percent over age sixty. In the same year, only 25 percent of the general population of São Paulo was past forty, and just 6 percent was past sixty.[16] Jews achieved their pattern of longevity independent of their immediate environment. Among the general population of the city, those over forty gained 5.5 percentage points between 1950 and 1968, reflecting improved health conditions; but the Jewish age distribution showed no material change over this eighteen-year period.

Within the Guatemalan community in 1965, over 100 individuals, or 10 percent of the Jewish population, were aged sixty-five and over. Comparable data do not exist for the Guatemalan population as a whole; but expectation of life at birth for the Guatemalan population was 49.5 in 1950 and had not changed significantly in 1973. It is thus most unlikely that 10 percent of Guatemaltecos live to age sixty-five.[17]

Since many of the health practices that eliminate infant mortality also work to prolong the life span, it is not arbitrary to conclude that life expectancy among Jews in areas for which no data exist approximates the modernized model shown for Buenos Aires more closely than it does the traditional rate still prevalent in most of Latin America. This conclusion is supported by substantial numbers of interviews, which also reveal one reason why this should be so. With expectation of life at birth standing at 48.5 years in the general population of Colombia, the Jewish community underwrites transportation to the United States and medical care there for any of its members in need of sophisticated medical assistance.

Low fertility, low infant mortality, and extended life expectancy among Jewish populations contrast with high fertility, high infant mortality, and low life expectancy among non-Jewish populations (with the exception of Argentina). The result is a higher median age for Jewish than for non-Jewish populations (see Table 6).

A longer life span, in addition to being its own reward, enables individuals to develop their skills to the utmost. The blighting of promising careers through early death is far less frequent among Jews than in the general population. Furthermore, survival into the sixties ensures that most parents are able to nurture their children to maturity. The phenomenon of parentless children is comparatively rare.

Family size. Small families are typical of Jewish populations. In countries that maintain traditionally high birth and death rates, the Jewish family stands out in sharp relief as having passed through a demographic transition: there are fewer wasted pregnancies, fewer children per family, and more of these children reach maturity. In Latin American nations that have passed as an entity through the demographic transition from traditional to modern patterns of family life, Jewish populations are less clearly differentiated—except in the matter of infant mortality.

The average family size of AMIA members diminished from 4.53 to 4.14 between 1920 and 1930. There is evidence that this generation was practicing birth control; Jewish families were smaller in Argentina than in central Europe.[18] By 1960, Jewish families were smaller than non-Jewish families in Buenos Aires, with an average 2.2 children being born to Jewish married women, as compared with 2.7 for non-Jewish women.[19] Jewish households averaged a fraction under 4 persons each. The downward trend shows up clearly in Quilmes (a district

Table 6. Median Age of Populations

Area and Date	Jewish	General
Argentina 1960*	34.7	27.0
São Paulo 1969†	33.78	27.2
Quilmes 1963‡	32.15	26.61
Guatemala 1965§	26–35	n.a.¶

* Schmelz and Della Pergola, *Hademografia*, p. 66.
† Rattner, *Tradição*, p. 23.
‡ AMIA, *Censo de la comunidad judía de Quilmes, 1963*, p. 19.
§ Jacob Shatzky, "Guatemala," p. 302.
¶ Not available. But with 46 percent under age 15, the median age could not lie in the 26–35 group.

of Gran Buenos Aires) in a 1963 survey that found an average 3.45 persons in Ashkenazic families.

Sephardic families tend to be somewhat larger (see Table 7). Modernization was a distinctively European phenomenon that Jews originating in Arabic or Balkan lands did not participate in as directly as did Jews of central, western, or even eastern Europe. There is thus a consistent difference in family size between Ashkenazic and Sephardic families in all communities for which we have data. Greater traditionalism in Sephardic life results in higher fertility rates and larger families. Even when Ashkenazic and Sephardic families are averaged together, Jewish families are smaller than families in the population as a whole, except in Quilmes. Family size is about the same among the general population of Buenos Aires as among Jews continentwide.

The less-developed countries, as is well known, are presently experiencing a population explosion. Forty-three percent of the population of Brazil, for example, is below the age of fifteen. The corresponding figure for São Paulo City is 36 percent for the general population; but it is just 21.3 percent for the Jewish population.[20] Urban families, whether Jewish or non-Jewish, tend to be smaller than rural families. But Jewish families are smaller than the São Paulo norm, and as a practical matter, since almost all Brazilian Jewish families are urban, Jewish families in Brazil are distinctly smaller than non-Jewish families.

There are age distribution charts for two other communities: that

Table 7. Family Size in Selected Cities

City and Date	Number of Family Members	
	Ashkenazim	Sephardim
Córdoba, 1960*	3.82	4.09
Quilmes 1963†	3.45	4.48
Tucumán, 1962‡	3.3	4.2
Valparaíso, 1960§	3.1	4.19
Mexico City, 1950¶	3.3	4.6

* Joseph Hodra, "Hayehudim ba-Córdoba," p. 34.
† AMIA, *Censo de la comunidad judía de Quilmes, 1963*, pp. 34–35.
‡ AMIA, *Primer censo de la población judía de la provincia de Tucumán*, p. 35.
§ Benny Bachrach, "Hayishuv hayehudi ba-Valparaíso, Chile," p. 43.
¶ Tovye Meisel, "Yidn in Meksike, *Algemeine Entsiclopedia*, p. 406.

of Guatemala and that of Argentina. The Guatemalan Jewish community consisted of 1,030 persons in 1965. In that year, 26 percent of the Jewish population was under age fifteen.[21] In the Guatemalan population as a whole, 46 percent of the population was below that age.

Twenty percent of Argentine Jews are under age fifteen, compared with 30 percent among the general population of the country.[22] An attempt to draw a Jewish "age pyramid" results in a boxlike graph, with each five-year cohort below age sixty containing an almost equal number of persons. Only two categories differ. The group that was aged fifty to fifty-four in 1960 contained larger numbers, men predominating, and reflected the migratory wave that peaked in the years just preceding World War I. The base of the "pyramid" narrows drastically, reflecting the declining birth rate and the assimilation of infants into the general population via the intermarriage of their parents.

Part of the gestalt of underdevelopment is a high dependency ratio. Families must provide for large numbers of children, many of whom do not survive to become themselves contributors to the family welfare. Jewish families, with their reduced number of children, do not suffer this handicap, but neither do they have the population reservoir out of which future growth might occur.

Rate of natural increase. The São Paulo Jewish population exhibits a rate of natural increase of 0.8 percent annually, based upon birth and death rates alone.[23] If one were to take into account emigration and outmarriage, for which no statistics exist, it is probable that the community would be found actually to be decreasing in numbers. Rattner believes that the demographic pattern revealed by his study is applicable to the rest of Brazil. Considering the present explosive population growth of the country, Jews—who already comprise fewer than 1 percent of the population—will be even more negligible statistically in the future, if present trends continue.

Other communities likewise report insufficient numbers of births to compensate for deaths. Paraguay, for example, declined from fifteen hundred to a thousand Jews in recent years.[24] The Bolivian community is in process of decay. In Mexico, where the Jewish community doggedly refuses to permit a census, the population estimate of thirty-five thousand offered by *Comunidades judías* in 1972 cannot be sustained by the estimated rate of natural increase of 1.5 percent. Without knowing the exact dimensions of the Jewish population, but having in mind its slow rate of growth as compared with explosive increase among the population at large, it is certain that the Jewish community

constitutes a less significant proportion of the Mexican population today than it did a generation ago.

Jewish demography is of an entirely different nature than the demography of the matrix populations among whom Jews live. The
matrix peoples have high rates of natural increase (Argentina is the
exception), preponderantly young populations, and a high growth potential capable of being unleashed by minimal expenditures on public
hygiene. But Jews passed through the period of population expansion
owing to better health care during the nineteenth century. They have
already responded to the enhanced life chances of infants by limiting
the number born. Thus, there is no scope for a Jewish "population
explosion" based on better health care. The only source of population growth among Jews would be an increase in the birth rate; and
such a trend was not observed in any country studied. To the contrary,
Jewish populations are aging, and their mortality at present tends to
run higher than among matrix populations. In this perspective, the
probable fate of Latin American Jewry, already an insignificant numerical minority, is to become still less significant numerically in future.

Urbanization. The history of the Jews of Latin America is one of
consolidation into metropolitan centers. Jews live in the cities, a majority in the great cities, and the largest number in the national capitals. In nations with just one major urban center, nearly the entire
Jewish population of the country is to be found in it (Costa Rica, El
Salvador, Guatemala, Honduras, Nicaragua, Paraguay, Peru, Uruguay).
Where a secondary city exists, the second largest Jewish community is
located there (Bolivia, Panama, Venezuela). In those nations characterized by many urban centers (Argentina, Brazil, Colombia), Jews are
found in all major cities and many minor ones (Mexico is the exception).

Argentine Jewry today is almost totally urban, despite its rural bias
at the beginning of the settlement period. The 1895 Argentine census
located 64 percent of israelitas in the rural province of Entre Ríos, and
only 12 percent in the capital. The Jewish farm population experienced uneven growth from 7,015 in 1897 to 19,361 in 1909. Meanwhile,
the Jewish population of the capital increased to 6,065 in 1904 and
16,589 in 1909. The JCA census of that year located almost 50,000 Jews
in the country of whom "close to 20,000 were in the agricultural colonies; 16,500 were in the capital, and the remainder scattered about
the country, in city and town."[25]

By World War I, half of Argentine Jewry lived in Buenos Aires. The agricultural colonies waxed and waned on a diminishing curve. A process of consolidation was taking place, as Jews moved from the farm to provincial towns and thence to the capital. In 1952, there were identifiable groups of Jews in 836 Argentine towns.[26] Two decades later, the *American Jewish Yearbook* estimated that there were Jews in some 600 localities. In other words, the process of consolidation into towns and larger cities was continuing.

This consolidation begins in the provinces of the interior. A breakdown of the Jewish population of the province of Tucumán at two dates fifteen years apart shows the rural Jewish population declining by 21 percent while the Jewish population of the provincial capital increased by 19 percent.[27] The process is replicated nationwide. Between the 1947 and 1960 national censuses, the Jewish population of Buenos Aires increased by 25 percent, from 186,000 to 231,955. During the same period, the number of Jews living elsewhere in Argentina decreased by 5 percent. Seventy-nine percent of Argentine Jews now live in Greater Buenos Aires, compared with 33 percent of the general population.[28] Four provinces hold almost all the rest of the Jewish population: Buenos Aires (exclusive of the capital), Entre Ríos, Santa Fé, and Córdoba. The densest concentrations of Jews are in the cities of Rosario, Córdoba, Santa Fé, La Plata, Tucumán, Bahía Blanca, Mendoza, San Cristobal, and Paraná.

For Brazil, census returns of 1900, 1940, and 1950 show Jews residing in most states and territories over the past fifty years. But growth occurred only in major commercial centers and in cities that industrialized: spectacularly so in the case of the former federal district (where Jews came to comprise over 1 percent of the population) and São Paulo. By 1940, these two communities had eclipsed the smaller (and in some cases much older) Jewish communities of Pôrto Alegre, Belo Horizonte, Curitiba, Recife, Salvador, and Belém.

The third largest national community of Jews is probably to be found in Uruguay. There, the great majority of Jews, like the majority of Uruguayos generally, live in the capital city of Montevideo. Data for Mexico, the fourth largest community, are, as usual, thin and unreliable. In 1948, Shatzky found that "apart from the city of México there exist another 17 cities with Jewish communities. Guadalajara has 480 souls, 40 percent of them Sephardim, and Monterrey 85 families. Little by little, Jews move from the small localities to the capital, in order to establish themselves among their co-religionists."[29] At that date, the Jewish population of Mexico was estimated to be twenty-five thousand. Its size may have increased in the intervening generation (though probably not by as high a factor as is generally believed), but 95 percent of this larger cohort is now living in the federal capital. The preponderance of the capital in Jewish cultural and political life quite dims the influence of scattered nuclei left over from the peddling era. At one time, these appeared to be the harbingers of a settled provincial Jewish population such as arose in Argentina. Today, they seem more like particles that have somehow escaped the centripetal pull of the capital. One cannot help but think that the difference in distribution can be attributed to the more secular nature of Argentine life, which makes small-town living and small-town schools tenable for Jewish families. In Mexico, the greater degree of attachment to medieval Catholic norms, the presence of a large autochthonous population that still equates judío and diablo, makes Jewish small-town life an exercise in endurance and encourages a move to the cosmopolitan atmosphere of Mexico City.

The concentration of Jews in Latin American metropolitan centers derives from three historic roots: urbanization of Jews in their countries of origin; the mass migration from farm to city that took place throughout Latin America; and the need of immigrants to integrate themselves into the economy.

"Jews massed into cities earlier than other population groups and at a faster tempo," writes Uriah Z. Engelman in his essay on "Sources of Jewish Statistics." From the Middle Ages onward, this trend was observable in Europe, the movement being accelerated by laws that forbade Jews to settle in rural areas or to own land. "By 1925 more than a fourth of all Jews in Europe and America lived in the fourteen cities with a million population or more, while only 5.7 percent of the total population of the two continents lived in them."[30] Jewish immigrants, settling in the major cities of Latin America, were continuing urban life styles they had developed on other continents.

Within the Latin American context, Jews were under the same economic constraints as other immigrants. We have seen that all immigrants were subject to urbanizing pressures, so that in Argentina, the country with the largest influx of immigrants, 70 percent of these had urbanized themselves by 1914. Jews, with a background in commerce and industry, were even more susceptible to these pressures, especially in the absence of desired services in the countryside.

Meanwhile, most of Latin America was undergoing intense urbanization, without reference to immigrants or, certainly, to Jews. Today, at least nine countries, including the most populous, are more than 50 percent urban. Had Jews resisted urbanization in order to remain internalized in rural areas, this phenomenon would surely have called for explication. As it is, the intense concentration of Jews in cities conforms to economic and social processes within the matrix societies as well as to the thrust of Jewish history.

A low birth rate, aging population, rising mortality rate, small family size, substantial emigration, and increasing rate of intermarriage characterize the Jewish population of Latin America and have caused it to begin to diminish in size. Urbanization tends to intensify these trends. City life often reinforces the desire to limit the size of one's family. Higher education paves the way for economic and social mobility, which in turn brings Jewish youth into contact with attractive non-Jewish potential mates. Life in the major population centers provides opportunity for mobility through emigration.

The nexus of causes underlying the atrophying of Latin American Jewish communities has been succinctly described in the case of Uruguay:

Various causes explain the decrease: the emigration to Israel and other countries, the high percentage of deaths among the older generation which is not compensated by natural increase, and the assimilation of marginal elements that have definitely separated themselves from Jewish life. Among the four Jewish communities . . . the new Comunidad Israelita (consisting of Jews originating from Central Europe) registers this process most dramatically. Today it has 1,160 members, that is to say, about 3,500 individuals. In September of 1961 it included almost double this number of members and counted some 6,000 individuals. The annual mortality rate is 60 and the number of births only twenty.[31]

Migration. The Jewish communities of Latin America have not added to their numbers through immigration since the dispersal of refugees in 1957. It is estimated that no more than 350 Jews were admitted to Argentina in any one year between 1953 and 1960. To the contrary, in the following decade, numbers of Jews apparently left Argentina. No figures exist for this emigration save in the case of Jews who settled in Israel. Between 1961 and 1973, from 16,000 to 18,000 Argentine Jews are known to have emigrated to the Jewish state. Others, for whom no figures exist, undoubtedly emigrated to the United States and elsewhere.[32]

In times of political and economic stress, Jews like other nationals tend to leave their homelands if they have the financial means. Chile is believed to have lost 6,000 Jews during the Allende years; Uruguay, which reported 55,000 Jews in 1970, claimed only 48,000 two years later, and the total has no doubt dropped still further in view of the large-scale flight of all population elements from that country. We have earlier seen how rural Jewish youth were drawn to the city by the prospect of higher education. There is evidence that this evacuation of the countryside by Jewish youth in quest of an education is being replicated on a broader scale as young men and women leave such hinterland communities as Quito, Lima, La Paz, and even Montevideo. An example of the way this process works occurred when the University of Montevideo was intervened for two years because of political unrest. Students who were locked out began to emigrate to attend school elsewhere. The reopening of the university in 1974 did not resolve the situation, as two years of entering classes were now backed up and had to wait their turn for admission. The pace of the exit of young would-be students from Uruguay accelerated at a time when, for economic and political reasons, there was in any event a large-scale exodus from the country by people of all socioeconomic levels. The difference for Jews is that, with a numerically small community to start with, departure of the college-bound reduces the number of potential mates so drastically that parents are encouraged to send abroad other children, particularly girls, whom they would otherwise have kept at home, but whom they wish to see marry endogamously. While some of these students remain within Latin America, many who are sent to the United States or Israel apparently depart with their parents' blessing to remain if possible. The result is to deprive Latin American economies of potential active elements, as well as to impoverish Jewish community life and challenge its ability to survive.

Intermarriage. It is not possible to know with precision just how many Jews marry non-Jewish mates in a given year; nor could one deduce from such a figure whether or not the individual continued to regard himself as a Jew and whether or not his children would be raised as Jews. Observation leads one to believe that substantial numbers of Jews do intermarry, that more men than women marry out of the Jewish faith, and that most children of mixed marriages are not raised as Jews. Several calculations enable us to advance beyond such observations in order to estimate the extent of assimilation among Argentine Jews.

First, the Argentine census of 1960 showed that more Jews married that year than could be accounted for in records of the Jewish community. Approximately 25 percent of Jews (male and female) who married in 1960 were married in non-Jewish rites (whether the partner was Jewish or not). Augmenting figures by 6 percent for marginal Jews and subtracting non-Jewish-rite marriages in which both partners may in fact have been Jews, we are left with an estimated rate of 30 percent of outmarriage.[33]

Second, clues derived from gaps in the statistical data confirm the observation that more men than women drop their affiliation with the Jewish community. In the age group fifteen to forty-four, there were 930 men for every 1,000 women, according to the 1960 census. The inference is that more young and middle-aged males than females declined to identify themselves as Jews.

Third, a distinction must be made between the completed fertility rate of Jewish women (including all their children) and the rate of Jewish births (including only those born who are considered Jewish and who thus increase the Jewish population). Using the first calculation, based on the number of live births reported by Jewish mothers, the current generation of Jewish women is not replacing itself. Schmelz and Della Pergola projected the 1960 birth rate onto the known number of Jewish women aged fifteen to forty-nine in 1960 and found a shortfall not of the anticipated 5 percent, but of 29 percent: 16,300 infants under the age of four in place of the expected 21,700. The difference represents infants born to Jewish mothers who had intermarried.[34]

The high and rising rate of intermarriage among Argentine Jews has been noted since Jews settled in that country. Its extent had never before been charted. Its ultimate impact, unless the trend should be reversed, would be the assimilation of Argentine Jews into the general population. Consistent with their hopes for Jewish survival, the tendency of Jewish organizations has been to deplore the trend to assimilation while continuing to count the offspring of mixed marriages as Jews. Recent research, however, forces the observer to face facts squarely. The Argentine Jewish community is steadily dwindling in size and faces a real question of viability.

Intermarriage and the assimilation to the majority culture that usually follows are universally regarded by Latin American Jews as the primary threat to their survival on the continent. The rapid and increasing rate of assimilation is deplored by Jewish leaders and is perceived by them as the most urgent item on the communal agenda. From the standpoint of non-Jewish Latin Americans, however, assimilation represents vindication of proimmigration forces who welcomed Jews to their shores. Assimilation continues the process that appeared first in the Curaçaoan Jewish community, then in the Dominican Republic, Venezuela, and elsewhere, a process at first confined to Sephardim. At first blush, Ashkenazim appeared to be more resistant to Hispanic and Portuguese cultures as well as to underlying indigenous and black elements. But German and French Jews assimilated quite readily and so eventually did the East Europeans. In the course of no more than three generations, substantial proportions of Jews have voluntarily abandoned their Jewish heritage in favor of an unalloyed national identity, despite the fact that there were few, if any, national institutions prepared to incorporate them together with their inherited culture. Persistent and diligent efforts on the part of other Jews to sustain and transmit their heritage on American soil failed to diminish the attraction Latin American cultures have exercised over the immigrants.

Abandonment of the Jewish heritage is almost always couched in secular terms: there are almost no conversions to Catholicism. Former Jews and their children tend to join the mass of the unchurched who are coming more and more to populate the Latin American urban centers. Anticlerical attitudes characteristic of this sector of the population transfer themselves readily to the Jewish "clerical" establishment, producing Jews who are "without confession," the equivalent of the "fallen away" Catholic. Where a secular milieu exists, Jews have shown themselves to be not only assimilable, but eager to assimilate.

The counterpart to assimilation may be emigration. Some Latin American Jews, rather than see their children abandon their Jewish identity, prefer to raise them in Israel or the United States, where their Jewish identity will be confirmed at the expense of their Latin identity. Jews at both ends of the spectrum—those who intermarry and ignore their Jewish heritage and those who emigrate in order to lead fuller lives as Jews—contribute to the cultural homogeneity of the Latin American peoples, who have not moved perceptibly toward adoption of an ideal of cultural pluralism.

9

Immigrants' Progress:
The Socioeconomic Status of
Jewish Communities Today

Most Jews entered the Latin American economies at the poverty level. Today, to the eyes of the observer, they appear to be middle or even upper class. The appearance is part truth, part illusion. Existing data on occupation and level of education, added to the demographic data presented earlier, enable us to develop a picture of the socioeconomic status of the Latin American Jewish communities. We can then turn to an exploration of the relationship between Jews as a class and the rest of society. This relationship is conditioned as much by myth as by reality.

Occupation

Analysis of the most recent Argentine census produced a coherent picture of the occupational distribution of Jews in that country. In 1960, 50 percent of Jewish males over age fourteen and 20 percent of women were in the work force. As compared with the total population of the country, this is a smaller percentage than average; the reason is the larger number of Jewish youth who attend school. As compared to the general population of Buenos Aires (where school attendance generally is higher), the Jewish proportion of employed is larger because many Jews are self-employed and do not abandon their business interests at age sixty-five.[1]

Among Jewish men in the Argentine work force, 37 percent are in commerce, 22 percent in industry, and 10 percent are executives and managers. For women, three groups each claim about 20 percent of the employed: secretaries, commerce, and the free professions. These percentages are all higher than for the general population.[2] In the younger age cohorts, fewer Jews are involved in commerce and more in the free professions and services. The number of farmers also dwindles with younger age groups. Most Argentine Jewish males are employers or self-employed. (The Argentine census defined "employer" as someone engaging at least one worker for pay.) Argentine Jewish women workers, on the other hand, are almost all employees.[3]

Schmelz and Della Pergola's analysis of the census data indicates clear differences between the Jewish and the general population. Jews are better educated; they are concentrated in white collar occupations; commerce is more significant among them; they tend to be employers or self-employed. These trends become more pronounced with younger age groups, except for the above-noted drop in commerce and rise in members of the free professions.[4]

Table 8 shows the chief occupations of Argentine Jews in 1960. It is clear that not all Argentine Jews have made it into the middle class. Ten thousand Jews remain in the old immigrant occupations of peddling or selling from a market stall or street kiosk; fifteen hundred persons, largely women, are servants in private homes. Twenty-four thousand production workers remain in the ranks of the Argentine proletariat.[5]

It took Argentine Jews four generations to achieve the mobility that Jewish immigrants to the United States achieved in two. This conclusion emerges from a recent study of Jewish males who joined the Khevra Kadisha (Burial Society, later Asociación Mutual Israelita Argentina, or AMIA) between the years 1895 and 1930. Contrary to general belief, Sofer finds that mobility during this period was fragile in the extreme: "The highest percentage of upwardly mobile workers are found . . . among those who arrived earliest and were able to establish themselves before class lines hardened. . . . The rising percentage of those sample members dying as workers . . . reflects an increased lack of mobility and hardening of class lines."[6]

During this thirty-five-year period, which encompasses the bulk of the Jewish migration, a surprising 80 to 90 percent of workers remained within three categories of occupation: skilled workers (the largest category at all six intervals sampled); "low nonmanuals" (including such occupations as street vendor, barber, railway station master, innkeeper, pawnbroker, hawker, bookkeeper); and "mid nonmanuals" (insurance

Table 8. *Jewish Participation in the Argentine Work Force,*
by Sex, Assorted Occupations, 1960

Occupation	Women	Men	Total
Total	23,652	95,409	119,061
Free Professions, including	4,731	7,471	12,202
Architects, engineers	91	1,481	1,572
Chemists, pharmacists	452	934	1,386
Physicians, surgeons, dentists	615	2,583	3,198
Teachers	2,542	686	3,228
Artists, writers	368	656	1,024
Executives, including	549	9,653	10,202
Managers, wholesale and retail stores	110	1,352	1,462
Owner-managers	405	7,851	8,256
Office employees, including	5,721	8,641	14,362
Accountants	1,090	1,861	2,951
Clerks	4,246	5,410	9,656
Commerce, including	5,155	35,415	40,570
Proprietors of stores	2,417	22,993	25,410
Peddlers, kiosk owners	2,510	5,784	8,294
Commercial agents	162	5,594	5,756
Market stalls, etc.	66	1,044	1,110
Farmers, hunters, fishermen, including	54	2,297	2,351
Owners, managers of farms	24	1,902	1,926
Miners, stonecutters	4	49	53
Transportation and Communication, including	36	1,133	1,169
Drivers	24	1,041	1,065
Factory workers, including	3,334	20,962	24,296
Textiles	479	2,695	3,174
Tailors, furriers	1,963	5,578	7,541
Shoemakers, tanners	179	1,652	1,831
Carpenters, woodworkers	26	1,888	1,914
Auto manufacture	69	1,180	1,249
Electricians (manufacture and repair)	27	991	1,018
Mechanics	35	1,516	1,551
Makers of precision instruments	75	1,569	1,644
Workers in service industries, including	2,014	1,704	3,718
Cooks, servants in private homes	1,529	40	1,569
Others and not known	2,058	8,133	10,191

Source: U. O. Schmelz and Sergio Della Pergola, *Hademografia shel hayehudim be-*
argentina ube-artzot aherot shel America ha-Latinit, pp. 119–20.

broker, warehouse keeper, manufacturer, import goods dealer, and so forth). There was a lot of movement back and forth between these groups, with self-employment filling intervals of unemployment. But it was very hard for these Ashkenazim to move up into the high non-manual or professional classes. Sixty percent of those who were workers when they joined the Khevra Kadisha were workers when the Khevra buried them. A range of 27 to 56 percent (depending on the year sampled) of those who were nonmanual workers when they joined the Khevra died in that same status.[7]

The garment industry employed more Jewish workers than any other: 64 percent of skilled workers in 1895, declining to 21 percent of the 1930 sample. The sweatshop, with its exploitative system of piece work in "inside" and "outside" shops, existed in Buenos Aires as it did in New York and London, with the difference that the cost of living was higher in Buenos Aires and that the country was so little developed that there was little demand for skilled labor outside the capital. Furniture workers and carpenters were the next largest category of skilled workers, their number starting at zero in the 1895 sample and rising to 23 percent toward the end of this period. Their upward mobility was more limited than that of the garment workers, possibly owing to the fact that it cost more for carpenters to buy themselves the needed machinery. Jewelers, who had the best working conditions of all, were less than 8 percent of any single sample.[8] The most common form of upward mobility was for a skilled worker to become a small shopkeeper. There was more lateral than upward movement, however, and substantial numbers of workers experienced downward mobility.[9] This poor performance is attributed to the fact that Argentina did not industrialize sufficiently during this period to generate opportunity for all immigrants. Official policy did not support local entrepreneurs— for example, by imposing tariffs to protect infant industry—and successive governments were never equal to the task of controlling inflation or relieving unemployment. It was only in 1945, with the accession to power of Juan Perón, that major modifications in the social structure finally took place. At that time, Jews began to approach the mobility patterns of Jews in the United States.[10] The Argentine case demonstrates clearly that opportunities for mobility are defined and limited by the economy and politics of the host society.

The way out of low-status occupations often ran through the university. In Argentina, this process, too, had to wait out a generation. A survey of fathers and their sons eighteen years old and older, which was conducted among Ashkenazim living in six Argentine cities in

1951, documents the process as it was just getting underway (see Table
9). Of the 1,899 families surveyed, the fathers of over half were first-
generation Argentine-born, 389 had one parent who was Argentine-
born, and 364 had two. Since we are talking about first, second, and
third-generation Argentinians, it is worth noting that the old immigrant occupations persist.

There were, however, differences between parent and son generations of 1951, among which the most significant were the near total
disappearance of the cuentanik, the halving of the percentage of merchants, the decline in the number of artisans, the doubling or more of
the percentage of Jews in the free professions, and the enrollment of
up to one-half of sons over age eighteen in the student population.

If we assume that members of the free professions hold a college
degree, then by adding these to the group of students, we can conclude
that at least one-half of the younger generation in this survey was col-

*Table 9. Occupations of Ashkenazic Fathers and Sons in
Six Argentine Communities, 1951 (percentages)*

Number of families surveyed	Mendoza 161	San Juan 94	Lanus 257	Córdoba 868	Santa Fé 392	Resistencia 127
Occupation of head of family						
Artisan	11.3	18.0	12.9	14.7	15.0	10.2
Merchant	59.5	57.8	49.0	53.2	52.4	76.4
Cuentanik	6.2	10.0	25.3	3.3	6.3	
Employee	3.2	5.6	4.3	5.8	11.0	4.0
Free professions	15.6	7.2	5.9	15.6	10.3	6.3
Workers			1.5	0.8	2.0	
Other	4.2	1.4	1.1	6.6	3.0	3.1
	100.0	100.0	100.0	100.0	100.0	100.0
Occupation of sons over age 18						
Artisan	3.2	2.1	7.9	5.3	10.4	5.7
Merchant	21.1	27.6	27.8	25.6	21.3	5.8
Cuentanik			5.9		1.2	
Employee	12.2	10.7	22.8	14.6	16.3	2.9
Free professions	31.6	35.0	12.9	28.8	27.6	28.6
Workers and Farmers		2.1	6.4	3.1	0.7	2.8
Unknown	1.9					
Student	30.0	22.5	16.3	22.6	22.5	54.2
	100.0	100.0	100.0	100.0	100.0	100.0

Source: Iejiel Harari, "Yahadut Argentina," pp. 22–23.

lege educated, with the exception of Lanus. An unknown percentage of "employees" might also be added to the cohort of universitarios. At the high point, nearly 62 percent of the younger group of Mendozan Jews were college educated. Resistencia shows all these trends in exaggerated fashion. This is the youngest of the six communities, and social ascent of its younger generation seems to have been correspondingly more rapid.

The dependence of immigrants upon prevailing economic and political conditions, which may prevent or compel, accelerate or deny, social mobility, is well illustrated by contrasting the Cuban with the Brazilian experience. We have seen that Jewish artisans in Cuba had great difficulty finding jobs in industry (because of the low level of industrialization) and even more difficulty hanging onto them (because of antiforeign labor legislation). The fact that they organized eight trade unions in the seven-year period 1929–36, in addition to joining Cuban unions where these existed, shows tremendous commitment to proletarian values, given the authoritarian nature of prevailing Cuban governments and the risks organizers ran of arrest and deportation. But all these unions shortly dissolved as their members were booted out of the proletariat and into the petite bourgeoisie. Their "upward mobility" was often more apparent than real in that many workers exchanged the regulated hours of factory work for unregulated exploitation in outside shops.

The success of these unwilling entrepreneurs was quite spectacular, as we learn from the dimensions of the Patronato that was dedicated in 1953. A contented Jewish bourgeousie was in fact created. A mere six years later, the revolution of 1959 altered the rules of the game once more. Fidel Castro and Che Guevara, in restructuring the Cuban economy along socialist lines, incidentally ruined the new Jewish entrepreneurs (many of whom, paradoxically, still cherished the socialist ideals of their youth). With the expropriation of their factories and shops, Jewish Cubans saw themselves reduced once more to the ranks of the proletariat, an event they perceived with a sense of déjà vu. They fled the island together with the rest of the middle class.

The Brazilian economic "miracle," taking off from a coup by modernizing military officers in 1964, created a milieu favorable to capitalism. An exceptionally prosperous class of Jewish entrepreneurs developed; at the date of writing, they exhibit great élan. Forty-one percent of the members of the Jewish community of São Paulo are in the work force. The occupational breakdown for the 11,926 economically active individuals contacted by Rattner's survey in 1968 showed that 27 percent were owners of firms and employers of a work force. Fifteen percent were directors and managers of business firms; another 15 percent were practicing one of the liberal professions; and 8.8 percent were self-employed artisans. Only 0.3 percent were manual workers.[11] By comparison, the Brazilian national census of 1960 showed 4.5 percent businessmen and managers in the general population, 1.5 percent in the liberal professions, and the vast majority in agriculture and manual labor. Although data are available for São Paulo only, it is likely that similar conclusions may be inferred for Jews elsewhere in Brazil and that, overall, Brazilian Jews, as classified by income and education, are upper-middle and lower-upper class. Rattner concludes, "On the evidence of data about the peculiar occupation structure of the Jewish community, corroborated by additional information about educational level, housing and land ownership in urban areas, travel overseas and general consumption patterns, we may assume that almost 2/3 of Brazilian Jews belong to the elite."[12]

Brazilian conditions have been favorable to immigrants generally, and the Jews' heady success should be seen in context: immigrants make up nearly half of paulista entrepreneurs and another third are the sons and grandsons of immigrants. Financial success, however, does not preclude the fact that Jews, along with other salient individuals, pay the price of political repression that is the other side of the coin of the economic miracle.

The remaining evidence we have for socioeconomic status of Latin American Jewry is more impressionistic. A survey of the Jews of Barranquilla, Colombia, in 1956 found that, of the 285 Sephardim in the city, 17 percent were in the highest income bracket, 41 percent were rated as somewhat lower, and 39 percent could be described in terms of their occupation and income as middle class. The class distribution of the 446 East Europeans was heavier at the lower end of the scale and lighter at the upper: 19 percent were making and selling shoes, 12 percent making and selling furniture. Among Sephardim, 96 percent of the work force were self-employed; among East Europeans, 95 percent. Interestingly, the figure for self-employed dropped to 68 percent among central European Jews, German-speakers being sought after as managers and foremen.[13]

When Barranquilla was surveyed again more than a decade later (together with two other Colombian communities), a more intense concentration in middle-class occupations was found and at a higher socioeconomic level. Among fathers of children attending Jewish parochial schools, 32 percent were owners of businesses or factories making such items as plastic, nylon, textiles, and metal; 42 percent owned small businesses employing fewer than ten persons; and 26 percent were members of the free professions.[14] As immigrants, the grandfathers of these children had been peddlers and workers (particularly shoemakers), with only a sprinkling of professionals. The grandchildren were making it into the petite (and in some cases, the haute) bourgeoisie.

Two self-studies of the Mexican Jewish community made three decades apart confirm the existence of a similar pattern. In 1940, 68.3 percent of economically active Ashkenazim were to be found in commerce, none in industry, and 2 percent in the liberal professions.[15] By 1970, these percentages were estimated at 60, 25, and 15 percent respectively.[16]

Every community reporting to *Comunidades judías* in its biennial editions (1966, 1968, 1970, 1971–72) notes a preponderance of its members in trade and industry, with a rising percentage of the upcoming generation entering the liberal professions. In this movement into professional life, the point of cathexis between the talents of immigrant children and the permeability of society at large is the university.

Education

Rural, preindustrial societies lack room or flexibility to accommodate persons who are different in custom or tradition. Access to positions of prestige and command is closed to immigrants in general and to Jews in particular. Only with the onset of industrialization does social mobility become possible for the outsider; often, his readiest channel of ascent is the university. As the need for an educated managerial and professional class becomes recognized, the immigrant finds that doors that were previously locked can be unlocked by the acquisition of needed technical and professional skills.

In the case of Jews, traditional emphasis on learning and the continuous provision of basic education to children equipped them to take advantage of the shift from traditional to modernizing attitudes in those countries where it occurred. In response to burgeoning opportunity in Brazil, Argentina, Chile, and elsewhere, they shifted their attention away from specifically Jewish studies to career-oriented curricula geared to local economies. In the process of this changeover, education for the purpose of perpetuating Jewish identity came to be replaced by education as a means of integrating themselves into the economies of their adoptive societies at successively higher levels.

Among the immigrants themselves, university education was a rarity.[17] Older sons of merchants and industrialists tended to enter their fathers' business; most had no time to go to college. It was their younger siblings, and more generally, their children, who benefited from university admissions policies in increasing numbers. The younger the age group, the more Jewish university students are found within it. In 1963, a self-study of Jewish residents of the Quilmes district of Buenos Aires showed that 3 percent of those aged fifty and over held a university degree. The percentage of *universitarios* rose to 12 percent for persons aged thirty to forty-nine and 19 percent for those aged twelve to twenty-nine.[18] Obviously, an age grouping that would bracket the usual university age more precisely should have yielded a higher percentage of students. This in fact emerged from the 1960 national census, which showed 40 percent of Jewish men and 21 percent of women aged twenty to twenty-four either attending college or with degree already in hand.[19]

A survey of the Jewish community of Valparaíso, Chile, in 1960, that reached 90 percent of avowed members or 1,050 individuals showed that 27 percent of sons born in the country were attending university. Concommitantly, the proportion of merchants dropped from 63 percent in the fathers' generation to 32 percent in the sons'. "Here as elsewhere," concludes the researcher, "youth move from trade to the free professions."[20]

In São Paulo today, nearly 66 percent of Jews aged twenty to twenty-four are enrolled at a university or higher technical school; an additional cohort of 24 percent of persons aged twenty-five to twenty-nine are so enrolled, as are 5 percent of persons aged thirty and over.[21] These figures contrast spectacularly with the 3.3 percent of the general population of the city who are receiving higher education.

The rush for a university education and its use as a means of social ascent is by no means restricted to Jews. Nisei (ethnic Japanese born in Brazil) comprise 10 percent of all matriculated students in São Paulo. The figures do not enable us to determine to what extent university enrollment is the result of some specifically Jewish factor and how much results from the situation of Jews as immigrants. But two-thirds enrollment of youth of university age is a fact that must be considered in delineating the profile of Brazilian Jews, as well as in assessing their contribution to culture and the economy.

The concentration of Jewish students in the free professions is marked for every community studied. The careers most heavily represented among Jewish universitarios of Quilmes were medicine, 27 percent; engineering, 12 percent; economics, 10 percent; pharmacy and biochemistry, 9 percent.[22] Twenty-six percent of second-generation Jews of Cali, Medellín, and Barranquilla, taken as a group, are presently practicing in the free professions, primarily in medicine, architecture, and engineering.[23] The most popular course pursued by Jewish university students of São Paulo is engineering (25 percent), followed by medicine (13 percent), economics and business administration (11 percent), and the law (11 percent).[24] Heavy representation in the law faculty indicates assurance on the part of students that they can make a living in this profession, which has traditionally exerted an attraction among Jews. One must then ask why a career in law is ignored by Jewish universitarios on the rest of the continent. Without data to guide us, intuition asserts that the lawyer, the *hombre de confianza*, [man of confidence], is a role to which Jews have not been admitted in the Spanish-speaking republics.

The data for São Paulo show that one-half of Jewish women aged twenty to twenty-four are attending university, where they comprise two-fifths of Jewish students. This is a continuation of the trend that appeared in earlier Argentine studies, which showed that in that country, 31 percent of Jewish students were women, as compared with 24 percent of women among university students generally (including the Jewish component).[25] The outcome of university education has been social mobility for women as well as for men. A recent survey of 125 Buenos Aires women engaged in stereotypically masculine professions found that a majority of the sample were daughters of immigrants; one-third of the cohort were Jews or daughters of Jews.[26]

The entry of Jews into the free professions in numbers far exceeding their proportion to the population conforms both to the patterns of Jewish history and to the developmental needs of their societies. That the latter is becoming more persuasive than the former is shown by the accelerating tendency to enter professions that relate to modernization, such as engineering, business administration, accounting, and architecture. Jews still become doctors, but there is more deployment throughout the economy. Rabbis, cantors, ritual slaughterers, and the other personnel of a religious life nowhere appear and must be imported from abroad.

Among the wealthiest group, there is a shift from communal schools at the elementary and secondary levels to prestigious secular schools in the private sector. The wealthiest Jewish families of Colombia no longer send their children to Jewish schools, but enroll them instead in United States–oriented private schools.[27] Mexican Jews show an increasing tendency to enroll their children in the more prestigious private schools, especially those where English is the language of instruction. The majority of Jewish youth of São Paulo who are of gymnasia or colegio age attend the great private schools of the city, those attended by the sons and daughters of the elite. There they not only learn their academic subjects but also make the professional and social contacts that will be invaluable to them in later life. The Jewish school, no matter how good academically—and some are very good indeed—cannot provide what is most desired by the present generation: entry into general society and upward mobility within it.

In seeking to gain acceptance, many Jews opt to forego their Jewish identity. This is a phenomenon common in the Western world since emancipation, but it appears to be most pronounced in Argentina. There society is even able to reward persons of Jewish descent who conform to the stereotyped ideals of Hispanic society. An interesting comparison has been made between the Argentine *Who's Who* (*Quien es Quien*) of 1939 and a directory of prominent individuals issued by the Jewish community in 1947.

Only 10 Eastern European Jews appeared among the almost 1500 entries in 1939 [*Quien es Quien*]. . . . Occupationally, they displayed patterns startingly different from the community as a whole. Six were authors, three were physicians, and one was an army colonel. Five married non-Jews and four married Jews. By 1947, there were 31 Jews listed among 2500 entries. Only two were women. *Only two of the total were involved in trade or industry.* [Emphasis supplied.] Doctors, attorneys, engineers, and authors accounted for 78 percent of the total. Of the 26 for whom marriage data were offered, 14 had married Jews while 12 did not. Between 1939 and 1947, newcomers to the *Quien es Quien* included seven Jewish lawyers, an accountant, a dentist, a pharmacist, and two industrialists involved in textiles and wearing apparel.[28]

Only one out of the forty-one Argentine Jews thought suitable for recognition by the general public was named in a directory of prominent Jews that appeared in 1947.

Cultural pluralism is not accepted as a valid ideal in Argentina, and Jews who are eager to join the mainstream often feel they must leave their Jewishness behind. This is most likely to occur during the university years, and the entry of increasing numbers of Jewish youth into university life has resulted in a noticeable lessening of the strength of the organized Jewish community. An anomalous situation arises from the fact that, particularly in Argentina, a significant number of intellectuals are of Jewish origin or are being taught by other intellectuals of Jewish origin. Their assimilationist course, which conforms to societal expectations, results in depriving Jewish communities of their intellectual leadership at a time when their full acceptance as citizens is by no means assured.

It was earlier shown that Jewish economic mobility, where it occurred, was a function of the ability of immigrants to fill a gap in the production and distribution of needed consumer goods. In similar fashion, Jewish social mobility may be seen as a function of the availability of educated Jewish personnel at times and in places where the demand for technically trained people was great enough to overcome traditional prejudices. Educational maintenance in community-sponsored schools, during periods when governments were failing to educate their own people, equipped Jews to participate in the economic development of their countries when attitudes had shifted sufficiently to permit them to do so. There can be no doubt, in surveying the occupations set forth in this chapter, that Jews added materially to the reservoir of skilled manpower so ardently desired by modernizing forces.

Social Class

It was said at the beginning of this chapter that the middle-class appearance of Latin American Jewry is both real and illusory. The reality is the spread of occupations and level of education displayed above, combined with the demographic variables presented in Chapter 8, all in the context of national economies that exhibit considerable polarity between rich and poor, the long-lived and the doomed. If we regard the term *middle class* as designating a statistical aggregation of persons exhibiting a middle range of measurable attributes, then Latin American Jewry is for the most part middle class. Jews earn intermediate levels of income, occupy comfortable housing, get a good education, have a long life expectancy, and are engaged in occupations that enable them to pass their bourgeois life style on to their children. Comprising a sector of the middle class as statistically aggregated, Jewish immigrants and their descendants have played an identifiable role in the modernization of the republics. If this population were to be treated as a separate entity on a chart delineating modernized characteristics,[29] they would show up together with Argentina, Uruguay, Chile, and portions of Brazil and Mexico as a modernized country. Considering their fragmentation, they might better be referred to as a modernized archipelago.

There are important caveats: 12 percent of the AMIA budget goes for social assistance, and its free kitchen continues to function as it did in immigrant days. The Jewish poor tend to be concealed because they are taken care of within the community and seldom come to the notice of public authority. Class structure is more complete among Jews of Argentina than in any other country; that is where the largest residue of Jews has gotten stuck in the lowest income categories—and Argentina is farthest away from the United States, the usual point of reference. It is possible also that anti-Semitic mythology operates here. Clichés such as "all Jews are rich," "the Jews control the pope," "Jews own Colombia," and the like, circulate freely in Latin America, creating an ambience in which the expectation is that the Jews one meets will be shockingly rich.

The expectation may appear to be borne out on first contact with mercantile and industrial Jewish entrepreneurs in the Caribbean basin. The prevailing ostentatious life style of the wealthy of this area is tempting and relatively easy to mimic, labor is cheap, and money will buy any amount of personal service. A life of conspicuous consumption, translated into North American labor costs, totals up to extremely high income levels. Actually, sloth can be sustained in Colombia or in Brazil quite cheaply, and a household with a dozen servants may be only middle class in terms of the size of estate of the head of household.

A more interesting way to look at the middle class is to ask in what way it functions within society. In an insightful analysis, Anthony Leeds points out that, in Europe and North America, middle-class persons perform certain "lubricating" functions, mediating and linking "the positions, networks, and organizations structuring the proletariats with those structuring the elites."[30] In this sense, the Jews' capacity to act as a middle class is severely circumscribed. There is a grave disconnection both socially and politically between Jews and their matrix societies, making it impossible for them as a group to exercise any of the linking or mediating functions usually associated with middle-class status. Thus, although from a North American perspective Latin American Jews are middle class, that status is illusory from an internal political point of view.

In both the Colombia studies cited in this work, the researchers found a wide discrepancy between income level and social status. The Jews of Barranquilla, whether foreign- or native-born, were aloof from politics in 1956, a phenomenon the author explains by reference to their commitment to business and their low social status. As of that date, no twentieth-century Jewish immigrant or son of an immigrant had ever held public office in Barranquilla.[31]

A decade and a half later, the same phenomenon was found to be at work in all three Colombian communities studied (Barranquilla, Medellín, Cali). Political participation among Jews was low. All reported voting regularly, but no one contributed to a political party, nor had anyone ever held public office. Political nonparticipation was attributed to "lack of acceptance in the upper social circles." This in turn was ascribed, not to anti-Semitism, but to social exclusion.[32] Upward links to the social elite did not exist for Jews.

Colombian Jewish communities illustrate the analytic worth of splitting the term "middle class" into categories: one reckoned by measurable attributes and one by mediatory functions. Rated by occupation, education, income level, place of residence, and other factors, Colombian Jews exhibit all the attributes of middle-class status. But performing traditional mediatory functions of a middle class is totally out of the question, for Jews are no more acceptable to the Colombian elite than they are to the Chibcha Indian. This disjuncture between income level and social status can be observed in every Jewish community. Though most Jews exercise a middle range of occupations and enjoy middle-class life styles, as a class they play no mediatory role in their societies.

Part of the Jews' lack of acceptability to other groups stems from their identification with commerce. Depreciation of entrepreneurial pursuits has been remarked on for all Latin American societies and has had a deleterious effect on all immigrants, not Jews only. Because entrepreneurs as a class lack social prestige, entrepreneurial talent tends to be drawn from the foreign-born or first-generation sons of Spanish and Italian immigrants. Of 119 high-level Argentine industrialists surveyed in 1959, only 11 were members of the criollo upper class.[33] Immigrant entrepreneurs and parvenus do not all at once achieve social status commensurate with their wealth; but within this deprecated group, Jews and Arabs find themselves "subordinated." Coming from the bottom rungs of the social ladder, they have a longer and a harder climb to the top. The obstacles they face are more numerous and more intractable than those that confront other parvenus.[34] Other immigrants attempted to compensate for their low social status by acquiring the outward symbols of upper-class grace, such as membership in the best social clubs and marriage into old families. But for Jews, social ascent is blocked: they cannot get into the "old boy" network. The extent of Jewish linkages upward varies from country to country but is everywhere limited. Nowhere do Jews have access to the traditional dominant triumvirate of the church, the armed forces, and the landowning oligarchy. Their exclusion from the first and last is a foregone conclusion. Less comprehensible is that they should also be excluded from the army officer corps. Record exists of one Jewish colonel in the Argentine army, but the possibility of a military career for Argentine Jews was foreclosed in the nationalistic thirties. Secret brotherhoods control access to crucial decision-making posts within the army, and during seven years (1966-73) of military control, their exclusivism became diffused to the national scene. In the opinion of one scholar, "Many Jews were removed as individuals from senior posts which they held in the administration. This political vulnerability of the Jews, as a group and as individuals, originates not only in their socio-economic stratification but also—and perhaps principally—in the fact that they are Jews."[35] It is also probable that Jewish officeholders were removed for partisan reasons bearing no relationship to their Jewishness. The effect, however, is the same: with a small population base to begin with, the removal from office of the few existing Jewish public officials results in a return to a policy of limpieza.

In Chile and Brazil, the presence of several Jewish officers in the armed forces was continually alluded to by respondents as evidence that Jews are well integrated into those countries. Jewish officers were not detected in other national armies. The assumption of respondents who were questioned on the matter was that a man who worked his way up through the military hierarchy would have to be one who had left his Jewish origins far behind. In Argentina, there was no way to put them far enough behind.

Brazil is the only republic in which Jewish officeholders can be identified on a continuing basis. In 1977, there were three Jews in the Chamber of Deputies, as well as several Jewish state legislators and councilmen. Two federal agencies—the National Housing Bank and the Brazilian Institute for Statistics and Geography—were headed by Jewish individuals. Curitiba, capital of the state of Paraná, has elected itself two Jewish mayors. The state secretary of transport for Rio de Janeiro, the state secretary of planning for São Paulo, and the state secretary of science, culture, and technology are posts that have been held by Jews in recent years.[36] Jewish participation in politics is relatively high, and Jews like other Brazilians pay the price of political involvement: in October 1975, Wladimir Herzog, director of educational television and a well-known journalist, died in military headquarters, where he had been brought for interrogation.

Jews are more diffused politically through the governing structures of Brazil than any other of the republics. Individuals from the important commercial families Lafer, Klabin, Moses, Bloch, and Levy have entered politics as ministers of state, bankers, and presidential advisers. There are Jews in numerous government posts and in significant military positions. The feeling of security engendered in Brazilian Jews by their political integration was, however, seriously undermined when, in November 1975, the Brazilian government voted in favor of United Nations Resolution 3379 equating Zionism with racism.[37]

Insofar as downward linkages are concerned, Jews as a group lack relationships with either the peasantry or the proletariat. This is a startling fact, considering that so large and so vocal a portion of Jewish immigrants arrived with leftist ideologies. But the Jewish labor activists who so alarmed conservative elites in Argentina, Uruguay, and Cuba in the early decades of this century were ahead of their time. They met little positive response from the masses, and severe political repression from the elite, both as activists and as Jews. Fear of further repression combined with economic opportunity to turn the majority of the Jewish proletariat into a bourgeoisie, with the results we have already surveyed: a Jewry that, in statistical terms, is almost completely middle class. Now that radical modes of thought are igniting the Latin American masses from one end of the continent to the other, the advantaged economic position of Jews is no longer conducive to alignment with leftist or populist forces. Bundism, communism, and the whole panoply of radical ideologies have been confined to the shadow play of kehillah elections.

Here lies a major source of dissension between old and young generations, for many Jewish universitarios accept the New Left position that being Jewish and being progressive are incompatible. Increasingly, Jewish youth cut their ties with their parents and with the Jewish community in order to earn credentials in progressive circles and join what they feel to be the wave of the future. But acceptance into radical forces is not automatic. Jews are not welcome in the Montoneros guerrilla movement in Argentina. They are excluded qua Jews from the Uruguay Tupumarus. Individual Jews have been associated with some governments of the Left, but this association has brought special problems' to the Jewish communities of those countries. For example, the Chileanization policies of President Salvador Allende Gossens (1970–

73), which aimed at creating a "socialist society through law," were in part designed by Senator Volodia Teitelboim, chief strategist of Chile's Communist party. These policies conformed both to the traditional Jewish demand for social justice and to the Chilean people's demand for equitable distribution of the wealth, as reflected in the election of Allende to the presidency. But they had the effect of provoking attacks upon the president because he was surrounded by Jews. The upsurge of anti-Semitism that accompanied the initiation of Allende's program took as its target not just those Jews who were members of his administration, but the entire community, which was held responsible for the fact that some Jews are Marxists. This was only one horn of the dilemma for Chilean Jews. The other was the flight from the country of the wealthiest members of the community, caused by fear of expropriation. As is well known, many middle-class Chileans abandoned their homeland at this time. The presence of Jews among their number (up to a fifth of the community) underscores the fact that Jews tend to behave more or less like everybody else; but their departure did little to mitigate attacks upon the community for harboring Marxists. At the same time, withdrawal of the emigrés' financial support badly damaged Jewish community services, a blow the now smaller and poorer community had difficulty absorbing.

In assuming control of Chile, the military junta that ousted Allende set about reestablishing a reassuring climate for business. Many middle-class persons, Jews among them, returned to the country. But Chilean Jews were newly aware of their dependence upon the goodwill of the powers that be; a strong conservative trend set in among Chilean Jews, who now felt that they would pay the price of social experimentation.

Attachment to a reactionary regime may not offer any greater security. Nicaraguan dictator Anastasio Somoza, an ally of the state of Israel on the international scene, attracted the allegiance of Nicaraguan Jews. In the wake of his fall from power in 1979, Nicaraguan Jews abandoned the country. Political losers have traditionally paid the price of imprisonment or exile from Latin America; but Jewish losers transmit their losses to the entire community.

The Jews' lack of acceptability to other groups lies in the endemic anti-Semitism of various strata of the Latin American populations. We have seen that anti-Semitism was an integral element of Spanish and Portuguese rule. The belief system that validated Jew hatred was transferred to the New World by the missionary and inquisitorial activities of the Catholic church. After a period of quiescence that may be ascribed to the fact that there were no longer any Jews around, anti-Semitism surfaced again in the twentieth century. It was exacerbated by commercial rivalry, real or imagined, and most notably by the Red scare of 1919, with the results issuing in Semana Trágica. In the 1970s, anti-Semitism is almost exclusively politically motivated.

There were at all times in the history of Latin America individuals and classes who were disinterested in scapegoating and concerned with the modernization of social attitudes, including the demythologizing of the Jews. Masonic lodges, with their history of opposition from the church, were receptive to Jews as allies. Positivists in Brazil and Mexico welcomed European Jews as modernizers. Anticlericals deprecated the teachings of the church with regard to the Jews and indeed often became pronounced philo-Semites, collecting Jewish and converso memorabilia and endowing themselves retroactively with Sephardic ancestors. It has been noted that individual nonconformists and rebels sometimes identified with the ultimate nonconformity of the Jews. In recent years, important elements within the hierarchy of the Catholic church, particularly in Peru and Chile, have collaborated with the organized Jewish communities to reduce the level of free-floating anti-Semitism in the spirit of the enlightened encyclicals of John XXIII.

Nevertheless, the Hispanic Catholic mold has been resistant to change. In Argentina, the nation that appeared most receptive to heterogenous immigration, two forms of anti-Semitism have been identified by the Argentine sociologist Gino Germani. One is rooted in the upper class, is ideological in nature, part of an authoritarian syndrome, and takes the form of exclusion of Jews from clubs and decision-making elites. The other is rooted in the mass of the people, is traditional in nature, linked to the medieval interpretation of Catholicism, and represents a passive acceptance of stereotypes.[38] This latent hatred of Jews has been little touched by aggiornamento, the movement to update the teachings of the Catholic church. It lies about the political landscape available for activation by parties of the right or of the left. Anti-Semitism began to color the national politics of Argentina in 1973-74, when a hate campaign was loosed against José Ber Gelbard, finance minister in the "Resurrection" government of Juan Perón. Gelbard, who never denied his origins as a Jew and a peddler, became the focus of an anti-Semitic attack aimed at splitting him from the president and weakening the administration. That a cabinet minister should come under attack for his policies is natural; but the fury of the racism that surfaced in this connection took the Jews of Buenos Aires by surprise and shook their self-confidence as Argentines. In Argentina, individual

9. *Covers of two anti-Semitic publications typical of those that circulate wide-ly in the Latin American republics. The discredited libel,* Protocols of the Elders of Zion, *is sold on many street corners along with lottery tickets and, for the superstitious, Stars of David. (Courtesy of the American Jewish Committee)*

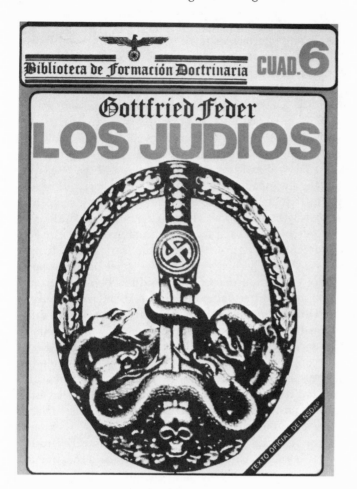

Jews may be, and have been, appointed to high office; but once there, they become vulnerable to attack as Jews.

The most active manipulators of anti-Semitic attitudes in recent years have been the cults centered around Nazi war criminals who found refuge in Latin America and Arab cadres who have forged a bond between Middle Eastern and Latin American guerrillas.

Numerous fascist organizations are currently operating in Argentina, fueled by ideas scavenged from the wreckage of the Third Reich. Anti-Semitic newspapers and magazines such as *El Fortín, Cabildo, Restauración,* and *Patria Peronista* are widely sold, and the principles they espouse are highly inflammatory, including one declaration that read: "We confirm that the white-slave trade and drug traffic are two instruments utilized by Zionist imperialism to corrupt our youth. This should be investigated as a conspiracy against our nation."[39] In February 1975, a government-controlled television station broadcast a dramatization of *La Bolsa,* the hoary anti-Semitic libel the newspapers had serialized three generations back. The "Andinia Plan," fabricated by the professional anti-Semite Walter Beveraggi Allende, continues to circulate, popularizing the paranoid delusion that there exists an international conspiracy to create a Jewish state in the south of Argentina.

Radical groups aligned with Arab terrorist groups in the Middle East have also become overtly anti-Semitic, disguising their prejudice as anti-Zionism. Argentine leftists attack Jews for having links with Israel and Israel for having links with imperialist powers that once held Argentina in a position of economic dependency. Ismael Jacinto Haiek, leader of a Montoneros commando cell in La Plata, is known to have been in contact with Yasir Arafat of the Palestine Liberation Organization and George Habash, head of the Popular Front for the Liberation of Palestine. Such contacts are not limited to Argentines. When, in December 1978, the PLO and Rejectionist Front offered their assistance to the Sandinista Front for the Liberation of Nicaragua, they issued a joint statement attacking "the racist state of Israel." There is evidence that the PLO is establishing relations with revolutionary groupings all over Latin America, to match its ties with Irish, Basque, and Japanese terrorist groups. The implications for Latin American Jews are threatening.

More than a thousand cases of Argentine Jews who have been arrested and detained without trial or notification of the charges against them are known to the Anti-Defamation League of the United States, which receives appeals from relatives and friends of the missing. Synagogues, Jewish schools, clubs, and newspapers have come under attack at an accelerating rate in recent years. It must be emphasized that these events are taking place in the context of civil war. There were eleven hundred political murders in Argentina in 1975. Eight thousand cases of political violence took place in the country between May 1973 and December 1975, according to the Argentine minister of the interior,[40] and priests figured in that number, as well as ordinary citizens and foreigners. The escalating violence of Argentine life is affecting all sectors of the population; other things being equal, it is probably not helpful to a political target to be Jewish.

Unrepresented in church, landed oligarchy, army, labor union, peasant syndicate, or guerrilla movement, Jews might, more than other middle-class sectors, look to the ballot box for political expression. But the electoral process functions only partially and intermittently in Latin America. This typically middle-class instrumentality is not available to Jews as a group any more than it is to other would-be power contenders who have failed to establish their capabilities by gaining control over a mass of "voters." One respondent, a teacher in a Jewish school who had lived in Mexico City for fifty years, reported: "I vote. They want you to vote. But of course I cannot participate in any of the decisions concerning whom I may vote for. That is quite closed to us foreigners." Taking the point a step farther, a respondent who was born in Mexico told of a conversation he had held with members of a Chamber of Commerce in a small city near the capital. He had asked what the chances were of getting political backing for a certain candidate (Jewish) for the national assembly. The gist of the reply was: "We are very glad to have you here, you Jews, you are good for business. But please, don't try to mix in our affairs."

Mexican xenophobia may be extreme, but respondents in all countries referred to the lack of channels for political expression. There is some scope for the practice of *shtadlanut* (the private approach to a ruler to redress some grievance or gain an advantage). By such means, Jewish associates of President Allende were apparently enabled to leave Chile when the military junta took over. But shtadlanut is no substitute for an institutionalized representative process. As an example, it is said that President Juan Perón made overtures to the Jewish community of Buenos Aires in search of their support; but today, a quarter of a million Jews live in the area without exerting any discernible impact on the administration of the city or of the country.

In the absence of political and social linkages, Jews are defined totally by their economic functions. Their character as an entrepreneurial community shows up in high relief against the background of a society and a culture that traditionally despised the entrepreneur. But political isolation results in even greater emphasis on economic activity because only wealth provides protection against disaster. Over the past twenty years, the size of Latin American Jewish communities has fluctuated with the rise and fall of governments favorable to the free enterprise system. Jews have been attracted to, and have remained in, nations that offered free scope to the entrepreneurial spirit and have abandoned republics whose social policies included the expropriation of private property. This has happened notwithstanding the fact that individual Jews have frequently been among the initiators and proponents of such policies.

While Cuba and Chile lost considerable numbers of Jews in the past two decades, Venezuela and Ecuador have gained. The Venezuelan Jewish community reported a 30 percent increase in numbers between 1970 and 1972 (estimates went from twelve to fifteen thousand to fifteen to seventeen thousand).[41] Allowing for the propensity of the communities to inflate their population figures, there was nevertheless visible growth. This is attributable to the boom in petroleum production, which caused the government to ease immigration restrictions in order to attract modernizing elements from abroad, among them, Jews. The Ecuadorean community, founded under conditions of stress, dwindled to one-fifth its original size as the country's economy stagnated in the postwar years. It has recently resumed growth as the development of a domestic petroleum industry sparked an economic boom. The new arrivals included entrepreneurs in flight from Allende's Chile.

These movements render the reduction of Jewish populations to a statistical table even riskier than originally set forth. Jews come closer than any other group to embodying the continental dream variously enunciated by Simon Bolívar and by Che Guevara: the dream of one united continent undivided by political barriers. Jews, excluded from political and social participation, tend to move from one Latin American country to another according to economic opportunity and the stress of the moment. In a way that would have surprised both Bolívar and Guevara, these movements can be read as a barometer of the capitalist system. The clustering of Jews in commercial and industrial activities, without extensive linkages upward and downward throughout society, leaves them more vulnerable to change in the marketplace than any other group. Unfavorable economic indicators are sufficient to set numbers of the group in motion, looking for economic security sufficient to offset the emotional insecurity with which they live.

Insecurity pervades Latin American Jewish communities today, not because they failed to act as the modernizers they were anticipated to be, but because they succeeded. That success now makes them a target of the new modernizers. Jews are not represented in those agencies that increasingly control the modernization process: the armed forces and revolutionary groupings. The breakup of existing economic organizations and the restructuring of national economies along communist or autarkic lines result in destruction of the economic base of Jewish communities. Such policies need not be anti-Semitic in order effectively to bring an end to Jewish life in the country, as the Cuban experience shows. Joined with anti-Semitism, such attacks could be devastating.

Faced with similar dilemmas in the past, Jews sought allies among liberals and progressives. But today, progressive sectors increasingly adopt anti-Jewish postures. The linkup between Latin American populists and Third World movements elsewhere, particularly in the Arab world, means adoption of anti-Israel policies, an orientation that cannot but transfer itself to the people who call themselves israelitas. As the old ideological issues dissipate and are replaced by others that agitate a broader mass of people, progressives make the same discovery long known to reactionaries: that in manipulating the masses, ancient religious hatreds can be useful.

10

Jews North and South:
A Comparison

Jewish life in the United States provides a useful base for examination
of Jewish life in Latin America. The contrast between the two communities points up differences that stem not from the immigrants (for they
were similar in their origins and part of the same migratory waves) but
from the nature of the host societies in which they settled.

Jews of the United States dwell within the boundaries of one of the
world's largest territorial sovereignties, characterized by pacific alterna-
tion of governments, secular norms, and a social milieu created by immigrants. Jews of Latin America are scattered throughout twenty-one
separate polities, characterized by volatile political scenes, hierarchical
religious norms, and a social milieu that was created long before their
arrival and to which they were expected to conform. Examining the
social structures of the two realms, one is struck over and over again by
the reluctance of Latin Americans to make the changes that would
have been necessary to integrate immigrants into their national societies. Although it cannot be said that the United States was totally accommodating in this regard, comparison shows the far more limited
flexibility of Latin American institutions and their near total imper-
meability by Jews.

The Jewish community of the United States came into existence
within a society that had been spun off from Europe in the Age of Enlightenment. The Jewish communities of Latin America came into
existence in societies that had been founded and still were grounded

238

in the pre-Enlightenment past. Jews were emancipated by their arrival in the United States; Jews of the Latin American republics have not been fully emancipated yet. Everything that distinguishes the Jewries of these two continents flows from this disparity.

Spain in America was a fragment of medieval Europe that, once loosed from its European context, evolved along its own internal lines of development. Incorporating Indians and then blacks into the lower rungs of the corporate and patrimonial structure, Latin American societies took on an American coloration but retained their medieval orientation. (In Louis Hartz's formulation, "the logic of feudal fragmentation" persisted, resulting in a "heartbreaking betrayal" of the Enlightenment.)[1] The conquistadors were the last and the most successful of the crusaders, and if the latifundia that were settled upon their successors were not precisely feudal estates, clearly they owed more to the institution of feudalism than they did to either freehold tenure or industrial capitalism. Spanish and Portuguese statism, revived and strengthened by transplantation into virgin territory overseas, met no countervailing power strong enough to challenge it, and consequently life in the Indies quickly settled down on foundations long familiar to the peninsulars.

If Spain and Portugal were able, as they were, to resist the forces of Protestant and of industrial revolutions, how much more resistant were the forces of tradition in these new nuclei of Iberia, whither only the orthodox could emigrate. Having destroyed the Amerindian civilizations, the conquerors grafted onto the ruins their own vision of the just society: Catholic, hierarchical, patrimonial. With certificates of cleanliness of blood, they purchased posts in government and church, becoming the bureaucrats and managers of empire. The tone of Latin American society was set by royal pensioners and true believers, whose allegiance for the next three centuries was to remain immutably fixed to their royal masters upon whom they depended for their wealth and status. They would never have left the kingdom had not the kingdom left them. When the French Revolution and Napoleon's invasion of Spain and Portugal cut the tie that bound, Enlightenment did not rush suddenly in. Instead, criollo elites took their nations out of the empire, generating "independence" revolutions that guaranteed that nothing in fact would change. Thus, medieval forms of life survived in Latin America long after their European originals had succumbed to modernizing forces. These medieval forms included legal and social inhibitions upon Jews.

North America began receiving European settlers two hundred

years later than South and Central America. During the intervening period, Europe exclusive of Iberia went through a great transformation. The Reformation and the wars of religion cracked forever the universal pretensions of the Catholic church, paving the way for religious competition. A wave of rationalism began the rout of all religions, a process that was to bring to birth the Age of Enlightenment and lead eventually to the emancipation of the Jews. Industrial revolution transformed Europe's modes of production, while capitalism began to alter the relationship between employer and employed. By the eighteenth century, Europe was entering the modern age, and Jews were beginning to be freed of the ages-old restrictions on residence, occupation, and family life that had trammeled them for centuries.

As a result of the difference in timing, the people who settled North America were different in mentality from those who had conquered the South. The eighteenth-century efflux of settlers out of England especially and North Europe generally were the unlicensed and the unemployed, dissenters from old religions and cast-offs of the new industrialism, looking for land and work to set their hands to. Devotees of eccentric cults, they had reason to fear state churches and came more and more to view religion as beyond the grasp of government. Catholics, Lutherans, and others who in Europe had belonged to state churches were now in a minority and in time would have to tailor their beliefs to the new American reality. The rational revolution was beginning to make its impact; many were prepared to believe that the world was subject to natural laws, or at least to the laws of nature's God, and that man's relationship to this God was a purely personal affair.

In contrast to the image of the deicide, the devil, the usurer, the bawd, that confronted Jewish immigrants to Spanish- and Portuguese-speaking lands, Jewish immigrants to the English colonies found elements favorable to themselves. South Carolina's charter had been drafted under the influence of John Locke, author of the first published appeal for emancipation of the Jews in the English-speaking world. The Puritans thought of themselves as Hebrews, "children of the covenant," who had been brought to New England's promised land by divine providence. Emphasis by fundamentalist sects upon the reading of the Old Testament led to the teaching of Hebrew in order that God's word could be heard in the original. Ancient Hebrew prophecy was one source of nourishment for the Enlightenment, and thus the climate of the colonies owed much to the Old Testament tradition. Jews coming into the colonies that inherited libertarian ideas found a

friendlier welcome than those who came to lands whose heritage—
never fully repudiated—included the Inquisition.

The nonconforming and dissenting colonists of the North rebelled
against royal authority on very slight pretext, when it seemed as though
Parliament was abandoning the liberal tradition. Placing power in the
hands of the people, the colonists devised a constitution that limited
the power that either government or church could wield over the citizen, by forbidding them to buttress one another. The anticlerical thrust
of the Enlightenment made inevitable the separation of church and
state, without the need to fight a war of religion on American soil.
Emancipation of the Jews was thus achieved in the United States without bloodshed and without reference to Jews, for there were almost
none in the country at the time. From the moment the republic was
launched, Jews enjoyed full civil, religious, and political equality.
There were to be no religious tests for office, no bar to the marriage or
burial of Jews, no limitations on place of residence or occupation.
Furthermore, the terms of revolution from the mother country offered
the promise that American society would continue to open outward,
rather than collapse in upon itself as had happened so quickly in Spanish and Portuguese realms. The break with Europe allowed Jews to
feel that they, too, had broken with the desolate past, that the United
States would be a different kind of diaspora, one where Jews could live
on equal terms with Gentiles because their values sprang from the same
sources and were compatible with one another.

Lacking an established church, the United States attracted immigrants of every religious persuasion and none. The diverse flow of peoples in turn confirmed the heterogeneous nature of American life. Immigrants arrived in such masses, into territory so nearly unpopulated,
that they created their own social norms, establishing as the national
ideal the actuality of their own existence: the plural society. No one
would deny that it was the dominant white, Protestant, Anglo-Saxon
male who set standards, but this dominance was not monolithic and
never so absolute as to exclude Jews. There was room for the Jewish
as for the non-Jewish immigrant; a variety of identities could coexist.
The social norm of cultural pluralism that developed in response to
the immigrant experience was never completely accepted. Curiously, it
was allowed to flourish side by side with the WASP ideal.

As a direct consequence, participation by Jews in the life of the
United States has regularly been welcomed as a sign that they were
becoming Americanized. This process went so far that by the mid-
twentieth century, Judaism was being accorded status as the third ma-

jor religious group in the country, despite the fact that Jews never accounted for more than 3.7 percent of the population.

In total contrast, the Jews of Latin America have had great difficulty overcoming the perception of themselves as foreigners, unwelcome and illegitimate intruders into national life, and even as corrupters of the national spirit. The Jewish immigrant to Latin America came to a continent already preempted by two powerful cultural traditions that either ignored him or were hostile to him. The first of these, the autochthonous one, was not attractive to Jews. The vestiges of Maya, Guaraní, Inca civilizations had nothing to offer either Ashkenazi or Sephardi; nor did Jews have a place in the indigenous world, save in that role of diablo to which the missionaries had consigned them. Entry into their new societies had to depend on identification with the Spanish or the Portuguese.

The same was true for all immigrants: the common meeting ground was the church. But the church, which had compassionately absorbed Indian and black, Italian and Pole, found Jews indigestible. The Jews were the one people whom the church had failed historically either to absorb or destroy. In the unreconstructed atmosphere of Latin Catholicism, where the line between church and state was blurred and overlapping jurisdiction persisted, Jews continued to be viewed as unassimilable. If they were outside the church, were they not also outside the state?

Until the present, national allegiances continue to be filtered through Catholic sensibilities. Most Latin American constitutions require that the president of the nation profess Roman Catholicism. The ubiquitous Christ figures displayed on mountain tops are a continual reminder of the Jews' inherited status as deicides. The more compassionate Catholic rendition of history, which reminds the faithful that Christ himself was a Jew, invites masochistic submission. The child in the classroom is daily asked to identify with either the crucified or the crucifiers. The choice of either role requires continual dissimulation and suppression. The Jewish child must either pretend to be that which he is not or pretend not to be that which he is. Either choice results in utilization of only half of his cultural heritage and the expenditure of a great deal of energy in suppressing the other half.

There are, of course, ecumenical efforts within the Latin American church. The number and influence of clerics working toward rapprochement varies from country to country. But the end toward which they strive—the reception of Jews into a brotherhood formerly restricted to Catholics—represents a difficult break with the past. This break, the all-important emancipation, occurred in the United States before the drafting of the Constitution.

On the part of the Jews, every attempt to identify with the majority culture brought them up against its essentially Catholic core, the centrality of the Inquisition mentality, and their own role as victims. Despite the lapse of centuries and the historical discontinuity between Spain and the Spanish-speaking republics, echoes of the Expulsion reverberated in immigrant ears. The principal park of Mexico City, the Alameda, where children play and Diego Rivera painted, was known to them as the site of the auto-da-fé, where New Christian pioneers were reduced to ashes by their Old Christian companions. One of the main streets of Lima was still known as Matajudíos, Kill-the-Jews; Havana boasted streets named Inquisador and Picoto (Gibbet). In colonial times, Jews had been pariahs. In modern times, omnipresent Catholic symbolism confirmed their status as outsiders, limited their access to education and to politics, and impeded their social acceptability.

We have seen that many Jewish immigrants to Latin America were alienated from their Jewish heritage and thus available for recruitment for life in lands where the survival of Judaism was not at all assured. Had the Latin American republics signaled their willingness to break with the past by developing secular national symbols with their origins in modern times, the way would have been paved for the acceptance of Jews into national life on the basis of equality. Hopeful immigrants at the turn of the century believed this was occurring. There is a world of difference between merging with a secular population on equal terms and accepting a subordinate position on a Catholic standard. To the degree that the Latin republics failed to evolve along secular lines, Jews were closed out of dominant social institutions. Where no neutral ground appeared between antagonistic Iberian and Jewish traditions, emergence of a Latin American Jewish identity was frustrated.

Pressure for conformity was felt by all immigrants, but a Jew had harder choices to make. He had to choose between continuing to feel a part of the Jewish people (which implied isolation from his fellow Bolivians or Argentinians) or starting anew as part (but not an integral part) of the Bolivian or Argentinian nation. The adjustment required was more demanding than that required of Catholic Italians and Spaniards. The terms in which the choice was presented were more urgent than the terms offered by societies that accepted cultural diversity. Those Jews who continued to identify primarily as Jews ended by constructing for themselves their own private societies, within which everyone was known to everyone else and responsible for their behavior. Jews who preferred to become fully functioning members of their national societies dropped their Jewish identity in order to gain acceptance.

Under these circumstances, it is difficult to forecast with confidence the emergence of a neo-Sephardic consciousness. Perhaps the nearest approximation surfaced in the words spoken by an elderly Jew in an attempt to summarize her life in Eucador. "We are Catholic Jews," she said. The phrase reflects acceptance of an ambiguous but tenable position as a subordinated minority within a patrimonial framework. It is not a status that would be acceptable to many persons in the post-Enlightenment world. As a subordinated minority, Jews are permitted to occupy a well-defined niche in society (usually defined in terms of commercial and financial services rendered) but are excluded from the centers of decision making. Expressions of creativity emerging from a specifically Jewish tradition are stifled by law, by social pressure, or by self-censorship.

In the United States, numerous institutions evolved that took as their task the Americanization of the immigrant. Foremost among these was the universal, tax-supported, public school. Notoriously, children were taught the pledge of allegiance before the alphabet. The primary interest of the state was in Americanizing the child; reading and writing could come later. A close adjunct to this process was the free night school for immigrants. It is not irrelevant that the prototype of such schools was opened in Baltimore in 1889 by Henrietta Szold, daughter of an immigrant Hungarian rabbi. Its first clients were Russian Jews, and the subjects taught were American history and the English language. The assumption of responsibility for this school by the city of Baltimore represented a clear acceptance of the obligation to teach the newcomers English and prepare them for citizenship. Subsequently, the system of adult night school education became a permanent part of the American educational scene and remains with us today.

Universal military conscription into the citizen army of the United States during World War I was another homogenizing experience for immigrants. Work in the industrial plant, where labor, like machines, was viewed as interchangeable, helped to obliterate distinctions between white ethnic groups, whether immigrant or Yankee. Standardization of behavior patterns was speeded by the continentwide network of transportation and communication, which made it possible for immigrants to blend to a national, rather than a merely regional, standard.

None of these nationalizing forces had free play in the Latin American republics. Burdened with some of the most difficult terrain in the world, Latin American communications and transportation responded to regional, not continental, exigencies. Industrialization did not really get under way until World War I; abstention from that conflict meant that citizen armies—the great democratizing force ever since the French Revolution—never came into being. To the contrary, in the anomie that followed independence, soldiering degenerated into banditry. As for public education, it was the victim of the most profound apathy and prejudice on the part of legislators.

In the absence of nationalizing institutions, immigrants to Latin America were left largely on their own when it came to restructuring their lives to suit the conditions of their new homes. Inevitably, they tended to perpetuate the pattern of life of the old country, since it was the only one they knew. This process operated on all nationality groups and marginalized them from the political process. Its impact on Jewish immigrants was particularly severe because Jews were themselves divided into numerous ethnic groups characterized by differences in language, custom, and religious practice. In their search for solidary relationships, Jews reproduced the varied institutions of their countries of origin. In the process, they unintentionally walled themselves off from one another as well as from the larger society. The result was that welter of interethnic rivalries that incapacitated the communities for concerted action.

Since Jewish immigrants to the United States originated in the same widely varied migrations, the same potential for divisiveness existed among them. Indeed, at the close of the colonial period, rivalry did develop between "aristocratic" Sephardim and "parvenu" Germans. Later, the aloof attitude of German Jews was to afflict impoverished East Europeans. But despite episodes of conflict, these interethnic feuds did not become institutionalized as they did in Latin America. Remnants of landsmenschaften survive in the United States, but they are utterly powerless and cater mostly to the social needs of the elderly. The representative and philanthropic bodies of active American Jewish life embrace Jews of every ethnic origin. In acculturating to a United States standard, Jews acculturated to one another.

The Americanization of immigrants was undertaken in religiously neutral terms. Development of secular public life in the United States

and the consignment of religious belief to the private sector enabled
Jews to identify with the nation and to adopt its symbols and heroes
without reservation. The religious affiliation of American presidents is
not regarded as relevant in public school textbooks. Old Glory, Mt.
Rushmore, and Monticello are national, not religious, symbols. No
school child is required to learn what church, if any, Davy Crockett
attended. Even the religious sensibilities of a Lincoln are transmuted
into a nonsectarian faith that is as acceptable to Jewish as to Christian
citizens. To be "religious" is a sufficient value in itself. It is regarded
as somewhat impolite to inquire as to which particular church one at-
tends.

It is a truism of Jewish history that the elements wherein Jewish
communities differ from one another are elements that have been
taken over from their host societies. We have seen that the rigidities of
Latin American Catholicism are replicated within the Jewish communities of that continent. Monopoly over the cemetery gives the kehillah
the same leverage as that exerted by the church. Rabbinical resistance
to reform parallels the opposition of Latin American prelates to the
innovations of Vatican II. In the United States, Jewish congregations
patterned themselves after the Protestant mold, refashioning Jewish
tradition in various ways and offering to the American Jew, as to the
American Protestant, a variety of religious styles. The Reform movement made a particularly swift and drastic adaptation to American
life, reflecting the emancipation psychology of the movement's German
founders. Conservatism threw a bridge between Reform and Orthodoxy, providing a way by which the East European migrants could
grow into the role of "third major religion" America was offering.
Later, Reconstructionism opened the way to continuously changing
interpretations of Judaism to keep it in touch with the evolution of
American life. The heterogeneity of American life made room for the
Orthodox as well and is now being extended to include nonconformists such as the Hasidim. Eclectic religious practice in the United States
contrasts strongly with the monopoly exercised by the church among
Catholics and by Orthodoxy among Jewish Latin Americans. The result is that third-generation American Jews are free to embrace their
Jewish identification while assimilating to American life. There is no
unbridgeable fracture between Protestantism and Judaism and ample
meeting ground for the two traditions.

But it is in the area of economics that comparison of the Jewish
situation in the North and in the South is most illuminating. The Jewish mode of entry into the North American economy included the same

reliance on peddling that has been noted for Latin America. Following an initial period of itinerancy and forced savings, many peddlers moved either into fixed commerce or manufacturing (principally in textiles and the clothing industry). The immigrants' behavior patterns were similar, but the receptive molds of the two societies were distinctly different. Industrialization began considerably earlier in the North, and purchasing power was more widely diffused throughout the population. In the North, there was none of that contempt for commerce which was so notable a feature of the Latin South. Moneymaking, striving to get ahead, and competition for status were all qualities approved by the culture; indeed, success at these activities was widely regarded as a sign of grace. Although the individual Jewish entrepreneur may have been as disliked by his non-Jewish competitor as was his coreligionist in the South by his, nevertheless northern culture, suffused by the Protestant ethic, supported his efforts to get ahead. Uncle Sam himself was a merchant. He provided quite a different role model than did the plundering *hidalgo* of Latin American mythology. There existed in the United States no counterpart to the obloquy that Hispanic culture had heaped upon the entrepreneur since the thirteenth century, unless it were contempt for the man who depended on inherited wealth for his status. Individuals with ingenuity and brains enough to turn potential into reality were admired—even if they were Jewish. With entrepreneurial talent widespread through the population, there was nothing mysterious about the process of making money, and no legend of a Jewish conspiracy was needed to explain the financial success of individual Jews. Nor was it necessary to compose fictitious Jewish genealogies for non-Jews who showed business acumen.

Very few of the Latin American Jewish communities ever achieved the buoyancy that characterizes Jewish life in the United States. One might name Curaçao under Dutch rule; Panama during the building of the canal; Chile during World War I; contemporary Brazil. The factor common to each was the existence of an expanding free enterprise economy. Jews have attained status in societies that measured them by their achievements, and they have been kept in a subordinate position where status was ascribed by the past.

Not all Jewish immigrants to the United States began as petty merchants; many were skilled craftsmen. Flowing into the labor-hungry industrial plant of the major East Coast cities, these immigrants integrated themselves into American life at the most meaningful level: the work force. Immigrants were widely regarded as machine fodder. Jews who flocked to the factories and sweatshops became subject to the homogenizing pressures of the industrial plant and, in the course of a generation and in the company of other immigrants, became "Americanized."

The reciprocal nature of immigrant acculturation and structural assimilation is nowhere clearer than in the field of labor organization. Jews were prime movers in the initiation of American labor unions. Workers with their roots in the Bund organized unions that set standards for the entire labor movement with respect to collective bargaining, the forty-hour week, medical insurance, workers' pensions, and the arbitration of grievances. In fact, it could be said that during their time in the factory, Jewish workers revolutionized the condition of the American working man and woman.

Along with their fellow activists, Jewish labor leaders suffered police repression at the start, not because they were Jews but because they were labor leaders. But the most forceful among them—people like Sidney Hillman, Morris Hillquit, Alex Rose, Rose Schneiderman, David Dubinsky—ultimately came to wield considerable influence in state and national politics. Merely to name them confirms the salience of Jewish labor leaders and their emergence from a parochial to a national stage. Their daily activities as they struggled to earn a living opened up key institutions in American society.

Not so in Latin America, where Jews have been confined to an almost exclusively economic role. After an initial honeymoon period when some Argentine parties went seeking the Jewish vote, Jewish political participation was not solicited or, often, accepted. Early union activity by Jews was met not only by police repression but by goon squad action against Jewish neighborhoods and homes. Over the course of a generation, as it became clear that a Jewish contribution to national political life was not acceptable, the ideals of the Bund were compressed into the hothouse atmosphere of the kehillah, where they could have no practical effect. Jewish labor leaders never gained national acceptability for their ideas, a failure shared by their non-Jewish colleagues. Socialism influenced the Latin American labor movement, but did not permeate the culture. Failure of the Radical party of Irigoyen in Argentina to act upon its principles is notorious. Socialism and communism alike were swamped in Argentina by Peronismo, which was a personalist movement that manipulated the loyalties of workers while reducing their unions to dependency on the chief executive. Egalitarian ideologies found no resonance in society as a whole.

In contrast to the political neutralization of Jews in Latin American politics, Jewish immigrants to the United States plunged into

local politics as soon as they had mastered the English language. By
the turn of the century, there were Jewish district captains, poll watch-
ers, ballot clerks, and campaign orators in the East Coast cities. Jews
were admitted to Tammany councils and nominated to municipal office. They were appointed corporation counsels and assistant district
attorneys; they sought election as assemblymen and aldermen, and
many went on to judicial appointments. The "Jewish vote" was being
sought in New York by 1905, and candidates campaigned vigorously in
Jewish wards.[2] Political activism among Jews depended not only on
their own proclivities (presumably shared by their cousins in Buenos
Aires) but on what has been called the democratic mold. The political
culture offered access to any group that could bring together sufficient
votes to force attention to their needs.

The pluralist society of the United States incorporated immigrant
Jews politically, as Latin American societies did not. The process was
crucial not just for immigrants, or only for Jews, but for the entire
working class, which was enabled to use the engines of major political
parties to bring about vast improvements in living conditions and to
achieve political status sufficient to guarantee that these gains would
be permanent.

The level of political activity among American Jews remains higher
today than it is among American non-Jews.[3] This involvement can be
documented at every level from the college campus up to and including national elections. American Jews today wield influence beyond the
weight of their numbers in many areas of political life, through jour-
nalism, party organization, volunteer work, and other activities. It is
noteworthy, however, that in a comparison of officeholders, Jews fall
back to a number consistent with their proportion in the population.
This reflects residual bars to entry into key social and political institutions, bars that reduce the availability of Jews as candidates for political office. A study by Stephen D. Isaacs found that "in the history of
the United States, 108 Jews have been elected to high office—governor,
senator, or congressman. Six-tenths of 1 percent of all congressmen
have been Jewish; nine-tenths of 1 percent of all senators have been
Jewish. Even today, with the enormously high level of activity by Jews,
they are represented proportionately—relatively speaking—in high offices: two are governors, three are senators, twelve are congressmen, or
2.9 percent of all the high elected officials in the nation."[4]

Although Isaacs deplores the low percentage of Jewish officeholders
by comparison with the high degree of political involvement among
Jews, the record is favorable when compared with officeholding by

Jews in the Spanish-speaking republics. Under conditions of democracy, four Jewish delegates were elected to the Argentine House of Representatives in 1958; two other Jews became the nation's first Jewish governors that same year. A few other Jews were elected in 1963, but officeholders were removed arbitrarily by the military coup of 1966.[5] In 1973, with the advent of the Peronista government of Hector Campora, two Jews were appointed to top positions: Finance Minister José Gelbard (who was the second Jew to reach cabinet rank in Argentine history) and an undersecretary of interior. The attacks upon Gelbard, charging sinister Jewish influence over Perón, demonstrated that participation by Jews in Argentine politics is still not acceptable to large sectors of the population. The contrast with the acceptability of Henry Kissinger as secretary of state of the United States is inescapable.

Government officials of Jewish descent have been noted in Venezuela. General Augusto Pinochet has made use of Jewish appointees within the Chilean government. In numbers alone, these isolated individuals are in no way representative of their communities. Though Jews have introduced important modernizing elements into their countries, they have not been permitted to play a commensurate political role. Instead, their position is continually being destabilized by shifts in the balance between other power contenders. Large numbers of Jews are displaced by every shift of government from right to left and back again. Political access is never quite good enough, and political activity itself has come to be feared, as exacting penalties disproportionate to the benefit to be gained. The electoral process, which has not functioned satisfactorily for the general population, has been even less satisfactory for Jews in terms of either representation or integration.

While American Jews can participate in elections and then sit back to watch their outcome with equanimity for their fate *as Jews*, Latin American Jews must constantly gauge the level of anti-Semitism among their governors. Jews are insufficient numerically to affect the outcome of elections, even if they were to vote as a unit (there is no evidence that they do) and even if elections were to be decided by a count of the ballots, which they usually are not. There is no effort to solicit Jewish support on the part of those whose duty it is to arrange elections. There is no "Jewish vote," nor any discussion of one, anywhere in Latin America.

Exclusion from local and national politics leaves Latin American Jews peculiarly vulnerable to shifts in political opinion in these areas that are traditionally volatile and where legal norms do not provide for their entry into society on equal terms. Jewish vulnerability under these circumstances does not depend on the ideology of the authority. Jews qua Jews fared well under the reactionary Trujillo of the Dominican Republic and the radical Fidel Castro of Cuba. The military junta of Chile has gone to considerable lengths to accommodate its Jewish community, while the equally authoritarian military junta in Argentina has not made a credible commitment to equal protection under the law. The common element is expedience. It may suit one government or another to accommodate Jewish interests or to squeeze them; nowhere (except perhaps in Chile) do legal and social norms provide for their treatment solely on the basis of their citizenship. Nowhere is the Catholic past so far distant that it cannot be called upon to justify current attacks on Jews. Latin American Jews are dependent on the goodwill of the powers that be, rather than on legal norms and ingrained habits of toleration. In this situation, it is probably irrelevant whether a government is of the right or of the left—anti-Semitism is a weapon available to either.

The absorption of immigrants is a reciprocal process: immigrants must learn new forms of behavior, adopting the cultural patterns of their host society; and the host society must be willing to move over and accommodate the immigrants. Seven variables of the assimilation process have been identified by Milton Gordon, each of them subject to an infinite number of variations. In his *Assimilation in American Life,* Gordon attempts to scale some American groups according to their degree of assimilation. He finds that American Jews have substantially acculturated (1), meaning that they have changed their cultural patterns to those of the host society. However, structural assimilation (2), which implies admission into cliques, clubs, and institutions, has not occurred. Nor are Jews universally acceptable as marriage partners (3). A sense of peoplehood based exclusively on the host society (4) has not fully developed among American Jews, and prejudice (5) against them remains, though overt discrimination (6) has been reduced. Civic assimilation (7), marked by the absence of conflict over values and power, has for the most part occurred.[6]

If we attempt to fit Latin American Jewry into this schema, we find that Jewish immigrants to Latin America acculturated with the same celerity, translating themselves from Yiddish and a host of other languages into Spanish or Portuguese in the course of a single generation. To a far greater degree than in the North, however, structural assimilation failed to occur. Jews were not granted access to the important sectors of their national societies.

On the other hand, Latin American Jews seem to enjoy greater acceptability as marital partners. The revelation that half the projected Argentine Jewish population simply does not exist testifies to the willingness of Jews to assimilate and the ease with which they may do so if they cease to regard themselves as Jews. As Magnus Mörner has pointed out, Latin Americans tend to interpret acculturation in biological terms.[7] They have already digested an astonishing variety of peoples, and their absorptive capacity includes Jews.

The rate of Jewish intermarriage is high not only in areas such as Argentina that are populated by other Europeans, but likewise in areas such as Cuba and Brazil, whose populations are exotic to Jews. "We fell in love with our children and married their mothers," as one early chronicler put it. Today, the trend toward intermarriage accelerates as more Jews enter the universities and go on to the free professions. Modern urban life styles support abandonment of religious affiliation, and intellectuals of Jewish descent fail with increasing frequency to identify with the Jewish people. This trend has now reached the point where increasing numbers of marriages between Jews take place by civil contract. Since the offspring of such marriages are not Jews, there is a possibility that the East Europeans will go the way of the Portuguese nation of Curaçao, the Alsatians of Mexico, and the Sephardim of the Amazon.

It is apparent that the dissolution of the Jewish people prepares the way for full-scale participation by the descendants of Jews in the peoplehood of each of the republics, the fourth stage of Gordon's schematic representation of the assimilatory process. For this to happen, social structures would have to open up. At this writing, however, it appears that they may actually be hardening.

The philo-Semite (and there are many in Latin America, even if one discounts the illiterates who wear a Star of David as a talisman) tries to destroy the prejudice by naming heroes he believes to have been Jewish: Christopher Columbus; Bartólome de las Casas, Apostle to the Indians; the poet-philosopher Sor Juana Inés de la Cruz; Antonio José Sucre, Liberator of Ecuador; Ferdinand the Catholic; Francisco Madera, revolutionary president of Mexico; not to mention all the inhabitants of Antioquia. It might be said that these claims and disclaimers muddy the waters even more, for they foster the myth of the Jew who is not what he seems to be. The reality of Jewish life on the continent is contained in the daily existence of Jews. The mystery of the Jew is manifest in persistent "accusations" of Marrano ancestry against politicians and families of the upper class; rumored plots by

Jewish bankers to take over entire countries in cohort with Jewish communists; and the omnipresent Christs whose vivid sufferings ordain, if not the punishment of the Jews, at least their subjugation. Among surface manifestations, one may note that anti-Semitic tracts, including the notorious libel *Protocols of the Elders of Zion*, are widely sold on Latin street corners, along with those other escapist fantasies of the disinherited, lottery tickets. Such folk anti-Semitism feeds the jealousies and hatreds of a people condemned to poverty by their own elite.

Adherence to such a value system ordained the near total exclusion of Jews from civic life. Five hundred years ago, Jews—and even Christians descended from Jews—were barred from settling in the New World. With the advent of independence, Jews were admitted to the republics but continued to suffer legal disabilities in relation to their civil status. School systems were based on philosophical tenets that Jews rejected and that rejected Jews. By the end of the nineteenth century, most legal prohibitions had been removed and a more promising environment created for non-Latin immigrants. But major social and political institutions continued to rebuff Jews. This can be demonstrated by the paucity of Jewish officeholders; the vulnerability of Jews in public life; the quarantine of Jewish press and publications; the absence of Jews from high ranks in the military; and the continued popularity of gross caricatures of Jews in the media.

The blockage of the entry of Jews into the core of national life represents, in a way, the compromise between proimmigration and anti-immigration forces: the Jews were admitted to the Latin republics, but they were not granted that great boon of North American Jewish life, civic assimilation. The process, which is so far advanced in the United States, has made a beginning in Brazil; but it has scarcely commenced in the Spanish-speaking republics. Jewish efforts to enter into the full responsibilities and rights of citizenship have consistently been blocked and their influence circumscribed, thus limiting the impact Jews individually or as a group can make upon society in any dimension other than the economic. Clearly, the chief limitation to the total assimilation of Latin American Jewry is the reluctance of society to admit Jews to membership.

Notes

Chapter 1

1. Benzion Netanyahu, in *The Marranos of Spain*, estimates the number of forced conversions in 1391 at two hundred thousand, with an equal number converting voluntarily in the years 1412–15 (pp. 241–43). Other historians believe the number of conversions cannot be reconstructed at this date. See Gerson D. Cohen's review of Netanyahu's work in *Jewish Social Studies* 29 (1967): 178–84, as well as Albert A. Sicroff's review in *Midstream* 12 (1966): 71–75.

2. Netanyahu, *Marranos*, p. 248. Netanyahu estimates the converso population of Spain at six to seven hundred thousand before the Edict. Other historians regard the figure as too high.

3. Ibid., pp. 211–15.

4. Ibid., p. 4.

5. Ibid., p. 3.

6. Antonio José Saraiva, *A Inquisição Portuguesa*.

7. Martin A. Cohen, "Some Misconceptions about the Crypto-Jews in Colonial Mexico," p. 281.

8. Martin A. Cohen, *Usque's Consolation for the Tribulations of Israel*, p. 5.

9. Albert Sicroff, *Les controverses des statuts de "pureté de sang" en Espagne du XVe au XVIIe siècles*, p. 25.

10. Ibid., p. 93.

11. Anita Novinsky, *Cristãos novos na Bahía*, pp. 47–48.

12. Sicroff, *Les controverses*, pp. 296–97.

13. Ronald Sanders, *Lost Tribes and Promised Lands*, p. 16.

14. Ibid., p. 87.

15. The most provocative synthesis of these theories is to be found in Sanders, *Lost Tribes*. The extent of the probabilities is probed by J. H. Eliot in his review of Sanders's book, which appeared in the *New York Review of Books* for 1 June 1978.

16. Charles Gibson, *The Spanish Tradition in America*, pp. 55–57.

17. Richard E. Greenleaf, *The Mexican Inquisition of the Sixteenth Century*, pp. 26–40. See also Seymour B. Liebman, "Hernando Alonso."

18. Henry Charles Lea, *The Inquisition in the Spanish Dependencies*, p. 193.

19. Seymour B. Liebman, *The Inquisition and the Jews in the New World*, pp. 50–54.

20. The literature on the Carvajal family is extensive. Among recent works, see Martin A. Cohen, *The Martyr*, and Seymour B. Liebman, *The Enlightened*.

21. Günter Friedlander, *Los héroes olvidados*, pp. 24–25.

22. Martin A. Cohen, ed., *The Jewish Experience in Latin America*, 1:xlv–xlvi.

23. Boleslao Lewin, "Esbozo de la historia judía de le Argentina desde 1580 hasta 1889," p. 39.

24. Ibid., pp. 44–45.

25. Charles R. Boxer, *Salvador de Sá and the Struggle for Brazil and Angola, 1602–1686*, pp. 80–81.

26. Arnold Wiznitzer, *Jews in Colonial Brazil*, p. 32.

27. Ibid., p. 146.

28. Novinsky, *Cristãos novos*, p. 145.

29. Ibid., pp. 59–60.

30. Anita Novinsky, "A Historical Bias," p. 142.

31. Novinsky, *Cristãos novos*, p. 201.

32. Novinsky, "A Historical Bias," pp. 151–53.

33. Ibid., p. 146.

34. George Alexander Kohut wrote about de Silva and other "Jewish Martyrs of the Inquisition in South America" in a now outdated article that was reprinted in Cohen, ed., *Jewish Experience*, 1:1–87. The article includes bibliographies of works by and about the dramatist.

35. Wiznitzer, *Jews in Colonial Brazil*, pp. 43–62.

36. Cohen, ed., *Jewish Experience*, 1:lviii.

37. Wiznitzer, *Jews in Colonial Brazil*, p. 72.

38. Cohen, ed., *Jewish Experience*, 1:lv.

39. Ibid., 1:lviii–lix.

40. Wiznitzer, *Jews in Colonial Brazil*, pp. 129–30.

41. Arnold Wiznitzer, "The Exodus from Brazil and Arrival in New Amsterdam of the Jewish Pilgrim Fathers, 1654," 1:329.

42. Frances P. Karner, *The Sephardics of Curaçao*, p. 9.

43. Isaac S. Emmanuel, *Jewish Education in Curaçao*, p. 1.

44. There are three major groups within the Jewish people: the Sephardim, who are descendants of those expelled from Spain and Portugal and who preserve their ancient homelands in their languages, Ladino (a compound of Hebrew and of fifteenth-century Castilian) and Portuguese; Oriental, or Arabic-speaking Jews who are often, in the Latin American context, grouped together with the Sephardim; and Ashkenazim, Yiddish-speaking Jews from eastern and central Europe, the basic stock of the Jewish community of the United States and Canada.

45. Isaac S. Emmanuel and Suzanne A. Emmanuel, *History of the Jews of the Netherlands Antilles*, 1:99.

46. Ibid., 1:115.

47. Karner, *Sephardics of Curaçao*, p. 12.

48. For Brazil, see Gilberto Freyre, *The Masters and the Slaves*; for Sephardim in New York, see Stephen Birmingham, *The Grandees*.

49. Harry Hoetink, *The Two Variants in Caribbean Race Relations*, p. 111.

50. Emmanuel and Emmanuel, *Netherlands Antilles*, p. 831.

51. Harry Hoetink, *El Pueblo Dominicano, 1850–1900*, pp. 49–50.

52. Harry Hoetink, "The Dominican Republic in the Nineteenth Century," p. 101.

53. Emmanuel and Emmanuel, *Netherlands Antilles*, 2:822.

54. Hoetink, *Variants*, p. 114. Magnus Mörner accurately observes that "with regard to the history of internal Latin American migrations that are of ethnic interest, almost everything remains to be done" (*Race and Class in Latin America*, p. 223).

55. Bernard D. Ansel, "The Beginnings of the Modern Jewish Community in Argentina, 1852–1891," p. 25.

56. Several anomalous sects today claim descent from Marranos: the fifty or so israelitas of Venta Prieta, a village not far from Mexico City; and some thirty mestizos of Cocula, in the state of Guerrero, also in Mexico. Neither these groups nor the several thousand members of Casa de Dios (House of God), who are converts from Protestantism, are recognized by the rabbinate of Mexico or by the state of Israel (*Encyclopedia Judaica* s.v. "Mexico"). These so-called "mestizo Jews," writes Seymour Liebman in "Mestizo Jews of Mexico," are neither Indians nor Jews, but mestizos. In the south of Chile live a group of "sabatistas" who claim to be descended from conversos who entered the country in the seventeenth century. They made themselves known to world Jewry in 1919 by addressing a letter to Justice Louis B. Brandeis of the United States Supreme Court. But their origin, according to Chilean historian Günter Böhm, is Protestant.

57. For a complete exposition of this phenomenon, see Joshua Trachtenberg, *The Devil and the Jews.*

58. Luis Kardúner, "La eliminación de las acepciones peyoritivas del diccionario de la lengua española," p. 256.

59. For example, it is customary to observe that El Inca Garcilaso de la Vega, son of a Spanish conquistador and an Inca princess who was later abandoned in favor of a Spanish wife, came to terms with his ambiguous heritage by writing the monumental *Royal Commentaries of the Inca.* It is less well known that Garcilaso's first published work was a translation from Italian into Spanish of the *Dialoghi d'Amore*, a book by the platonic philosopher Leon Hebreo, né Judah Abravanel, a Spanish Jew whose family had been expelled from Spain in 1492.

Chapter 2

1. For an examination of positivism, see the works of Leopoldo Zea.
2. Magnus Mörner, *Race Mixture in the History of Latin America*, pp. 141–42.
3. Carl Solberg, *Immigration and Nationalism*, p. 20.
4. Jacob Lestchinsky, "Jewish Migrations, 1840–1956," p. 1538.
5. Arthur Ruppin, "The Jewish Population of the World," p. 349.
6. Leib Hersch, "Jewish Migrations during the Last Hundred Years," p. 407.
7. Mark Wischnitzer, *To Dwell in Safety*, p. 4.
8. *Registro oficial de la Republica*, Buenos Aires, 1879, 1:92, Item 189.5.
9. Bernard Ansel, "The Beginnings of the Modern Jewish Community in Argentina, 1852–1891," pp. 9–12.
10. Juan Batista Alberdi, *Organización política de la confederación argentina*, p. 27.
11. Ansel, "Beginnings," p. 94.
12. Solberg, *Immigration and Nationalism*, pp. 4 and 26.
13. Ibid., p. 8.
14. Juan A. Alsina, *La inmigración en el primer siglo de la independencia*, p. 222.
15. Solberg, *Immigration and Nationalism*, p. 29.
16. Gino Germani, "Mass Immigration and Modernization in Argentina," p. 292.
17. Torcuato di Tella and Gino Germani, *Argentina, sociedad de masas*, pp. 26–28.

18. Gino Germani, *Política y sociedad en una época de transición*, p. 183.
19. Ansel, "Beginnings."
20. Ibid., p. 101.
21. Ibid., pp. 117 ff.
22. Bernard Ansel, "European Adventurer in Tierra del Fuego."
23. Robert Ricard, "L'emigration des Juifs marocains en Amérique du Sud," p. 237.
24. A German Jewish woman now in her seventies told me that her mother forbade her to go out with a certain young man, on the ground that he came from Argentina.
25. Ansel, "Beginnings," p. 210.
26. Solberg, *Immigration and Nationalism*, pp. 35–36.
27. Gunther Böhm, "Judíos en Chile durante el siglo XIX," p. 341.
28. After the French Revolution, French Freemasonry followed the example of the Republic in cutting all ties with institutional Christianity. From that time forward, there was no bar to the entry of Jews into lodges. Freemasonry became an important element in the emancipation of European Jews, providing a springboard by means of which they could enter society without passing through the fire of the Catholic church. We have already seen that Sephardim migrating from Curaçao to Santo Domingo utilized Freemasonry to integrate themselves into society, and the same process was at work in Chile.
29. J. Lloyd Mecham, *Church and State in Latin America*, pp. 343–44.
30. Corinne Azen Krause, "The Jews in Mexico," pp. 17 ff.
31. Ibid., pp. 31–32.
32. Ibid., pp. 49–58.
33. Ibid., p. 107.
34. Ibid., pp. 83–92.
35. Ibid., p. 65.
36. Salomão Serebrenick, *Quatro séculos de vida judaica no Brasil*, p. 95.
37. Mörner, *Race Mixture*, p. 140.
38. Kurt Loewenstamm, *Vultos judaicos no Brasil*, 2:25.
39. Anita Novinsky, "Os Israelitas em São Paulo," p. 118.
40. Loewenstamm, *Vultos*, 2:99–100.
41. Novinsky, "Os Israelitas," p. 118.
42. Ibid., p. 119.
43. Robert G. Nachman, "Positivism, Modernization, and the Middle Class in Brazil," p. 23.
44. Mecham, *Church and State*, p. 274.
45. Ibid., p. 160.
46. Francis Merriman Stanger, "Church and State in Peru during the First Century of Independence," p. 150.
47. *Breve reseña historiográfica*, pp. 11–12.
48. Yaacov Hasson, "Iquitos," p. 367.
49. William J. Griffith, "Attitudes toward Foreign Colonization," p. 78.
50. Ibid., p. 75.
51. Jacob Shatzky, *Comunidades judías en Latinoamérica*, p. 133.
52. Harry Hoetink, *El Pueblo Dominicano, 1850–1900*, p. 53.
53. Hans Kohn, "The Jew Enters Western Culture," p. 291.
54. Andre N. Chouraqui, *Between East and West*, p. 120.

Chapter 3

1. A recurring problem of Jewish historiography is the continuing imbalance between Ashkenazic and Sephardic sources. A great deal more is known about the former than about the latter, at least in part because modern Jewish historians have tended to come from the Ashkenazic world.

2. Juan A. Alsina, *La inmigración en el primer siglo de la independencia*, pp. 49–50.

3. Bernard D. Ansel, "The Beginnings of the Modern Jewish Community in Argentina," p. 237.

4. Iaacov Rubel, "Argentina, ¿sí o no?," p. 290.

5. Ansel, "Beginnings," pp. 289 ff.

6. Ira Rosenswaike, "The Jewish Population of Argentina," p. 197.

7. The Jewish Colonization Association entered Jewish history as "IKO," Yiddishe Kolonizatsie Organizatsie, but the English initials are used in the present study.

8. Jewish Colonization Association, *Report*.

9. But not all rusos were Jews.

10. Pinie Wald, "Di Yiddishe Arbeter-Bavegung in Argentina," p. 119.

11. Harry O. Sandberg, "The Jews of Latin America," p. 45.

12. Wald, "Arbeter-Bavegung," pp. 118–19.

13. This phenomenon is paralleled by the experience of the United States. One-fourth of all immigrant and skilled industrial labor who came to this country were Jews, who supplied almost half of immigrant craftsmen in tailoring and watchmaking, a third of all printing workers, and more than 40 percent of all immigrant leather workers (Jacob Lestchinsky, "Jewish Migrations, 1840–1956," pp. 1569–70).

14. Eugene F. Sofer, "From Pale to Pampa," pp. 184–85.

15. Victor A. Mirelman, "The Semana Trágica of 1919 and the Jews of Argentina," p. 62.

16. Ricardo Rojas, Preface to *La condición del extranjero en América*, by Domingo F. Sarmiento, pp. 11–12.

17. *Los gauchos judíos* consists of a series of sketches of East European Jewish life on the Argentine pampas, as these religious town dwellers come to grips with life in the "desert." Gauchesque elements of eroticism and violence intrude upon them as they grapple with their strange surroundings. A mounted gaucho snatches a Jewish bride out from under the wedding canopy. She goes willingly. Love conquers fear of the unknown. Her elders, who celebrate Argentine holidays and march behind the Argentine flag, cannot make this leap with her, but the implication is that her sisters will. This Argentine variant of *Abie's Irish Rose* consummates the marriage of two cultures through kidnapping and rape, probably the only way it could have been done under the circumstances. Gerchunoff himself came into the heritage of the pampas directly: his father was murdered by a gaucho.

18. Francisco Luis Bernardez, "Gerchunoff, clásico de verdaderos," p. 32.

19. Hymen Alpern and José Martel, *El teatro hispano-americano*, p. 76.

20. Silvano Santander, "Tres personalidades judeo-argentinas," p. 75.

21. Robert Alan Goodman, "The Image of the Jew in Argentine Literature as Seen by Argentine Jewish Writers," p. 38.

22. Moisés Senderey, *Di Geshikhte fun dem Yiddishn Yishuv in Chile*, p. 71.

23. Sandberg, "Jews of Latin America," pp. 62–63.

Notes to Pages 63–83

24. The lower estimate by Jacob Shatzky, *Comunidades judías in Latinoamerica*, p. 113; the higher by Sandberg, "Jews of Latin America," p. 89.

25. Harriet Sara Lesser, "A History of the Jewish Community of Mexico City, 1912–1970," p. 11.

26. Corinne Azen Krause, "The Jews in Mexico," p. 98.

27. Salomão Serebrenick, *Quatro séculos de vida judaica no Brasil, 1500–1900*, p. 99.

28. Frida Alexandr, *Filipson*.

29. Itzhak Z. Raizman, "Yidn in Brazil," p. 147.

30. Eliahu Lipiner, "A nova imigraçco judaica no Brasil," p. 115.

31. Sandberg, "Jews of Latin America," p. 56.

32. *Breve reseña historiográfica*, p. 43.

33. Jacob Beller, *Jews in Latin America*, p. 136.

34. Comité Judío Americano, *Comunidades judías de Latinoamérica*, 1971–72, p. 188.

35. J. Lloyd Mecham, *Church and State in Latin America*, p. 339.

36. Eliahu Trotzky, "Yidn in Uruguay," p. 1.

37. Ibid., p. 3.

38. Sandberg, "Jews of Latin America," pp. 69–70.

39. *Comunidades judías*, 1971–72, p. 192.

40. Sandberg, "Jews of Latin America," p. 67.

41. Jacob Shatzky, *Yiddishe yishuvim in Lateyn America*, p. 88.

42. Marco Pitchon, *José Martí y la compresión humana, 1853–1953*.

43. Leizer Ran, "Cuba," p. 423.

44. *Comunidades judías*, 1971–72, p. 226.

45. Isidoro Aizenberg, "Coro, Venezuela," p. 386.

46. *Comunidades judías*, 1971–72, p. 228.

47. Sandberg, "Jews of Latin America," p. 37.

48. A sociological study of the shtetl may be found in Mark Zborowsky, *Life Is with People*. The novels of Sholom Aleichem portray this world sympathetically; those of Isaac Bashevis Singer undertake its rediabolization.

49. Sandberg, "Jews of Latin America," p. 43.

Chapter 4

1. Mark Wischnitzer, *To Dwell in Safety*, p. 291.

2. *Encyclopedia Judaica*, "Latin America."

3. Wischnitzer, *To Dwell*, p. 293.

4. Ilya M. Dijour, "Jewish Migration in the Post-war Period," p. 80.

5. Carl Solberg, *Immigration and Nationalism*, p. 93.

6. Ibid., pp. 132–33.

7. José Luis de Imaz, *Los que mandan*, p. 216.

8. John Raymond Hebert, "The Tragic Week of January, 1919, in Buenos Aires," p. 172.

9. Ibid., p. 174.

10. *Encyclopedia Judaica*, "Argentina."

11. Hebert, "Tragic Week," p. 225.

12. Natan Lerner, "Anti-Semitism and the Nationalist Ideology in Argentina," pp. 135–38.

13. Gino Germani, "Antisemitismo ideológico y antisemitismo tradicional," p. 190.
14. Jerry W. Knudsen, "The Bolivian Immigration Bill of 1942."
15. Arthur D. Morse, *While Six Million Died*, p. 275.
16. Wischnitzer, *To Dwell*, p. 198.
17. Ibid., pp. 198–99.
18. Ibid., p. 238.
19. Salo Baron, "Jewish Emancipation," p. 396.
20. Boris Sapir, *The Jewish Community of Cuba*, p. 22.
21. Sander M. Kaplan, "Jewish Robinson Crusoes," *Havaner Lebn*, 12 October 1934. What does a Jewish editor write on El Día de la Raza? With what element of Cuba's "races" does he identify?
22. Y. O. Pinis, *Hatuey*.
23. D. M. Hermelin, *Clara*.
24. Eliezer Aronowsky, *Maceo-poema*.
25. Abraham M. Matterin, *Martí y las discriminaciónes raciales*.
26. Marco Pitchon, *José Martí y la compresión humana, 1853–1953*.
27. Sapir, *Jewish Community*, p. 34.
28. Leizer Ran, "Cuba," p. 435.
29. Abraham J. Dubelman, "Cuba," pp. 481–85.
30. Harry O. Sandberg, "The Jews of Latin America," p. 56; and Eliahu Lipiner, "A nova imigração judaica no Brasil," p. 118.
31. Henrique Rattner, *Tradição e mudança*, p. 98.
32. Memo by Cecilia Rozovsky Davidson, 11 October 1937, p. 23, Brazilian file, American Joint Distribution Committee Archives, New York.
33. Wischnitzer, *To Dwell*, p. 293.
34. See his introduction to *Tristes Tropiques: A World on the Wane*.
35. Robert M. Levine, "Brazil's Jews during the Vargas Era and after," pp. 48–54.
36. Kurt Loewenstein, *Brazil Under Vargas*, p. 181.
37. Lipiner, "A nova imigração," p. 114.
38. Dijour, "Jewish Migration," p. 80.
39. Marcos Margulies, "Ayer y mañana," p. 326.
40. U. O. Schmelz and Sergio Della Pergola, *Hademografia shel hayehudim be-argentina ube-artzot aherot shel America halatinit*, p. 5.
41. Ibid., p. 82.
42. Rattner, *Tradição*, pp. 189–90.
43. Ira Rosenswaike, "The Jewish Population of Argentina," p. 212.
44. Raphael Patai, *Tents of Jacob*, p. 288.
45. Gino Germani, "Mass Immigration and Modernization in Argentina," p. 291.
46. Jacob Beller, *Jews in Latin America*.
47. Patai, *Tents*, p. 160.
48. Jerry W. Knudsen, "Anti-Semitism in Latin America," p. 30.

Chapter 5

1. "Hacer la américa" was the expression immigrants of all origins used to describe their struggle to force their new homelands to yield them the means of survival. For the memoirs of a Spanish immigrant who failed, see Juan F. Marsal, *Hacer la América: Biografía de un emigrante* (Buenos Aires, 1972).
2. Simon Guberek, *Yo vi crecer un país*, p. 29.

3. Haim Avni, "Argentine Jewry," part 1, p. 144.

4. *Havaner Lebn*, 26 April 1935.

5. Eliahu Trotzky, "Yidn in Uruguay," p. 5.

6. *Havaner Lebn*, 5 April 1935.

7. Moisés Senderey, *Historia de la colectividad israelita de Chile*, p. 217.

8. Tovye Meisel, "Yidn in Meksike," in *Algemeine Entsiclopedia*, p. 409.

9. Harriet Sara Lesser, "A History of the Jewish Community of Mexico City, 1912–1970," p. 23.

10. Meisel, "Yidn in Meksike," p. 409.

11. Memo by Noel Aronovici, 20 August 1940, Bolivia file, Joint Distribution Committee Archives, New York.

12. Boris Sapir, "Jews in Cuba," p. 112.

13. *Havaner Lebn*, 12 October 1934.

14. Ibid., 12 April 1935.

15. Alberto Lleras Camargo, "A Humble Jewish Revolution."

16. Eugene Sofer, "From Pale to Pampa," pp. 125–26.

17. Ibid., chapter 4.

18. Pinie Wald, "Di Yiddishe Arbeter-Bavegung in Argentina," p. 124.

19. Sofer, "From Pale to Pampa," p. 178.

20. Ibid., p. 285.

21. Ibid., p. 163.

22. Henrique B. Veltman, "Crônica do judaísmo carioca," p. 54.

23. Alfred Hirschberg, "The Economic Adjustment of Jewish Refugees in São Paulo," pp. 37–38.

24. Boris Sapir, *The Jewish Community of Cuba*, pp. 29–30.

25. Leizer Ran, "Cuba," p. 426.

26. Sapir, *Jewish Community of Cuba*, p. 34.

27. Ran, "Cuba," p. 426.

28. This industry has now migrated to Israel and to New York City.

29. Senderey, *Chile*, pp. 218–19.

30. Ibid., p. 219.

31. Ibid., p. 224.

32. Lesser, "Mexico City," pp. 158–59.

33. Memo by S. Lipschitz, "The Jewish Situation in Mexico," May–June 1931, American Jewish Committee Archives, New York.

34. Jacob Levitz, "The Acculturation of East European Jews in Mexico City, 1920–1946," p. 83.

35. Meisel, "Yidn in Meksike," p. 410.

36. Memo by Max Weiser, "Report of the Anti-Semitic Current in Ecuador," 29 December 1948, American Joint Distribution Committee Archives, New York.

37. Veltman, "Carioca," p. 58.

38. Simon Kuznets, "Economic Structure and Life of the Jews," pp. 1598–1603.

39. Seymour Martin Lipset and A. Solari, eds., *Elites in Latin America*, p. 51.

40. Paul Deutschman et al., *Communication and Social Change in Latin America*, p. 13.

41. Tomas Roberto Fillol, *Social Factors in Economic Development*.

42. Gino Germani, "Mass Immigration and Modernization in Argentina," pp. 297–98.

43. José Luis de Imaz, *Los que mandan*, p. 143.

44. Carl Solberg, *Immigration and Nationalism*, p. 64.
45. Aaron Lipman, "Social Backgrounds of the Bogotá Entrepreneur," p. 231.
46. Everett E. Hagen, *On the Theory of Social Change*, pp. 371–72.

Chapter 6

1. James R. Scobie, *Revolution on the Pampas*, p. 31.
2. Arieh Tartakower, *Hahityashvut hayehudit bagolah*, p. 162.
3. Baron Maurice de Hirsch, "My Views on Philanthropy," p. 416.
4. Kurt Grunwald, *Turkenhirsch*, pp. 76–77.
5. Scobie, *Revolution*, p. 124.
6. Lázaro Schallman, "Dramática historia de los 'Pampistas' o 'Stambuler,'" p. 154.
7. Morton D. Winsberg, "Jewish Agricultural Colonization in Entre Ríos," part 1, p. 286.
8. Haim Avni, "Argentine Jewry," part 1, pp. 137–38.
9. Jacob Lestchinsky, "Economic and Social Development of the Jewish People," p. 377.
10. Jewish Colonization Association, *Su obra en la Argentina, 1891–1941*, p. iii.
11. Tartakower, *Hahityashvut*, p. 167.
12. This was common practice in all the colonies; the colonist did not receive actual title to the land until all payments were completed and all debts with the company were canceled (Scobie, *Revolution*, p. 58).
13. S. Y. Horowitz, "Di cooperativn in di yiddishe kolonies in Argentina," p. 81.
14. Winsberg, "Entre Ríos," part 3, p. 180.
15. Ibid., part 2, p. 423.
16. Tartakower, *Hahityashvut*, p. 167.
17. Winsberg, "Entre Ríos," part 1, pp. 287–88.
18. Scobie, *Revolution*, p. 128.
19. Gino Germani, "Mass Immigration and Modernization in Argentina," p. 298.
20. Oscar E. Cornblit, "European Immigrants in Argentine Industry and Politics," pp. 223–24.
21. Winsberg, *Colonia Baron Hirsch*, pp. 54–55.
22. U. O. Schmelz and Sergio Della Pergola, *Hademografia shel hayehudim be-argentina ube-artzot aherot shel America halatinit*, p. 132.
23. Ira Rosenswaike, "The Jewish Population of Argentina," p. 204.
24. Schmelz and Della Pergola, *Hademografia*, pp. 132–35.
25. As it was, considerable hostility was directed at JCA schools as centers of alien influence. See Solberg, *Immigration and Nationalism in Argentina and Chile*, pp. 148–49.
26. Mark Wischnitzer, *To Dwell in Safety*, p. 65.
27. Harry Hoetink, *El Pueblo Dominicano, 1850–1900*, p. 75.
28. The motive for this offer has been the subject of speculation. Perhaps it was a move to counter unfavorable publicity generated by Trujillo's slaughter and expulsion of Haitians the year before.
29. Hyman Kisch, "The Jewish Settlement from Central Europe in the Dominican Republic," pp. 1–20.

30. Alexander T. Edelmann, in *Latin American Government and Politics*, p. 197, defines minifundia as five hectares or less.

31. Jacob Shatzky, *Yiddishe yishuvim in Lateyn America*, p. 89.

32. Hochschild was a German Jew who came to Bolivia in the 1920s by way of Chile. Starting as a broker of tin sales, he went on to become one of the "big three" of Bolivian tin mining, only to be nationalized, along with his competitors, in 1952.

33. All information on the Bolivian settlement is taken from files of the American Joint Distribution Committee in New York.

34. Edelmann, *Government and Politics*, p. 197.

35. Jerry W. Knudsen, "The Bolivian Immigration Bill of 1942," p. 139.

36. Memo by J. B. Lightman and T. Berelejis, "Report on Bolivia," 21 July 1948, Joint Distribution Committee Archives, New York.

37. Tartakower, *Hahityashvut*, p. 175.

38. Irving Louis Horowitz, "The Jewish Community of Buenos Aires," p. 201.

Chapter 7

1. Günther Böhm, "Judíos en Chile durante el siglo XIX," p. 360.

2. Zvi Beitner, "Origins and Development of the Ashkenazic Jewish Community of Montevideo," p. 8.

3. Corinne Azen Krause, "The Jews in Mexico," p. 167.

4. S. Y. Horowitz, "Di cooperativn in di yiddishe kolonies in Argentina," pp. 79–80.

5. Ibid., pp. 90–95.

6. Morton D. Winsberg, "Jewish Agricultural Colonization in Entre Ríos," part 3, p. 189.

7. Memo by Noel Aronovici, "Interim Report on Bolivia," 20 August 1940, Joint Distribution Committee Archives, New York.

8. An exhaustive list appears in Lázaro Schallman, "Historia del periodismo judío en la Republica Argentina," pp. 149–73. In 1898, the publisher of *Viderkol* engraved his four-page newspaper in stone, in the absence of Hebrew type. The paper went just three issues.

9. Haim Avni, "Argentine Jewry: Its Socio-Political Status and Organizational Patterns," part 3, p. 162.

10. Moisés Senderey, *Historia de la colectividad israelita de Chile*, pp. 58–60.

11. Avni, "Argentine Jewry," p. 158.

12. Irving Louis Horowitz, "The Jewish Community of Buenos Aires," p. 212.

13. Marshall Meyer, "Una década de judaísmo conservador en Latinoamerica," p. 182.

14. Ibid., p. 183.

15. Ibid., p. 187.

16. Comite Judío Americano, *Comunidades judias de Latinoamérica*, 1970, p. 117.

17. Henrique Rattner and Gabriel Bolaffi, "Jewish University Students in Face of Judaism," p. 21.

18. *Havaner Lebn*, 12 February 1933.

19. Ultimately, no fewer than seventy-eight were established.

20. The report is quoted in full in Horowitz, "Di cooperativn," pp. 77 ff.

21. Carl Solberg, *Immigration and Nationalism*, p. 148.

22. Iejiel Harari, "Yahadut Argentina," p. 28.

23. Tzila Chelminsky, "La educación judía en México," p. 221.

24. Ibid., and Tovye Meisel, "Yidn in Meksike," *Algemeine Entsiclopedia*, pp. 415–19.

25. Benny Bachrach, "Hayishuv hayehudi ba-Valparaíso, Chile," pp. 45–47.

26. Henrique Rattner, *Tradição*, p. 131.

27. Simja Sneh, "La red escolar judía en la República Argentina," pp. 136–37.

28. Rattner, *Tradição*, p. 66.

29. Antonio León Pinelo was born in Valladolid, Spain, shortly after the flight of his parents from Portugal. The family established itself in Tucumán in 1604 and moved to Córdoba shortly thereafter, where the father, Diego López de Lisboa, was named *regidor del cabildo*, or secretary to the town. Diego ultimately became chaplain and majordomo to the archbishop of Lima, Fernando Arías de Ugarte, and one of his sons, Diego de León Pinelo, became rector of the University of San Marcos in that city. Antonio was named *procurador* of Buenos Aires in 1621 and while in that position went to Spain (illegally; he paid five hundred ducats to the governor to be allowed to sail) to plead for the opening of the port. He is also known as the author of a voluminous work that locates the site of the Garden of Eden in Amazonia. The grandfather of this family, Juan López, was burned at the stake for judaizing. See Rosa Arciniega, "Antonio de León Pinelo, el erudito de fantasia desbordada," and Boleslao Lewin, "Esbozo de la historia judía en la Argentina desde 1580 hasta 1889."

30. The Cali school is named for Jorge Isaacs (b. 1837 at Cali, died 1895 at Ibaqué), author of *María*, the first Spanish-American romantic novel. Isaacs's father was a British Jew from Jamaica.

31. John Kenneth Smith, "Jewish Education in Colombia," p. 102.

32. Horowitz, "Buenos Aires," p. 208.

33. Jacob Schatzky, *Comunidades judías en Latinoamérica*, pp. 143–44.

34. Perla Reicher, "Hapoalim hayehudim ba-Uruguay," pp. 105–8.

35. Zvi Gitelman, *Jewish Nationality and Soviet Politics*, pp. 34–35.

36. Beitner, "Montevideo," p. 12.

37. Ibid., p. 13.

38. Reicher, "Hapoalim," p. 107.

39. Horowitz, "Buenos Aires," p. 207. It is true, as Horowitz states, that kehillah politics in Buenos Aires are mimetic, but they imitate, not the politics of Argentina, but the politics of Israel. The kehillah has representation in the World Jewish Congress and the World Zionist Organization, but not in the Argentine legislature.

40. Teresa Kaplanski de Caryevschi, "The Organized Jewish Community of Buenos Aires—A.M.I.A.," pp. 154–55.

41. AMIA claimed 53,487 members (presumed heads of families) in 1974. Of this number, 38,200 paid their dues. Two hundred were in arrears, and a round 10,000 had dropped out of sight. Only 900 new members per year were being added (Nathan Lerner, *Jewish Organization in Latin America*, p. 29).

42. In recent years, couples who applied to be married by a rabbi were obliged to register as members of AMIA. A recent sample of Jews not affiliated with AMIA showed that 42 percent of them were married under civil law only. Large numbers of Jews are also showing up in municipal cemetery records, but not in the AMIA register. Lerner concludes, "If we bear in mind that one of the main motivations for registration as a Community member is to have a burial place in the Jewish cem-

etery, then we may draw regrettable conclusions as to the interest shown in the Jewish Community" (ibid., p. 29).

43. See, for example, Bernard Ansel, "Discord among Western and Eastern European Jews in Argentina."

44. This remark was made to me by the president of one of the largest kehillot on the continent.

45. Rattner and Bolaffi, "Jewish University Students," pp. 4–5.

46. Nissim Elnecavé, "Sephardic Jews in Argentina," p. 56.

Chapter 8

1. The United States Current Population Survey of 1957 posed a religious question in a trial run for the 1960 census. The results were suppressed at the instance of Jewish organizations that regarded the collection of separate official statistics on religion as a breach of the First Amendment. The figures were released ten years later as a result of passage of the Freedom of Information Act and have been a fertile source of information; but no religious question was included in the 1970 census.

2. U. O. Schmelz, *Jewish Population Studies, 1961–1968*, p. 104.

3. Comité Judío Americano, *Comunidades judías de Latinoamérica*, 1970, p. 100.

4. U. O. Schmelz and Sergio Della Pergola, *Hademografia shel hayehudim beargentina ube-artzot aherot shel America halatinit.*

5. Henrique Rattner, *Tradição e mudança.*

6. Tovye Meisel, "Yidn in Meksike," in *Algemeine Entsiclopedia.*

7. Ira Rosenwaike, "The Jewish Population of Argentina."

8. Ibid., p. 201.

9. Ibid., p. 202. At that date, the League of Nations *Statistical Yearbook* gave the Argentine birth rate as 29.7, death rate 12.8, and rate of natural increase 16.9 per 1,000 for the country as a whole.

10. U. O. Schmelz, *Jewish Population Studies, 1961–1968*, p. 38.

11. National demographic data drawn from Charles L. Taylor and Michael C. Hudson, *World Handbook of Political and Social Indicators.*

12. Schmelz, *Population Studies*, p. 14.

13. Schmelz and Della Pergola, *Hademografia*, p. 54.

14. Eduard E. Arriaga, *New Life Tables for Latin American Populations in the Nineteenth and Twentieth Centuries*, pp. 1–4.

15. Meisel, "Yidn in Meksike," p. 407.

16. Rattner, *Tradição*, pp. 23–24.

17. Jacob Shatzky, "Guatemala," p. 302.

18. Eugene F. Sofer, "From Pale to Pampa," pp. 12–13.

19. Schmelz and Della Pergola, *Hademografia*, p. 45.

20. Rattner, *Tradição*, pp. 24 and 178.

21. Schatzky, "Guatemala," p. 302.

22. Schmelz and Della Pergola, *Hademografia*, p. 65.

23. Rattner, *Tradição*, p. 33.

24. Comité Judío Americano, *Comunidades judías de Latinoamérica*, 1971–72, p. 193.

25. Rosenswaike, "The Jewish Population of Argentina," p. 200.

26. Jacob Schatzky, *Comunidades judías en Latinoamérica*, p. 11.

27. AMIA, *Primer censo de la población judía de la provincia de Tucumán*, p. 18.
28. Schmelz and Della Pergola, *Hademografia*, p. 131.
29. Shatzky, *Comunidades*, p. 138.
30. Uriah Z. Engelman, "Sources of Jewish Statistics," p. 1531.
31. *Comunidades judías*, 1971–72, pp. 213–14.
32. Schmelz and Della Pergola, *Hademografia*, p. 59.
33. Ibid., p. 33.
34. Ibid., pp. 46–47.

Chapter 9

1. U. O. Schmelz and Sergio Della Pergola, *Hademografia shel hayehudim be-Argentina ube-artzot aherot shel America halatinit*, pp. 106–7.
2. Ibid., p. 111.
3. Ibid., p. 128.
4. Ibid., p. 130.
5. Ibid., pp. 119–20.
6. Eugene F. Sofer, "From Pale to Pampa," p. 164.
7. Ibid., p. 163.
8. Ibid., pp. 163–66.
9. Ibid., pp. 285–86.
10. Ibid., p. 130.
11. Henrique Rattner, *Tradição e mudança*, p. 43.
12. Henrique Rattner, "Occupational Structure of Jews in Brazil," pp. 8–9.
13. Celia S. Rosenthal, "The Jews of Barranquilla," pp. 265–66.
14. John Kenneth Smith, "Jewish Education in Colombia," p. 28.
15. Tovye Meisel, "Yidn in Meksike," *Algemeine Entsiclopedia*, p. 408.
16. Comité Judíos Americano, *Comunidades judías de latinoamérica*, 1970, p. 107.
17. For the autobiography of one immigrant who did succeed in putting himself through medical school, see Mario Schteingard, *Mis memorias*.
18. AMIA, *Censo de la comunidad judía de Quilmes*, p. 69.
19. Schmelz and Della Pergola, *Hademografia*, p. 102.
20. Benny Bachrach, "Hayishuv hayehudi ba-Valparaíso, Chile," pp. 44–45.
21. Rattner, *Tradição*, p. 75.
22. AMIA, *Quilmes*, p. 68.
23. Smith, "Jewish Education in Colombia," p. 29.
24. Rattner, *Tradição*, p. 72.
25. AMIA, *Quilmes*, p. 70.
26. Nora Scott Kinzer, "Women Professionals in Buenos Aires," pp. 163–64.
27. Smith, "Jewish Education in Colombia," pp. 103–4.
28. Sofer, "From Pale to Pampa," p. 283.
29. Such as that developed by José Nun in "A Latin American Phenomenon."
30. "First, then, the term [middle class] refers to a large, loosely internally-organized bounded aggregate of people—a class—which has certain kinds of functions, most of which are what one might call 'lubricatory': the making effective of transactions involving the strategic resources of society; the implementation of the exchanges of resources, including money; collection of information; transmission of knowledge; the processing of information for ultimate users—all of which I have

elsewhere called functionary activities. These lubricatory or functionary activities are the operational aspects of the kinds of positions and organisations to which the people designated as 'middle class' are attached. The *function* of these activities is the linkage of the positions, networks, and organizations structuring the proletariats with those structuring the elites in such a way that the necessarily interdependent societal functions of *these* two aggregates can be made to operate more or less predictably.

"Second, the term refers to . . . relatively minor . . . scalar attributes of intermediate levels of income, types of housing, kinds of occupation . . . styles of living, etc." (Anthony Leeds, "Economic-Social Changes and the Future of the Middle Class," p. 53).

31. Rosenthal, "Barranquilla," p. 268.

32. Smith, "Jewish Education in Colombia," p. 30.

33. José Luis de Imaz, *Los que mandan*, p. 145.

34. Ibid., p. 161.

35. Haim Avni, "Argentine Jewry," part 1, p. 153.

36. American Jewish Committee, *American Jewish Yearbook 1977*, p. 356.

37. Because the roll call vote on the resolution has been widely viewed as an index of anti-Jewish sentiment (as contrasted with resolutions relating to the state of Israel only), it is worth recording the votes of the Latin American republics on this issue. Three voted in favor: Brazil, Cuba, and Mexico. Eight voted against: Costa Rica, Dominican Republic, El Salvador, Haiti, Honduras, Nicaragua, Panama, and Uruguay. The remainder, including Argentina, abstained. Information on this subject is in *American Jewish Yearbook 1977*, pp. 97–126.

The United States delegate, Daniel Patrick Moynihan, in voting against this resolution, said that it "projected a political lie of a variety well known to the twentieth century . . . [and that it constituted] a massive attack on the moral realities of the world."

38. Gino Germani, "Antisemitismo ideológico y antisemitismo tradicional," pp. 177–90.

39. Argentine anti-Semitic organizations include Tacuara, Falange de Fé (Córdoba), Centuria Universitaria Nacionalista, Falange Restauradora Nacionalista, Centuria Nacionalist, Agrupación Nacionalista Argentina, and Partido Acción Nacionalista (*American Jewish Yearbook 1977*, p. 346).

40. Ibid., p. 335. The account continues: "Most political analysts felt that this number fell short of reality. Terrorist forces were estimated at 400,000 at the end of 1975, as compared with 200,000 in 1974."

41. *Comunidades judías*, 1970 and 1972.

Chapter 10

1. Louis D. Hartz, *The Founding of New Societies*, p. 28.

2. Charles S. Bernheimer, *The Russian Jew in the United States*, pp. 256–61.

3. The most recent survey of the subject will be found in Stephen D. Isaacs, *Jews and American Politics*.

4. Ibid., p. 11.

5. Haim Avni, "Argentine Jewry," part 1, p. 152.

6. Milton M. Gordon, *Assimilation in American Life*, pp. 71–76.

7. Magnus Mörner, *Race Mixture in the History of Latin America*, p. 5.

Bibliography

Aizenberg, Isidoro. "Coro, Venezuela: Primera corriente de inmigración al país." In Comité Judío Americano, *Comunidades judías de Latino-américa*, pp. 379–87. Buenos Aires: Américalee, S.R.L., 1971–72.

Alberdi, Juan B. *Organización de la confederación argentina*. New ed. 2 vols. Buenos Aires: P. García y Cia, 1913.

Alexandr, Frida. *Filipson: Memorias da primeira colônia judaica no Rio Grande do Sul*. São Paulo: Editôra Fulgor, 1967.

Algemeine Entsiclopedia. Vol. 5. New York: Dubnow Fund and Encyclopedia Committee, 1957.

Alpern, Hymen, and Martel, José. *El teatro hispano-americano*. New York: Odyssey Press, 1956.

Alsina, Juan A. *La inmigración en el primer siglo de la independencia*. Buenos Aires, 1910.

American Jewish Committee. *American Jewish Yearbook*. New York: American Jewish Committee. Vol. [1]+ (1899–1900+).

Anderson, Charles. "Political Factors in Latin American Economic Development." *Journal of International Affairs* 20, no. 2 (1966): 235–54.

Andrade, Eurico. "Não, são judeus!" *Realidade* (São Paulo), April 1968.

Angel, Marc D. "The Sephardim of the United States: An Exploratory Study." *American Jewish Yearbook* 74 (1973): 77–138.

Ansel, Bernard D. "The Beginnings of the Modern Jewish Community in Argentina, 1852–1891." Ph.D. dissertation, University of Kansas, 1969.

————. "Discord among Western and Eastern European Jews in Argentina." *American Jewish Historical Quarterly* 60 (December 1970): 151–58.

————. "European Adventurer in Tierra del Fuego: Julio Popper." *Hispanic American Historical Review* 50 (February 1970): 89–110.

Arciniega, Rosa. "Antonio de Leon Pinelo, el erudito de fantasia desbordada." In *Breve reseña historiográfica*, pp. 197–200. Lima, 1970.

Argentiner IWO Schriftn. Buenos Aires. Vol. 1+ (1941+).

Aronowsky, Eliezer. *Kubaner lider*. Havana: Oifgang Presse, 1928.

————. *Maceo-poema*. Havana: Ediciones Bené Brith Maimonides, 1950.

Arriaga, Edward E. *New Life Tables for Latin American Populations in the Nineteenth and Twentieth Centuries*. Population Monograph Series No. 3. Berkeley: University of California Press, 1968.

Bibliography

Asociación Feminina Hebrea de Cuba. *Almanaque conmemorativo de la caja de préstamos.* Havana, 1952.

Asociación Mutual Israelita Argentina (AMIA). Instituto de Investigaciones Sociales. *Primer censo de la población judía de la provincia de Tucumán: Datos y comentarios.* Buenos Aires, 1963.

————. Instituto de Investigaciones Sociales y Estadistica. *Censo de la comunidad judía de Quilmes, 1963.* Buenos Aires, 1968.

————. *Pinkus fun der kehilla in ihr 75stn aniversar.* Buenos Aires, 1969. Dual title: *Anales de la comunidad israelita de Buenos Aires, 1963–68.*

————. *Yohrbuch fun yiddishn yishuv in Argentina.* Edited by Nehemia Zucker. Buenos Aires, 1945–46.

————. *Yohrbuch fun der yiddisher kehillah in Buenos Aires, 1953–54.* Edited by Abraham Mittelberg. Buenos Aires, 1953.

————. *Yohrbuch fun der yiddisher kehillah in Buenos Aires, 1954–55.* Edited by Abraham Mittelberg. Buenos Aires, 1954.

Austri-Dan, Isaiah. "The Jewish Community of Mexico." *Dispersion and Unity* 2 (1963): 51–73.

————. "Unser Lateyn-Amerikanisher yiddishkeit." *Havaner Lebn Almanac,* January 1958, pp. 30–32.

Avni, Haim. "The Agricultural Settlements of Baron Hirsch in Argentina." Ph.D. dissertation, Hebrew University, 1968.

————. *Argentina, ha'aretz hayavda.* [Argentina, promised land.] Jerusalem: Magnes Press, 1973.

————. "Argentine Jewry: Its Socio-Political Status and Organizational Patterns." *Dispersion and Unity* 12 (1971): 128–62; 13/14 (1971-72): 161–208; 15 (1972–73): 158–215.

————. "Jewish Communities in Latin America." In *World Politics and the Jewish Condition,* edited by Louis Henkin, pp. 256–74. New York: Quadrangle Books, 1972.

————. *Jewish Students and the Argentinian Jewish Community.* Jerusalem: Seminar in the home of the President of Israel, 1971.

————. "Profile of Latin American Jewry." In *Yahadut america halatinit be'idan shel temurot,* edited by Haim Avni, et al., pp. 9–19. Jerusalem: Hebrew University, 1972.

————; Glick, Asher Dov; Lorch, Nathaniel; and Lazar, Moshe. *Yahadut america halatinit be'idan shel temurot.* [Latin American Jewry in a changing world.] A Symposium. Jerusalem: Hebrew University, Institute of Contemporary Jewry, 1972.

Bachi, Roberto. *Population Trends of World Jewry.* Jerusalem: Institute of Contemporary Jewry, Hebrew University, 1976.

Bachrach, Benny. "Hayishuv hayehudi ba-Valparaíso, Chile." [The Jewish community of Valparaíso, Chile.] *Dispersion and Unity* 2 (June 1960): 40–47.

Baer, Yitzhak Fritz. *A History of the Jews in Christian Spain.* Translated from the Hebrew by Louis Schoffman. 2 vols. Philadelphia: Jewish Publication Society, 1961–66.

Banks, Arthur S., and Textor, Robert B. "A Cross-Polity Survey." In *Studies in Comparative Politics*, edited by Frank Munger, pp. 247–310. New York: Thomas Crowell Co., 1967.

Barcía, José Rubia, ed. *Américo Castro and the Meaning of Spanish Civilization.* Berkeley: University of California Press, 1976.

Baron, Salo. "Jewish Emancipation." *Encyclopedia of the Social Sciences.* New York: Macmillan Co., 1937.

———. "Who Is a Jew?" In *History and Jewish Historians. Essays and Addresses by Salo Wittmayer Baron.* Compiled with a foreword by Arthur Hertzberg and Leon A. Feldman, pp. 5–22. Philadelphia: Jewish Publication Society of America, 1964.

Basseches, Bruno. *Bibliografia das fontes de historia dos judeus no Brasil, incluindo obras sobre judaismo publicadas no Brasil.* Rio de Janeiro, 1961.

Becker, Larry M. "The Jewish Community of Cuba." *Congress Bulletin* (U.S.), May-June 1971.

Beitner, Zvi. "Origins and Development of the Ashkenazic Jewish Community of Montevideo." Typescript of paper submitted to Yeshiva University, 1958.

Beller, Jacob. *Jews in Latin America.* New York: Jonathan David Publishers, 1969.

Benítez, Fernando. "Domingo de Ramos." *Siempre* (Mexico, D.F.) 414 (14 January 1970): 2–16. Reprinted as CIDOC 70/201, Cuernavaca.

Berman, Hyman. "A Cursory View of the Jewish Labor Movement: An Historiographical Survey." *American Jewish Historical Quarterly* 52 (December 1962): 79–97.

Berman, Yitzchak. "Jewish Colonization in Brazil Disappears." *Dispersion and Unity* 2 (June 1960): 51.

Bernardez, Francisco Luis. "Gerchunoff, clásico de los verdaderos." *Comentario* (Buenos Aires) 63 (November-December 1968): 32–33.

Bernheimer, Charles S. *The Russian Jew in the United States.* Philadelphia: John C. Winston Co., 1905.

Blecher, J. "Hastatistika shel hayehudim be-Argentina." [Statistics of Argentine Jewry.] In *Am yisroel b'doreynu*, edited by Shaul Esh, pp. 34–40. Jerusalem: Hebrew University, 1964.

Böhm, Günther. "Judíos en Chile durante el siglo XIX." In Comité Judío Americano, *Comunidades judías de Latinoamérica*, pp. 340–66. Buenos Aires: Américalee, S.R.L., 1971–72.

———. *Nuevos antecedentes para una historia de los judíos en Chile colonial.* Santiago: Editorial Universitaria S.A., 1963. A chapter of this book, "Los apellidos de los conversos," reprinted in Comité Judío Americano, *Comunidades judías de Latinoamérica*, pp. 196–208. Buenos Aires, 1966.

Bolaffi, Gabriel. "Socialização e resocialização num grupo juvenil informal." Mimeographed. São Paulo, n.d.

Bibliography

Boxer, Charles R. *Salvador de Sá and the Struggle for Brazil and Angola, 1602–1686.* London: Athlone Press, University of London, 1952.

Breve reseña historiográfica: Cien años de vida judía en el Perú, 1870–1970. Lima, 1970.

Brookings Institution. *Refugee Settlement in the Dominican Republic.* Washington: Brookings Institution, 1942.

B'tfutzot hagolah. Magazine of the World Zionist Organization, Jerusalem. Issue of June 1960 devoted to Latin American Jewish Communities. [Hebrew.] Subsequently published as *Dispersion and Unity*; now *Forum.*

Bustamente, Norberto R., et al. "Discriminación y marginalidad social en latinoamérica." *Comentario* 72 (May-June 1970): 3–23.

Castanien, Donald B. *El Inca Garcilaso de la Vega.* New York: Twayne Publishers, Inc., 1969.

Castro, Américo. *The Spaniards: An Introduction to Their History.* Berkeley: University of California Press, 1971.

Central Yiddish Culture Organization. *The Jewish People: Past and Present.* 3 vols. New York: Marstin Press, 1946–48.

Chacon, Vamireh. "Consciéncia nacional e judaísmo no Brasil." *Revista do Instituto de Estudos Brasileiros* (São Paulo), no. 10 (1971), pp. 7–26.

Chelminksy, Tzila. "La educación judía en México." In Comité Judío Americano, *Comunidades judías de Latinoamérica*, pp. 221–29. Buenos Aires: Editorial Candelabro, 1970.

Chouraqui, Andre N. *Between East and West: A History of the Jews of North Africa.* Philadelphia: Jewish Publication Society, 1968.

Cochrane, Thomas Childs. *Entrepreneurship in Argentine Culture: Torcuato di Tella.* Philadelphia: University of Pennsylvania Press, 1962.

Cohen, Hayyim. "Sephardi Jews in the United States: Marriage with Ashkenazim and Non-Jews." *Dispersion and Unity* 13/14 (1971): 151–60.

Cohen, Martin A. "Antonio Diaz de Cáceres: Marrano Adventurer in Colonial Mexico." *American Jewish Historical Quarterly* 60 (December 1970): 169–84.

———. *The Martyr. Luis de Carvajal. The Story of a Secret Jew and the Mexican Inquisition in the Sixteenth Century.* Philadelphia: Jewish Publication Society, 1973.

———. "Some Misconceptions about the Crypto-Jews in Colonial Mexico." *American Jewish Historical Quarterly* 61 (June 1972): 277–93.

———. *Usque's Consolation for the Tribulations of Israel.* Translated from the Portuguese by Martin A. Cohen. Philadelphia: Jewish Publication Society, 1965.

———, ed. *The Jewish Experience in Latin America.* 2 vols. Philadelphia: American Jewish Historical Society, 1971.

Comité Judío Americano. *Comunidades judias de Latinoamérica.* Buenos Aires: Editorial Candelabro, 1966, 1968, 1970, 1971–72.

———. *Conferencia sobre identidad e identificación judia.* [Eleven pamphlets issued between the years 1965–67.] Buenos Aires and Santiago.

Bibliography

————. *Estudio demográfico-piloto de la comunidad judía de Guadalajara.* Mexico City: 1970.

Cornblit, Oscar E. "European Immigrants in Argentine Industry and Politics." In *The Politics of Conformity in Latin America*, edited by Claudio Veliz, pp. 221–48. London: Oxford University Press, 1967.

Crozier, Brian. *Franco.* Boston and Toronto: Little, Brown & Co., 1967.

Cúneo, Dardo; Mafud, Julio; Sánchez Sívori, Amalia; and Schallman, Lázaro. *Inmigración y nacionalidad.* Biblioteca de Psicología Social y Sociología. Buenos Aires: Editorial Paidós, n.d.

Dajes, Marta de. "Los estudiantes judíos universitarios de Bogotá." In Comité Judío Americano, *Comunidades judías de Latinoamérica*, pp. 307–22. Buenos Aires: Américalee, S.R.L., 1971–72.

Davis, Moshe. "Mercazei yehudim bayevashot America: Gisha hashvatit" [Centers of Jewry in the Western Hemisphere: A comparative approach.] In *Am yisroel b'doreynu*, edited by Shaul Esh. Jerusalem: Hebrew University, 1964. Reprinted in *Jewish Journal of Sociology* 5 (June 1963): 4–26.

————. "Mixed Marriage in Western Jewry." *Jewish Journal of Sociology* 10 (December 1968): 177–220.

Delegación de Asociaciones Israelitas Argentinas (DAIA). "Estudio sobre la identidad judía." Mimeographed. Buenos Aires, n.d.

Deutschman, Paul, et al. *Communication and Social Change in Latin America.* New York: Praeger, 1968.

Dickmann, Enrique. *Recuerdos de un militante socialista.* Buenos Aires: Editorial de Vanguardia, 1949.

Dijour, Ilya M. "Jewish Migration in the Post-war Period." *Jewish Journal of Sociology* 4 (June 1962): 72–81.

Di Tella, Torcuato; Germani, Gino; Graciarena, Jorge; et al. *Argentina, sociedad de masas.* Buenos Aires: Editorial Universitario de Buenos Aires, 1965.

Dominican Republic Settlement Association (Dorsa). *Sosua, Haven for Refugees in the Dominican Republic.* Pamphlet No. 4. New York, 24 September 1941.

Dubelman, Abraham J. "Cuba." *American Jewish Yearbook* 63 (1962): 481–85.

————. *Oif Kubaner Erd.* Havana, 1953.

Dubnow, Semon. *History of the Jews in Russia and Poland from the Earliest Times until the Present Day.* Translated from the Russian by I. Friedlaender. 2 vols. New York: Ktav Publishing House, 1975. Reprint of edition published by Jewish Publication Society of America, Philadelphia, 1916.

Duker, Abraham C., and Ben-Horin, Meir, eds. *Emancipation and Counter-Emancipation.* New York: Ktav Publishing House, 1974.

Edelmann, Alexander T. *Latin American Government and Politics.* Rev. ed. Homewood, Ill.: Dorsey Press, 1969.

Eisenstadt, Shmuel N. *The Absorption of Immigrants.* London: Routledge & Kegan Paul, 1954.

273

Bibliography

————. *Modernization: Protest and Change.* Englewood Cliffs, N.J.: Prentice-Hall, 1966.

Elbogen, Ismar. *A Century of Jewish Life.* Philadelphia: Jewish Publication Society, 1953.

Elkin, Judith Laikin. "History of the Jews of Latin America in the Nineteenth and Twentieth Centuries." Ph.D. dissertation, The University of Michigan, 1976.

————. "Goodnight, Sweet Gaucho: A Revisionist View of the Jewish Agricultural Experiment in Argentina." *American Jewish Historical Quarterly* 67 (March 1978): 208–23.

Elnecavé, Nissim. "Sephardic Jews in Argentina." *Dispersion and Unity* 2 (June 1960): 56–57.

Emmanuel, Isaac S. *Jewish Education in Curaçao.* Philadelphia: American Jewish Historical Society, 1955.

————. *The Jews of Coro, Venezuela.* Monographs of the AJA, no. 8. Cincinnati: American Jewish Archives, HUC-JIR, 1973.

————. *Precious Stones of the Jews of Curaçao, 1656–1957.* New York: Bloch Publishing Co., 1957.

————, and Emmanuel, Suzanne A. *History of the Jews of the Netherlands Antilles.* 2 vols. Assen: Royal Van Gorcum, Ltd., 1970, and Cincinnati: American Jewish Archives, 1970.

Encyclopedia Judaica. 16 vols. New York: Macmillan Co., and Jerusalem: Keter Publishing House, Ltd., 1971–72.

Engleman, Uriah Z. "Sources of Jewish Statistics." In *The Jews: Their History, Culture, and Religion,* edited by Louis Finkelstein, pp. 1510–35. 2 vols. 3d ed. New York: Harper & Bros., 1960.

Esh, Shaul, ed. *Am yisroel b'doreynu.* [Studies in contemporary Jewish life.] Papers delivered at the section of Contemporary Jewry of the Third World Congress of Jewish Studies, Jerusalem, 1961. Jerusalem: Hebrew University, Institute of Contemporary Jewry, 1964.

Experts Conference on Latin America and the Future of Its Jewish Communities. *Proceedings.* New York, 3–4 June 1972. London: Institute of Jewish Affairs, 1973.

Federacão Israelita do Estado de São Paulo. *Guia das Instituições Israelitas do Estado de São Paulo.* São Paulo, 1967.

Feinberg, David. "Historical Survey of the Colonization of Russian Jews in Argentina." *American Jewish Historical Quarterly* 43 (September 1953): 37–69. Reprinted in *The Jewish Experience in Latin America,* edited by Martin A. Cohen, 2:331–63. 2 vols. Philadelphia: American Jewish Historical Society, 1971.

Feingold, Henry L. *Zion in America.* New York: Hippocrene Books, Inc., 1974.

Fillol, Thomas Roberto. *Social Factors in Economic Development: The Argentine Case.* Cambridge: M.I.T. Press, 1961.

Bibliography

Finkelstein, Louis, ed. *The Jews: Their History, Culture, and Religion.* 2 vols. 3d ed. New York: Harper & Bros., 1960.

Fischerman, Joaquin. "Etnocentrismo y antisemitismo." *Indice* (Buenos Aires) 1 (December 1967): 17–24. Reprinted in *La cuestión judía,* edited by Juan José Sebreli, pp. 191–204. Buenos Aires: Editorial Tiempo Contemporaneo, n.d.

Freid, Jacob, ed. *Jews in the Modern World.* New York: Twayne Publishers, 1962.

Friedlander, Günter. *Los héroes olvidados.* Santiago: Editorial Nascimiento, 1966.

Garfunkle, Boris. *Narro mi vida.* Buenos Aires, 1963.

Gendler, Everett. "Holy Days in Havana." *Conservative Judaism* 23 (Winter 1969): 15–24. Reprinted in *Religion in Cuba Today: A New Church in a New Society,* edited by Alice Hageman, pp. 80–92. New York: Association Press, 1971.

Gerchunoff, Alberto. *Jewish Gauchos of the Pampas.* New York: Abelard-Schuman, 1955.

———. *El pino y el palmero.* Buenos Aires: Sociedad Hebraica Argentina, 1952.

Germani, Gino. "Antisemitismo ideológico y antisemitismo tradicional." In Juan José Sebreli, ed., *La cuestión judía en la Argentina,* pp. 177–90. Buenos Aires: Editorial Tiempo Contemporaneo, n.d.

———. *Estructura social de la Argentina: Analisis estadistico.* Buenos Aires: Editorial Raigal, 1955.

———. "Mass Immigration and Modernization in Argentina." In *Masses in Latin America,* edited by Irving Louis Horowitz, pp. 289–330. New York: Oxford University Press, 1970. Reprinted in *Latin American Radicalism: A Documentary Report on Left and Nationalist Movements,* edited by Irving L. Horowitz; Jesue de Castro; and Frank Gerassi. New York: Vintage, 1971.

———. *Política y sociedad en una época de transición.* Buenos Aires: Editorial Paidós, 1962.

Gibson, Charles. *The Spanish Tradition in America.* Columbia: University of South Carolina Press, 1968.

Gillin, John. "Ethos Components in Modern Latin American Culture." *American Anthropologist* 57 (1955): 488–500.

Ginzberg, Eli. *Kavim le-heker haye hakalkalah shel yehudei hatefutsot.* [Notes for the study of the economic life of the Jews of the diaspora.] Study Circle on Diaspora Jewry in the home of the President of Israel. Jerusalem: Hebrew University, Institute of Contemporary Jewry, 1972.

Gitelman, Zvi. *Jewish Nationality and Soviet Politics.* Princeton, N.J.: Princeton University Press, 1972.

Glantz, Jacobo. *Notes sobre la formación de la comunidad judía de México, Israel y la diaspora en el año 5721 (1960–61).* Edited by Enrique Chemilsky. Mexico City, 1962.

275

Bibliography

Glauert, Earl T. "Ricardo Rojas and the Emergence of Argentine Cultural Nationalism." *Hispanic American Historical Review* 43 (1963): 1–13.

Glazer, Nathan. *American Judaism.* Chicago: University of Chicago Press, 1957.

———, and Moynihan, Daniel. *Beyond the Melting Pot.* Cambridge: M.I.T. Press, 1970.

Glick, Asher Dov. "The Military in Latin America." In *Yahadut america halatinit*, edited by Haim Avni, et al., pp. 20–25. Jerusalem: Hebrew University, 1972.

Gonçalves Salvador, José. *Cristãos-Novos, jesuitas e inquisição.* São Paulo: Livraria Pioneira Editôra, 1969.

Goodman, Robert Alan. "The Image of the Jew in Argentine Literature as Seen by Argentine Jewish Writers." Ph.D. dissertation, State University of New York, 1972.

Gordon, Milton M. *Assimilation in American Life.* New York: Oxford University Press, 1964.

Gori, Gaston. *Inmigración y colonización en la Argentina.* Buenos Aires, 1964.

Greenleaf, Richard E. *The Mexican Inquisition of the Sixteenth Century.* Albuquerque: University of New Mexico Press, 1969.

Griffith, William J. "Attitudes toward Foreign Colonization." In *Applied Enlightenment: Nineteenth Century Liberalism*, edited by Margaret Harrison and Robert Wauchope, pp. 71–110. Middle American Research Institute. New Orleans: Tulane University Press, 1972.

Grunwald, Kurt: *Turkenhirsch: A Study of Baron Maurice de Hirsch.* New York: Transaction Books, 1966.

Guberek, Simon: *Yo vi crecer un país.* Bogotá, 1974.

Gudiño Kramer, Luis. "Colonización judía en el litoral." *Davar* (Buenos Aires) 14 (November 1947).

Hagen, Everett E. *On the Theory of Social Change: How Economic Growth Begins.* Homewood, Ill.: Dorsey Press, 1962.

Hanke, Lewis, ed. *Do the Americas Have a Common History?* New York: Alfred Knopf, 1964.

Harari, Iejiel. "Yahadut Argentina." [Argentine Jewry.] *Dispersion and Unity* 2 (June 1960): 16–34.

———, and Lewin, Itzjak. "Resultado de la encuesta sobre profesiones, idiomas, y crecimiento de la colectividad judía." *Nueva Sion* (Buenos Aires), 24 February 1950 and 14 July 1950.

Haring, Clarence. *Empire in Brazil.* Cambridge: Harvard University Press, 1958.

Hartz, Louis D. *The Founding of New Societies.* New York: Harcourt, Brace and World, 1964.

Hasson, Yaacov. "Elementos para el estudio histórico y pedagógico de la educación judía en el Perú." In Comité Judío Americano, *Comunidades judias de Latinoamérica*, pp. 240–44. Buenos Aires: Editorial Candelabro, 1970.

Bibliography

————. "Iquitos: Alma judía en la Amazonia peruana." In Comité Judío Americano, *Comunidades judías de Latinoamérica*, pp. 367–73. Buenos Aires: Américalee, S.R.L., 1971–72.

Havaner Lebn. Weekly issues, 1934–59; and *Almanac*, various dates.

————. *Un cuarto de siglo vida habañera, 1932–1957*. Edited by Sander M. Kaplan and Alexander J. Dubelman. Havana, 1958.

Hebert, John Raymond. "The Tragic Week of January, 1919, in Buenos Aires: Background, Events, Aftermath." Ph.D. dissertation, Georgetown University, 1972.

Hebrew University. *Jews in Latin America*. Bibliography and Exhibition Catalogue. Jerusalem, 1972.

Hendel, Samuel. "Los orígenes de la comunidad israelita." In *Judíos en el Uruguay*. Montevideo: World Jewish Congress, 1968.

Henkin, Louis, ed. *World Politics and the Jewish Condition*. New York: Quadrangle Books, 1972.

Hermelin, D. M. *Clara: An Historical Romance*. Serialized in *Havaner Lebn* beginning 18 November 1932.

Hersch, Leib. "Jewish Migrations during the Last Hundred Years." In Central Yiddish Culture Organization, *The Jewish People: Past and Present*, 1: 407–30. 3 vols. New York: Marstin Press, 1946–48.

Hertzberg, Arthur. *The French Enlightenment and the Jews*. New York: Columbia University Press, 1968.

Hexter, Maurice Beck. *The Jews in Mexico*. New York: New York City Emergency Committee on Jewish Refugees, 1926. Reprinted in *Jewish Social Service Quarterly* 2 (March-June 1926): 188–96, 274–86.

Hirsch, Baron Maurice de. "My Views on Philanthropy." *North American Review* 2 (July 1891): 416.

Hirschberg, Alfred. "The Economic Adjustment of Jewish Refugees in São Paulo." *Jewish Social Studies* 7 (January 1945): 31–40.

Hirschberg, Alice Irene. *Desafio e resposta: A história da Congregação Israelita Paulista*. São Paulo, 1976.

Hochstein, Joshua. "La colaboración hispano–israelita en la América." In *América: Revista de la Asociación de escritores y artistas americanos*. Havana, September 1939.

————. "La inmigración judía de la post-guerra." In *América: Revista de la asociación de escritores y artistas americanos*. Havana, October 1939.

Hodra, Joseph. "Hayehudim ba-Córdoba." [The Jews of Córdoba.] *Dispersion and Unity* 2 (June 1960): 34–51.

Hoetink, Harry. "The Dominican Republic in the Nineteenth Century: Some Notes on Immigration, Stratification, and Race." In *Race and Class in Latin America*, edited by Magnus Mörner. New York: Columbia University Press, 1970.

————. *El Pueblo Dominicano, 1850–1900: Apuntes para su sociologia histórica*. 2d ed. Santiago de los Caballeros: Universidad Católica Madre y Maestra, 1971.

Bibliography

————. *The Two Variants in Caribbean Race Relations.* New York: Oxford University Press, 1967.

Horowitz, Irving Louis. "The Jewish Community of Buenos Aires." *Jewish Social Studies* 24 (October 1962): 195–222.

————. "Jewish Ethnicism and Latin American Nationalism." *Midstream* 18 (November 1972): 22–28.

Horowitz, S. Y. "Di cooperativn in di yiddishe kolonies in Argentina." *Argentiner IWO Schriftn* 1 (1941): 59–116.

Hurvitz, Nathan. "Sources of Motivation and Achievement of American Jews." *Jewish Social Studies* 23 (October 1961): 217–34.

Imaz, José Luis de. *Los que mandan.* Translated and with an introduction by Carlos A. Astiz. Albany: State University of New York Press, 1970.

Isaacs, Stephen D. *Jews and American Politics.* New York: Doubleday, 1974.

Jewish Colonization Association. *Report.* Buenos Aires, 1909.

————. *Su obra en la Argentina, 1891–1941.* Buenos Aires, 1942.

Johnson, John J. *Continuity and Change in Latin America.* Stanford: Stanford University Press, 1964.

————. *Political Change in Latin America: The Emergence of the Middle Sectors.* Stanford: Stanford University Press, 1958.

Kahan, Arcadius. "A Note on Methods of Research on the Economic History of the Jews." In *For Max Weinreich on his Seventieth Birthday,* pp. 173–82. The Hague: Mouton, 1964.

Kahl, J. A. *Measurement of Modernism: A Study of Values in Brazil and Mexico.* Austin: University of Texas Press, 1970.

Kahn, Solomon. *Meksikanishe refleksn.* Mexico City: Farlag "Selbsthilf," 1954.

————. *Yidish-Meksikanish.* Mexico City: Farlag "Selbsthilf," 1945.

Kaplan, Sander M. "Jewish Robinson Crusoes." *Havaner Lebn,* 12 October 1934.

Kaplanski de Caryevschi, Teresa. "The Organized Jewish Community of Buenos Aires—A.M.I.A." *Dispersion and Unity* 11 (1970): 147–78.

Kardúner, Luis. "La eliminación de las acepciones peyoritivas del diccionario de la lengua española." In Comité Judío Americano, *Comunidades judías de Latinoamérica,* pp. 251–72. Buenos Aires: Américalee, S.R.L., 1971–72.

Karner, Frances P. *The Sephardics of Curaçao: A Study of Sociolcultural Patterns in Flux.* Assen: Van Gorcum & Co., 1969.

Katz, Jacob. *Jews and Freemasons in Europe, 1723–1939.* Translated from Hebrew by Leonard Oschry. Cambridge: Harvard University Press, 1970.

Kayserling, M. *Christopher Columbus and the Participation of the Jews in the Spanish and Portuguese Discoveries.* New York: Hermon Press, 1968.

Kinzer, Nora Scott. "Women Professionals in Buenos Aires." In *Female and Male in Latin America,* edited by Ann Pescatello, pp. 159–90. Pittsburgh: University of Pittsburgh Press, 1973.

Bibliography

Kisch, Hyman. "The Jewish Settlement from Central Europe in the Dominican Republic." Ph.D. dissertation, Jewish Theological Seminary, 1970.

Kitron, Moshe. *Hayishuv hayehudi ba-amerikah halatinit.* [Jewish settlement in Latin America.] Jerusalem: World Jewish Congress, 1960.

———. "La 'alia' latinoaméricana en Israel." In Comité Judío Americano, *Comunidades judías de Latinoamérica*, pp. 143–59. Buenos Aires: Editorial Candelabro, 1968.

———. "Latin American Jewry in Our Time." *Dispersion and Unity* 4 (1964–65): 53–78.

Klein, Alberto. "Cronología de la comunidad Israelita Argentina." In Comité Judío Americano, *Comunidades judías de Latinoamérica*, pp. 101–24. Buenos Aires, 1966.

Knudsen, Jerry W. "Anti-Semitism in Latin America." *Patterns of Prejudice* (London) 6 (September–October 1972): 1–10; and 6 (November–December 1972): 22–30.

———. "The Bolivian Immigration Bill of 1942: A Case Study in Latin American Anti-Semitism." *American Jewish Archives* 22 (November 1970): 138–58.

Kochanski, Mendel. "The Jewish Community in Cuba." *Jewish Frontier* 18 (September 1951): 25–27.

Kohn, Hans. "The Jew Enters Western Culture." *Menorah Journal* 18 (April 1930): 291–302.

Kovadloff, Jacobo. "La sociedad Hebraica Argentina de Buenos Aires." In Comité Judío Americano, *Comunidades judías de Latinoamérica*, pp. 180–85. Buenos Aires, 1966.

Krause, Corinne Azen. "The Jews in Mexico: A History with Special Emphasis on the Period from 1857 to 1930." Ph.D. dissertation, University of Pittsburgh, 1970.

———. "Mexico—Another Promised Land? A Review of Projects for Jewish Colonization in Mexico: 1881–1925." *American Jewish Historical Quarterly* 61 (June 1972): 325–41.

Krause, José. *Un judío de México opina.* Mexico City, 1969.

Kriesberg, Louis. "Entrepreneurs in Latin America and the Role of Cultural and Situational Processes." *International Social Science Journal* 15 (1963): 581–94.

Kritschmar, Najum. "Der itziker matzav fun di yidishe kolonies." In Asociación Mutual Israelita Argentina, *Pinkus fun der kehillah*, pp. 282–95. Buenos Aires, 1969.

Kuznets, Simon. "Economic Structure and Life of the Jews." In *The Jews: Their History, Culture, and Religion*, edited by Louis Finkelstein, pp. 1597–1666. 2 vols. 3d ed. New York: Harper & Bros., 1960.

———. *Economic Structure of U.S. Jewry: Recent Trends.* Jerusalem: Hebrew University, Institute of Contemporary Jewry, 1972.

Landorff, Gabriel. "La producción literaria en idisch en la Argentina en

1967." In Comité Judío Americano, *Comunidades judías de Latinoamérica*, pp. 238–43. Buenos Aires: Editorial Candelabro, 1968.

Lapide, Pinchas. *Three Popes and the Jews*. New York: Hawthorn Books, Inc., 1967.

Lat, Netam. "From Sosua to Azua." *Hadassah Magazine* 53 (November 1971): 16–17, 38–39.

Lazar, Moshe. "The Spiritual Background." In *Yahadut america halatinit*, edited by Haim Avni, et al., pp. 32–34. Jerusalem: Hebrew University, 1972.

Lea, Henry Charles. *The Inquisition in the Spanish Dependencies*. New York: Macmillan Co., 1908.

League of Nations. *Statistical Yearbook, 1933/34*. Geneva, 1934.

Lee, Samuel James. *Moses of the New World*. Cranbury, N.J.: A. S. Barnes, 1970.

Leeds, Anthony. "Economic-Social Changes and the Future of the Middle Class." In Experts Conference on Latin America and the Future of its Jewish Communities, *Proceedings*, pp. 48–71. London: Institute of Jewish Affairs, 1973.

Leite Filho, Solidonio. *Os judeus no Brasil*. Rio de Janeiro: J. Leite & Cia., 1923.

Lemle, Henrique. "Jews in Northern Brazil." *Reconstructionist*, 3 March 1967.

Lerner, Falik. "La producción literaria judía de la Argentina en el último lustro." In Comité Judío Americano, *Comunidades judías de Latinoamérica*, pp. 173–79. Buenos Aires, 1966.

Lerner, Ira T. *Mexican Jewry in the Land of the Aztecs*. Mexico City, 1973.

Lerner, Natan. "Anti-Semitism and the Nationalist Ideology in Argentina." *Dispersion and Unity* 17/18 (1973): 131–39.

———. "Argentina's First Anti-Semitic Novel." *Patterns of Prejudice* (London) 5 (September–October 1971): 25–27.

———. *Jewish Organization in Latin America*. Tel Aviv: David Horowitz Institute, Tel Aviv University, 1974.

Lesser, Harriet Sara. "A History of the Jewish Community of Mexico City, 1912–1970." Ph.D. dissertation, Jewish Teachers' Seminary and Columbia University, 1972.

Lestchinsky, Jacob. *De lage fun yidn in lateyn-amerikaner lender*. [The situation of Jews in Latin American lands.] New York: World Congress for Jewish Affairs, 1948.

———. "Economic and Social Development of the Jewish People." In Central Yiddish Culture Organization, *The Jewish People: Past and Present*, 1: 361–90. 3 vols. New York: Marstin Press, 1946–48.

———. "The Economic Development of the Jews of the United States." In Central Yiddish Culture Organization, *The Jewish People: Past and Present*, 1:391–406. 3 vols. New York: Marstin Press, 1946–48.

———. "Jewish Migrations, 1840–1956." In *The Jews: Their History, Cul-*

Bibliography

ture, and Religion, edited by Louis Finkelstein, 2:1536–96. 2 vols. 3d ed. New York: Harper & Bros., 1960.

Levine, Robert M. "Brazil's Jews during the Vargas Era and after." *Luso-Brazilian Review* 5 (Summer 1968): 45–58.

Levitz, Jacob. "The Acculturation of East European Jews in Mexico City, 1920–1946." Master's thesis, Wayne University, 1946.

———. "The Jewish Community in Mexico: Its Life and Education." Ph.D. dissertation, Dropsie College, 1954.

———. "Mexico." *American Jewish Yearbook* 58 (1957): 410.

Lewin, Boleslao. *El judío en la época colonial; Un aspecto de la historia rioplatense.* Buenos Aires: Colegio libre de estudios superiores, 1939.

———. "Esbozo de la historia judía de la Argentina desde 1580 hasta 1889." In Asociación Mutual Israelita Argentina, *Pinkus fun der kehillah*, pp. 37–66. Buenos Aires, 1969.

———. *Martires y conquistadores judíos en latinoamérica.* Also published as *Yidishe deroberer un martiren in lateyn-america.* Buenos Aires: Asociación pro-cultura judía, 1968.

———. "The Struggle against Jewish Immigration into Latin America in Colonial Times." *YIVO Annual of Jewish Social Science* 7 (1952): 212–28.

Liebman, Seymour B. "The Cuban Jewish Community in South Florida." *American Jewish Year Book* 70 (1969): 238–46.

———. *The Enlightened: The Writings of Luis de Carvajal, El Mozo.* Translated, edited, and with introduction and epilogue by Seymour B. Liebman. Coral Gables: University of Miami Press, 1967.

———. "Hernando Alonso: The First Jew on the North American Continent." *Journal of Inter-American Studies* 5 (April 1963): 291–96.

———. *The Inquisition and the Jews in the New World. Summaries of Procesos, 1500–1810, and Bibliographic Guide.* Coral Gables: University of Miami Press, 1974.

———. *The Jews in New Spain: Faith, Flame, and the Inquisition.* Coral Gables: University of Miami Press, 1970.

———. "The Jews of Colonial Mexico." *Hispanic American Historical Review* 43 (February 1963): 95–108.

———. "Latin American Jews: Ethnicity and Nationalism." *Jewish Frontier* 40 (July–August 1973): 8–13.

———. "The Mestizo Jews of Mexico." *American Jewish Archives* 19 (November 1967): 144–74.

———. *Mexican Jewry: A Guide to Jewish References in Mexico—Colonial Era, 1521–1821.* Philadelphia: University of Pennsylvania Press, 1964.

———. "Research Problems in Mexican Jewish History." *American Jewish Historical Quarterly* 54 (December 1964): 165–80.

———. "Understanding Latin American Jewry." *Reconstructionist*, 3 March 1967.

Bibliography

Lipiner, Eliahu. "A nova imigração judaica no Brasil." Part II of *Breve historia dos judeus no Brasil*. Rio de Janeiro: Ed. Biblos, 1962.

————. *Os Judaizantes nas Capitanias de Cima*. São Paulo: Editôra Brasiliense, 1969.

————. "Yidn in Brazil." *Algemeine Entsiclopedia* 5 (1957): 385–404.

Lipman, Aaron. "Social Backgrounds of the Bogotá Entrepreneur." *Journal of Inter-American Studies* 7 (1965): 227–35.

Lipset, Seymour Martin. "The Study of Jewish Communities in a Comparative Context." *Jewish Journal of Sociology* 5 (1963): 156–60.

————, and Solari, A., eds. *Elites in Latin America*. New York: Oxford University Press, 1967.

————, and Bendix, Reinhard. *Movilidad social*. Buenos Aires: Editorial Universitaria de Buenos Aires, 1963.

Litvinoff, Norberto. "Estudio de actitudes en la comunidad judía Argentina." *Indice* (Buenos Aires) 2 (April 1969): 88–102.

Lleras Camargo, Alberto. "A Humble Jewish Revolution." *Vision* (1972?).

Loewenstamm, Kurt. *Vultos judaicos no Brasil*. Vol. 1, *Tempo colonial, 1500–1822*. Vol. 2, *Imperio, 1822–1899*. Rio de Janeiro: 1949 and 1956.

Loewenstein, Kurt. *Brazil under Vargas*. New York: Macmillan, 1942.

Lorch, Nathaniel. "Decline of the Jewish Community." In *Yahadut america halatinit*, edited by Haim Avni, et al., pp. 25–31. Jerusalem: Hebrew University, 1972.

Luftig, Roman. "La comunidad israelita de San Pablo." In Comité Judío Americano, *Comunidades judias de Latinoamérica*, pp. 211–14. Buenos Aires: Editorial Candelabro, 1970.

————. "Sistema y estensión de la asistencia social en San Pablo." In Comité Judío Americano, *Comunidades judias de Latinoamérica*, pp. 156–59. Buenos Aires: Editorial Candelabro, 1968.

Malamud, Samuel. "Contribución judía al desarrollo del Brasil en las 150 años de la independencia." In Comité Judío Americano, *Comunidades judias de Latinoamérica*, pp. 330–39. Buenos Aires: Américalee, S.R.L., 1971–72.

Maller, Julius B. "The Role of Education in Jewish History." In *The Jews: Their History, Culture, and Religion*, edited by Louis Finkelstein, 2: 1234–53. 2 vols. 3d ed. New York: Harper & Bros., 1960.

Malloy, James M. *Bolivia: The Unfinished Revolution*. Pittsburgh: University of Pittsburgh Press, 1970.

Maloof, Louis J. "A Sociological Study of Arabic-speaking People in Mexico." Ph.D. dissertation, University of Florida, 1959.

Marcus, Jacob Rader. *The Colonial American Jews, 1492–1776*. Vol. 3, Bibliography. Detroit: Wayne State University Press, 1970.

Margolis, Max, and Marx, Alexander. *History of the Jewish People*. Philadelphia: Jewish Publication Society of America, 1958.

Margulies, Marcos. "Ayer y mañana: Demografía de las comunidades judías

Bibliography

en el Brasil." In Comité Judío Americano, *Comunidades judías de Latinoamérica*, pp. 323–29. Buenos Aires: Américalee, S.R.L., 1971–72.

————. *Judaica brasiliensis repertorio bibliografico comentado*. Rio de Janeiro: Editôra Documentário, 1974.

Matterin, Abraham M. *Martí y las discriminaciónes raciales*. Havana, 1953.

McClelland, David. *The Achieving Society*. Princeton, N.J.: Van Nostrand, 1961.

Mecham, J. Lloyd. *Church and State in Latin America*. Rev. ed. Chapel Hill: University of North Carolina Press, 1966.

Meisel, Tovye. *Yidn in Meksike*. *YIVO Bletter* 27 (1946): 213–330.

————. "Yidn in Meksike." *YIVO Annual of Jewish Social Science* 2–3 (1947–48): 295–312.

————. "Yidn in Meksike." *Algemeine Entsiclopedia* 5 (1957): 405–20.

Meyer, Marshall. "Una década de judaísmo conservador en Latinoamérica." In Comité Judío Americano, *Comunidades judías de Latinoamérica*, pp. 182–93. Buenos Aires: Editorial Candelabro, 1970.

Mirelman, Victor A. "The Early History of the Jewish Community of Buenos Aires: 1860–1892." Master's thesis, Columbia University, 1968.

————. "The Jews in Argentina (1890–1930): Assimilation and Particularism." Ph.D. dissertation, Columbia University, 1973.

————. "A Note on Jewish Settlement in Argentina, 1881–1892." *Jewish Social Studies* 33 (January 1971): 3–12. Reprinted in Comité Judío Americano, *Comunidades judias de Latinoamérica*, pp. 292–306. Buenos Aires: Américalee, S.R.L., 1971–72.

————. "The Semana Trágica of 1919 and the Jews of Argentina." *Jewish Social Studies* 37 (January 1975): 61–73.

Monk, Abraham, and Rogovsky, Eduardo I. "Survey of Attitudinal Trends of the Buenos Aires Jewish Community: Attitudes of Young Jewish Married Couples." Buenos Aires, 1964. American Jewish Committee typescript.

Mörner, Magnus. *Race Mixture in the History of Latin America*. Boston: Little, Brown and Co., 1967.

————, ed. *Race and Class in Latin America*. New York: Columbia University Press, 1970.

Morse, Arthur D. *While Six Million Died*. New York: Random House, 1967.

Morse, Richard. "The Heritage of Latin America." In *The Founding of New Societies*, edited by Louis Hartz, pp. 123–77. New York: Harcourt, Brace and World, 1964.

Nachman, Robert G. "Positivism, Modernization, and the Middle Class in Brazil." *Hispanic American Historical Review* 57 (February 1977): 1–23.

Netanyahu, Benzion. *The Marranos of Spain*. Millwood, N.Y.: Kraus Reprint Co., 1973.

Nicolaiewsky, Eva. *Israelitas no Rio Grande do Sul*. Porto Alegre: Editôra Garatuja, 1975.

Novinsky, Anita. *Cristãos novos na Bahia*. São Paulo: Editôra Perspectiva, 1972.

Bibliography

————. "Fontes para a história econômica e social do Brasil. Inventários dos bens de condenados pela Inquisição. (Brasil, século XVIII)." *Revista de História* (São Paulo), no. 98 (1974), pp. 359–92.

————. "A Historical Bias: The New Christian Collaboration with the Dutch Invaders of Brazil (Seventeenth Century)." Jerusalem: Fifth World Congress of Jewish Studies, 1972.

————. "Impedimentos ao trabalho livre no período inquisitorial e as respostas da realidade Brasileira." *Anais do VI simpósio nacional dos professôres universitários de história* (São Paulo) (1973): 231–54.

————. "Os israelitas em São Paulo." In *São Paulo: Espírito, povo, instituições*, edited by J. V. Freitas Marcondes and Osmar Pimentel, pp. 109–26. São Paulo: Livraria Pioneira Editôra, 1974.

————. "Uma fonte inédita para a história do Brasil." *Revista de História* (São Paulo), no. 94 (1973), pp. 563–72.

Nun, José. "A Latin American Phenomenon: The Middle-Class Military Coup." In *Latin America: Reform or Revolution?* edited by James Petras and Maurice Zeitlin, pp. 145–85. Greenwich, Conn.: Fawcett Publications, 1968.

Oddone, Juan Antonio. *La formación del Uruguay moderno—La inmigración y el desarrollo económico-social.* Buenos Aires: Editorial Universitaria, 1966.

Omegna, Nelson. *Diabolização dos judeus: Martírio e presença dos sefardins no Brasil colonial.* Rio de Janeiro: Distribuidora Record, 1969.

Pan American Union and New York Public Library. *Indice general de publicaciones periódicas latinoamericanas: Humanidades y ciencias sociales.* 8 vols. New York, 1960. *Supplement* 1961–65.

Patai, Raphael. "Indios Israelitas of Mexico." *Menorah Journal* 38, no. 1 (1950): 54–67.

————. *Tents of Jacob.* Englewood Cliffs, N.J.: Prentice-Hall, 1971.

Peñolosa, Fernando. "Latin American Immigrants in Israel." *Jewish Social Studies* 34 (April 1972): 122–39.

Perera, Victor. "Growing up Jewish in Guatemala." *Present Tense* 1 (Winter 1974): 55–59.

Perez, Leon S. "The Problems of Jewish University Youth in the Argentine." *Dispersion and Unity* 2 (1963): 89–98.

Pessah, Alberto. "La Asociación Communidad Israelita Sefardí de Buenos Aires." In Comité Judío Americano, *Comunidades judías de Latinoamérica*, pp. 194–96. Buenos Aires, Editorial Candelabro, 1970.

Petras, James, and Zeitlin, Maurice, eds. *Latin America: Reform or Revolution?* Greenwich, Conn.: Fawcett Publications, 1968.

Pinis, Y. O. *Hatuey: An Epic Poem.* Havana, 1931.

Pitchon, Marco. *José Martí y la compresión humana, 1853–1953.* Havana, 1957.

Poppino, Rollie E. *Brazil: The Land and People.* New York: Oxford University Press, 1968.

Bibliography

Presse. XX Aniversario de Di Presse. Buenos Aires, 1938.

Raizman, Itzhak Z. "Yidn in Brazil." *Jewish Review* 4 (October 1946): 139–53.

Ramos Mejía, José M. *Las multitudes Argentinas.* Buenos Aires: Talleres Gráficos, 1934.

Ran, Leizer, ed. *Continuidad hebrea en tierra Cubana.* Almanaque conmemorativo del 25 aniversario del Centro Israelita de Cuba. 1925–50. Dual title: *Hemshej oif kubaner erd.* Havana, 1951.

————. "Cuba." *Algemeine Entsiclopedia* 5 (1957): 421–36.

Rattner, Henrique, ed. *Nos caminhos da diaspora.* Centro Brasileiro de Estudos Judaicos. São Paulo, 1972.

————. "Occupational Structure of Jews in Brazil: Trends and Perspectives." Mimeographed paper prepared for the Sixth World Congress of Jewish Studies, Jerusalem, August 1973.

————. "Persistencia de padroes tradicionais." *Sociologia* (São Paulo) 27, no. 2 (June 1965).

————. "Sociological Research & Census of the Jewish Community in São Paulo, 1968." Preliminary Report. *American Jewish Yearbook* 70 (1969): 382.

————. *Tradição e mudança: A comunidade judaica em São Paulo.* São Paulo: Atica, 1970.

————, and Bolaffi, Gabriel. "Jewish University Students in Face of Judaism." Mimeographed. São Paulo, 1966.

Reicher, Perla. "Hapoalim hayehudim ba-Uruguay." [Jewish workers in Uruguay.] Tel Aviv University, Institute for Zionist Research, 1971.

————. "Safrut, itoniyot, ukruzim shel yahadut Uruguay." [Books, newspapers, and posters of Uruguayan Jewry.] University of Tel Aviv, Institute for Zionist Research, 1970.

Rennie, Ysabel F. *The Argentine Republic.* New York: Macmillan Co., 1945.

"Requiem for a Jewish Community." *Jewish Chronicle* (London), 10 August 1962.

Ricard, Robert. "L'emigration des Juifs marocains en Amérique du Sud," *Société de Géographie du Maroc* (Casablanca) 8° Tome 7, 1928: 237–40.

Rieier, Jacques. "The Jewish Colony of Cuba." Typescript. N.p., 1942.

Rischin, Moses. "The Jewish Labor Movement in America: A Social Interpretation." In *Labor History* 4, no. 3 (Fall 1963): 227–47.

Rivkin, Ellis. "The Utilization of Non-Jewish Sources for the Reconstruction of Jewish History." *Jewish Quarterly Review* n.s., 48 (October 1957): 183–203.

Rogovsky, Eduardo; Widucynski, Elias; and Winograd, Fanny K. de. "Una investigación del departamento de estudios sociales del Comité Judío Americano." In Comité Judío Americano, *Comunidades judías de Latinoamérica,* pp. 233–37. Buenos Aires, Editorial Candelabro, 1968.

Rojas, Ricardo. Preface to *La condición del extranjero en América,* by Domingo F. Sarmiento. Buenos Aires: Librería "La Facultad," 1928.

Bibliography

————. *La restauración nacionalista.* Buenos Aires: Ministerio de Justicia e Instrucción Pública, 1909.

Rosen, Joseph A. "New Neighbors in Sosua." *Survey Graphic,* September 1941.

Rosenswaike, Ira. "The Jewish Population of Argentina." *Jewish Social Studies* 22 (October 1960): 195–214.

Rosenthal, Celia S. "The Jews of Barranquilla." *Jewish Journal of Sociology* 18 (1956): 262–74.

Rozitchner, Leon. *Ser judío.* Buenos Aires: Talleres Gráficos Garamond S.C.A., 1968.

Rubel, Iaacov. "Argentina, ¿sí o no?" In Comité Judío Americano, *Comunidades judías de Latinoamérica,* pp. 273–91. Buenos Aires: Américalee, S.R.L., 1971–72.

Ruppin, Arthur. "The Jewish Population of the World." In Central Yiddish Culture Organization, *The Jewish People: Past and Present,* 1:348–60. 3 vols. New York: Marstin Press, 1946–48.

Russett, Bruce M., et al. *World Handbook of Political and Social Indicators.* New Haven: Yale University Press, 1964.

Sable, Martin H. *Latin American Jewry: A Research Guide.* Cincinnati: Hebrew Union College Press, 1978.

Sandberg, Harry O. "The Jews of Latin America." *American Jewish Yearbook* 19 (1917–18): 35–105.

Sanders, Ronald. *Lost Tribes and Promised Lands: The Origins of American Racism.* Boston: Little, Brown, 1978.

Santander, Silvano. "Tres personalidades judeo-argentinas." In Asociación Mutal Israelita Argentina *Anales de la comunidad israelita de Buenos Aires, 1963–68,* pp. 75–82. Buenos Aires, 1969.

Sapir, Boris. *The Jewish Community of Cuba.* Translated by Simon Wolin. New York: Jewish Teachers' Seminary Press, 1948.

————. "Jewish Organizations in Cuba." *Jewish Review* 4 (January–March 1947): 263–81.

————. "Jews in Cuba." *Jewish Review* 5 (July–September 1946): 109–44.

————. "Tsu der geshikhte fun yidn in Cuba." *YIVO Bletter* 25, no. 3 (May–June 1945): 335–66.

Sapolinsky, Asher. "The Jewry of Uruguay." *Dispersion and Unity* 2 (1963): 74–88.

Sapolnik, Jaime. *A contribução judaica a independencia do Brasil.* Bahía: Sec. Ed. e Cultura, Estado de Bahia, 1973.

Saraiva, Antonio José. *A inquisição portuguesa.* Lisbon, 1956.

Sarmiento, Domingo F. *La condición del extranjero en América.* Preface by Ricardo Rojas. Buenos Aires: Librería "La Facultad," 1928.

Schallman, Lázaro. "Dramática historia de los 'Pampistas' o 'Stambuler,'" in Comité Judío Americano, *Comunidades judías de Latinoamérica,* pp. 151–72. Buenos Aires, 1966.

————. "Historia de los 'Pampistas.'" Biblioteca Popular Judía. Buenos Aires: Congreso Judío Latinoamericano, 1971.

Bibliography

————. "Historia del periodismo judío en la Republica Argentina." In Comité Judío Americano, *Comunidades judías de Latinoamérica*, pp. 149–73. Buenos Aires: Editorial Candelabro, 1970.

————. "Las primeras agrupaciones de mujeres judías en la Argentina." *OSFA* (Buenos Aires) 36 (December 1972): 37.

————. *Los pioneros de la colonización judía en la Argentina.* Buenos Aires: Congreso Judío Latinoamericano, 1969.

————. "Orígenes de la colonización agrícola judía en la república Argentina." *Comentario* (Buenos Aires) 40 (1964): 23–34.

————. "Proceso histórico de la colonización agrícola." In *Inmigración y nacionalidad*, edited by D. J. Cúneo et al., pp. 145–209. Buenos Aires: Editorial Paidós, n.d.

Scharfstein, Zevi. "Jewish Education in Latin America." In Central Yiddish Culture Organization, *The Jewish People: Past and Present*, 2:172–78. 3 vols. New York: Marstin Press, 1946–48.

Schers, David, and Singer, Hadassa. "The Jewish Communities of Latin America: External and Internal Factors in Their Development." *Jewish Social Studies* 39 (Summer 1977): 241–58.

Schmelz, U. O. "Critical Assessment of Jewish Population Estimates for Argentina and Latin America." In *Studies in Jewish Demography: Survey for 1969–1971*, edited by U. O. Schmelz et al., pp. 25–52. Jerusalem: Hebrew University, 1975.

————. "Evaluation of Jewish Population Estimates." *American Jewish Yearbook* 70 (1969): 273–88.

————. *Infant and Early Childhood Mortality among Jews of the Diaspora.* Jerusalem: Hebrew University, Institute of Contemporary Jewry, 1971.

————. *Jewish Demography and Statistics, 1920–1960.* 2 vols. Jerusalem: Hebrew University, Institute of Contemporary Jewry, 1961.

————. *Jewish Population Studies, 1961–1968.* Jerusalem: Hebrew University, Institute of Contemporary Jewry; London: Institute of Jewish Affairs, 1970.

————, and Della Pergola, Sergio. *Hademografia shel hayehudim be-Argentina ube-artzot aherot shel America halatinit.* [The demography of the Jews in Argentina and in other countries of Latin America.] Tel Aviv: Tel Aviv University, August 1974.

Schneider, Joseph. "Shpurn fun di Yiddisher fargangenheit in der alter Havana." *Havaner Lebn*, 12 October 1934.

Schteingard, Mario. *Mis memorias.* Buenos Aires: By the Author, 1956.

Schusheim, A. L. "Tsu de geshichte fun der antsteiung fun dem idishn kibuts in Buenos Aires." *Yohrbuch 5714 (1953–54).* Buenos Aires: Asociación Mutual Israelita Argentina, 1954.

————, and Bottachanski, J. "The Jewish Community in Argentina." *Algemeine Entsiclopedia* 5 (1957): 342–84.

Schwartz, Ernst, and TeVelde, Johan C. "Jewish Agricultural Settlement in

Bibliography

Argentina: The ICA Experiment." *Hispanic American Historical Review* 19 (May 1939): 185–93.

Scobie, James R. *Revolution on the Pampas.* Latin American Monographs, no. 1. Institute of Latin American Studies. Austin: University of Texas Press, 1964.

Sebreli, Juan José, ed. *La cuestion judía en la Argentina.* Buenos Aires: Editorial Tiempo Contemperaneo, n.d.

Senderey, Moisés. "Brazil under Vargas." In *Havaner Lebn: Un cuarto de siglo, vida habañera 1932–1957,* edited by Sander M. Kaplan and Alexander J. Dubelman. Havana, 1958.

———. *Historia de la colectividad israelita de Chile.* Santiago: Editorial "Dos Ydische Wort," 1956. Also published as *Di Geshikhte fun dem Yiddishn Yishuv in Chile.* Santiago, 1956.

Serebrenick, Salomão. *Quatro séculos de vida judaica no Brasil, 1500–1900.* Part I of *Breve historia dos judeus no Brasil.* Rio de Janeiro: Edições Biblos, Ltda., 1962.

Sharot, Stephen. "Minority Situation and Religious Acculturation: A Comparative Analysis of Jewish Communities." *Comparative Studies in Society and History* 16 (June 1974): 329–54.

Shatzky, Jacob. *Comunidades judías en Latinoamérica.* Buenos Aires: American Jewish Committee, 1952. Also published as *Yiddishe yishuvim in Lateyn America.* Buenos Aires, 1952.

———. "Guatemala." *Jewish Journal of Sociology* 7 (December 1965): 302–3.

Sicroff, Albert. *Les controverses des statuts de "pureté de sang" en Espagne du XVe au XVIIe siècles.* Paris: Didier, 1960.

Sidicaro, Luis. "La comunidad sefardi de habla española de Buenos Aires." In Comité Judío Americano, *Comunidades judias de Latinoamérica,* pp. 197–202. Buenos Aires: Editorial Candelabro, 1970.

Silvert, Kalman H. "The Annual Political Cycle in Argentina." American University Field Staff Reports Service (East Coast South America Series) 8 (1961), no. 6.

Sklare, Marshall. *The Jew in American Society.* New York: Behrman House, 1974.

Smith, John Kenneth. "Jewish Education in Colombia: Group Survival versus Assimilation." Ph.D. dissertation, University of Wisconsin, 1972.

Smith, T. Lynn. *Brazil: Portrait of Half a Continent.* New York: Dryden Press, 1951.

———. "Changing Functions of Latin American Cities." *Américas* 25 (July 1968): 70–83.

Sneh, Simja. "La red escolar judía en la república Argentina." In Comité Judío Americano, *Comunidades judias de Latinoamérica,* pp. 129–42. Buenos Aires: Editorial Candelabro, 1968.

Sobel, Louis H. "Jewish Community Life in Latin America." *American Jewish Yearbook* 47 (1945–46): 119–40.

Sofer, Eugene F. "From Pale to Pampa: Eastern European Jewish Social Mo-

Bibliography

bility in Gran Buenos Aires, 1890–1945." Ph.D. dissertation, University of California, Los Angeles, 1976.

Solberg, Carl. *Immigration and Nationalism: Argentina and Chile, 1890–1914.* Austin: University of Texas Press, 1970.

Sourasky, Leon. *História de la comunidad israelita de Mexico (1917–1942).* Mexico City: By the Author, 1965.

Speist, Robbie. "Jews of Cuba." *Morning Freiheit*, 14 June 1970.

Stanger, Francis Merriman. "Church and State in Peru during the First Century of Independence." *Hispanic American Historical Review* 2, no. 4 (November 1927): 418–37. Reprinted in *The Conflict between Church and State in Latin America*, edited by Frederick B. Pike, pp. 143–53. New York: Alfred A. Knopf, 1964.

Steinberg, I. N. "Jewish Colonization in the Americas: Argentina." In Central Yiddish Culture Organization, *The Jewish People: Past and Present*, 2: 81–87. 3 vols. New York: Marstin Press, 1946–48.

Stern, Norton B. *Baja California: Jewish Refuge and Homeland.* Los Angeles: Dawson's Book Shop, 1973.

Strassman, Paul W. "The Industrialist." In *Continuity and Change in Latin America*, edited by John J. Johnson, pp. 161–85. Stanford: Stanford University Press, 1964.

Szajkowski, Zosa. "Baron Hirsch's bamiyungen l'teives di rusishe yidn un der crisis in der ICA kurz far zein toit." *Davke* (Buenos Aires), no. 2 (1950–51), pp. 401–16.

Tartakower, Arieh. *Hahityashvut hayehudit bagolah.* [Jewish colonization in the Diaspora.] "Argentina." 2:156–94. 2 vols. Tel Aviv: M. Neuman, 1969.

Taylor, Charles L., and Hudson, Michael C. *World Handbook of Political and Social Indicators.* New Haven: Yale University Press, 1972.

Trachtenberg, Joshua. *The Devil and the Jews.* New Haven: Yale University Press, 1943.

Trotzky, Eliahu. "Yidn in Uruguay." Mimeographed. N.d.

United Nations. *Demographic Yearbook.* New York: United Nations, 1973–74.

Uslar-Pietri, Arturo. "La escuela y el destino de América Latina." *Cuadernos* (Paris) 76 (September 1963): 3–8.

Vainsencher, Isaac. "No miento ni cedo." Montevideo: Editorial Zriah, 1973.

Varon, Benjamin. *Si yo fuera paraguayo.* Asunción: By the Author, 1972.

Vasertzug, S. "La kehilla de Buenos Aires y el vaad hakehillot de la Argentina." In Comité Judío Americano, *Comunidades judías de Latinoamérica*, pp. 143–55. Buenos Aires, 1966.

Veltman, Henrique B. "Crônica do judaísmo carioca." *Comentario* (Rio de Janeiro) 13 (1° trimestre 1972): 51–59.

Wald, Pinie. "Di Yiddishe Arbeter-Bavegung in Argentina." In Asociación Mutual Israelita Argentina, *Pinkus fun der kehilla*, pp. 109–43. Buenos Aires, 1954–55.

Weill, Simon. *Población israelita en la república Argentina.* Buenos Aires, 1936.

Bibliography

Weiner, Akiva. "A Chapter from the Recent Past in Cuba." In *Havaner Lebn: Un cuarto de siglo vida habañera*, edited by Sander M. Kaplan and Alexander J. Dubelman, pp. 40–44. Havana, January 1958.

Weiser, Benno. "Ecuador: Eight Years on Ararat." *Commentary* 3 (June 1947): 531–36.

———. "Latin America." *American Jewish Yearbook* 54 (1953): 201–15.

Willems, Emilio. "A assimilação dos judeus." *Sociologia* (São Paulo) 7 (1945): 54–67.

———. *Latin American Culture: An Anthropological Synthesis*. New York: Harper and Row, 1975.

Williams, Eric E. *From Columbus to Castro: The History of the Caribbean, 1492–1969*. New York: Harper and Row, 1971.

Winsberg, Morton D. *Colonia Baron Hirsch: A Jewish Agricultural Colony in Argentina*. University of Florida Monographs, Social Sciences No. 19. Gainesville: University of Florida Press, 1964.

———. "Jewish Agricultural Colonization in Entre Ríos." *American Journal of Economics and Sociology* 27 (July 1968): 285–95; 27 (October 1968): 423–28; 28 (April 1969): 179–91.

Winter, Olga M. de. "La educación judía en la Argentina." In Comité Judíos Americano, *Comunidades judías de Latinoamérica*, pp. 133–42. Buenos Aires, 1966.

Wischnitzer, Mark. "Historical Background of Settlement of Jewish Refugees in Santo Domingo." *Journal of Social Studies* 4, no. 1 (1942): 50–58.

———. "Jewish Communal Organization in Modern Times." In Central Yiddish Culture Organization, *The Jewish People: Past and Present*, 2:201–16. 3 vols. New York: Marstin Press, 1946–48.

———. "The Sosua Settlement." *Ort Economic Bulletin* 2 (1941) no. 3.

———. *To Dwell in Safety*. Philadelphia: Jewish Publication Society, 1948.

Wiznitzer, Arnold. "Crypto-Jews in Mexico during the Sixteenth Century." *American Jewish Historical Society Quarterly* 51 (1961–62): 168–214, 222–68.

———. "The Exodus from Brazil and Arrival in New Amsterdam of the Jewish Pilgrim Fathers, 1654." In *The Jewish Experience in Latin America*, edited by Martin A. Cohen, 2:313–30. 2 vols. Philadelphia: American Jewish Historical Society, 1971.

———. *Jews in Colonial Brazil*. New York: Columbia University Press, 1960.

———. *Records of the Earliest Jewish Community in the New World*. With a foreword by Salo Baron. Philadelphia: American Jewish Historical Society, 1954.

Woodward, Ralph Lee. *Positivism in Latin America: 1850–1900*. Lexington, Mass.: D. C. Heath & Co., 1971.

World Jewish Conference. *Judíos en el Uruguay*. Montevideo, 1968.

Yerushalmi, Yosef Hayim. *From Spanish Court to Italian Ghetto. Isaac Cardoso: A Study in 17th Century Marranism and Jewish Apologetics*. New York: Columbia University Press, 1971.

Bibliography

YIVO–Institute for Jewish Research. *Bibliography of American and Canadian Jewish Memoirs and Autobiographies in Yiddish, Hebrew, and English.* New York, 1970.

Yidishe Zaitung, Di. Yovl Bukh. Sakh ha-koln fun 50 yohr yidish lebn in Argentina. Edited by Hirsch Trivacks. Buenos Aires, 1940.

Zborowsky, Mark. *Life Is with People: The Culture of the Shtetl.* New York: Schocken Books, 1962.

Zea, Leopoldo. *The Latin American Mind.* Norman: University of Oklahoma Press, 1963.

———. *Positivism in Mexico.* Austin: University of Texas Press, 1974.

Zenner, Walter P. "International Networks in a Migrant Ethnic Group." In *Migration and Anthropology.* Proceedings of the 1970 Annual Spring Meeting of the American Ethnological Society. Seattle: University of Washington Press, 1971.

Index

Index

Index

in Peru, 11–12; in Brazil, 14; in Portugal, 16; abolished, 19, 21
Intermarriage: in Spain, 4; in Bahía, 14; in Dominican Republic, 19, 147; in Argentina, 33, 170, 211–12; in Chile, 38; in Mexico, 40; in Peru, 47–48; in Venezuela, 70; and the linke, 185; United States and Latin America compared, 252
Irigoyen, Hipólito, 82
Isaacs, Jorge, 265 (n. 30)
Israelita, 22

JCA (Jewish Colonization Association), 57, 64, 125; founded, 127–30; scope of plan, 130–32; number of colonists, 133–34; assessment of, 133–43; bureaucracy, 134–36, 141–42, 152; education in, 138, 172–73; migration to cities, 140–41; credit co-ops, 160–61
Jecker, Jean Baptiste, 41
Jewish ethnicity, 18, 58, 94, 97; in kehillot, 180–82, 186–90; definition of, 256 (n. 44)
Jewish identity: and the Catholic church, 171, 177; and the linke, 185; sports clubs, 189; for census purposes, 194–96; and continental mobility, 236; image, 240–42; and nationality, 242–44; alienation from Judaism, 243; "mestizo" Jews, 257 (n. 56). See also Intermarriage
Jewish migrations: global, 27–28; periodization, 28–29, 54–56, 76–86; origins, 54–55, 94–99; settlement pattern, 73–74, 78–80, 85–86, 96; and prosperity, 236; United States and Latin America compared, 238–53
Jewish population profile: 1889, 50–53; 1917, 72–75; 1970, 94–99; mentality, 99, 120; as economic actors, 119–24; political subordination, 225–37
John XXIII (pope), 86
Joint (Joint Distribution Committee or JDC), 88, 91, 159, 162–63
Judaizers, 5–6, 10–11, 13–14. See also Marranos
Juárez, Benito, 39–40; Ley Juárez, 39

Kaplan, Sander M., 88
Kehillah (pl. kehillot): description of, 178; in Argentina, 178–81 (see AMIA); internal politics, 181–87; in Mexico, 181; Uruguay, 182–84; and Zionism, 185–86

Kessel, Joseph, 62
Khevra Kadisha (Burial Society), 156–57, 215
Klabin, Mauricio, 119

La Bolsa, 57, 234. See also Anti-Semitism
Ladino, 23, 256 (n. 44)
Lafer, Horacio, 119
Language: in education, 172; surveys of use: Argentina, 173; Mexico, 173–75; Chile, 175; Brazil, 175; in kehillot, 181
La Plata, 12–13
La Protesta, 60
Latifundia: in Argentina, 31–32, 125–26, 136–38, 140–42; Dominican Republic, 146; Bolivia, 149; and failure of colonization, 152; origin of, 239
La Vangardia, 60
"Law of 50 Percent," 87, 90, 113
León Pinelo, Antonio, 265 (n. 29)
León Pinelo, Diego de, 265 (n. 29)
Levi, León, 115
Lévi-Strauss, Claude, 92
Levy, Alexandre, 45
Levy sisters, 34
Limantour, José Yves, 41
Lima y Sola, Manuel de, 37
Limpieza de sangre: definition, 7; in Spain, 7; in Portugal, 7–8; in the Indies, 9–11; defamatory use, 20–21; and gauchismo, 32; and commerce, 121; and university admissions, 121; and public service, 239
"Linke" (Jewish leftists): synagogue, 166; in Uruguay, 182–84; and Semana Trágica, 182; expelled from kehillot, 185
Loewenthal, Wilhelm, 127
Los gauchos judíos, 61, 259 (n. 17)
Lucienville (Basavilbaso), 157, 161

Maldonado de Silva, Francisco, 12
Marranos, 5, 6, 20, 23; myth of Antioquia, 123. See also conversos
Martí, José, 22, 89
Maskillim. See Haskalah
Matterin, Abraham, 89
Mauricio, 135. See also JCA
Meiggs, Henry, 46–47
Mexico, 79, 85, 86; toleration, 38–41; immigration policy, 39; origins of Jewish immigrants, 39–42, 63–64, 79–80; occupations, 41–42, 104–5, 115–17; census, 42, 195; anti-Semitism, 116, 235; welfare, 158–59; religious observance,